S0-AWU-475

ALGORITHMS

IN A NUTSHELL

Second Edition

George T. Heineman,
Gary Pollice
& Stanley Selkow

Beijing · Boston · Farnham · Sebastopol · Tokyo

Algorithms in a Nutshell

by George T. Heineman, Gary Pollice, and Stanley Selkow

Copyright © 2016 George Heineman, Gary Pollice and Stanley Selkow. All rights reserved.

Printed in the United States of America.

Published by O'Reilly Media, Inc., 1005 Gravenstein Highway North, Sebastopol, CA 95472.

O'Reilly books may be purchased for educational, business, or sales promotional use. Online editions are also available for most titles (*http://safaribooksonline.com*). For more information, contact our corporate/institutional sales department: 800-998-9938 or *corporate@oreilly.com*.

Editors: Andy Oram and Mary Treseler	**Indexer:** Judy McConville
Production Editor: Colleen Lobner	**Interior Designer:** David Futato
Copyeditor: Christina Edwards	**Cover Designer:** Karen Montgomery
Proofreader: Jasmine Kwityn	**Illustrator:** Rebecca Demarest

October 2008:   First Edition
March 2016:   Second Edition

Revision History for the Second Edition
2016-03-09:   First Release

See *http://oreilly.com/catalog/errata.csp?isbn=9781491948927* for release details.

Nutshell Handbook, the Nutshell Handbook logo, and the O'Reilly logo are registered trademarks of O'Reilly Media, Inc. *Algorithms in a Nutshell*, the cover image of a hermit crab, and related trade dress are trademarks of O'Reilly Media, Inc.

While the publisher and the authors have used good faith efforts to ensure that the information and instructions contained in this work are accurate, the publisher and the authors disclaim all responsibility for errors or omissions, including without limitation responsibility for damages resulting from the use of or reliance on this work. Use of the information and instructions contained in this work is at your own risk. If any code samples or other technology this work contains or describes is subject to open source licenses or the intellectual property rights of others, it is your responsibility to ensure that your use thereof complies with such licenses and/or rights.

978-1-491-94892-7

[LSI]

Table of Contents

Preface to the Second Edition. vii

1. Thinking in Algorithms. 1
   Understand the Problem   1
   Naïve Solution   3
   Intelligent Approaches   3
   Summary   8
   References   8

2. The Mathematics of Algorithms. 9
   Size of a Problem Instance   9
   Rate of Growth of Functions   10
   Analysis in the Best, Average, and Worst Cases   14
   Performance Families   18
   Benchmark Operations   31
   References   33

3. Algorithm Building Blocks. 35
   Algorithm Template Format   35
   Pseudocode Template Format   36
   Empirical Evaluation Format   37
   Floating-Point Computation   38
   Example Algorithm   42
   Common Approaches   46
   References   52

4. Sorting Algorithms. 53
   Transposition Sorting   57

Selection Sort   61
Heap Sort   62
Partition-Based Sorting   67
Sorting without Comparisons   74
Bucket Sort   74
Sorting with Extra Storage   81
String Benchmark Results   85
Analysis Techniques   87
References   89

5. Searching. 91
Sequential Search   92
Binary Search   95
Hash-Based Search   99
Bloom Filter   114
Binary Search Tree   119
References   131

6. Graph Algorithms. 133
Graphs   134
Depth-First Search   137
Breadth-First Search   143
Single-Source Shortest Path   147
Dijkstra's Algorithm for Dense Graphs   152
Comparing Single-Source Shortest-Path Options   157
All-Pairs Shortest Path   159
Minimum Spanning Tree Algorithms   163
Final Thoughts on Graphs   167
References   168

7. Path Finding in AI. 169
Game Trees   169
Path-Finding Concepts   173
Minimax   174
NegMax   180
AlphaBeta   183
Search Trees   189
Depth-First Search   192
Breadth-First Search   198
A*Search   201
Comparing Search-Tree Algorithms   211
References   214

8. **Network Flow Algorithms**...................................... 217
    Network Flow   218
    Maximum Flow   220
    Bipartite Matching   231
    Reflections on Augmenting Paths   234
    Minimum Cost Flow   238
    Transshipment   239
    Transportation   240
    Assignment   242
    Linear Programming   242
    References   243

9. **Computational Geometry**.. 245
    Classifying Problems   246
    Convex Hull   249
    Convex Hull Scan   250
    Computing Line-Segment Intersections   258
    LineSweep   259
    Voronoi Diagram   268
    References   281

10. **Spatial Tree Structures**.. 283
    Nearest Neighbor Queries   284
    Range Queries   285
    Intersection Queries   285
    Spatial Tree Structures   285
    Nearest Neighbor Queries   288
    Range Query   298
    Quadtrees   305
    R-Trees   311
    References   323

11. **Emerging Algorithm Categories**................................. 325
    Variations on a Theme   325
    Approximation Algorithms   326
    Parallel Algorithms   332
    Probabilistic Algorithms   336
    References   344

12. **Epilogue: Principles of Algorithms**............................. 345
    Know Your Data   345
    Decompose a Problem into Smaller Problems   346

Choose the Right Data Structure   347
Make the Space versus Time Trade-Off   349
Construct a Search   350
Reduce Your Problem to Another Problem   350
Writing Algorithms Is Hard—Testing Algorithms Is Harder   351
Accept Approximate Solutions When Possible   352
Add Parallelism to Increase Performance   353

A. Benchmarking. 355

Index. 367

Preface to the Second Edition

Revising a book for a new edition is always an arduous task. We wanted to make sure that we retained all the good qualities of the first edition, published in 2009, while fixing some of its shortcomings and adding additional material. We continue to follow the principles outlined in the first edition:

- Use real code, not just pseudocode to describe algorithms
- Separate the algorithm from the problem being solved
- Introduce just enough mathematics
- Support mathematical analysis empirically

As we updated this second edition, we reduced the length of our text descriptions and simplified the layout to make room for new algorithms and additional material. We believe we continue to offer a *Nutshell* perspective on an important area of computer science that has significant impact on practical software systems.

Changes to the Second Edition

In updating this book for the second edition, we followed these principles:

Select New Algorithms

After the publication of the first edition, we often received comments such as "Why was **Merge Sort** left out?" or "Why didn't you cover **Fast Fourier Transform** (FFT)?" It was impossible to satisfy all of these requests, but we were able to add the following algorithms:

- **Fortune's algorithm**, to compute the Voronoi Diagram for a set of points ("Voronoi Diagram" on page 268)

- **Merge Sort**, for both internal memory data as well as external files ("Merge Sort" on page 81)

- Multithreaded **Quicksort** ("Parallel Algorithms" on page 332)

- **AVL Balanced Binary Tree** implementation ("Solution" on page 121)

- A new *Spatial Algorithms* chapter (Chapter 10) contains **R-Trees** and **Quadtrees**

In total, the book covers nearly 40 essential algorithms.

Streamline Presentation

To make room for the new material, we revised nearly every aspect of the first edition. We simplified the template used to describe each algorithm and reduced the accompanying descriptions.

Add Python Implementations

Rather than reimplement existing algorithms in Python, we intentionally used Python to implement most of the new algorithms added.

Manage Code Resources

The code for the first edition was made available as a ZIP file. We have since transitioned to a GitHub repository (*https://github.com/heineman/algorithms-nutshell-2ed*). Over the years we improved the quality of the code and its documentation. We have incorporated a number of blog entries that were written after the publication of the first edition. There are over 500 unit test cases and we use code coverage tools to ensure coverage of 99% of our Java code. In total, the code repository consists of over 110 KLOC.

Audience

We intend this book to be your primary reference when seeking practical information on how to implement or use an algorithm. We cover a range of existing algorithms for solving a large number of problems and adhere to the following principles:

- When describing each algorithm, we use a stylized template to properly frame each discussion and explain the essential points of each algorithm

- We use a variety of languages to implement each algorithm (including C, C++, Java, and Python). In doing so, we make concrete the discussion of algorithms and speak using languages you are already familiar with

- We describe the expected performance of each algorithm and empirically provide evidence to support these claims

We intend this book to be most useful to software practitioners, programmers, and designers. To meet your objectives, you need access to a quality resource that explains real solutions to practical algorithms you need to solve real problems. You already know how to program in a variety of programming languages. You know about the essential computer science data structures, such as arrays, linked lists, stacks, queues, hash tables, binary trees, and undirected and directed graphs. You don't need to implement these data structures, since they are typically provided by code libraries.

We expect you will use this book to learn about tried and tested solutions to solve problems efficiently. You will learn some advanced data structures and novel ways to apply standard data structures to improve the efficiency of algorithms. Your problem-solving abilities will improve when you see the key decision for each algorithm that make for efficient solutions.

Conventions Used in This Book

The following typographical conventions are used in this book:

Code
All code examples appear in this typeface.

This code is replicated directly from the code repository and reflects real code. All code listings are "pretty-printed" to highlight the appropriate syntax of the programming language.

Italic
Indicates key terms used to describe algorithms and data structures. Also used when referring to variables within a pseudocode description of an example.

Constant width
Indicates the name of actual software elements within an implementation, such as a Java class, the name of an array within a C implementation, and constants such as true or false.

We cite numerous books, articles, and websites throughout the book. These citations appear in text using parentheses, such as (Cormen et al., 2009), and each chapter closes with a listing of references used within that chapter. When the reference citation immediately follows the name of the author in the text, we do not duplicate the name in the reference. Thus, we refer to the *Art of Computer Programming* books by Donald Knuth (1998) by just including the year in parentheses.

All URLs used in the book were verified as of January 2016, and we tried to use only URLs that should be around for some time. We include small URLs, such as *http://www.oreilly.com*, directly within the text; otherwise, they appear in footnotes and within the references at the end of a chapter.

Using Code Examples

Supplemental material (code examples, exercises, etc.) is available for download at *https://github.com/heineman/algorithms-nutshell-2ed*.

This book is here to help you get your job done. In general, if example code is offered with this book, you may use it in your programs and documentation. You do not need to contact us for permission unless you're reproducing a significant portion of the code. For example, writing a program that uses several chunks of code from this book does not require permission. Selling or distributing a CD-ROM of examples from O'Reilly books does require permission. Answering a question by citing this book and quoting example code does not require permission. Incorporating a significant amount of example code from this book into your product's documentation does require permission.

We appreciate, but do not require, attribution. An attribution usually includes the title, author, publisher, and ISBN. For example: "*Algorithms in a Nutshell, Second Edition* by George T. Heineman, Gary Pollice, and Stanley Selkow. Copyright 2016 George Heineman, Gary Pollice and Stanley Selkow, 978-1-4919-4892-7."

If you feel your use of code examples falls outside fair use or the permission given above, feel free to contact us at *permissions@oreilly.com*.

Safari® Books Online

Safari Books Online is an on-demand digital library that delivers expert content in both book and video form from the world's leading authors in technology and business.

Technology professionals, software developers, web designers, and business and creative professionals use Safari Books Online as their primary resource for research, problem solving, learning, and certification training.

Safari Books Online offers a range of plans and pricing for enterprise, government, education, and individuals.

Members have access to thousands of books, training videos, and prepublication manuscripts in one fully searchable database from publishers like O'Reilly Media, Prentice Hall Professional, Addison-Wesley Professional, Microsoft Press, Sams, Que, Peachpit Press, Focal Press, Cisco Press, John Wiley & Sons, Syngress, Morgan Kaufmann, IBM Redbooks, Packt, Adobe Press, FT Press, Apress, Manning, New Riders, McGraw-Hill, Jones & Bartlett, Course Technology, and hundreds more. For more information about Safari Books Online, please visit us online.

How to Contact Us

Please address comments and questions concerning this book to the publisher:

O'Reilly Media, Inc.
1005 Gravenstein Highway North
Sebastopol, CA 95472

800-998-9938 (in the United States or Canada)
707-829-0515 (international or local)
707-829-0104 (fax)

We have a web page for this book, where we list errata, examples, and any additional information. You can access this page at *http://bit.ly/algorithms_nutshell_2e*.

To comment or ask technical questions about this book, send email to *bookquestions@oreilly.com*.

For more information about our books, courses, conferences, and news, see our website at *http://www.oreilly.com*.

Find us on Facebook: *http://facebook.com/oreilly*

Follow us on Twitter: *http://twitter.com/oreillymedia*

Watch us on YouTube: *http://www.youtube.com/oreillymedia*

Acknowledgments

We would like to thank the book reviewers for their attention to detail and suggestions, which improved the presentation and removed defects from earlier drafts: From the first edition: Alan Davidson, Scot Drysdale, Krzysztof Duleba, Gene Hughes, Murali Mani, Jeffrey Yasskin, and Daniel Yoo. For the second edition: Alan Solis, Robert P. J. Day, and Scot Drysdale.

George Heineman would like to thank those who helped instill in him a passion for algorithms, including Professors Scot Drysdale (Dartmouth College) and Zvi Galil (Columbia University, now Dean of Computing at Georgia Tech). As always, George thanks his wife, Jennifer, and his children Nicholas (who has now started learning how to program) and Alexander (who loves making origami creations from the printed rough drafts of this edition).

Gary Pollice would like to thank his wife Vikki for 46 great years. He also wants to thank the WPI computer science department for a great environment and a great job.

Stanley Selkow would like to thank his wife, Deb. This book was another step on their long path together.

1

Thinking in Algorithms

Algorithms matter! Knowing which algorithm to apply under which set of circumstances can make a big difference in the software you produce. Let this book be your guide to learning about a number of important algorithm domains, such as sorting and searching. We will introduce a number of general approaches used by algorithms to solve problems, such as the Divide and Conquer or Greedy strategy. You will be able to apply this knowledge to improve the efficiency of your own software.

Data structures have been tightly tied to algorithms since the dawn of computing. In this book, you will learn the fundamental data structures used to properly represent information for efficient processing.

What do you need to do when choosing an algorithm? We'll explore that in the following sections.

Understand the Problem

The first step in designing an algorithm is to understand the problem you want to solve. Let's start with a sample problem from the field of computational geometry. Given a set of points, P, in a two-dimensional plane, such as shown in Figure 1-1, picture a rubberband that has been stretched around the points and released. The resulting shape is known as the *convex hull* (i.e., the smallest convex shape that fully encloses all points in P). Your task is to write an algorithm to compute the convex hull from a set of two-dimensional points.

Given a convex hull for P, any line segment drawn between any two points in P lies totally within the hull. Let's assume we order the points in the hull clockwise. Thus, the hull is formed by a clockwise ordering of h points $L_0, L_1, \ldots, L_{h-1}$ as shown in Figure 1-2. Each sequence of three hull points L_i, L_{i+1}, L_{i+2} creates a right turn.

1

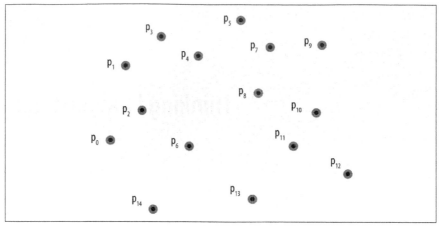

Figure 1-1. Sample set of 15 points in plane

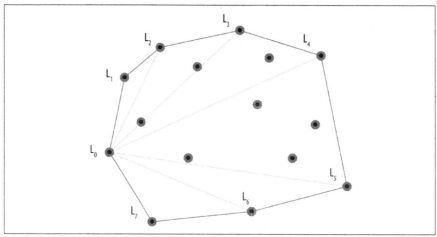

Figure 1-2. Computed convex hull for points

With just this information, you can probably draw the convex hull for any set of points, but could you come up with an *algorithm* (i.e., a step-by-step sequence of instructions that will efficiently compute the convex hull for any set of points)?

What we find interesting about the convex hull problem is that it doesn't seem to be easily classified into existing algorithmic domains. There doesn't seem to be any linear sorting of the points from left to right, although the points are ordered in clockwise fashion around the hull. Similarly, there is no obvious search being performed, although you can identify a line segment on the hull because the remaining $n - 2$ points are "to the right" of that line segment in the plane.

Naïve Solution

Clearly a convex hull exists for any collection of three or more points. But how do you construct one? Consider the following idea. Select any three points from the original collection and form a triangle. If any of the remaining $n - 3$ points are contained within this triangle, then they cannot be part of the convex hull. We'll describe the general process using pseudocode, and you will find similar descriptions for each of the algorithms in the book.

Slow Hull Summary

Best, Average, Worst: $O(n^4)$

```
slowHull (P)
  foreach p0 in P do
    foreach p1 in {P-p0} do
      foreach p2 in {P-p0-p1} do ❶
        foreach p3 in {P-p0-p1-p2} do
          if p3 is contained within Triangle(p0,p1,p2) then
            mark p3 as internal ❷

  create array A with all non-internal points in P
  determine leftmost point, left, in A
  sort A by angle formed with vertical line through left ❸
  return A
```

❶ Points *p0*, *p1*, *p2* form a triangle.

❷ Points *not marked* as internal are on convex hull.

❸ These angles (in degrees) range from –90 to 90.

In the next chapter, we will explain the mathematical analysis that shows why this approach is considered to be inefficient. This pseudocode summary explains the steps that produce a convex hull for each input set; in particular, it created the convex hull in Figure 1-2. Is this the best we can do?

Intelligent Approaches

The numerous algorithms in this book are the results of striving for more efficient solutions to existing code. We identify common themes in this book to help you solve your problems. There are many different ways to compute a convex hull. In sketching these approaches, we give you a sample of the material in the chapters that follow.

Greedy

Here's a way to construct the convex hull one point at a time:

1. Remove from P its lowest point, *low*, which must be part of the hull.

2. Sort the remaining $n - 1$ points in *descending* order by the angle formed in relation to a vertical line through *low*. These angles range from 90 degrees for points to the left of the line down to −90 degrees for points to the right. p_{n-2} is the rightmost point and p_0 is the leftmost point. Figure 1-3 shows the vertical line and the angles to it from each point as light lines.

3. Start with a partial convex hull formed from three points in this order $\{p_{n-2}, low, p_0\}$. Try to extend the hull by considering, in order, each of the points p_1 to p_{n-2}. If the last three points of the partial hull ever turn left, the hull contains an incorrect point that must be removed.

4. Once all points are considered, the partial hull completes. See Figure 1-3.

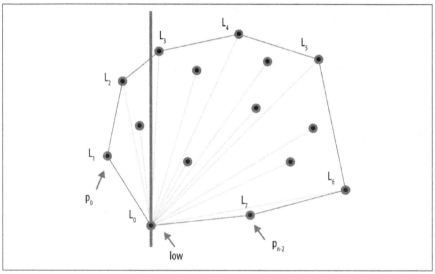

Figure 1-3. Hull formed using a Greedy approach

Divide and Conquer

We can divide the problem in half if we first sort all points, P, left to right by x coordinate (breaking ties by considering their y coordinate). From this sorted collection, we first compute the upper *partial* convex hull by considering points in order left to right from p_0 to p_{n-1} in the clockwise direction. Then the lower partial convex hull is constructed by processing the same points in order right to left from p_{n-1} to p_0 again in the clockwise direction. **Convex Hull Scan** (described in Chapter 9) computes these partial hulls (shown in Figure 1-4) and merges them together to produce the final convex hull.

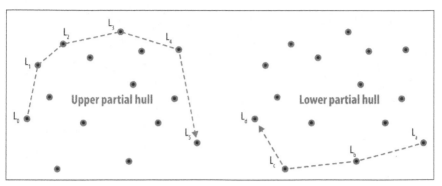

Figure 1-4. Hull formed by merging upper and lower partial hulls

Parallel

If you have a number of processors, partition the initial points by x coordinate and have each processor compute the convex hull for its subset of points. Once these are completed, the final hull is *stitched* together by the repeated merging of neighboring partial solutions. A parallel approach divides subproblems among a number of processors to speed up the overall solution.

Figure 1-5 shows this approach on three processors. Two neighboring hulls are stitched together by adding two tangent lines—one on the top and one on the bottom—and then eliminating the line segments contained within the quadrilateral formed by these two lines.

Approximation

Even with these improvements, there is still fixed *lower bound* performance for computing the convex hull that cannot be beaten. However, instead of computing the exact answer, perhaps you would be satisfied with an approximate answer that can be computed quickly and whose error *can be accurately determined*.

The **Bentley–Faust–Preparata** algorithm constructs an approximate convex hull by partitioning the points into vertical strips (Bentley et al., 1982). Within each strip, the maximum and minimum points (based on y coordinate) are identified (they are drawn in Figure 1-6 with squares around the points). Together with the leftmost point and the rightmost point in P, these extreme points are stitched together to form the approximate convex hull. In doing so, it may happen that a point falls outside the actual convex hull, as shown for point p_1 in Figure 1-6.

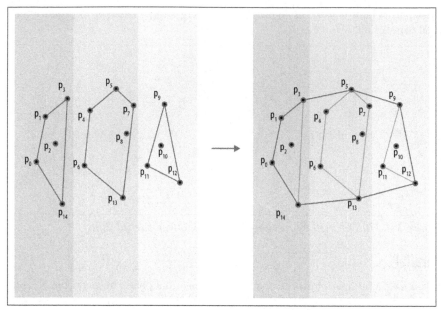

Figure 1-5. Hull formed by parallel constructions and stitching

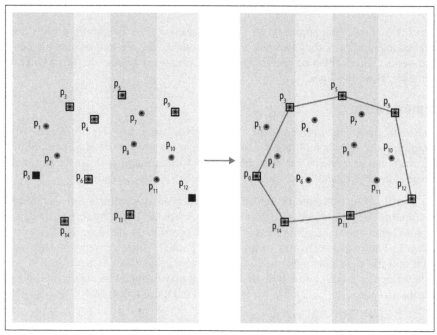

Figure 1-6. Hull formed by approximate computation

Generalization

It is often possible to solve a more general problem whose solution can be readily converted to solve your specific problem. The *Voronoi diagram* (Preparata and Shamos, 1993) is a geometric structure that divides a set of points in a plane into regions, each one of which is *anchored* by one of the original points in the input set *P*. Each region R_i is the set of points (x, y) in the plane closer to the anchor point, p_i, than any other point in *P*. Once the Voronoi diagram is computed, these regions can be visualized as shown in Figure 1-7. The gray regions are *semi-infinite* and you can observe that these match directly to the points on the convex hull. This observation leads to the following algorithm:

1. Compute the Voronoi diagram for *P*.

2. Initialize the hull with the lowest point, *low*, in *P* and start at its associated region.

3. In clockwise fashion, visit the neighboring region that shares an infinitely long side and add that region's anchor point to the hull.

4. Continue adding points until the original region is encountered.

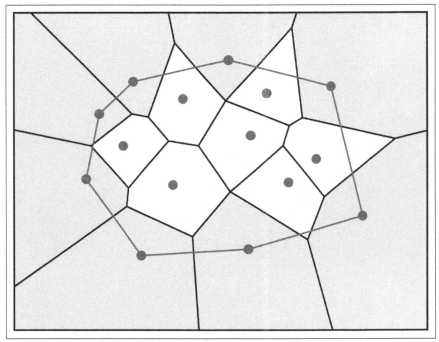

Figure 1-7. Hull computed from Voronoi diagram

Summary

An efficient algorithm is often not at all obvious to discover, and very different algorithms may be the best ones to choose for different data sets, different processing environments (such as where you can exploit parallelism), and different goals. This brief introduction only scratched the surface of algorithms. Hopefully you are now inspired to learn more about these different approaches as well as the variety of algorithms we have collected in this book. We have implemented all algorithms and provided suitable documentation and explanations to help you understand how to use these algorithms and even implement them yourselves.

References

Bentley, J. L., F. Preparata, and M. Faust, "Approximation algorithms for convex hulls," *Communications of the ACM*, 25(1): 64–68, 1982, *http://doi.acm.org/10.1145/358315.358392*.

Preparata, F. and M. Shamos, *Computational Geometry: An Introduction*, Springer, 1993.

2

The Mathematics of Algorithms

One of the most important factors for choosing an algorithm is the speed with which it is likely to complete. Characterizing the expected computation time of an algorithm is inherently a mathematical process. This chapter presents the mathematical tools behind this time prediction. After reading the chapter, you should understand the various mathematical terms used throughout this book—and in the rest of the literature that describes algorithms.

Size of a Problem Instance

An instance of a problem is a particular input data set given to a program. In most problems, the execution time of a program increases with the size of this data set. At the same time, overly compact representations (possibly using compression techniques) may unnecessarily slow down the execution of a program. It is surprisingly difficult to define the optimal way to encode an instance because problems occur in the real world and must be translated into an appropriate representation to be solved by a program.

When evaluating an algorithm, we want as much as possible to assume the encoding of the problem instance is not the determining factor in whether the algorithm can be implemented efficiently. Your representation of a problem instance should depend just on the type and variety of operations that need to be performed. Designing efficient algorithms often starts by selecting the proper data structures in which to represent the problem.

Because we cannot formally define the size of an instance, we assume an instance is encoded in some generally accepted, concise manner. For example, when sorting n integers, we adopt the general convention that each of the n numbers fits into a 32-bit word in the computing platform, and the size of an instance to be sorted is n. In case some of the numbers require more than one word—but only a constant, fixed number of words—our measure of the size of an instance is off *only by a multiplicative constant*. So an algorithm that performs a computation using integers stored using 64 bits may take twice as long as a similar algorithm coded using integers stored in 32 bits.

Algorithmic researchers accept that they are unable to compute with pinpoint accuracy the costs involved in using a particular encoding in an implementation. Therefore, they assert that performance costs that differ by a multiplicative constant are *asymptotically equivalent*, or in other words, will not matter as the problem size continues to grow. As an example, we can expect 64-bit integers to require more processing time than 32-bit integers, but we should be able to ignore that and assume that a good algorithm for a million 32-bit integers will also be good for a million 64-bit integers. Although such a definition would be impractical for real-world situations (who would be satisfied to learn they must pay a bill that is 1,000 times greater than expected?), it serves as the universal means by which algorithms are compared.

For all algorithms in this book, the constants are small for virtually all platforms. However, when implementing an algorithm in production code, you must pay attention to the details reflected by the constants. This asymptotic approach is useful since it can predict the performance of an algorithm on a large problem instance based on the performance on small problem instances. It helps determine the largest problem instance that can be handled by a particular algorithm implementation (Bentley, 1999).

To store collections of information, most programming languages support *arrays*, contiguous regions of memory indexed by an integer i to enable rapid access to the ith element. An array is one-dimensional when each element fits into a word in the platform (e.g., an array of integers or Boolean values). Some arrays extend into multiple dimensions, enabling more complex data representations.

Rate of Growth of Functions

We describe the behavior of an algorithm by representing the *rate of growth of its execution time* as a function of the size of the input problem instance. Characterizing an algorithm's performance in this way is a common abstraction that ignores numerous details. To use this measure properly requires an awareness of the details hidden by the abstraction. Every program is run on a computing platform, which is a general term meant to encompass:

- The computer on which the program is run, its CPU, data cache, floating-point unit (FPU), and other on-chip features
- The programming language in which the program is written, along with the compiler/interpreter and optimization settings for generated code
- The operating system
- Other processes being run in the background

We assume that changing the platform will change the execution time of the program by a constant factor, and that we can therefore ignore platform differences in conformance with the asymptotically equivalent principle described earlier.

To place this discussion in context, we briefly discuss the **Sequential Search** algorithm, presented later in Chapter 5. **Sequential Search** examines a list of $n \geq 1$ distinct elements, one at a time, until a desired value, v, is found. For now, assume that:

- There are n distinct elements in the list
- The list contains the desired value v
- Each element in the list is equally likely to be the desired value v

To understand the performance of **Sequential Search**, we must know how many elements it examines "on average." Since v is known to be in the list and each element is equally likely to be v, the average number of examined elements, $E(n)$, is the sum of the number of elements examined for each of the n values divided by n. Mathematically:

$$E(n) = \frac{1}{n} \sum_{i=1}^{n} i = \frac{n(n+1)}{2n} = \frac{1}{2}n + \frac{1}{2}$$

Thus, **Sequential Search** examines about half of the elements in a list of n distinct elements subject to these assumptions. If the number of elements in the list doubles, then **Sequential Search** should examine about twice as many elements; the expected number of probes is a *linear* function of n. That is, the expected number of probes is "about" $c*n$ for some constant c; here, $c = 0.5$. A fundamental fact of performance analysis is that the constant c is unimportant in the long run, because the most important cost factor is the size of the problem instance, n. As n gets larger and larger, the error in claiming that:

$$\frac{1}{2}n \approx \frac{1}{2}n + \frac{1}{2}$$

becomes less significant. In fact, the ratio between the two sides of this approximation approaches 1. That is:

$$\lim_{n \to \infty} \frac{\left(\frac{1}{2}n\right)}{\left(\frac{1}{2}n + \frac{1}{2}\right)} = 1$$

although the error in the estimation is significant for small values of n. In this context, we say the rate of growth of the expected number of elements that **Sequential Search** examines is linear. That is, we ignore the constant multiplier and are concerned only when the size of a problem instance is large.

When using the abstraction of the rate of growth to choose between algorithms, remember that:

Constants matter
> That's why we use supercomputers and upgrade our computers on a regular basis.

Size of n is not always large
> We will see in Chapter 4 that the rate of growth of the execution time of **Quicksort** is less than the rate of growth of the execution time of **Insertion Sort**. Yet **Insertion Sort** outperforms **Quicksort** for small arrays on the same platform.

An algorithm's rate of growth determines how it will perform on increasingly larger problem instances. Let's apply this underlying principle to a more complex example.

Consider evaluating four sorting algorithms for a specific sorting task. The following performance data was generated by sorting a block of n random strings. For string blocks of size $n = 1 - 512$, 50 trials were run. The best and worst performances were discarded, and Figure 2-1 shows the average running time (in microseconds) of the remaining 48 results. The variance between the runs is surprising.

One way to interpret these results is to try to design a function that will predict the performance of each algorithm on a problem instance of size n. We are unlikely to guess such a function, so we use commercially available software to compute a trend line with a statistical process known as regression analysis. The "fitness" of a trend line to the actual data is based on a value between 0 and 1, known as the R^2 value. R^2 values near 1 indicate high fitness. For example, if $R^2 = 0.9948$, there is only a 0.52% chance the fitness of the trend line is due to random variations in the data.

Sort-4 is clearly the worst performing of these sort algorithms. Given the 512 data points as plotted in a spreadsheet, the trend line to which its performance conforms is:

$$y = 0.0053*n^2 - 0.3601*n + 39.212$$

$$R^2 = 0.9948$$

Having an R^2 confidence value so close to 1 declares this an accurate estimate. **Sort-2** offers the fastest implementation over the given range of points. Its behavior is characterized by the following trend line equation:

$$y = 0.05765*n*log(n) + 7.9653$$

Sort-2 marginally outperforms **Sort-3** initially, and its ultimate behavior is perhaps 10% faster than **Sort-3**. **Sort-1** shows two distinct behavioral patterns. For blocks of 39 or fewer strings, the behavior is characterized by:

$$y = 0.0016*n^2 + 0.2939*n + 3.1838$$

$$R^2 = 0.9761$$

However, with 40 or more strings, the behavior is characterized by:

$$y = 0.0798*n*log(n) + 142.7818$$

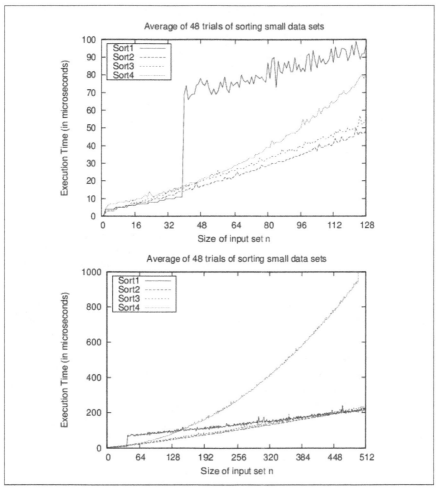

Figure 2-1. Comparing four sort algorithms on small data sets

The numeric coefficients in these equations are entirely dependent upon the platform on which these implementations execute. As described earlier, such incidental differences are not important. The long-term trend as *n* increases dominates the computation of these behaviors. Indeed, Figure 2-1 graphs the behavior using two different ranges to show that the real behavior for an algorithm may not be apparent until n is large enough.

Algorithm designers seek to understand the behavioral differences that exist between algorithms. **Sort-1** reflects the performance of `qsort` on Linux 2.6.9. When reviewing the source code (which can be found through any of the available Linux code repositories), we discover the following comment: "Qsort routine from Bentley & McIlroy's Engineering a Sort Function." Bentley and McIlroy (1993) describe how to optimize **Quicksort** by varying the strategy for problem sizes less than 7, between 8 and 39, and for 40 and higher. It is satisfying to see that the empirical results presented here confirm the underlying implementation.

Analysis in the Best, Average, and Worst Cases

One question to ask is whether the results of the previous section will be true for all input problem instances. How will the behavior of **Sort-2** change with different input problem instances of the same size?

- The data could contain large runs of elements already in sorted order
- The input could contain duplicate values
- Regardless of the size n of the input set, the elements could be drawn from a much smaller set and contain a significant number of duplicate values

Although **Sort-4** from Figure 2-1 was the slowest of the four algorithms for sorting n random strings, it turns out to be the fastest when the data is already sorted. This advantage rapidly fades away, however; with just 32 random items out of position, as shown in Figure 2-2, **Sort-3** now has the best performance.

However, suppose an input array with n strings is "nearly sorted"—i.e., $n/4$ of the strings (25% of them) are swapped with another position just four locations away. It may come as a surprise to see in Figure 2-3 that **Sort-4** outperforms the others.

The conclusion to draw is that for many problems, no single optimal algorithm exists. Choosing an algorithm depends on understanding the problem being solved and the underlying probability distribution of the instances likely to be treated, as well as the behavior of the algorithms being considered.

To provide some guidance, algorithms are typically presented with three common cases in mind:

Worst case
> Defines a class of problem instances for which an algorithm exhibits its worst runtime behavior. Instead of trying to identify the specific input, algorithm designers typically describe *properties* of the input that prevent an algorithm from running efficiently.

Defines the expected behavior when executing the algorithm on random problem instances. While some instances will require greater time to complete because of some special cases, the vast majority will not. This measure describes the expectation an average user of the algorithm should have.

Best case

Defines a class of problem instances for which an algorithm exhibits its best runtime behavior. For these instances, the algorithm does the least work. In reality, the best case rarely occurs.

By knowing the performance of an algorithm under each of these cases, you can judge whether an algorithm is appropriate to use in your specific situation.

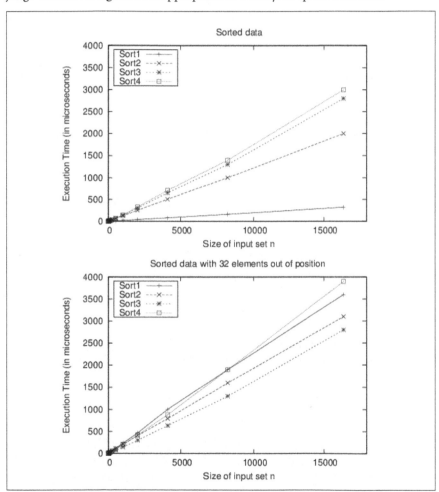

Figure 2-2. Comparing sort algorithms on sorted/nearly sorted data

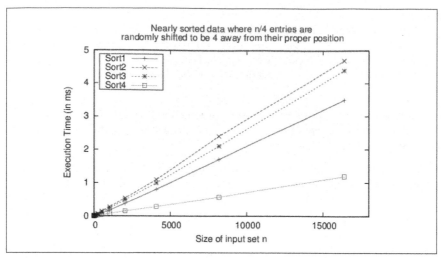

Figure 2-3. Sort-4 wins on nearly sorted data

Worst Case

For any particular value of n, the work done by an algorithm or program may vary dramatically over all the instances of size n. For a given program and a given value n, the worst-case execution time is the maximum execution time, where the maximum is taken over all instances of size n.

We are interested in the worst-case behavior of an algorithm because it often is the easiest case to analyze. It also explains how slow the program could be in any situation.

More formally, if S_n is the set of instances s_i of size n, and $t()$ is a function that measures the work done by an algorithm on each instance, then work done by an algorithm on S_n in the worst case is the maximum of $t(s_i)$ over all $s_i \in S_n$. Denoting this worst-case performance on S_n by $T_{wc}(n)$, the rate of growth of $T_{wc}(n)$ defines the worst-case complexity of the algorithm.

There are not enough resources to compute each individual instance s_i on which to run the algorithm to determine empirically the one that leads to worst-case performance. Instead, an adversary crafts a worst-case problem instance given the description of the algorithm.

Average Case

Consider a telephone system designed to support a large number n of telephones. In the worst case, it must be able to complete all calls where $n/2$ people pick up their phones and call the other $n/2$ people. Although this system will never crash because of overload, it would be prohibitively expensive to construct. In reality, the probability that each of $n/2$ people calls a unique member of the other $n/2$ people is exceedingly small. Instead, we could design a system that is cheaper to build and use mathematical tools to consider the probability of crash due to overload.

For the set of instances of size n, we associate a probability distribution $Pr\{s_i\}$, which assigns a probability between 0 and 1 to each instance s_i such that the sum of the probabilities over all instances of size n is 1. More formally, if S_n is the set of instances of size n, then:

$$\sum_{s_i \in S_n} Pr\{s_i\} = 1$$

If $t()$ measures the work done by an algorithm on each instance, then the average-case work done by an algorithm on S_n is:

$$T_{ac}(n) = \sum_{s_i \in S_n} t(s_i) \, Pr\{s_i\}$$

That is, the actual work done on instance s_i, $t(s_i)$, is weighted with the probability that s_i will actually be presented as input. If $Pr\{s_i\} = 0$, then the actual value of $t(s_i)$ does not impact the expected work done by the program. Denoting this average-case work on S_n by $T_{ac}(n)$, then the rate of growth of $T_{ac}(n)$ defines the average-case complexity of the algorithm.

Recall that when describing the rate of growth of work or time, we consistently ignore constants. So when we say that **Sequential Search** of n elements takes, on average:

$$\frac{1}{2}n + \frac{1}{2}$$

probes (subject to our earlier assumptions), then by convention we simply say that subject to these assumptions, we expect **Sequential Search** will examine a *linear* number of elements, or *order n*.

Best Case

Knowing the best case for an algorithm is useful even though the situation rarely occurs in practice. In many cases, it provides insight into the optimal circumstance for an algorithm. For example, the best case for **Sequential Search** is when it searches for a desired value, v, which ends up being the first element in the list. Consider a slightly different approach, which we'll call **Counting Search**, that counts the number of times that v appears in a list. If the computed count is zero, then the item was not found, so it returns false; otherwise, it returns true. Note that **Counting Search** always searches through the entire list; therefore, even though its worst-case behavior is $O(n)$—the same as **Sequential Search**—its best-case behavior remains $O(n)$, so it is unable to take advantage of either the best-case or average-case situations in which it could have performed better.

Lower and Upper Bounds

We simplify the presentation of the "Big O" notation in this book. The goal is to classify the behavior of an algorithm as it solves problem instances of increasing size, n. The classification is stated as $O(f(n))$ where $f(n)$ is most commonly a function such as n, n^3, or 2^n.

For example, assume there is an algorithm whose worst-case performance *is never greater than* directly proportional to the size of the input problem instance, once the size is "large enough." More precisely, there exists some constant $c > 0$ such that $t(n) \leq c^*n$ for all $n > n_0$, where n_0 is the point where each problem instance is "large enough." In this case, the classification would be the function $f(n) = n$ and we would use the notation $O(n)$. For this same algorithm, assume that its best-case performance *is never smaller than* directly proportional to the size of the input problem instance. In this case, there exists a different constant c and a different threshold problem size, n_0, and $t(n) \geq c^*n$ for all $n > n_0$. Here classification once again is $f(n) = n$ and we would use the notation $\Omega(n)$.

To summarize, the actual formal notation is as follows:

- The *lower bound* for the execution time of an algorithm is classified as $\Omega(f(n))$ and corresponds to the best-case scenario
- The *upper bound* for the execution time is classified as $O(f(n))$ and corresponds to the worst-case scenario

It is necessary to consider both scenarios. The careful reader will note that we could just as easily have used a function $f(n) = c^*2^n$ to classify the algorithm discussed above as $O(2^n)$, though this describes much slower behavior. Indeed, doing so would provide little information—it would be like saying you need no more than 1 week to perform a 5-minute task. In this book, we always present an algorithm's classification using its closest match.

In complexity theory, there is another notation, $\Theta(f(n))$, which combines these concepts to identify an accurate *tight bound*—that is, when the lower bound is determined to be $\Omega(f(n))$ and the upper bound is also $O(f(n))$ for the same classification $f(n)$. We chose the widely accepted (and more informal use) of $O(f(n))$ to simplify the presentations and analyses. We ensure that when discussing algorithmic behavior, there is no more accurate $f'(n)$ that can be used to classify the algorithms we identify as $O(f(n))$.

Performance Families

We compare algorithms by evaluating their performance on problem instances of size n. This methodology is the standard means developed over the past half-century for comparing algorithms. By doing so, we can determine which algorithms scale to solve problems of a nontrivial size by evaluating the running time needed by the algorithm in relation to the size of the provided input. A secondary performance evaluation is to consider how much memory or storage an algorithm needs; we address these concerns within the individual algorithm descriptions, as appropriate.

We use the following classifications, which are ordered by *decreasing* efficiency:

- Constant: $O(1)$
- Logarithmic: $O(\log n)$
- Sublinear: $O(n^d)$ for $d < 1$
- Linear: $O(n)$
- Linearithmic: $O(n \log n)$
- Quadratic: $O(n^2)$
- Exponential: $O(2^n)$

When evaluating the performance of an algorithm, keep in mind that you must identify the most expensive computation within an algorithm to determine its classification. For example, consider an algorithm that is subdivided into two tasks, a task classified as linear followed by a task classified as quadratic. The overall performance of the algorithm must therefore be classified as quadratic.

We'll now illustrate these performance classifications by example.

Constant Behavior

When analyzing the performance of the algorithms in this book, we frequently claim that some primitive operations provide constant performance. Clearly this claim is not an absolute determinant for the actual performance of the operation since we do not refer to specific hardware. For example, comparing whether two 32-bit numbers x and y are the same value should have the same performance regardless of the actual values of x and y. A constant operation is defined to have $O(1)$ performance.

What about the performance of comparing two 256-bit numbers? Or two 1,024-bit numbers? It turns out that for a predetermined fixed size k, you can compare two k-bit numbers in constant time. The key is that the problem size (i.e., the values x and y being compared) cannot grow beyond the fixed size k. We abstract the extra effort, which is multiplicative in terms of k, using the notation $O(1)$.

Log *n* Behavior

A bartender offers the following $10,000 bet to any patron: "I will choose a secret number from 1 to 1,000,000 and you will have 20 chances to guess my number. After each guess, I will either tell you Too Low, Too High, or You Win. If you guess my number in 20 or fewer questions, I give you $10,000. If none of your 20 guesses is my secret number you must give me $10,000." Would you take this bet? You should, because you can always win. Table 2-1 shows a sample scenario for the range 1–8 that asks a series of questions, reducing the problem size by about half each time.

Table 2-1. Sample behavior for guessing number from 1–8

Number	First round	Second round	Third round	Fourth round
1	Is it 4? Too High	Is it 2? Too High	Must be 1! You Win	
2	Is it 4? Too High	Is it 2? You Win		
3	Is it 4? Too High	Is it 2? Too Low	Must be 3! You Win	
4	Is it 4? You Win			
5	Is it 4? Too Low	Is it 6? Too High	Must be 5! You Win	
6	Is it 4? Too Low	Is it 6? You Win		
7	Is it 4? Too Low	Is it 6? Too Low	Is it 7? You Win	
8	Is it 4? Too Low	Is it 6? Too Low	Is it 7? Too Low	Must be 8! You Win

In each round, depending upon the specific answers from the bartender, the size of the potential range containing the secret number is cut in about half each time. Eventually, the range of the secret number will be limited to just one possible number; this happens after $1 + \lfloor log_2(n) \rfloor$ rounds, where $log_2(x)$ computes the logarithm of x in base 2. The floor function $\lfloor x \rfloor$ rounds the number x down to the largest integer smaller than or equal to x. For example, if the bartender chooses a number between 1 and 10, you could guess it in $1 + \lfloor log_2(10) \rfloor = 1 + \lfloor 3.32 \rfloor$, or four guesses. As further evidence of this formula, if the bartender chooses one of two numbers, then you need two rounds to guarantee that you will guess the number, or $1 + \lfloor log_2(2) \rfloor = 1 + 1 = 2$. Remember, according to the bartender's rules, you *must guess the number out loud*.

This same approach works equally well for 1,000,000 numbers. In fact, the **Guessing** algorithm shown in Example 2-1 works for any range [*low*, *high*] and determines the value of the hidden number, *n*, in $1 + \lfloor log_2(high\text{-}low + 1) \rfloor$ rounds. If there are 1,000,000 numbers, this algorithm will locate the number in at most $1 + \lfloor log_2(1{,}000{,}000) \rfloor = 1 + \lfloor 19.93 \rfloor$, or 20 guesses (the worst case).

Example 2-1. Java code to guess number in range [low, high]

```java
// Compute number of turns when n is guaranteed to be in range [low,high].
public static int turns (int n, int low, int high) {
  int turns = 0;
  // Continue while there is a potential number to guess
  while (high >= low) {
    turns++;
    int mid = (low + high)/2;
    if (mid == n) {
      return turns;
    } else if (mid < n) {
      low = mid + 1;
    } else {
      high = mid - 1;
    }
  }
  return turns;
}
```

Logarithmic algorithms are extremely efficient because they rapidly converge on a solution. These algorithms succeed because they reduce the size of the problem by about half each time. The **Guessing** algorithm reaches a solution after at most $k = 1 + \lfloor log_2 (n) \rfloor$ iterations, and at the ith iteration ($0 < i \le k$), the algorithm computes a guess that is known to be within $\pm\epsilon = 2^{k-i} - 1$ from the actual hidden number. The quantity ϵ is considered the error, or uncertainty. After each iteration of the loop, ϵ is cut in half.

For the remainder of this book, whenever we refer to *log* (*n*) it is assumed to be computed in base 2, so we will drop the subscript log_2 (*n*).

Another example showing efficient behavior is the **Bisection** algorithm, which computes a root of an equation in one variable; namely, for what values of *x* does a continuous function *f*(*x*) = 0? You start with two values, *a* and *b*, for which *f*(*a*) and *f*(*b*) are opposite signs—that is, one is positive and one is negative. At each step, the method *bisects* the range [*a*, *b*] by computing its midpoint, *c*, and determines in which half the root must lie. Thus, with each round, *c* approximates a root value and the method cuts the error in half.

To find a root of *f*(*x*) = $x^*sin(x) - 5^*x - cos(x)$, start with *a* = −1 and *b* = 1. As shown in Table 2-2, the algorithm converges on the solution of *f*(*x*) = 0, where *x* = −0.189302759 is a root of the function.

Table 2-2. Bisection method

n	a	b	c	f(c)
1	−1	1	0	−1
2	−1	0	−0.5	1.8621302
3	−0.5	0	−0.25	0.3429386

n	a	b	c	f(c)
4	−0.25	0	−0.125	−0.3516133
5	−0.25	−0.125	−0.1875	−0.0100227
6	−0.25	−0.1875	−0.21875	0.1650514
7	−0.21875	−0.1875	−0.203125	0.0771607
8	−0.203125	−0.1875	−0.1953125	0.0334803
9	−0.1953125	−0.1875	−0.1914062	0.0117066
10	−0.1914062	−0.1875	−0.1894531	0.0008364
11	−0.1894531	−0.1875	−0.1884766	−0.0045945
12	−0.1894531	−0.1884766	−0.1889648	−0.0018794
13	−0.1894531	−0.1889648	−0.189209	−0.0005216
14	−0.1894531	−0.189209	−0.1893311	0.0001574
15	−0.1893311	−0.189209	−0.18927	−0.0001821
16	−0.1893311	−0.18927	−0.1893005	−0.0000124

Sublinear $O(n^d)$ Behavior for $d < 1$

In some cases, the behavior of an algorithm is better than *linear*, yet not as efficient as *logarithmic*. As discussed in Chapter 10, a *k*-d tree in multiple dimensions can partition a set of *n* *d*-dimensional points efficiently. If the tree is balanced, the search time for range queries that conform to the axes of the points is $O(n^{1-1/d})$. For two-dimensional queries, the resulting performance is $O(sqrt(n))$.

Linear Performance

Some problems clearly seem to require more effort to solve than others. A child can evaluate 7 + 5 to get 12. How much harder is the problem 37 + 45?

Specifically, how hard is it to add two *n*-digit numbers $a_{n-1}...a_0 + b_{n-1}...b_0$ to result in an *n* + 1-digit number $c_n...c_0$ digit value? The primitive operations used in this **Addition** algorithm are as follows:

$$c_i \leftarrow (a_i + b_i + carry_i) \bmod 10$$
$$carry_{i+1} \leftarrow \begin{cases} 1 \text{ if } a_i + b_i + carry_i \geq 10 \\ \qquad 0 \text{ otherwise} \end{cases}$$

A sample Java implementation of **Addition** is shown in Example 2-2, where an *n*-digit number is represented as an array of int values whose most significant (i.e., leftmost) digit is in index position 0. For the examples in this section, it is assumed that each of these values is a decimal digit *d* such that $0 \leq d \leq 9$.

Example 2-2. Java implementation of add

Mathematics
of
Algorithms

```java
public static void add (int[] n1, int[] n2, int[] sum) {
  int position = n1.length-1;
  int carry = 0;
  while (position >= 0) {
    int total = n1[position] + n2[position] + carry;
    sum[position+1] = total % 10;
    if (total > 9) { carry = 1; } else { carry = 0; }
    position--;
  }
  sum[0] = carry;
}
```

As long as the input problem can be stored in memory, add computes the addition of the two numbers as represented by the input integer arrays n1 and n2 and stores the result in the array sum. Would this implementation be as efficient as the following plus alternative, listed in Example 2-3, which computes the exact same answer using different computations?

Example 2-3. Java implementation of plus

```java
public static void plus(int[] n1, int[] n2, int[] sum) {
  int position = n1.length;
  int carry = 0;
  while (--position >= 0) {
    int total = n1[position] + n2[position] + carry;
    if (total > 9) {
      sum[position+1] = total-10;
      carry = 1;
    } else {
      sum[position+1] = total;
      carry = 0;
    }
  }
  sum[0] = carry;
}
```

Do these small implementation details affect the performance of an algorithm? Let's consider two other potential factors that can impact the algorithm's performance:

- add and plus can trivially be converted into C programs. How does the choice of language affect the algorithm's performance?

- The programs can be executed on different computers. How does the choice of computer hardware affect the algorithm's performance?

The implementations were executed 10,000 times on numbers ranging from 256 digits to 32,768 digits. For each digit size, a random number of that size was generated; thereafter, for each of the 10,000 trials, these two numbers were circular shifted (one left and one right) to create two different numbers to be added. Two different programming languages were used (C and Java). We start with the hypothesis that as the problem size doubles, the execution time for the algorithm doubles as well. We would like to know that this overall behavior occurs regardless of the machine, programming language, or implementation variation used. Each variation was executed on a set of configurations:

g
   C version was compiled with debugging information included.

O1, O2, O3
   C version was compiled under these different optimization levels. Increasing numbers imply better performance.

Java
   Java implementation of algorithm.

Table 2-3 contains the results for both add and plus. The eighth and final column compares the ratio of the performance of plus on problems of size *2n* versus problems of size *n*. Define $t(n)$ to be the actual running time of the **Addition** algorithm on an input of size *n*. This growth pattern provides empirical evidence of the time to compute plus for two *n*-digit numbers.

Table 2-3. Time (in milliseconds) to execute 10,000 add/plus invocations on random digits of size n

n	Add-g	Add-java	Add-O3	Plus-g	Plus-java	Plus-O3	Ratio
256	33	19	10	31	20	11	
512	67	22	20	58	32	23	2.09
1024	136	49	40	126	65	46	2.00
2048	271	98	80	241	131	95	2.07
4096	555	196	160	489	264	195	2.05
8192	1107	392	321	972	527	387	1.98
16384	2240	781	647	1972	1052	805	2.08
32768	4604	1554	1281	4102	2095	1721	2.14
65536	9447	3131	2572	8441	4200	3610	2.10
131072	19016	6277	5148	17059	8401	7322	2.03

n	Add-g	Add-java	Add-O3	Plus-g	Plus-java	Plus-O3	Ratio
262144	38269	12576	10336	34396	16811	14782	2.02
524288	77147	26632	21547	69699	35054	30367	2.05
1048576	156050	51077	53916	141524	61856	66006	2.17

We can classify the **Addition** algorithm as being *linear* with respect to its input size n. That is, there is some constant $c > 0$ such that $t(n) \leq c*n$ for "large enough" n, or more precisely, all $n > n_0$. We don't actually need to compute the actual value of c or n_0; we just know they exist and they can be computed. An argument can be made to establish a linear-time lower bound on the complexity of **Addition** by showing that every digit must be examined (consider the consequences of not checking one of the digits).

For all plus executions (regardless of language or compilation configuration) of **Addition**, we can set c to $1/7$ and choose n_0 to be 256. Other implementations of **Addition** would have different constants, yet their overall behavior would still be *linear*. This result may seem surprising given that most programmers assume integer arithmetic is a constant time operation; however, constant time addition is achievable only when the integer representation (such as 16-bit or 64-bit) uses a fixed integer size n.

When considering differences in algorithms, the constant c is not as important as knowing the rate of growth of the algorithm. Seemingly inconsequential differences result in different performance. The plus implementation of **Addition** attempts to improve efficiency by eliminating the modulo operator (%). Still, when compiling both plus and add using -O3 optimization, add is nearly 30% faster. This is not to say that we ignore the value of c. Certainly if we execute **Addition** a large number of times, even small changes to the actual value of c can have a large impact on the performance of a program.

Linearithmic Performance

A common behavior in efficient algorithms is best described by this performance family. To explain how this behavior occurs in practice, let's define $t(n)$ to represent the time an algorithm takes to solve an input problem instance of size n. Divide and Conquer is an efficient way to solve a problem in which a problem of size n is divided into (roughly equal) subproblems of size $n/2$, which are solved recursively. The solutions of these subproblems are combined together *in linear time* to solve the original problem of size n. Mathematically, this can be stated as:

$$t(n) = 2*t(n/2) + c*n$$

That is, $t(n)$ includes the cost of the two subproblems together with no more than a linear time cost (i.e., $c*n$) to merge the results. Now, on the right side of the equation, $t(n/2)$ is the time to solve a problem of size $n/2$; using the same logic, this can be represented as:

$$t(n/2) = 2*t(n/4) + c*n/2$$

and so the original equation is now:

$$t(n) = 2*[2*t(n/4) + c*n/2] + c*n$$

If we expand this out once more, we see that:

$$t(n) = 2*[2*[2*t(n/8) + c*n/4] + c*n/2] + c*n$$

This last equation reduces to $t(n) = 8*t(n/8) + 4*c*n/4 + 2*c*n/2 + c*n$, which can be simplified as $8*t(n/8) + 3*c*n$. We can then say that $t(n) = (2^k)*t(n/2^k) + k*c*n$. This expansion ends when $2^k = n$ (i.e., when $k = log(n)$). In the final base case when the problem size is 1, the performance $t(1)$ is a constant d. Thus, the closed-form formula for $t(n) = n*d + c*n*log(n)$. Because $c*n*log(n)$ is asymptotically greater than $d*n$ for any fixed constants c and d, $t(n)$ can be simply written as O($n \ log \ n$).

Quadratic Performance

Now consider a similar problem where two integers of size n are multiplied together. Example 2-4 shows an implementation of **Multiplication**, an elementary school algorithm, using the same n-digit representation used earlier when adding numbers.

Example 2-4. mult implementation of Multiplication in Java

```java
public static void mult (int[] n1, int[] n2, int[] result) {
  int pos = result.length-1;

  // clear all values
  for (int i = 0; i < result.length; i++) { result[i] = 0; }
  for (int m = n1.length-1; m>=0; m--) {
    int off = n1.length-1 - m;
    for (int n = n2.length-1; n>=0; n--,off++) {
      int prod = n1[m]*n2[n];

      // compute partial total by carrying previous digit's position
      result[pos-off] += prod % 10;
      result[pos-off-1] += result[pos-off]/10 + prod/10;
      result[pos-off] %= 10;
    }
  }
}
```

Once again, an alternative program is written, times, which eliminates the need for the costly modulo operator, and skips the innermost computations when n1[m] is zero (note that times is not shown here, but can be found in the provided code repository). The times variation contains 203 lines of generated Java code to remove the two modulo operators. Does this variation show cost savings that validate the extra maintenance and development cost in managing this generated code?

Table 2-4 shows the behavior of these implementations of **Multiplication** using the same random input set used when demonstrating **Addition**. Figure 2-4 graphically depicts the performance, showing the parabolic growth curve that is the trademark of *quadratic* behavior.

Table 2-4. Time (in milliseconds) to execute 10,000 multiplications

n	$mult_n$(ms)	$times_n$(ms)	$mult_{2n}/mult_n$
4	2	41	
8	8	83	4
16	33	129	4.13
32	133	388	4.03
64	530	1276	3.98
128	2143	5009	4.04
256	8519	19014	3.98
512	34231	74723	4.02

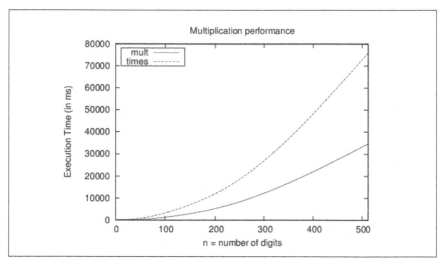

Figure 2-4. Comparison of mult versus times

Even though the times variation is twice as slow, both times and mult exhibit the same asymptotic performance. The ratio of $mult_{2n}/mult_n$ is roughly 4, which demonstrates that the performance of **Multiplication** is *quadratic*. Let's define $t(n)$ to be the actual running time of the **Multiplication** algorithm on an input of size n. By this definition, there must be some constant $c > 0$ such that $t(n) \le c*n^2$ for all $n > n_0$. We don't actually need to know the full details of the c and n_0 values, just that they exist. For the mult implementation of **Multiplication** on our platform, we can set c to 1/7 and choose n_0 to be 16.

Once again, individual variations in implementation are unable to "break" the inherent quadratic performance behavior of an algorithm. However, other algorithms exist (Zuras, 1994) to multiply a pair of *n*-digit numbers that are significantly faster than quadratic. These algorithms are important for applications such as data encryption, in which one frequently multiplies large integers.

Less Obvious Performance Computations

In most cases, reading the description of an algorithm (as shown in **Addition** and **Multiplication**) is sufficient to classify an algorithm as being *linear* or *quadratic*. The primary indicator for *quadratic*, for example, is a nested loop structure. But some algorithms defy such straightforward analysis. Consider the GCD algorithm in Example 2-5, designed by Euclid to compute the greatest common divisor between two integers.

Example 2-5. Euclid's GCD algorithm

```
public static void gcd (int a[], int b[], int gcd[]) {
  if (isZero (a)) { assign (gcd, a); return; }
  if (isZero (b)) { assign (gcd, b); return; }

  a = copy (a);      // Make copies to ensure
  b = copy (b);      // that a and b are not modified

  while (!isZero (b)) {
    // last argument to subtract represents sign of results which
    // we can ignore since we only subtract smaller from larger.
    // Note compareTo (a, b) is positive if a > b.
    if (compareTo (a, b) > 0) {
      subtract (a, b, gcd, new int[1]);
      assign (a, gcd);
    } else {
      subtract (b, a, gcd, new int[1]);
      assign (b, gcd);
    }
  }

  // value held in a is the computed gcd of original (a,b)
  assign (gcd, a);
}
```

This algorithm repeatedly compares two numbers (a and b) and subtracts the smaller number from the larger until zero is reached. The implementations of the helper methods (isZero, assign, compareTo, subtract) can be found in the accompanying code repository.

This algorithm produces the greatest common divisor of two numbers, but there is no clear answer as to how many iterations will be required based on the size of the input. During each pass through the loop, either a or b is reduced and never becomes negative, so we can guarantee that the algorithm will terminate, but some GCD requests take longer than others; for example, using this algorithm, gcd(1000,1) takes 999 steps! Clearly the performance of this algorithm is more sensitive to its inputs than **Addition** or **Multiplication**, in that there are different problem instances of the same size that require very different computation times. This GCD algorithm exhibits its worst-case performance when asked to compute the GCD of $(10^k-1, 1)$; it needs to process the while loop $n = 10^k-1$ times! Since we have already shown that **Addition** is $O(n)$ in terms of the input size n—and so is subtraction, by the way—GCD can be classified as $O(n^2)$.

The GCD implementation in Example 2-5 is outperformed handily by the ModGCD algorithm described in Example 2-6, which relies on the modulo operator to compute the integer remainder of a divided by b.

Example 2-6. ModGCD algorithm for GCD computation

```
public static void modgcd (int a[], int b[], int gcd[]) {
  if (isZero(a)) { assign (gcd, a); return; }
  if (isZero(b)) { assign (gcd, b); return; }

  // align a and b to have same number of digits and work on copies
  a = copy(normalize(a, b.length));
  b = copy(normalize(b, a.length));

  // ensure a is greater than b. Also return trivial gcd
  int rc = compareTo(a,b);
  if (rc == 0) { assign (gcd, a); return; }
  if (rc < 0) {
    int t[] = b;
    b = a;
    a = t;
  }

  int quot[] = new int[a.length];
  int remainder[] = new int[a.length];
  while (!isZero(b)) {
    int t[] = copy (b);
    divide (a, b, quot, remainder);
    assign (b, remainder);
    assign (a, t);
  }
```

```
// value held in a is the computed gcd of (a,b).
  assign (gcd, a);
}
```

ModGCD arrives at a solution more rapidly because it won't waste time subtracting really small numbers from large numbers within the while loop. This difference is not simply an implementation detail; it reflects a fundamental shift in how the algorithm solves the problem.

The computations shown in Figure 2-5 (and enumerated in Table 2-5) show the result of generating 142 random n-digit numbers and computing the GCD of all 10,011 pairs of these numbers.

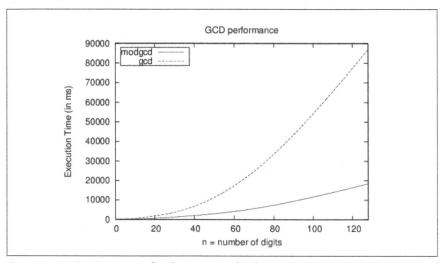

Figure 2-5. Comparison of gcd versus modgcd

Table 2-5. Time (in milliseconds) to execute 10,011 gcd computations

n	modgcd	gcd	modgcd$_{2n}$/modgcd$_n$
4	68	45	0.23
8	226	408	3.32
16	603	1315	2.67
32	1836	4050	3.04
64	5330	18392	2.9
128	20485	76180	3.84

Even though the ModGCD implementation is nearly three times faster than the corresponding GCD implementation on random computations, the performance of ModGCD is *quadratic*, or O(n^2). The analysis is challenging and it turns out that the

---

worst-case performance for ModGCD occurs for two successive Fibonacci numbers. Still, from Table 2-5 we can infer that the algorithm is quadratic because the performance appears to quadruple as the problem size doubles.

More sophisticated algorithms for computing GCD have been designed—though most are impractical except for extremely large integers—and analysis suggests that the problem allows for more efficient algorithms.

Exponential Performance

Consider a lock with three numeric dials in sequence, each of which contains the digits from 0 to 9. Each dial can be set independently to one of these 10 digits. Assume you have a found such a lock, but don't have its combination; it is simply a matter of some manual labor to try each of the 1,000 possible combinations, from 000 to 999. To generalize this problem, assume the lock has n dials, then the total number of possibilities is 10^n. Solving this problem using a brute-force approach would be considered exponential performance or $O(10^n)$, in this case in base 10. Often, the exponential base is 2, but this performance holds true for any base $b > 1$.

Exponential algorithms are practical only for very small values of n. Some algorithms might have a worst-case behavior that is exponential, yet still are heavily used in practice because of their average-case behavior. A good example is the **Simplex** algorithm for solving linear programming problems.

Summary of Asymptotic Growth

An algorithm with better asymptotic growth will *eventually* execute faster than one with worse asymptotic growth, regardless of the actual constants. The actual breakpoint will differ based on the actual constants, but it exists and can be empirically evaluated. In addition, during asymptotic analysis we only need to be concerned with the fastest-growing term of the $t(n)$ function. For this reason, if the number of operations for an algorithm can be computed as $c*n^3 + d*n*log(n)$, we would classify this algorithm as $O(n^3)$ because that is the dominant term that grows far more rapidly than $n*log(n)$.

Benchmark Operations

The Python operator ** rapidly performs exponentiation. The sample computation 2**851 is shown here.

```
1501503365760940045994231539101851372262351918709900707335
5798781525263125238463415894820397160662761697108038369410
9252383653813326044865235229218132798103200794538451818
05154673256699778290824639959535835805252308660678089369234
23852922777447919533214924 8
```

In Python, computations are relatively independent of the underlying platform (i.e., computing 2^{851} in Java or C on most platforms would cause numeric overflow). But a fast computation in Python yields the result shown in the preceding example. Is it an advantage or a disadvantage that Python abstracts away the underlying architecture? Consider the following two hypotheses:

Hypothesis H1
> Computing 2^n has consistent behavior, regardless of the value of n.

Hypothesis H2
> Large numbers (such as shown previously in expanded form) can be treated in the same way as any other number, such as 123,827 or 997.

To refute hypothesis H1, we conduct 10,000 evaluations of 2^n. The total execution time for each value of n is shown in Figure 2-6.

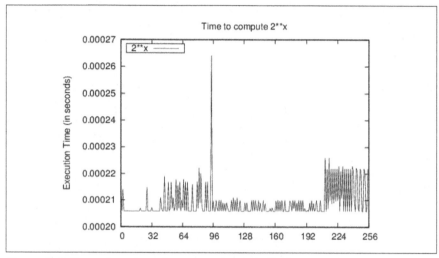

Figure 2-6. Execution times for computing 2^x in Python

Oddly enough, the performance seems to have different behaviors, one for x smaller than 16, a second for x values around 145, and a third for x greater than 200. This behavior reveals that Python uses an **Exponentiation By Squaring** algorithm for computing powers using the ** operator. Manually computing 2^x using a for loop would cause *quadratic* performance.

To refute hypothesis H2, we conduct an experiment that precomputes the value of 2^n and then evaluates the time to compute $\pi*2^n$. The total execution time of these 10,000 trials is shown in Figure 2-7.

Why do the points in Figure 2-7 not appear on a straight line? For what value of x does the line break? The multiplication operation (*) appears to be overloaded. It does different things depending on whether the numbers being multiplied are floating-point numbers, or integers that each fit into a single word of the machine, or integers that are so large they must each be stored in several words of the machine, or some combination of these.

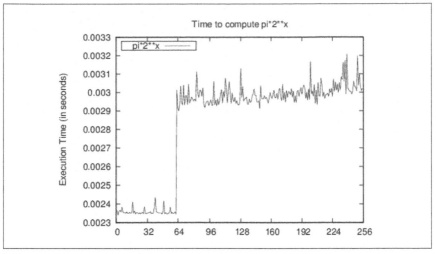

Figure 2-7. Execution times for computing large multiplication

The break in the plot occurs for $x = \{64,65\}$ and appears to correspond to a shift in the storage of large floating-point numbers. Again, there may be unexpected slow-downs in computations that can only be uncovered by such benchmarking efforts.

References

Bentley, J., *Programming Pearls*. Second Edition. Addison-Wesley Professional, 1999.

Bentley, J. and M. McIlroy, "Engineering a sort function," *Software—Practice and Experience*, 23(11): 1249–1265, 1993. *http://dx.doi.org/10.1002/spe.4380231105*

Zuras, D., "More on squaring and multiplying large integers," *IEEE Transactions on Computers*, 43(8): 899–908, 1994, *http://dx.doi.org/10.1109/12.295852.*

3

Algorithm Building Blocks

We build software to solve problems. But programmers are often too focused on solving a problem to determine whether a solution to the problem already exists. Even if the programmer knows the problem has been solved in similar cases, it's not clear that the existing code will actually fit the specific problem facing the programmer. Ultimately, it isn't easy to find code in a given programming language that can be readily modified to solve the problem.

We can think of algorithms in different ways. Many practitioners are content to look up an algorithm in a book or on some website, copy some code, run it, maybe even test it, and then move on to the next task. In our opinion, this process does not improve one's understanding of algorithms. In fact, this approach can lead you down the wrong path where you select a specific implementation of an algorithm.

The question is how to locate the right algorithm for the job quickly and understand it well enough to ensure you've made a good choice. And once you've chosen the algorithm, how do you implement it efficiently? Each book chapter groups together a set of algorithms solving a standard problem (such as Sorting or Searching) or related problems (such as Path Finding). In this chapter, we present the format we use to describe the algorithms in this book. We also summarize the common algorithmic approaches used to solve problems.

Algorithm Template Format

The real power of using a template to describe each algorithm is that you can quickly compare and contrast different algorithms and identify commonalities in seemingly different algorithms. Each algorithm is presented using a fixed set of sections that conform to this template. We may omit a section if it adds no value to the algorithm description or add sections as needed to illuminate a particular point.

Name

A descriptive name for the algorithm. We use this name to communicate concisely the algorithm to others. For example, if we talk about using a **Sequential Search**, it conveys exactly what type of search algorithm we are talking about. The name of each algorithm is always shown in **Bold Font**.

Input/Output

Describes the expected format of input data to the algorithm and the resulting values computed.

Context

A description of a problem that illustrates when an algorithm is useful and when it will perform at its best. A description of the properties of the problem/solution that must be addressed and maintained for a successful implementation. They are the things that would cause you to choose this algorithm specifically.

Solution

The algorithm description using real working code with documentation. All code solutions can be found in the associated code repository.

Analysis

A synopsis of the analysis of the algorithm, including performance data and information to help you understand the behavior of the algorithm. Although the analysis section is not meant to "prove" the described performance of an algorithm, you should be able to understand why the algorithm behaves as it does. We will provide references to actual texts that present the appropriate lemmas and proofs to explain why the algorithms behave as described.

Variations

Presents variations of the algorithm or different alternatives.

Pseudocode Template Format

Each algorithm in this book is presented with code examples that show an implementation in a major programming language, such as Python, C, C++, and Java. For readers who are not familiar with all of these languages, we first introduce each algorithm in pseudocode with a small example showing its execution.

Consider the following sample performance description, which names the algorithm and classifies its performance clearly for all three behavior cases (best, average, and worst) described in Chapter 2.

Sequential Search Summary

Best: $O(1)$ **Average, Worst:** $O(n)$

```
search (A,t)
  for i=0 to n-1 do ❶
    if A[i] = t then
      return true
  return false
end
```

❶   Access each element in order, from position *0* to *n-1*.

The pseudocode description is intentionally brief. Keywords and function names are described in boldface text. All variables are in lowercase characters, whereas arrays are capitalized and their elements are referred to using $A[i]$ notation. The indentation in the pseudocode describes the scope of conditional **if** statements and looping **while** and **for** statements.

You should refer to each algorithm summary when reading the provided source-code implementations. After each summary, a small example (such as the one shown in Figure 3-1) is provided to better explain the execution of the algorithm. These figures show the dynamic behavior of the algorithms, typically with time moving "downward" in the figure to depict the key steps of the algorithm.

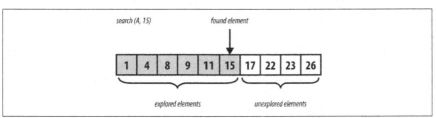

Figure 3-1. Example of Sequential Search executing

Empirical Evaluation Format

We confirm the performance of each algorithm by executing with a series of benchmark problems appropriate for each individual algorithm. Appendix A provides more detail on the mechanisms used for timing purposes. To properly evaluate the performance, a test suite is composed of a set of k individual trials (typically $k \geq 10$). The best and worst performers are discarded as outliers, the remaining $k - 2$ trials are aggregated, and the average and standard deviations are computed. Tables are shown with problem instances typically ranging in size from $n = 2$ to 2^{20}.

Floating-Point Computation

Because several algorithms in this book involve numerical computations, we need to describe the power and limitations of how modern computers process these computations. Computers perform basic computations on values stored in registers by a central processing unit (CPU). These registers have grown in size as computer architectures have evolved from the 8-bit Intel processors popular in the 1970s to today's widespread acceptance of 64-bit architectures (such as Intel's Itanium and Sun Microsystems Sparc processor). The CPU often supports basic operations —such as ADD, MULT, DIVIDE, and SUB—over integer values stored within these registers. Floating-point units (FPUs) can efficiently process floating-point computations according to the IEEE Standard for Binary Floating-Point Arithmetic (IEEE 754).

Mathematical computations over integer-based values (such as Booleans, 8-bit shorts, and 16- and 32-bit integers) have traditionally been the most efficient CPU computations. Programs are often optimized to take advantage of this historic performance differential between integer and floating-point calculations. However, modern CPUs have dramatically improved the performance of floating-point computations relative to their integer counterparts. It is thus important that developers become aware of the following issues when programming using floating-point arithmetic (Goldberg, 1991).

Performance

It is commonly accepted that computations over integer values will be more efficient than their floating-point counterparts. Table 3-1 lists the computation times of 10,000,000 operations including the Linux results (from the first edition of this book) and results for a 1996 Sparc Ultra-2 machine. As you can see, the performance of individual operations can vary significantly from one platform to another. These results show the tremendous speed improvements in processors over the past two decades. Some of the results show 0.0000 timing because they are faster than the available timing mechanism.

Table 3-1. Performance computations of 10,000,000 operations

Operation	Sparc Ultra-2 (time in seconds)	Linux i686 (time in seconds)	Current (time in seconds)
32-bit integer CMP	0.811	0.0337	0.0000
32-bit integer MUL	2.372	0.0421	0.0000
32-bit float MUL	1.236	0.1032	0.02986
64-bit double MUL	1.406	0.1028	0.02987
32-bit float DIV	1.657	0.1814	0.02982
64-bit double DIV	2.172	0.1813	0.02980

Operation	Sparc Ultra-2 (time in seconds)	Linux i686 (time in seconds)	Current (time in seconds)
128-bit double MUL	36.891	0.2765	0.02434
32-bit integer DIV	3.104	0.2468	0.0000
32-bit double SQRT	3.184	0.2749	0.0526

Rounding Error

Any computation using floating-point values may introduce rounding errors because of the nature of the floating-point representation. In general, a floating-point number is a finite representation designed to approximate a real number whose representation may be infinite. Table 3-2 shows information about floating-point representations and the specific representation for the value 3.88f.

Table 3-2. Floating-point representation

Primitive type	Sign	Exponent	Mantissa
Float	1 bit	8 bits	23 bits
Double	1 bit	11 bits	52 bits

Sample Representation of 3.88f as (0x407851ec)

01000000 01111000 01010001 11101100 (total of 32 bits)

seeeeeee emmmmmmm mmmmmmmm mmmmmmmm

The next three consecutive 32-bit floating-point representations (and values) following 3.88f are:

- 0x407851ed: 3.8800004
- 0x407851ee: 3.8800006
- 0x407851ef: 3.8800008

Here are the floating-point values for three randomly chosen 32-bit values:

- 0x1aec9fae: 9.786529E-23
- 0x622be970: 7.9280355E20
- 0x18a4775b: 4.2513525E-24

In a 32-bit floating-point value, one bit is used for the sign, 8 bits form the exponent, and 23 bits form the mantissa (also known as the *significand*). In the Java float representation, "the power of two can be determined by interpreting the exponent bits as a positive number, and then subtracting a bias from the positive number. For a float, the bias is 126" (Venners, 1996). The exponent stored is 128, so the actual exponent value is 128 – 126, or 2.

To achieve the greatest precision, the mantissa is always normalized so that the left-most digit is always 1; this bit *does not have to actually be stored*, but is understood by the floating-point processor to be part of the number. In the previous example, the mantissa is

.[1]111100001010001111101100 = [1/2] + 1/4 + 1/8 + 1/16 + 1/32 + 1/1,024 + 1/4,096 + 1/65,536 + 1/131,072 + 1/262,144 + 1/524,288 + 1/2,097,152 + 1/4,194,304

which evaluates exactly to 0.9700000286102294921875 if the full sum of fractions is carried out.

When storing 3.88f using this representation, the approximate value is + 1*0.9700000286102294921875*2², which is exactly 3.88000011444091796875. The error inherent in the value is ~0.0000001. The most common way of describing floating-point error is to use the term *relative error*, which computes the ratio of the absolute error with the desired value. Here, the relative error is 0.0000001144091796875/3.88, or 2.9E-8. It is quite common for these relative errors to be less than 1 part per million.

Comparing Floating-Point Values

Because floating-point values are only approximate, the simplest operations in floating point become suspect. Consider the following statement:

```
if (x == y) { ... }
```

Is it truly the case that these two floating-point numbers must be exactly equal? Or is it sufficient for them to be simply approximately equal (for which we use the symbol ≅)? Could it ever occur that two values are different though close enough that they should be considered to be the same? Let's consider a practical example: three points $p_0 = (a, b)$, $p_1 = (c, d)$, and $p_2 = (e, f)$ in the Cartesian plane define an ordered pair of line segments (p_0, p_1) and (p_1, p_2). The value of the expression $(c - a)*(f - b) - (d - b)*(e - a)$ can determine whether these two line segments are collinear (i.e., on the same line). If the value is:

- 0 then the segments are collinear
- < 0 then the segments are turning to the left (or counterclockwise)
- > 0 then the segments are turning to the right (or clockwise)

To show how floating-point errors can occur in Java computations, consider defining three points using the values of a to f in Table 3-3.

Table 3-3. Floating-point arithmetic errors

	32-bit floating point (float)	64-bit floating point (double)
$a = 1/3$	0.33333334	0.3333333333333333
$b = 5/3$	1.6666666	1.6666666666666667

	32-bit floating point (float)	64-bit floating point (double)
$c = 33$	33.0	33.0
$d = 165$	165.0	165.0
$e = 19$	19.0	19.0
$f = 95$	95.0	95.0
$(c - a)*(f - b) - (d - b)*(e - a)$	4.8828125 E-4	-4.547473508864641 E - 13

As you can readily determine, the three points p_0, p_1, and p_2 are collinear on the line $y = 5*x$. When computing the floating-point computation test for collinearity, however, the errors inherent in floating-point arithmetic affect the result of the computation. Using 32-bit floating-point values, the calculation results in 0.00048828125; using 64-bit floating-point values, the computed value is actually a very small negative number! This example shows that both 32-bit and 64-bit floating-point representations fail to capture the true mathematical value of the computation. And in this case, the result is a disagreement over whether the points represent a clockwise turn, a counterclockwise turn, or collinearity. Such is the world of floating-point computations.

One common solution to this situation is to introduce a small value δ to determine ≅ (approximate equality) between two floating-point values. Under this scheme, if $|x - y| < δ$, then we consider x and y to be equal. Still, by this simple measure, even when $x ≅ y$ and $y ≅ z$, it's possibly not true that $x ≅ z$. This breaks the principle of *transitivity* in mathematics and makes it really challenging to write correct code. Additionally, this solution won't solve the collinearity problem, which used the sign of the value (0, positive, or negative) to make its decision.

Special Quantities

While all possible 64-bit values could represent valid floating-point numbers, the IEEE standard defines several values that are interpreted as special numbers (and are often not able to participate in the standard mathematical computations, such as addition or multiplication), shown in Table 3-4. These values have been designed to make it easier to recover from common errors, such as divide by zero, square root of a negative number, overflow of computations, and underflow of computations. Note that the values of positive zero and negative zero are also included in this table, even though they can be used in computations.

Table 3-4. Special IEEE 754 quantities

Special quantity	64-bit IEEE 754 representation
Positive infinity	0x7ff0000000000000L
Negative infinity	0xfff0000000000000L

Special quantity	64-bit IEEE 754 representation
Not a number (NaN)	`0x7ff0000000000001L` through `0x7fffffffffffffffL` and `0xfff0000000000001L` through `0xffffffffffffffffL`
Negative zero	`0x8000000000000000`
Positive zero	`0x0000000000000000`

These special quantities can result from computations that go outside the acceptable bounds. The expression `1/0.0` in Java computes to be the quantity positive infinity. If the statement had instead read `double x=1/0`, then the Java virtual machine would throw an `ArithmeticException` since this expression computes the integer division of two numbers.

Example Algorithm

To illustrate our algorithm template, we now describe the **Graham's Scan** algorithm for computing the convex hull for a collection of points. This was the problem presented in Chapter 1 and illustrated in Figure 1-3.

Name and Synopsis

Graham's Scan computes the convex hull for a collection of Cartesian points. It locates the lowest point, *low*, in the input set *P* and sorts the remaining points { *P – low* } in *reverse* polar angle with respect to the lowest point. With this order in place, the algorithm can traverse *P* clockwise from its lowest point. Every left turn of the last three points in the hull being constructed reveals that the last hull point was incorrectly chosen so it can be removed.

Input/Output

A convex hull problem instance is defined by a collection of points, *P*.

The output will be a sequence of (*x*, *y*) points representing a clockwise traversal of the convex hull. It shouldn't matter which point is first.

Context

This algorithm is suitable for Cartesian points. If the points, for example, use a different coordinate system where increasing *y* values reflect lower points in the plane, then the algorithm should compute *low* accordingly. Sorting the points by polar angle requires trigonometric calculations.

Graham's Scan Summary

Best, Average, Worst: O(*n log n*)

```
graham(P)
  low = point with lowest y coordinate in P ❶
  remove low from P
  sort P by descending polar angle with respect to low ❷

  hull = {P[n-2], low} ❸
  for i = 0 to n-1 do
    while (isLeftTurn(secondLast(hull), last(hull), P[i])) do
      remove last point in hull ❹

    add P[i] to hull

  remove duplicate last point ❺
  return hull
```

❶   Ties are broken by selecting the point with lowest *x* coordinate.

❷   P[0] has max polar angle and P[n – 2] has min polar angle.

❸   Form hull clockwise starting with min polar angle and low.

❹   Every turn to the left reveals last hull point must be removed.

❺   Because it will be P[n – 2].

Solution

If you solve this problem by hand, you probably have no trouble tracing the appropriate edges, but you might find it hard to explain the exact sequence of steps you took. The key step in this algorithm is sorting the points by descending polar angle with respect to the lowest point in the set. Once ordered, the algorithm proceeds to "walk" along these points, extending a partially constructed hull and adjusting its structure if the last three points of the hull ever form a left turn, which would indicate a nonconvex shape. See Example 3-1.

Example 3-1. GrahamScan implementation

```java
public class NativeGrahamScan implements IConvexHull {
  public IPoint[] compute (IPoint[] pts) {
    int n = pts.length;
    if (n < 3) { return pts; }

    // Find lowest point and swap with last one in points[] array,
    // if it isn't there already
```

```
int lowest = 0;
double lowestY = pts[0].getY();
for (int i = 1; i < n; i++) {
  if (pts[i].getY() < lowestY) {
    lowestY = pts[i].getY();
    lowest = i;
  }
}

if (lowest != n-1) {
  IPoint temp = pts[n-1];
  pts[n-1] = pts[lowest];
  pts[lowest] = temp;
}

// sort points[0..n-2] by descending polar angle with respect
// to lowest point points[n-1].
new HeapSort<IPoint>().sort(pts, 0, n-2,
                            new ReversePolarSorter(pts[n-1]));

// three points *known* to be on the hull are (in this order) the
// point with lowest polar angle (points[n-2]), the lowest point
// (points[n-1]), and the point with the highest polar angle
// (points[0]). Start with first two
DoubleLinkedList<IPoint> list = new DoubleLinkedList<IPoint>();
list.insert(pts[n-2]);
list.insert(pts[n-1]);

// If all points are collinear, handle now to avoid worrying about later
double firstAngle = Math.atan2(pts[0].getY() - lowest,
                               pts[0].getX() - pts[n-1].getX());
double lastAngle = Math.atan2(pts[n-2].getY() - lowest,
                              pts[n-2].getX() - pts[n-1].getX());
if (firstAngle == lastAngle) {
  return new IPoint[] { pts[n-1], pts[0] };
}

// Sequentially visit each point in order, removing points upon
// making mistake. Because we always have at least one "right
// turn," the inner while loop will always terminate
for (int i = 0; i < n-1; i++) {
  while (isLeftTurn(list.last().prev().value(),
                    list.last().value(),
                    pts[i])) {
    list.removeLast();
  }

  // advance and insert next hull point into proper position
  list.insert(pts[i]);
}

// The final point is duplicated, so we take n-1 points starting
```

```
  // from lowest point.
  IPoint hull[] = new IPoint[list.size()-1];
  DoubleNode<IPoint> ptr = list.first().next();
  int idx = 0;
  while (idx < hull.length) {
    hull[idx++] = ptr.value();
    ptr = ptr.next();
  }

  return hull;
}

/** Use Collinear check to determine left turn. */
public static boolean isLeftTurn(IPoint p1, IPoint p2, IPoint p3) {
  return (p2.getX() - p1.getX())*(p3.getY() - p1.getY()) -
         (p2.getY() - p1.getY())*(p3.getX() - p1.getX()) > 0;
}
}

/** Sorter class for reverse polar angle with respect to a given point. */
class ReversePolarSorter implements Comparator<IPoint> {
  /** Stored x,y coordinate of base point used for comparison. */
  final double baseX;
  final double baseY;

  /** PolarSorter evaluates all points compared to base point. */
  public ReversePolarSorter(IPoint base) {
    this.baseX = base.getX();
    this.baseY = base.getY();
  }

  public int compare(IPoint one, IPoint two) {
    if (one == two) { return 0; }

    // make sure both have computed angle using atan2 function.
    // Works because one.y is always larger than or equal to base.y
    double oneY = one.getY();
    double twoY = two.getY();
    double oneAngle = Math.atan2(oneY - baseY, one.getX() - baseX);
    double twoAngle = Math.atan2(twoY - baseY, two.getX() - baseX);

    if (oneAngle > twoAngle) { return -1; }
    else if (oneAngle < twoAngle) { return +1; }

    // if same angle, then must order by decreasing magnitude
    // to ensure that the convex hull algorithm is correct
    if (oneY > twoY) { return -1; }
    else if (oneY < twoY) { return +1; }

    return 0;
  }
}
```

If all $n > 2$ points are collinear then in this special case, the hull consists of the two extreme points in the set. The computed convex hull might contain multiple consecutive points that are collinear because no attempt is made to remove them.

Analysis

Sorting n points requires $O(n\ log\ n)$ performance, as described in Chapter 4. The rest of the algorithm has a for loop that executes n times, but how many times does its inner while loop execute? As long as there is a left turn, a point is removed from the hull, until only the first three points remain. Since no more than n points are added to the hull, the inner while loop can execute no more than n times in total. Thus, the performance of the for loop is $O(n)$. The result is that the overall algorithm performance is $O(n\ log\ n)$ since the sorting costs dominates the cost of the whole computation.

Common Approaches

This section presents the fundamental algorithm approaches used in the book. You need to understand these general strategies for solving problems so you see how they can be applied to solve specific problems. Chapter 10 contains additional strategies, such as seeking an acceptable approximate answer rather than the definitive one, or using randomization with a large number of trials to converge on the proper result rather than using an exhaustive search.

Greedy

A Greedy strategy completes a task of size n by incrementally solving the problem in steps. At each step, a Greedy algorithm will make the best local decision it can given the available information, typically reducing the size of the problem being solved by one. Once all n steps are completed, the algorithm returns the computed solution.

To sort an array A of n numbers, for example, the Greedy **Selection Sort** algorithm locates the largest value in $A[0, n - 1]$ and swaps it with the element in location $A[n - 1]$, which ensures $A[n - 1]$ is in its proper location. Then it repeats the process to find the largest value remaining in $A[0, n - 2]$, which is similarly swapped with the element in location $A[n - 2]$. This process continues until the entire array is sorted. For more detail, see Chapter 4.

You can identify a Greedy strategy by the way that subproblems being solved shrink very slowly as an algorithm processes the input. When a subproblem can be completed in $O(log\ n)$ then a Greedy strategy will exhibit $O(n\ log\ n)$ performance. If the subproblem requires $O(n)$ behavior, as it does here with **Selection Sort**, then the overall performance will be $O(n^2)$.

Divide and Conquer

A Divide and Conquer strategy solves a problem of size n by dividing it into two independent subproblems, each about half the size of the original problem. Quite often the solution is recursive, terminating with a base case that can be solved trivially. There must be some *resolution* computation that can determine the solution for a problem when given two solutions for two smaller subproblems.

To find the largest element in an array of n numbers, for example, the recursive function in Example 3-2 constructs two subproblems. Naturally, the maximum element of the original problem is simply the larger of the maximum values of the two subproblems. Observe how the recursion terminates when the size of the subproblem is 1, in which case the single element *vals[left]* is returned.

Example 3-2. Recursive Divide and Conquer approach to finding maximum element in array

```
/** Invoke the recursion. */
public static int maxElement (int[] vals) {
  if (vals.length == 0) {
    throw new NoSuchElementException("No Max Element in Empty Array.");
  }
  return maxElement(vals, 0, vals.length);
}

/** Compute maximum element in subproblem vals[left, right).
 * Note that the right endpoint is not part of the range. */
static int maxElement (int[] vals, int left, int right) {
  if (right - left == 1) {
    return vals[left];
  }

  // compute subproblems
  int mid = (left + right)/2;
  int max1 = maxElement(vals, left, mid);
  int max2 = maxElement(vals, mid, right);

  // Resolution: compute result from results of subproblems
  if (max1 > max2) { return max1; }
  return max2;
}
```

A Divide and Conquer algorithm structured as shown in Example 3-2 will exhibit $O(n)$ performance if the *resolution* step can be accomplished in constant $O(1)$ time, as it does here. When the resolution step itself requires $O(n)$ computations, then the overall performance will be $O(n \log n)$. Note that you can more rapidly find the largest element in a collection by scanning each element and storing the largest one found. Let this be a brief reminder that Divide and Conquer will not always provide the fastest implementation.

Dynamic Programming

Dynamic Programming is a variation on Divide and Conquer that solves a problem by subdividing it into a number of simpler subproblems that are solved in a specific order. It solves each smaller problem just once and stores the results for future use to avoid unnecessary recomputation. It then solves problems of increasing size, *composing* together solutions from the results of these smaller subproblems. In many cases, the computed solution is provably optimal for the problem being solved.

Dynamic Programming is frequently used for optimization problems where the goal is to minimize or maximize a particular computation. The best way to explain Dynamic Programming is to show a working example.

Scientists often compare DNA sequences to determine their similarities. If you represent such a DNA sequence as a string of characters—A, C, T, or G—then the problem is restated as computing the *minimum edit distance* between two strings. That is, given a base string s_1 and a target string s_2 determine the fewest number of edit operations that transform s_1 into s_2 if you can:

- Replace a character in s_1 with a different character
- Remove a character in s_1
- Insert a character into s_1

For example, given a base string, s_1, representing the DNA sequence "GCTAC" you only need three edit operations to convert this to the target string, s_2, whose value is "CTCA":

- Replace the fourth character ("A") with a "C"
- Remove the first character ("G")
- Replace the last "C" character with an "A"

This is not the only such sequence of operations, but you need at least three edit operations to convert s_1 to s_2. For starters, the goal is to compute the *value* of the optimum answer—i.e., the number of edit operations—rather than the actual sequence of operations.

Dynamic Programming works by storing the results of simpler subproblems; in this example, you can use a two-dimensional matrix, $m[i][j]$, to record the result of computing the minimum edit distance between the first i characters of s_1 and the first j characters of s_2. Start by constructing the following initial matrix:

```
0  1  2  3  4
1  .  .  .  .
2  .  .  .  .
```

3 . . . .

4 . . . .

5 . . . .

In this table, each row is indexed by i and each column is indexed by j. Upon completion, the entry $m[0][4]$ (the top-right corner of the table) will contain the result of the edit distance between the first 0 characters of s_1 (i.e., the empty string "") and the first four characters of s_2 (i.e., the whole string "CTCA"). The value of $m[0][4]$ is 4 because you have to insert four characters to the empty string to equal s_2. Similarly, $m[3][0]$ is 3 because starting from the first three characters of s_1 (i.e., "GCT") you have to delete three characters to equal the first zero characters of s_2 (i.e., the empty string "").

The trick in Dynamic Programming is an optimization loop that shows how to compose the results of these subproblems to solve larger ones. Consider the value of $m[1][1]$, which represents the edit distance between the first character of s_1 ("G") and the first character of s_2 ("C"). There are three choices:

- Replace the "G" character with a "C" for a cost of 1
- Remove the "G" and insert the "C" for a cost of 2
- Insert a "C" character and then delete the "G" character for a cost of 2

You clearly want to record the minimum cost of each of these three choices, so $m[1][1] = 1$. How can you generalize this decision? Consider the computation shown in Figure 3-2.

These three options for computing $m[i][j]$ represent the following:

Replace cost
> Compute the edit distance between the first $i - 1$ characters of s_1 and the first $j - 1$ characters of s_2 and then add 1 for replacing the jth character of s_2 with the ith character of s_1, if they are different.

Remove cost
> Compute the edit distance between the first $i - 1$ characters of s_1 and the first j characters of s_2 and then add 1 for removing the ith character of s_1.

Insert cost
> Compute the edit distance between the first i characters of s_1 and the first $j - 1$ characters of s_2 and then add 1 for inserting the jth character of s_2.

Visualizing this computation, you should see that Dynamic Programming must evaluate the subproblems in the proper order (i.e., from top row to bottom row, and left to right within each row, as shown in Example 3-3). The computation proceeds from row index value $i = 1$ to $len(s_1)$. Once the matrix m is populated with its initial values, a nested for loop computes the minimum value for each of the subproblems in order until all values in *m* are computed. This process is not recursive, but rather, it uses results of past computations for smaller problems. The result of the full problem is found in $m[len(s_1)][len(s_2)]$.

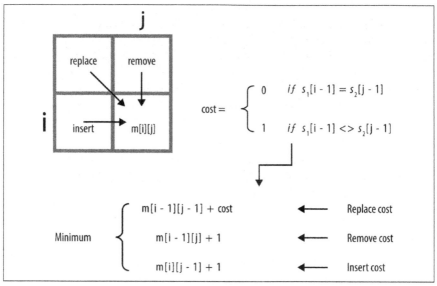

Figure 3-2. Computing m[i][j]

Example 3-3. Minimum edit distance solved using Dynamic Programming

```
def minEditDistance(s1, s2):
  """Compute minimum edit distance converting s1 -> s2."""
  len1 = len(s1)
  len2 = len(s2)

  # Create two-dimensional structure such that m[i][j] = 0
  # for i in 0 .. len1 and for j in 0 .. len2
  m = [None] * (len1 + 1)
  for i in range(len1+1):
    m[i] = [0] * (len2+1)

  # set up initial costs on horizontal and vertical
  for i in range(1, len1+1):
    m[i][0] = i
  for j in range(1, len2+1):
    m[0][j] = j

  # compute best
  for i in range(1,len1+1):
    for j in range(1,len2+1):
      cost = 1
```

```
    if s1[i-1] == s2[j-1]: cost = 0

    replaceCost = m[i-1][j-1] + cost
    removeCost  = m[i-1][j] + 1
    insertCost  = m[i][j-1] + 1
    m[i][j]     = min(replaceCost,removeCost,insertCost)

return m[len1][len2]
```

Table 3-5 shows the final value of *m*.

Table 3-5. Result of all subproblems

0	1	2	3	4
1	1	2	3	4
2	1	2	2	3
3	2	1	2	3
4	3	2	2	2
5	4	3	2	3

The cost of subproblem $m[3][2] = 1$ which is the edit distance of the string "GCT" and "CT". As you can see, you only need to delete the first character which validates this cost is correct. This code only shows how to compute the minimum edit distance; to actually record the sequence of operations that would be performed, a *prev*[*i*][*j*] matrix records which of the three cases was selected when computing the minimum value of *m*[*i*][*j*]. To recover the operations, trace backwards from $m[len(s_1)][len(s_2)]$ using decisions recorded in *prev*[*i*][*j*] stopping once *m*[0][0] is reached. This revised implementation is shown in Example 3-4.

Example 3-4. Minimum edit distance with operations solved using Dynamic Programming

```
REPLACE = 0
REMOVE  = 1
INSERT  = 2

def minEditDistance(s1, s2):
    """Compute minimum edit distance converting s1 -> s2 with operations."""
    len1 = len(s1)
    len2 = len(s2)

    # Create two-dimensional structure such that m[i][j] = 0
    # for i in 0 .. len1 and for j in 0 .. len2
    m = [None] * (len1 + 1)
    op = [None] * (len1 + 1)
    for i in range(len1+1):
```

```python
    m[i] = [0] * (len2+1)
    op[i] = [-1] * (len2+1)

# set up initial costs on horizontal and vertical
for j in range(1, len2+1):
    m[0][j] = j
for i in range(1, len1+1):
    m[i][0] = i

# compute best
for i in range(1,len1+1):
    for j in range(1,len2+1):
        cost = 1
        if s1[i-1] == s2[j-1]: cost = 0

        replaceCost = m[i-1][j-1] + cost
        removeCost  = m[i-1][j] + 1
        insertCost  = m[i][j-1] + 1
        costs       = [replaceCost,removeCost,insertCost]
        m[i][j]     = min(costs)
        op[i][j]    = costs.index(m[i][j])

ops = []
i = len1
j = len2
while i != 0 or j != 0:
    if op[i][j] == REMOVE or j == 0:
        ops.append('remove {}-th char {} of {}'.format(i,s1[i-1],s1))
        i = i-1
    elif op[i][j] == INSERT or i == 0:
        ops.append('insert {}-th char {} of {}'.format(j,s2[j-1],s2))
        j = j-1
    else:
        if m[i-1][j-1] < m[i][j]:
            fmt='replace {}-th char of {} ({}) with {}'
            ops.append(fmt.format(i,s1,s1[i-1],s2[j-1]))
        i,j = i-1,j-1

return m[len1][len2], ops
```

References

Goldberg, D., "What Every Computer Scientist Should Know About Floating-Point Arithmetic," *ACM Computing Surveys*, March 1991, *http://docs.sun.com/source/ 806-3568/ncg_goldberg.html.*

Venners, B., "Floating-point arithmetic: A look at the floating-point support of the Java virtual machine," *JavaWorld*, 1996, *http://www.javaworld.com/article/2077257/ learn-java/floating-point-arithmetic.html.*

Sorting Algorithms

Numerous computations and tasks become simple by properly sorting information in advance. The search for efficient sorting algorithms dominated the early days of computing. Indeed, much of the early research in algorithms focused on sorting collections of data that were too large for the computers of the day to store in memory. Because today's computers are so much more powerful than the ones of 50 years ago, the size of the data sets being processed is now on the order of terabytes of information. Although you may not be called on to sort such huge data sets, you will likely need to sort large numbers of items. In this chapter, we cover the most important sorting algorithms and present results from our benchmarks to help you select the best sorting algorithm to use in each situation.

Terminology

A collection of comparable elements A is presented to be sorted in place; we use the notations $A[i]$ and a_i to refer to the ith element of the collection. By convention, the first element in the collection is $A[0]$. We use $A[low, low + n)$ to refer to the sub-collection $A[low] \ldots A[low + n - 1]$ of n elements, whereas $A[low, low + n]$ contains $n + 1$ elements.

To sort a collection, you must reorganize the elements A such that if $A[i] < A[j]$, then $i < j$. If there are duplicate elements, these elements must be contiguous in the resulting ordered collection—that is, if $A[i] = A[j]$ in a sorted collection, then there can be no k such that $i < k < j$ and $A[i] \neq A[k]$. Finally, the sorted collection A must be a permutation of the elements that originally formed A.

Representation

The collection may already be stored in the computer's random access memory (RAM), but it might simply exist in a file on the filesystem, known as secondary storage. The collection may be archived in part on tertiary storage (such as tape libraries and optical jukeboxes), which may require extra processing time just to locate the information; in addition, the information may need to be copied to secondary storage (such as hard disk drives) before it can be processed.

Information stored in RAM typically takes one of two forms: pointer-based or value-based. Assume we want to sort the strings "eagle," "cat," "ant," "dog," and "ball." Using pointer-based storage, shown in Figure 4-1, an array of information (i.e., the contiguous boxes) contains pointers to the actual information (i.e., the strings in ovals) rather than storing the information itself. Such an approach enables arbitrarily complex records to be stored and sorted.

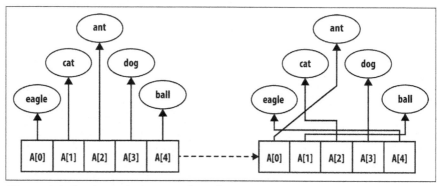

Figure 4-1. Sorting using pointer-based storage

By contrast, value-based storage packs a collection of n elements into record blocks of a fixed size, s, which is better suited for secondary or tertiary storage. Figure 4-2 shows how to store the same information shown in Figure 4-1 using a contiguous block of storage containing a set of rows of exactly $s = 5$ bytes each. In this example, the information is shown as strings, but it could be any collection of structured, record-based information. The "¬" character represents a padding character that cannot be part of any string; in this encoding, strings of length s need no padding character. The information is contiguous and can be viewed as a one-dimensional array $B[0, n*s)$. Note that $B[r*s + c]$ is the cth letter of the rth word (where $c \geq 0$ and $r \geq 0$); also, the ith element of the collection (for $i \geq 0$) is the subarray $B[i*s,(i + 1)*s)$.

Information is usually written to secondary storage as a value-based contiguous collection of bytes. The algorithms in this chapter can also be written to work with disk-based information simply by implementing swap functions that transpose bytes within the files on disk; however, the resulting performance will differ because of the increased input/output costs in accessing secondary storage. **Merge Sort** is particularly well-suited for sorting data in secondary storage.

Whether pointer-based or value-based, a sorting algorithm updates the information (in both cases, the boxes) so that $A[0, n)$ is ordered. For convenience, we use the $A[i]$ notation to represent the ith element, even when value-based storage is being used.

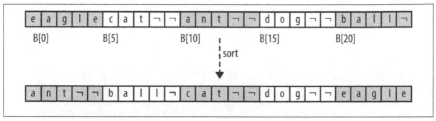

Figure 4-2. Sorting using value-based storage

Comparable Elements

The elements in the collection being compared must admit a total ordering. That is, for any two elements p and q in a collection, exactly one of the following three predicates is true: $p = q$, $p < q$, or $p > q$. Commonly sorted primitive types include integers, floating-point values, and characters. When composite elements are sorted (such as strings of characters), lexicographical ordering is imposed on each individual element of the composite, thus reducing a complex sort into individual sorts on primitive types. For example, the word "alphabet" is considered to be less than "alternate" but greater than "alligator" by comparing each individual letter, from left to right, until a word runs out of characters or an individual character in one word is different from its partner in the other word (thus "ant" is less than "anthem").

This question of ordering is far from simple when considering capitalization (is "A" greater than "a"?), diacritical marks (is "è" less than "ê"?), and diphthongs (is "æ" less than "a"?). Note that the powerful Unicode standard (*http://www.unicode.org/versions/latest*) uses encodings, such as UTF-16, to represent each individual character using up to four bytes. The Unicode Consortium (*http://www.unicode.org*) has developed a sorting standard (known as "the collation algorithm") that handles the wide variety of ordering rules found in different languages and cultures (Davis and Whistler, 2008).

The algorithms presented in this chapter assume you can provide a comparator function, cmp, which compares element p to q and returns 0 if $p = q$, a negative number if $p < q$, and a positive number if $p > q$. If the elements are complex records, the cmp function might only compare a "key" value of the elements. For example, an airport terminal might list outbound flights in ascending order of destination city or departure time while flight numbers appear to be unordered.

Stable Sorting

When the comparator function cmp determines that two elements, a_i and a_j, in the original unordered collection are equal, it may be important to maintain their relative ordering in the sorted set—that is, if $i < j$, then the final location for a_i must be to the left of the final location for a_j. Sorting algorithms that guarantee this property are considered to be *stable*. For example, the left four columns of Table 4-1 show an original collection of flight information already sorted by time of flight during the day (regardless of airline or destination city). If a stable sort orders this collection using a comparator function that orders flights by destination city, the only possible result is shown in the right four columns of Table 4-1.

Table 4-1. Stable sort of airport terminal information

Destination	Airline	Flight	Departure Time (Ascending)	→	Destination (Ascending)	Airline	Flight	Departure Time
Buffalo	Air Trans	549	10:42 AM		Albany	Southwest	482	1:20 PM
Atlanta	Delta	1097	11:00 AM		Atlanta	Delta	1097	11:00 AM
Baltimore	Southwest	836	11:05 AM		Atlanta	Air Trans	872	11:15 AM
Atlanta	Air Trans	872	11:15 AM		Atlanta	Delta	28	12:00 PM
Atlanta	Delta	28	12:00 PM		Atlanta	Al Italia	3429	1:50 PM
Boston	Delta	1056	12:05 PM		Austin	Southwest	1045	1:05 PM
Baltimore	Southwest	216	12:20 PM		Baltimore	Southwest	836	11:05 AM
Austin	Southwest	1045	1:05 PM		Baltimore	Southwest	216	12:20 PM
Albany	Southwest	482	1:20 PM		Baltimore	Southwest	272	1:40 PM
Boston	Air Trans	515	1:21 PM		Boston	Delta	1056	12:05 PM
Baltimore	Southwest	272	1:40 PM		Boston	Air Trans	515	1:21 PM
Atlanta	Al Italia	3429	1:50 PM		Buffalo	Air Trans	549	10:42 AM

You will note that all flights that have the same destination city are also sorted by their scheduled departure time; thus, the sort algorithm exhibited stability on this collection. An unstable algorithm pays no attention to the relationships between element locations in the original collection (it might maintain relative ordering, but it also might not).

Criteria for Choosing a Sorting Algorithm

To choose the sorting algorithm to use or implement, consider the qualitative criteria in Table 4-2.

Table 4-2. Criteria for choosing a sorting algorithm

Criteria	Sorting algorithm
Only a few items	**Insertion Sort**
Items are mostly sorted already	**Insertion Sort**
Concerned about worst-case scenarios	**Heap Sort**
Interested in a good average-case behavior	**Quicksort**
Items are drawn from a uniform dense universe	**Bucket Sort**

Criteria	Sorting algorithm
Desire to write as little code as possible	**Insertion Sort**
Require stable sort	**Merge Sort**

Transposition Sorting

Early sorting algorithms found elements in the collection A that were out of place and moved them into their proper position by *transposing* (or swapping) elements in A. **Selection Sort** and (the infamous) **Bubble Sort** belong to this sorting family. But these algorithms are outperformed by **Insertion Sort**, which we now present.

Insertion Sort

Insertion Sort repeatedly invokes an `insert` helper function to ensure $A[0, i]$ is properly sorted; eventually, i reaches the rightmost element, sorting A entirely.

Insertion Sort Summary

Best: O(n)   Average, Worst: O(n^2)

```
sort (A)
  for pos = 1 to n-1 do
    insert (A, pos, A[pos])
end

insert (A, pos, value)
  i = pos - 1
  while i >= 0 and A[i] > value do ❶
    A[i+1] = A[i]
    i = i-1
  A[i+1] = value ❷
end
```

❶   Shifts elements greater than `value` to the right.

❷   Inserts `value` into proper location.

Figure 4-3 shows how **Insertion Sort** operates on an unordered collection A of size $n = 16$. The 15 rows that follow depict the state of A after each invocation of *insert*.

A is sorted in place by incrementing $pos = 1$ up to $n - 1$ and inserting the element $A[pos]$ into its rightful position in the growing sorted region $A[0, pos]$, demarcated on the right by a bold vertical line. The elements shaded in gray were shifted to the right to make way for the inserted element; in total, **Insertion Sort** executed 60 neighboring transpositions (a movement of just one place by an element).

Context

Use **Insertion Sort** when you have a small number of elements to sort or the elements in the initial collection are already "nearly sorted." Determining when the array is "small enough" varies from one machine to another and by programming language. Indeed, even the type of element being compared may be significant.

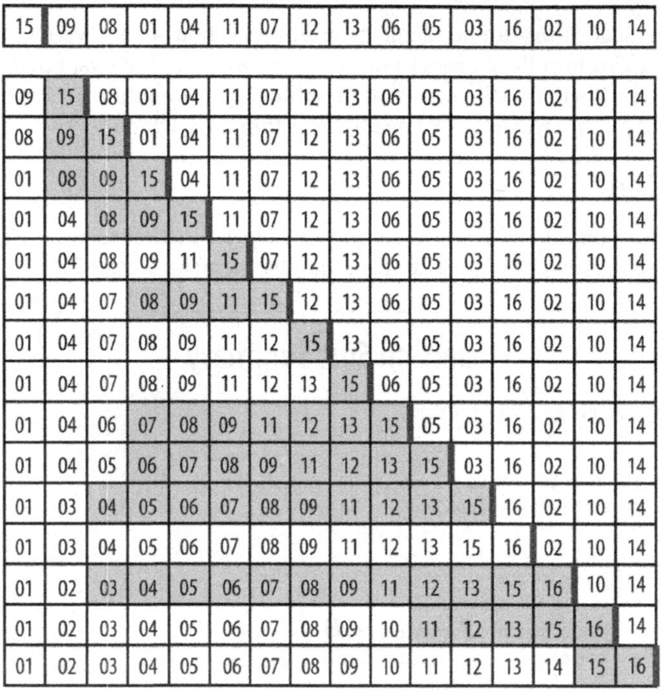

15	09	08	01	04	11	07	12	13	06	05	03	16	02	10	14

09	15	08	01	04	11	07	12	13	06	05	03	16	02	10	14
08	09	15	01	04	11	07	12	13	06	05	03	16	02	10	14
01	08	09	15	04	11	07	12	13	06	05	03	16	02	10	14
01	04	08	09	15	11	07	12	13	06	05	03	16	02	10	14
01	04	08	09	11	15	07	12	13	06	05	03	16	02	10	14
01	04	07	08	09	11	15	12	13	06	05	03	16	02	10	14
01	04	07	08	09	11	12	15	13	06	05	03	16	02	10	14
01	04	07	08	09	11	12	13	15	06	05	03	16	02	10	14
01	04	06	07	08	09	11	12	13	15	05	03	16	02	10	14
01	04	05	06	07	08	09	11	12	13	15	03	16	02	10	14
01	03	04	05	06	07	08	09	11	12	13	15	16	02	10	14
01	03	04	05	06	07	08	09	11	12	13	15	16	02	10	14
01	02	03	04	05	06	07	08	09	11	12	13	15	16	10	14
01	02	03	04	05	06	07	08	09	10	11	12	13	15	16	14
01	02	03	04	05	06	07	08	09	10	11	12	13	14	15	16

Figure 4-3. The progression of Insertion Sort on a small array

Solution

When the information is stored using pointers, the C program in Example 4-1 sorts an array ar of items that can be compared using a comparison function, cmp.

Example 4-1. Insertion Sort with pointer-based values

```
void sortPointers (void **ar, int n,
                   int (*cmp)(const void *, const void *)) {
  int j;
  for (j = 1; j < n; j++) {
    int i = j-1;
    void *value = ar[j];
    while (i >= 0 && cmp (ar[i], value) > 0) {
      ar[i+1] = ar[i];
```

```
        i--;
      }
    ar[i+1] = value;
  }
}
```

When *A* is represented using value-based storage, it is packed into *n* rows of a fixed element size of *s* bytes. Manipulating the values requires a comparison function as well as the means to copy values from one location to another. Example 4-2 shows a suitable C program that uses memmove to transfer the underlying bytes efficiently for a set of contiguous entries in *A*.

Example 4-2. Insertion Sort using value-based information

```
void sortValues (void *base, int n, int s,
                 int (*cmp)(const void *, const void *)) {
  int j;
  void *saved = malloc (s);
  for (j = 1; j < n; j++) {
    int i = j-1;
    void *value = base + j*s;
    while (i >= 0 && cmp (base + i*s, value) > 0) { i--; }

    /* If already in place, no movement needed. Otherwise save value
     * to be inserted and move intervening values as a LARGE block.
     * Then insert into proper position. */
    if (++i == j) continue;

    memmove (saved, value, s);
    memmove (base+(i+1)*s, base+i*s, s*(j-i));
    memmove (base+i*s, saved, s);
  }
  free (saved);
}
```

The optimal performance occurs when the array is already sorted, and arrays sorted in reverse order produce the worst performance for **Insertion Sort**. If the array is already mostly sorted, **Insertion Sort** does well because there is less need to transpose elements.

Insertion Sort requires very little extra space to function; it only needs to reserve space for a single element. For value-based representations, most language libraries offer a block memory move function to make transpositions more efficient.

Analysis

In the best case, each of the *n* items is in its proper place and thus **Insertion Sort** takes linear time, or $O(n)$. This may seem to be a trivial point to raise (how often are you going to sort a set of already sorted elements?), but it is important because

Insertion Sort is the only comparison-based sorting algorithm that has this best-case behavior.

Much real-world data is already partially sorted, so optimism and realism might coincide to make **Insertion Sort** an effective algorithm to use. The efficiency of **Insertion Sort** increases when duplicate items are present, since there are fewer swaps to perform.

Unfortunately, **Insertion Sort** is too conservative when all n items are distinct and the array is randomly organized (i.e., all permutations of the data are equally likely) because each item starts on average $n/3$ positions in the array from its final position. The program numTranspositions.c in the code repository empirically validates this claim for small n up to 12 (also see Trivedi, 2001). In the average and worst case, each of the n items must be transposed a linear number of positions, thus **Insertion Sort** requires $O(n^2)$ quadratic time.

Insertion Sort operates inefficiently for value-based data because of the amount of memory that must be shifted to make room for a new value. Table 4-3 contains direct comparisons between a naïve implementation of value-based **Insertion Sort** and the implementation from Example 4-2. Ten random trials of sorting n elements were conducted, and the best and worst results were discarded. This table shows the average of the remaining eight runs. Note how the implementation improves by using a block memory move rather than individual memory swapping. Still, as the array size doubles, the performance time approximately quadruples, validating the $O(n^2)$ behavior of **Insertion Sort**. Even with the bulk move improvement, **Insertion Sort** still remains quadratic.

Table 4-3. Insertion Sort bulk move versus Insertion Sort (in seconds)

n	Insertion Sort bulk move (B_n)	Naïve Insertion Sort (S_n)
1,024	0.0039	0.0130
2,048	0.0153	0.0516
4,096	0.0612	0.2047
8,192	0.2473	0.8160
16,384	0.9913	3.2575
32,768	3.9549	13.0650
65,536	15.8722	52.2913
131,072	68.4009	209.2943

When **Insertion Sort** operates over pointer-based input, swapping elements is more efficient; the compiler can even generate optimized code to minimize costly memory accesses.

Selection Sort

One common sorting strategy is to select the largest value from the range $A[0, n)$ and swap its location with the rightmost element $A[n - 1]$. This process is repeated, subsequently, on each successive smaller range $A[0, n - 1)$ until A is sorted. We discussed **Selection Sort** in Chapter 3 as an example of a Greedy approach. Example 4-3 contains a C implementation.

Example 4-3. Selection Sort implementation in C

```c
static int selectMax (void **ar, int left, int right,
                      int (*cmp)(const void *, const void *)) {
  int  maxPos = left;
  int  i = left;
  while (++i <= right) {
    if (cmp(ar[i], ar[maxPos]) > 0) {
      maxPos = i;
    }
  }

  return maxPos;
}

void sortPointers (void **ar, int n,
                   int (*cmp)(const void *, const void *)) {
  /* repeatedly select max in ar[0,i] and swap with proper position */
  int i;
  for (i = n-1; i >= 1; i--) {
    int maxPos = selectMax (ar, 0, i, cmp);
    if (maxPos != i) {
      void *tmp = ar[i];
      ar[i] = ar[maxPos];
      ar[maxPos] = tmp;
    }
  }
}
```

Selection Sort is the slowest of all the sorting algorithms described in this chapter; it requires quadratic time even in the best case (i.e., when the array is already sorted). It repeatedly performs almost the same task without learning anything from one iteration to the next. Selecting the largest element, *max*, in A takes $n - 1$ comparisons, and selecting the second largest element, *second*, takes $n - 2$ comparisons —not much progress! Many of these comparisons are wasted, because if an element is smaller than *second*, it can't possibly be the largest element and therefore has no impact on the computation for *max*. Instead of presenting more details on this poorly performing algorithm, we now consider **Heap Sort**, which shows how to more effectively apply the principle behind **Selection Sort**.

Heap Sort

We always need at least $n - 1$ comparisons to find the largest element in an unordered array A of n elements, but can we minimize the number of elements that are compared directly? For example, sports tournaments find the "best" team from a field of n teams without forcing the ultimate winner to play all other $n - 1$ teams. One of the most popular basketball events in the United States is the NCAA championship tournament, where essentially a set of 64 college teams compete for the national title. The ultimate champion team plays five teams before reaching the final determining game, and so that team must win six games. It is no coincidence that $6 = log\ (64)$. **Heap Sort** shows how to apply this behavior to sort a set of elements.

Heap Sort Summary

Best, Average, Worst: $O(n\ log\ n)$

```
sort (A)
  buildHeap (A)
  for i = n-1 downto 1 do
    swap A[0] with A[i]
    heapify (A, 0, i)
end

buildHeap (A)
  for i = n/2-1 downto 0 do
    heapify (A, i, n)
end

# Recursively enforce that A[idx,max) is valid heap
heapify (A, idx, max)
  largest = idx    ❶
  left = 2*idx + 1
  right = 2*idx + 2

  if left < max and A[left] > A[idx] then
    largest = left    ❷
  if right < max and A[right] > A[largest] then
    largest = right    ❸
  if largest ≠ idx then
    swap A[idx] and A[largest]
    heapify (A, largest, max)
end
```

❶ Assume parent A[idx] is larger than or equal to either of its children.

❷ Left child is larger than its parent.

❸ Right child is larger than either its parent or left sibling.

Figure 4-4 shows the execution of `buildHeap` on an array of six values.

Start with unordered array which is to be converted into heap:

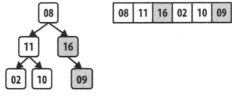

1. Calling heapify (A,2,6) first swaps **09** and **16**

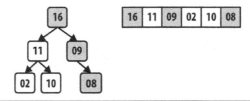

2. Calling heapify (A,1,6) makes no change because **11** is greater than both of its children, **02** and **10**

3. Calling heapify (A,0,6) first swaps **08** and **16** and then recursively calls heapify (A,2,6) which swaps **08** and **09**

Figure 4-4. Heap Sort example

A heap is a binary tree whose structure ensures two properties:

Shape property
> A leaf node at depth $k > 0$ can exist only if all 2^{k-1} nodes at depth $k - 1$ exist. Additionally, nodes at a partially filled level must be added "from left to right." The root node has a depth of 0.

Heap property
> Each node in the tree contains a value greater than or equal to either of its two children, if it has any.

The sample heap in Figure 4-5(a) satisfies these properties. The root of the binary tree contains the largest element in the tree; however, the smallest element can be found in any leaf node. Although a heap only ensures a node is greater than either of its children, **Heap Sort** shows how to take advantage of the shape property to efficiently sort an array of elements.

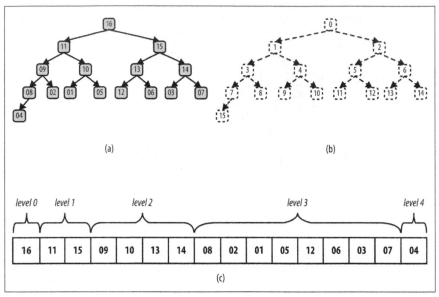

Figure 4-5. (a) Sample heap of 16 unique elements; (b) labels of these elements;
(c) heap stored in an array

Given the rigid structure imposed by the *shape property*, a heap can be stored in an array A without losing any of its structural information. Figure 4-5(b) shows an integer label assigned to each node in the heap. The root is labeled 0. For a node with label i, its left child (should it exist) is labeled $2*i + 1$; its right child (should it exist) is labeled $2*i + 2$. Similarly, for a non-root node labeled i, its parent node is labeled $\lfloor (i - 1)/2 \rfloor$. Using this labeling scheme, we can store the heap in an array by storing the element value for a node in the array position identified by the node's label. The array shown in Figure 4-5(c) represents the heap shown in Figure 4-5(a). The order of the elements within A can be simply read from left to right as deeper levels of the tree are explored.

Heap Sort sorts an array, A, by first converting that array in place into a heap using buildHeap which makes repeated calls to heapify. heapify(A, i, n) updates the array, A, to ensure that the tree structure rooted at $A[i]$ is a valid heap. Figure 4-6 shows details of the invocations of heapify that convert an unordered array into a heap. The progress of buildHeap on an already sorted array is shown in Figure 4-6. Each numbered row in this figure shows the result of executing heapify on the initial array from the midway point of $\lfloor (n/2) \rfloor - 1$ down to the leftmost index 0.

As you can see, large numbers are eventually "lifted up" in the resulting heap (which means they are swapped in A with smaller elements to the left). The grayed squares in Figure 4-6 depict the element pairs swapped in heapify—a total of 13—which is far fewer than the total number of elements swapped in **Insertion Sort** as depicted in Figure 4-3.

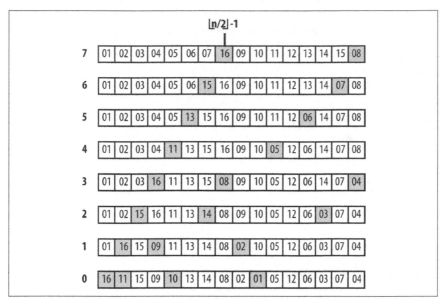

Figure 4-6. buildHeap processing an initially sorted array

Heap Sort processes an array A of size n by treating it as two distinct subarrays, $A[0, m)$ and $A[m, n)$, which represent a heap of size m and a sorted subarray of $n - m$ elements, respectively. As i iterates from $n - 1$ down to 1, **Heap Sort** grows the sorted subarray $A[i, n)$ downward by swapping the largest element in the heap (at position $A[0]$) with $A[i]$; it then reconstructs $A[0, i)$ to be a valid heap by executing heapify. The resulting nonempty subarray $A[i, n)$ will be sorted because the largest element in the heap represented in $A[0, i)$ is guaranteed to be smaller than or equal to any element in the sorted subarray $A[i, n)$.

Context

Heap Sort is not a stable sort. **Heap Sort** avoids many of the nasty (almost embarrassing!) cases that cause **Quicksort** to perform badly. Nonetheless, in the average case, **Quicksort** outperforms **Heap Sort**.

Solution

A sample implementation in C is shown in Example 4-4.

Example 4-4. Heap Sort implementation in C

```
static void heapify (void **ar, int (*cmp)(const void *, const void *),
                     int idx, int max) {
  int left = 2*idx + 1;
  int right = 2*idx + 2;
  int largest;
```

```
/* Find largest element of A[idx], A[left], and A[right]. */
if (left < max && cmp (ar[left], ar[idx]) > 0) {
  largest = left;
} else {
  largest = idx;
}

if (right < max && cmp (ar[right], ar[largest]) > 0) {
  largest = right;
}

/* If largest is not already the parent then swap and propagate. */
if (largest != idx) {
  void *tmp;
  tmp = ar[idx];
  ar[idx] = ar[largest];
  ar[largest] = tmp;

  heapify (ar, cmp, largest, max);
  }
}

static void buildHeap (void **ar,
                       int (*cmp)(const void *, const void *), int n) {
  int i;
  for (i = n/2-1; i>=0; i--) {
    heapify (ar, cmp, i, n);
  }
}

void sortPointers (void **ar, int n,
                   int (*cmp)(const void *, const void *)) {
  int i;
  buildHeap (ar, cmp, n);
  for (i = n-1; i >= 1; i--) {
    void *tmp;
    tmp = ar[0];
    ar[0] = ar[i];
    ar[i] = tmp;

    heapify (ar, cmp, 0, i);
  }
}
```

Analysis

heapify is the central operation in **Heap Sort**. In buildHeap, it is called $\lfloor (n/2) \rfloor - 1$ times, and during the actual sort it is called $n - 1$ times, for a total of $\lfloor (3*n/2) \rfloor - 2$ times. Because of the *shape property*, the depth of the heap will always be $\lfloor \log n \rfloor$ where n is the number of elements in the heap. As you can see, it is a recursive operation with no more than *log n* recursive calls until the heap is corrected or the end of the heap is reached. However, `heapify` will stop prematurely once the heap is corrected; as it turns out, no more than $2*n$ comparisons are needed in total (Cormen et al., 2009), which means that `buildHeap` behaves in linear time or $O(n)$.

Variations

The code repository contains a nonrecursive **Heap Sort** implementation and Table 4-4 presents a benchmark comparison of running 1,000 randomized trials of both implementations, discarding the best and worst performances of each.

Table 4-4. Comparing Heap Sort versus nonrecursive Heap Sort (in seconds)

n	Nonrecursive Heap Sort	Recursive Heap Sort
16,384	0.0048	0.0064
32,768	0.0113	0.0147
65,536	0.0263	0.0336
131,072	0.0762	0.0893
262,144	0.2586	0.2824
524,288	0.7251	0.7736
1,048,576	1.8603	1.9582
2,097,152	4.566	4.7426

At first, there is a noticeable improvement in eliminating recursion in **Heap Sort**, but this difference reduces as *n* increases.

Partition-Based Sorting

A Divide and Conquer strategy solves a problem by dividing it into two independent subproblems, each about half the size of the original problem. You can apply this strategy to sorting as follows: find the *median* element in the collection A and swap it with the middle element of A. Now swap elements in the left half that are greater than A[*mid*] with elements in the right half that are less than or equal to A[*mid*]. This subdivides the original array into two distinct subarrays that can be recursively sorted in place to sort the original collection A.

Implementing this approach is challenging because it might not be obvious how to compute the median element of a collection without sorting the collection first! It turns out that you can use any element in A to partition A into two subarrays; if you choose "wisely" each time, then both subarrays will be more or less the same size and you will achieve an efficient implementation.

Assume there is a function $p = partition$ (A, $left$, $right$, $pivotIndex$) that uses a special *pivot* value in A, $A[pivotIndex]$, to modify A and return the location p in A such that:

- $A[p] = pivot$
- All elements in $A[left, p)$ are less than or equal to *pivot*
- All elements in $A[p + 1, right]$ are greater than *pivot*

If you are lucky, when *partition* completes, the size of these two subarrays are more or less half the size of the original collection. Example 4-5 shows a C implementation of `partition`.

Example 4-5. C implementation to partition ar[left,right] around a given pivot element

```
/**
 * In linear time, group the subarray ar[left, right] around a pivot
 * element pivot=ar[pivotIndex] by storing pivot into its proper
 * location, store, within the subarray (whose location is returned
 * by this function) and ensuring all ar[left,store) <= pivot and
 * all ar[store+1,right] > pivot.
 */
int partition (void **ar, int (*cmp)(const void *, const void *),
               int left, int right, int pivotIndex) {
  int idx, store;
  void *pivot = ar[pivotIndex];

  /* move pivot to the end of the array */
  void *tmp = ar[right];
  ar[right] = ar[pivotIndex];
  ar[pivotIndex] = tmp;

  /* all values <= pivot are moved to front of array and pivot inserted
   * just after them. */
  store = left;
  for (idx = left; idx < right; idx++) {
    if (cmp (ar[idx], pivot) <= 0) {
      tmp = ar[idx];
      ar[idx] = ar[store];
      ar[store] = tmp;
      store++;
    }
  }

  tmp = ar[right];
  ar[right] = ar[store];
  ar[store] = tmp;
  return store;
}
```

The **Quicksort** algorithm, introduced by C. A. R. Hoare in 1960, selects an element in the collection (sometimes randomly, sometimes the leftmost, sometimes the middle one) to partition an array into two subarrays. Thus, **Quicksort** has two steps. First, the array is partitioned and then each subarray is recursively sorted.

Quicksort Summary

Best, Average: O($n \log n$), **Worst:** O(n^2)

```
sort (A)
  quicksort (A, 0, n-1)
end

quicksort (A, left, right)
  if left < right then
    pi = partition (A, left, right)
    quicksort (A, left, pi-1)
    quicksort (A, pi+1, right)
end
```

This pseudocode intentionally doesn't specify the strategy for selecting the pivot index. In the associated code, we assume there is a `selectPivotIndex` function that selects an appropriate index. We do not cover here the advanced mathematical analytic tools needed to prove that **Quicksort** offers O($n \log n$) average behavior; further details on this topic are available in Cormen (2009).

Figure 4-7 shows **Quicksort** in action. Each of the black squares represents a pivot selection. The first pivot selected is "2," which turns out to be a poor choice since it produces two subarrays of size 1 and size 14. During the next recursive invocation of **Quicksort** on the right subarray, "12" is selected to be the pivot (shown in the fourth row down), which produces two subarrays of size 9 and 4, respectively. Already you can see the benefit of using *partition* since the last four elements in the array are, in fact, the largest four elements, although they are still unordered. Because of the random nature of the pivot selection, different behaviors are possible. In a different execution, shown in Figure 4-8, the first selected pivot nicely subdivides the problem into two more or less comparable tasks.

Context

Quicksort exhibits worst-case quadratic behavior if the partitioning at each recursive step only divides a collection of n elements into an "empty" and "large" set, where one of these sets has no elements and the other has $n - 1$ (note that the pivot element provides the last of the n elements, so no element is lost).

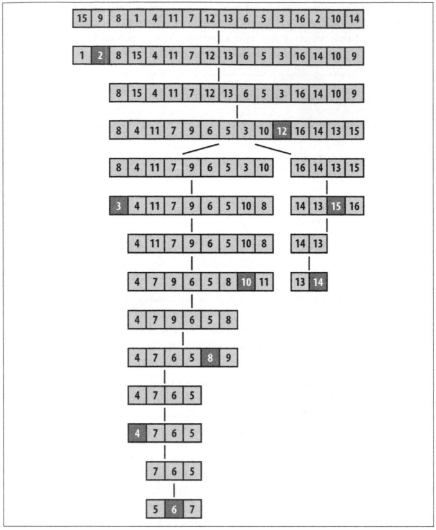

Figure 4-7. Sample Quicksort execution

Solution

The **Quicksort** implementation shown in Example 4-6 includes standard optimization to use **Insertion Sort** when the size of the subarray to be sorted falls below a predetermined minimum size.

Example 4-6. Quicksort implementation in C

```
/**
 * Sort array ar[left,right] using Quicksort method.
 * The comparison function, cmp, is needed to properly compare elements.
 */
void do_qsort (void **ar, int (*cmp)(const void *, const void *),
               int left, int right) {
  int pivotIndex;
  if (right <= left) { return; }

  /* partition */
  pivotIndex = selectPivotIndex (ar, left, right);
  pivotIndex = partition (ar, cmp, left, right, pivotIndex);

  if (pivotIndex-1-left <= minSize) {
    insertion (ar, cmp, left, pivotIndex-1);
  } else {
    do_qsort (ar, cmp, left, pivotIndex-1);
  }
  if (right-pivotIndex-1 <= minSize) {
    insertion (ar, cmp, pivotIndex+1, right);
  } else {
    do_qsort (ar, cmp, pivotIndex+1, right);
  }
}

/**  Qsort straight */
void sortPointers (void **vals, int total_elems,
                   int (*cmp)(const void *, const void *)) {
  do_qsort (vals, cmp, 0, total_elems-1);
}
```

The external method selectPivotIndex(ar, left, right) chooses the *pivot* value on which to partition the array.

Analysis

Surprisingly, using a random element as pivot enables **Quicksort** to provide an average-case performance that usually outperforms other sorting algorithms. In addition, there are numerous enhancements and optimizations researched for **Quicksort** that have achieved the most efficiency out of any sorting algorithm.

In the ideal case, partition divides the original array in half and **Quicksort** exhibits its O(*n log n*) performance. In practice, **Quicksort** is effective with a randomly selected *pivot*.

In the worst case, the largest or smallest item is picked as the pivot. When this happens, **Quicksort** makes a pass over all elements in the array (in linear time) to sort just a single item in the array. If this process is repeated $n - 1$ times, it will result in $O(n^2)$ worst-case behavior.

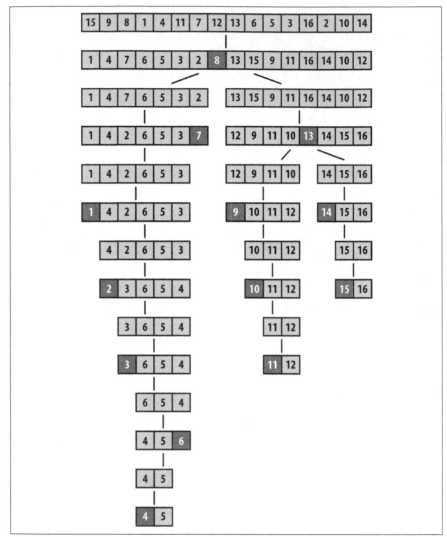

Figure 4-8. A different Quicksort behavior

Variations

Quicksort is the sorting method of choice on most systems. On Unix-based systems, there is a built-in library function called `qsort`. Often, the operating system uses optimized versions of the default **Quicksort** algorithm. Two of the commonly cited sources for optimizations are by Sedgewick (1978) and Bentley and McIlroy

(1993). It is instructive that some versions of the Linux operating system implement qsort using **Heap Sort**.

Various optimizations include:

- Create a stack that stores the subtasks to be processed to eliminate recursion
- Choose the pivot based on median-of-three strategy
- Set the minimum partition size below which to use **Insertion Sort** instead which varies by implementation and machine architecture; in JDK 1.8, the threshold value is set to 7
- When processing the two subproblems, minimize the total size of the recursive stack by solving the smaller subproblem first

However, none of these optimizations will eliminate the $O(n^2)$ worst-case behavior of **Quicksort**. The only way to ensure an $O(n\ log\ n)$ worst-case performance is to use a partition function that can guarantee it finds a "reasonable approximation" to the actual median of that set. The Blum-Floyd-Pratt-Rivest-Tarjan (BFPRT) partition algorithm (Blum et al., 1973) is a provably linear time algorithm, but it has only theoretical value. An implementation of BFPRT is provided with the code repository.

Picking a pivot

Selecting the pivot element from a subarray $A[left, left + n)$ must be an efficient operation; it shouldn't require checking all n elements of the subarray. Some alternatives are:

- Select first or last: $A[left]$ or $A[left + n - 1]$
- Select random element in $A[left, left + n - 1]$
- Select median-of-k: the middle value of k elements taken from $A[left, left + n - 1]$

Often one chooses median-of-three; Sedgewick reports that this approach returns an improvement of 5%, but note that some arrangements of data will force even this alternative into subpar performance (Musser, 1997). A median-of-five pivot selection has also been used. Performing further computation to identify the proper pivot rarely provides beneficial results because of the extra computational costs.

Processing the partition

In the partition method shown in Example 4-5, elements less than or equal to the selected pivot are inserted toward the front of the subarray. This approach might skew the size of the subarrays for the recursive step if the selected pivot has many duplicate elements in the array. One way to reduce the imbalance is to place elements equal to the pivot alternatively in the first and second subarrays.

Processing subarrays

Quicksort yields two recursive invocations of **Quicksort** on smaller subarrays. While processing one, the activation record of the other is pushed onto the execution stack. If the larger subarray is processed first, it is possible to have a linear number of activation records on the stack at the same time (although modern compilers may eliminate this observed overhead). To minimize the possible depth of the stack, process the smaller subarray first. If the depth of the recursion is a foreseeable issue, then perhaps **Quicksort** is not appropriate for your application.

Using simpler insertion sort technique for small subarrays

On small arrays, **Insertion Sort** is faster than **Quicksort**, but even when used on large arrays, **Quicksort** ultimately decomposes the problem to require numerous small subarrays to be sorted. One commonly used technique to improve the recursive performance of **Quicksort** is to invoke **Quicksort** for large subarrays only, and use **Insertion Sort** for small ones, as shown in Example 4-6.

Sedgewick (1978) suggests that a combination of median-of-three and using **Insertion Sort** for small subarrays offers a speedup of 20%–25% over pure **Quicksort**.

IntroSort

Switching to **Insertion Sort** for small subarrays is a local decision that is made based upon the size of the subarray. Musser (1997) introduced a **Quicksort** variation called **IntroSort**, which monitors the recursive depth of **Quicksort** to ensure efficient processing. If the depth of the **Quicksort** recursion exceeds $log (n)$ levels, then **IntroSort** switches to **Heap Sort**. The SGI implementation of the C++ Standard Template Library (*http://www.sgi.com/tech/stl/sort.html*) uses **IntroSort** as its default sorting mechanism.

Sorting without Comparisons

At the end of this chapter, we will show that no comparison-based sorting algorithm can sort n elements in better than $O(n \ log \ n)$ performance. Surprisingly, there are potentially faster ways to sort elements if you know something about those elements in advance. For example, if you have a fast hashing function that uniformly partitions a collection of elements into distinct, ordered buckets, you can use the following **Bucket Sort** algorithm for linear $O(n)$ performance.

Bucket Sort

Given a set of n elements, **Bucket Sort** constructs a set of n ordered buckets into which the elements of the input set are partitioned; **Bucket Sort** reduces its processing costs at the expense of this extra space. If a hash function, hash($A[i]$), can uniformly partition the input set of n elements into these n buckets, **Bucket Sort** can sort, in the worst case, in $O(n)$ time. Use **Bucket Sort** when the following two properties hold:

Uniform distribution

The input data must be uniformly distributed for a given range. Based on this distribution, n buckets are created to evenly partition the input range.

Ordered hash function

The buckets are ordered. If $i < j$, elements inserted into bucket b_i are lexico-graphically smaller than elements in bucket b_j.

Bucket Sort Summary

Best, Average, Worst: O(n)

```
sort (A)
  create n buckets B
  for i = 0 to n-1 do ❶
    k = hash(A[i])
    add A[i] to the k-th bucket B[k]
  extract (B, A) ❷
end

extract (B, A)
  idx = 0
  for i = 0 to n-1 do
    insertionSort (B[i]) ❸
    foreach element e in B[i] ❹
      A[idx++] = e
end
```

❶ Create bucket list and hash all elements to proper bucket.

❷ Process all buckets to extract values back into A in sorted order.

❸ If more than one element in bucket, sort first.

❹ Copy elements back into proper position in A.

Bucket Sort is not appropriate for sorting arbitrary strings, for example, because typically it is impossible to develop a hash function with the required characteristics. However, it could be used to sort a set of uniformly distributed floating-point numbers in the range [0, 1).

Once all elements to be sorted are inserted into the buckets, **Bucket Sort** extracts the values from left to right using **Insertion Sort** on the contents of each bucket. This orders the elements in each respective bucket as the values from the buckets are extracted from left to right to repopulate the original array. An example execution is shown in Figure 4-9.

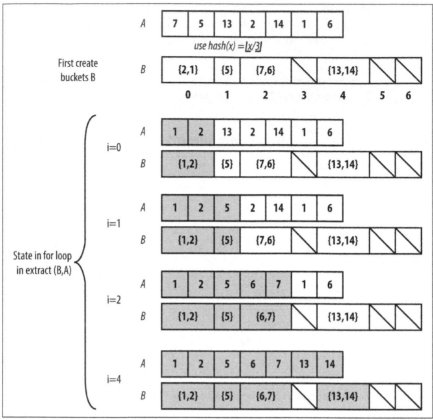

Figure 4-9. Small example demonstrating Bucket Sort

Solution

In the C implementation for **Bucket Sort**, shown in Example 4-7, each bucket stores a linked list of elements that were hashed to that bucket. The functions `numBuckets` and `hash` are provided externally, based upon the input set.

Example 4-7. Bucket Sort implementation in C

```
extern int hash (void *elt);
extern int numBuckets (int numElements);

/* linked list of elements in bucket. */
typedef struct entry {
  void          *element;
  struct entry  *next;
} ENTRY;

/* maintain count of entries in each bucket and pointer to its first entry */
```

```
typedef struct {
  int        size;
  ENTRY      *head;
} BUCKET;

/* Allocation of buckets and the number of buckets allocated */
static BUCKET *buckets = 0;
static int num = 0;

/** One by one remove and overwrite ar */
void extract (BUCKET *buckets, int (*cmp)(const void *, const void *),
              void **ar, int n) {
  int i, low;
  int idx = 0;
  for (i = 0; i < num; i++) {
    ENTRY *ptr, *tmp;
    if (buckets[i].size == 0) continue;   /* empty bucket */

    ptr = buckets[i].head;
    if (buckets[i].size == 1) {
      ar[idx++] = ptr->element;
      free (ptr);
      buckets[i].size = 0;
      continue;
    }

    /* insertion sort where elements are drawn from linked list and
     * inserted into array. Linked lists are released. */
    low = idx;
    ar[idx++] = ptr->element;
    tmp = ptr;
    ptr = ptr->next;
    free (tmp);

    while (ptr != NULL) {
      int i = idx-1;
      while (i >= low && cmp (ar[i], ptr->element) > 0) {
        ar[i+1] = ar[i];
        i--;
      }
      ar[i+1] = ptr->element;
      tmp = ptr;
      ptr = ptr->next;
      free (tmp);
      idx++;
    }
    buckets[i].size = 0;
  }
}

void sortPointers (void **ar, int n,
                   int (*cmp)(const void *, const void *)) {
```

```
    int i;
    num = numBuckets (n);
    buckets = (BUCKET *) calloc (num, sizeof (BUCKET));
    for (i = 0; i < n; i++) {
      int k = hash(ar[i]);

      /** Insert each element and increment counts */
      ENTRY *e = (ENTRY *) calloc (1, sizeof (ENTRY));
      e->element = ar[i];
      if (buckets[k].head == NULL) {
        buckets[k].head = e;
      } else {
        e->next = buckets[k].head;
        buckets[k].head = e;
      }

      buckets[k].size++;
    }

    /* now sort, read out, and overwrite ar. */
    extract (buckets, cmp, ar, n);

    free (buckets);
}
```

For numbers drawn uniformly from [0, 1), Example 4-8 contains sample implementations of the hash and numBuckets functions to use.

Example 4-8. Hash and numBuckets functions for [0, 1) range

```
static int num;

/** Number of buckets to use is the same as the number of elements. */
int numBuckets (int numElements) {
  num = numElements;
  return numElements;
}

/**
 * Hash function to identify bucket number from element. Customized
 * to properly encode elements in order within the buckets. Range of
 * numbers is from [0, 1), so we subdivide into buckets of size 1/num;
 */
int hash (double *d) {
  int bucket = num*(*d);
  return bucket;
}
```

The buckets could also be stored using fixed arrays that are reallocated when the buckets become full, but the linked list implementation is about 30%–40% faster.

Analysis

The sortPointers function of Example 4-7 sorts each element from the input into its associated bucket based upon the provided hash function; this takes $O(n)$ time. Because of the careful design of the hash function, we know that all elements in bucket b_i are smaller than the elements in bucket b_j if $i < j$.

As the values are extracted from the buckets and written back into the input array, **Insertion Sort** is used when a bucket contains more than a single element. For **Bucket Sort** to exhibit $O(n)$ behavior, we must guarantee that the total time to sort each of these buckets is also $O(n)$. Let's define n_i to be the number of elements partitioned in bucket b_i. We can treat n_i as a random variable (using statistical theory). Now consider the expected value $E[n_i]$ for each bucket b_i. Each element in the input set has probability $p = 1/n$ of being inserted into a given bucket because each of these elements is uniformly drawn from the range [0, 1). Therefore, $E[n_i] = n*p = n*(1/n) = 1$, while the variance $Var[n_i] = n*p*(1 - p) = (1 - 1/n)$. It is important to consider the variance because some buckets will be empty, and others may have more than one element; we need to be sure that no bucket has too many elements. Once again, we resort to statistical theory, which provides the following equation for random variables:

$$E[n_i^2] = Var[n_i] + E^2[n_i]$$

From this equation we can compute the expected value of n_i^2. This is critical because it is the factor that determines the cost of **Insertion Sort**, which runs in a worst case of $O(n^2)$. We compute $E[n_i^2] = (1 - 1/n) + 1 = (2 - 1/n)$, which shows that $E[n_i^2]$ can be considered a constant. This means that when we sum up the costs of executing **Insertion Sort** on all n buckets, the expected performance cost remains $O(n)$.

Variations

Instead of creating n buckets, **Hash Sort** creates a suitably large number of buckets k into which the elements are partitioned; as k grows in size, the performance of **Hash Sort** improves. The key to **Hash Sort** is a hashing function hash(e) that returns an integer for each element e such that hash(a_i) ≤ hash(a_j) if a_i is lexicographically smaller than a_j.

The hash function hash(e) defined in Example 4-9 operates over elements containing just lowercase letters. It converts the first three characters of the string (using base 26 representation) into an integer value; for the string "abcdefgh," its first three characters ("abc") are extracted and converted into the value 0*676 + 1*26 + 2 = 28. This string is thus inserted into the bucket labeled 28.

Example 4-9. hash and numBuckets functions for Hash Sort

```
/** Number of buckets to use. */
int numBuckets (int numElements) {
  return 26*26*26;
}

/**
 * Hash function to identify bucket number from element. Customized
 * to properly encode elements in order within the buckets.
 */
int hash (void *elt) {
  return (((char*)elt)[0] - 'a')*676 +
         (((char*)elt)[1] - 'a')*26 +
         (((char*)elt)[2] - 'a');
}
```

The performance of **Hash Sort** for various bucket sizes and input sets is shown in Table 4-5. We show comparable sorting times for **Quicksort** using the median-of-three approach for selecting the pivotIndex.

Table 4-5. Sample performance for Hash Sort with different numbers of buckets, compared with Quicksort (in seconds)

n	26 buckets	676 buckets	17,576 buckets	Quicksort
16	0.000005	0.000010	0.000120	0.000004
32	0.000006	0.000012	0.000146	0.000005
64	0.000011	0.000016	0.000181	0.000009
128	0.000017	0.000022	0.000228	0.000016
256	0.000033	0.000034	0.000249	0.000033
512	0.000074	0.000061	0.000278	0.000070
1,024	0.000183	0.000113	0.000332	0.000156
2,048	0.000521	0.000228	0.000424	0.000339
4,096	0.0016	0.000478	0.000646	0.000740
8,192	0.0058	0.0011	0.0011	0.0016
16,384	0.0224	0.0026	0.0020	0.0035
32,768	0.0944	0.0069	0.0040	0.0076
65,536	0.4113	0.0226	0.0108	0.0168
131,072	1.7654	0.0871	0.0360	0.0422

Note that with 17,576 buckets, **Hash Sort** outperforms **Quicksort** for $n > 8,192$ items (and this trend continues with increasing n). However, with only 676 buckets, once $n > 32,768$ (for an average of 48 elements per bucket), **Hash Sort** begins its inevitable slowdown with the accumulated cost of executing **Insertion Sort** on increasingly larger sets. Indeed, with only 26 buckets, once $n > 256$, **Hash Sort** begins to quadruple its performance as the problem size doubles, showing how too few buckets leads to $O(n^2)$ performance.

Sorting with Extra Storage

Most sorting algorithms sort a collection in place without requiring any noticeable extra storage. We now present **Merge Sort**, which offers $O(n \log n)$ behavior in the worst case while using $O(n)$ extra storage. It can be used to efficiently sort data that is stored externally in a file.

Merge Sort

To sort a collection A, divide it evenly into two smaller collections, each of which is then sorted. A final phase merges these two sorted collections back into a single collection of size n. A naïve implementation of this approach, shown here, uses far too much extra storage:

```
sort (A)
  if A has less than 2 elements then
    return A
  else if A has 2 elements then
    swap elements of A if out of order
    return A

  sub1 = sort(left half of A)
  sub2 = sort(right half of A)

  merge sub1 and sub2 into new array B
  return B
end
```

Each recursive call of sort will require space equivalent to the size of the array, or $O(n)$, and there will be $O(\log n)$ such recursive calls; thus the storage requirement for this naïve implementation is $O(n \log n)$. Fortunately there is a way to use only $O(n)$ storage, as we now discuss.

Input/Output

The output of the sort is returned in place within the original collection A. The internal storage *copy* is discarded.

Merge Sort Summary

Best, Average, Worst: O(*n log n*)

```
sort (A)
  copy = copy of A ❶
  mergeSort (copy, A, 0, n)
end

mergeSort (A, result, start, end) ❷
  if end - start < 2 then return
  if end - start = 2 then
    swap elements of result if out of order
    return

  mid = (start + end)/2
  mergeSort (result, A, start, mid) ❸
  mergeSort (result, A, mid, end)

  merge left and right halves of A into result ❹
end
```

❶ Make full copy of all elements.

❷ Place elements of A[start,end) into result[start,end) in sorted order.

❸ Sort results[start,mid) into A[start,mid).

❹ Merge sorted subarrays in A back into result.

Solution

Merge Sort merges the left- and right-sorted subarrays using two indices *i* and *j* to iterate over the left (and right) elements, always copying the smaller of A[*i*] and A[*j*] into its proper location *result[idx]*. There are three cases to consider:

- The right side is exhausted (*j* ≥ *end*), in which case the remaining elements are taken from the left side

- The left side is exhausted (*i* ≥ *mid*), in which case the remaining elements are taken from from the right side

- The left and right side have elements; if A[*i*] < A[*j*], insert A[*i*] otherwise insert A[*j*]

Once the for loop completes, *result* has the merged (and sorted) elements from the original A[*start*, *end*). Example 4-10 contains the Python implementation of **Merge Sort**.

Example 4-10. Merge Sort implementation in Python

```python
def sort (A):
  """merge sort A in place."""
  copy = list (A)
  mergesort_array (copy, A, 0, len(A))

def mergesort_array (A, result, start, end):
  """Mergesort array in memory with given range."""
  if end - start < 2:
    return
  if end - start == 2:
    if result[start] > result[start+1]:
      result[start],result[start+1] = result[start+1],result[start]
    return

  mid = (end + start) // 2
  mergesort_array (result, A, start, mid)
  mergesort_array (result, A, mid, end)

  # merge A left- and right- side
  i = start
  j = mid
  idx = start
  while idx < end:
    if j >= end or (i < mid and A[i] < A[j]):
      result[idx] = A[i]
      i += 1
    else:
      result[idx] = A[j]
      j += 1

    idx += 1
```

Analysis

Merge Sort completes the "merge" phase in O(*n*) time after recursively sorting the left- and right-half of the range A[*start*, *end*), placing the properly ordered elements in the array referenced as result.

Because *copy* is a true copy of the entire array A, the terminating base cases of the recursion will work *because it references the original elements of the array directly at their respective index locations.* This observation is a sophisticated one and is key to the algorithm. In addition, the final merge step requires only O(*n*) operations, which ensures the total performance remains O(*n log n*). Because *copy* is the only extra space used by the algorithm, the total space requirement is O(*n*).

Variations

Of all the sorting algorithms, **Merge Sort** is the easiest one to convert to working with external data. Example 4-11 contains a full Java implementation using memory mapping of data to efficiently sort a file containing binary-encoded integers. This sorting algorithm requires the elements to all have the same size, so it can't easily be adapted to sort arbitrary strings or other variable-length elements.

Example 4-11. External Merge Sort implementation in Java

```java
public static void mergesort (File A) throws IOException {
  File copy = File.createTempFile ("Mergesort", ".bin");
  copyFile(A, copy);

  RandomAccessFile src = new RandomAccessFile (A, "rw");
  RandomAccessFile dest = new RandomAccessFile (copy, "rw");
  FileChannel srcC = src.getChannel();
  FileChannel destC = dest.getChannel();
  MappedByteBuffer srcMap = srcC.map (FileChannel.MapMode.READ_WRITE,
                                 0, src.length());
  MappedByteBuffer destMap = destC.map (FileChannel.MapMode.READ_WRITE,
                                 0, dest.length());

  mergesort (destMap, srcMap, 0, (int) A.length());

  // The following two invocations are only needed on Windows platform:
  closeDirectBuffer (srcMap);
  closeDirectBuffer (destMap);
  src.close();
  dest.close();
  copy.deleteOnExit();
}

static void mergesort (MappedByteBuffer A, MappedByteBuffer result,
                       int start, int end) throws IOException {
  if (end - start < 8) {
    return;
  }

  if (end - start == 8) {
    result.position (start);
    int left = result.getInt();
    int right = result.getInt();
    if (left > right) {
      result.position (start);
      result.putInt (right);
      result.putInt (left);
    }
    return;
  }
```

```
int mid = (end + start)/8*4;
mergesort (result, A, start, mid);
mergesort (result, A, mid, end);

result.position (start);
for (int i = start, j = mid, idx=start; idx < end; idx += 4) {
  int Ai = A.getInt (i);
  int Aj = 0;
  if (j < end) { Aj = A.getInt (j); }
  if (j >= end || (i < mid && Ai < Aj)) {
    result.putInt (Ai);
    i += 4;
  } else {
    result.putInt (Aj);
    j += 4;
  }
}
}
```

The structure is identical to the **Merge Sort** implementation, but it uses a memory-mapped structure to efficiently process data stored on the file system. There are issues on Windows operating systems that fail to properly close the MappedByte Buffer data. The repository contains a work-around method closeDirect Buffer(MappedByteBuffer) that will handle this responsibility.

String Benchmark Results

To choose the appropriate algorithm for different data, you need to know some properties about your input data. We created several benchmark data sets on which to show how the algorithms presented in this chapter compare with one another. Note that the actual values of the generated tables are less important because they reflect the specific hardware on which the benchmarks were run. Instead, you should pay attention to the relative performance of the algorithms on the corresponding data sets:

Random strings
Throughout this chapter, we have demonstrated performance of sorting algorithms when sorting 26-character strings that are permutations of the letters in the alphabet. Given there are $n!$ such strings, or roughly $4.03*10^{26}$ strings, there are few duplicate strings in our sample data sets. In addition, the cost of comparing elements is not constant, because of the occasional need to compare multiple characters.

Double-precision floating-point values
Using available pseudorandom generators available on most operating systems, we generate a set of random numbers from the range [0, 1). There are essentially no duplicate values in the sample data set and the cost of comparing two

elements is a fixed constant. The results of these data sets are not included here, but can be found in the code repository.

The input data provided to the sorting algorithms can be preprocessed to ensure some of the following properties (not all are compatible):

Sorted
> The input elements can be presorted into ascending order (the ultimate goal) or in descending order.

Killer median-of-three
> Musser (1997) discovered an ordering that ensures that **Quicksort** requires $O(n^2)$ comparisons when using median-of-three to choose a pivot.

Nearly sorted
> Given a set of sorted data, we can select k pairs of elements to swap and the distance d with which to swap (or 0 if any two pairs can be swapped). Using this capability, you can construct input sets that might more closely match your input set.

The upcoming tables are ordered left to right, based on how well the algorithms perform on the final row in the table. To produce the results shown in Tables 4-6 through 4-8, we executed each trial 100 times and discarded the best and worst performers. The average of the remaining 98 trials is shown in these tables. The columns labeled "Quicksort BFPRT[4] minSize = 4" refer to a **Quicksort** implementation that uses BFPRT (with groups of 4) to select the partition value, switching to **Insertion Sort** when a subarray to be sorted has four or fewer elements.

Because the performance of **Quicksort** median-of-three degrades so quickly, only 10 trials were executed in Table 4-8.

Table 4-6. Performance results (in seconds) on random 26-letter permutations of the alphabet

n	Hash Sort 17,576 buckets	Quicksort median-of-three	Merge Sort	Heap Sort	Quicksort BFPRT[4] minSize = 4
4,096	0.000631	0.000741	0.000824	0.0013	0.0028
8,192	0.0011	0.0016	0.0018	0.0029	0.0062
16,384	0.0020	0.0035	0.0039	0.0064	0.0138
32,768	0.0040	0.0077	0.0084	0.0147	0.0313
65,536	0.0107	0.0168	0.0183	0.0336	0.0703
131,072	0.0359	0.0420	0.0444	0.0893	0.1777

Table 4-7. Performance (in seconds) on sorted random 26-letter permutations of the alphabet

n	Insertion Sort	Merge Sort	Quicksort median-of-three	Hash Sort 17,576 buckets	Heap Sort	Quicksort BFPRT[4] minSize = 4
4,096	0.000029	0.000434	0.00039	0.000552	0.0012	0.0016
8,192	0.000058	0.000932	0.000841	0.001	0.0026	0.0035
16,384	0.000116	0.002	0.0018	0.0019	0.0056	0.0077
32,768	0.000237	0.0041	0.0039	0.0038	0.0123	0.0168
65,536	0.000707	0.0086	0.0085	0.0092	0.0269	0.0364
131,072	0.0025	0.0189	0.0198	0.0247	0.0655	0.0834

Table 4-8. Performance (in seconds) on killer median data

n	Merge Sort	Hash Sort 17,576 buckets	Heap Sort	Quicksort BFPRT[4] minSize = 4	Quicksort median-of-three
4,096	0.000505	0.000569	0.0012	0.0023	0.0212
8,192	0.0011	0.0010	0.0026	0.0050	0.0841
16,384	0.0023	0.0019	0.0057	0.0108	0.3344
32,768	0.0047	0.0038	0.0123	0.0233	1.3455
65,536	0.0099	0.0091	0.0269	0.0506	5.4027
131,072	0.0224	0.0283	0.0687	0.1151	38.0950

Analysis Techniques

When analyzing a sorting algorithm, we must explain its best-case, worst-case, and average-case performance (as discussed in Chapter 2). The average case is typically hardest to accurately quantify and relies on advanced mathematical techniques and estimation. It also assumes a reasonable understanding of the likelihood that the input may be partially sorted. Even when an algorithm has been shown to have a desirable average-case cost, its implementation may simply be impractical. Each sorting algorithm in this chapter is analyzed both by its theoretical behavior and by its actual behavior in practice.

A fundamental result in computer science is that no algorithm that sorts by comparing elements can do better than O($n \log n$) performance in the average or worst case. We now sketch a proof. Given n items, there are $n!$ permutations of these elements. Every algorithm that sorts by pairwise comparisons corresponds to a binary decision tree. The leaves of the tree correspond to an underlying permutation, and every permutation must have at least one leaf in the tree. The nodes on a path from the root to a leaf correspond to a sequence of comparisons. The *height* of such a tree is the number of comparison nodes in the longest path from the root to a leaf node; for example, the height of the tree in Figure 4-10 is 5 because only five comparisons are needed in all cases (although in four cases only four comparisons are needed).

Construct a binary decision tree where each internal node of the tree represents a comparison $a_i \le a_j$ and the leaves of the tree represent one of the $n!$ permutations. To sort a set of n elements, start at the root and evaluate the statements shown in each node. Traverse to the left child when the statement is true; otherwise, traverse to the right child. Figure 4-10 shows a sample decision tree for four elements.

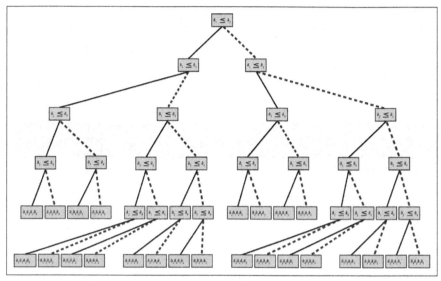

Figure 4-10. Binary decision tree for ordering four elements

We could construct many different binary decision trees. Nonetheless, we assert that given any such binary decision tree for comparing n elements, we can compute its minimum height h—that is, there must be some leaf node that requires h comparison nodes in the tree from the root to that leaf. Consider a complete binary tree of height h in which all nonleaf nodes have both a left and right child. This tree contains a total of $n = 2^h - 1$ nodes and height $h = log(n + 1)$; if the tree is not complete, it could be unbalanced in strange ways, but we know that $h \ge \lceil log(n + 1) \rceil$. Any binary decision tree with $n!$ leaf nodes already demonstrates that it has at least $n!$ nodes in total. We need only compute $h = \lceil log(n!) \rceil$ to determine the height of any such binary decision tree. We take advantage of the following properties of logarithms: $log(a*b) = log(a) + log(b)$ and $log(x^y) = y*log(x)$.

$$h = log(n!) = log(n * (n - 1) * (n - 2) * \ldots * 2 * 1)$$

$$h > log(n * (n - 1) * (n - 2) * \ldots * n/2)$$

$$h > log((n/2)^{n/2})$$

$$h > (n/2) * log(n/2)$$

$$h > (n/2) * (log(n) - 1)$$

Thus, $h > (n/2)*(log(n) - 1)$. What does this mean? Well, given n elements to be sorted, there will be at least one path from the root to a leaf of size h, which means an algorithm that sorts by comparison requires at least this many comparisons to sort the n elements. Note that h is computed by a function $f(n)$; here in particular, $f(n) = (1/2)*n*log(n) - n/2$, which means any sorting algorithm using comparisons will require $O(n \log n)$ comparisons to sort.

References

Bentley, J. and M. McIlroy, "Engineering a sort function," *Software—Practice and Experience*, 23(11): 1249–1265, 1993, *http://dx.doi.org/10.1002/spe.4380231105*.

Blum, M., R. Floyd, V. Pratt, R. Rivest, and R. Tarjan, "Time bounds for selection," *Journal of Computer and System Sciences*, 7(4): 448–461, 1973, *http://dx.doi.org/10.1016/S0022-0000(73)80033-9*.

Cormen, T. H., C. Leiserson, R. Rivest, and C. Stein, *Introduction to Algorithms*. Third Edition. MIT Press, 2009.

Davis, M. and K. Whistler, "Unicode Collation Algorithm, Unicode Technical Standard #10," June 2015, *http://unicode.org/reports/tr10/*.

Gilreath, W., "Hash sort: A linear time complexity multiple-dimensional sort algorithm," Proceedings, First Southern Symposium on Computing, 1998, *http://arxiv.org/abs/cs.DS/0408040*.

Musser, D., "Introspective sorting and selection algorithms," *Software—Practice and Experience*, 27(8): 983–993, 1997.

Sedgewick, R., "Implementing Quicksort programs," *Communications ACM*, 21(10): 847–857, 1978, *http://dx.doi.org/10.1145/359619.359631*.

Trivedi, K. S., *Probability and Statistics with Reliability, Queueing, and Computer Science Applications*. Second Edition. Wiley-Blackwell Publishing, 2001.

5
Searching

Given a collection *C* of elements, there are two fundamental queries:

Existence
Does C contain a target element? Given a collection *C*, we often simply want to know whether the collection already contains a given element *t*. The response to such a query is `true` if an element exists in the collection that matches the desired target *t*, or `false` if this is not the case.

Associative lookup
Return information associated in collection *C* with a target key value *k*. A key is usually associated with a complex structure called a value. The lookup retrieves or replaces this value.

The algorithms in this chapter describe specific ways to structure data to more efficiently process search queries. For example, you might order the collection *C* using the sorting algorithms previously covered in Chapter 4. As we will see, sorting improves the performance of queries, but there are other costs involved in maintaining a sorted collection, especially when elements are frequently inserted or deleted.

Ultimately the performance is based on how many elements an algorithm inspects as it processes a query. Use the following guide to select the best algorithm for you:

Small collections
Sequential Search offers the simplest implementation and is implemented as a basic construct in many programming languages. Use this algorithm when the collection is available only sequentially, as with an *iterator*.

Restricted memory
    When the collection is an array that doesn't change and you want to conserve memory, use **Binary Search**.

Dynamic membership
    If the elements in the collection change frequently, consider **Hash-Based Search** and **Binary Search Tree** for their ability to spread out the costs associated with maintaining their data structures.

Sorted access
    Use **Binary Search Tree** when you need *dynamic membership* and the ability to process elements in the collection in sorted order.

Don't forget to account for any upfront preprocessing required by the algorithm to structure data in advance of handling search queries. Choose an appropriate structure that not only speeds up the performance of individual queries, but also minimizes the overall cost of maintaining the collection structure in the face of both dynamic access and multiple queries.

We assume the existence of a set U (the universe) of possible values. The collection C contains elements drawn from U, and the target element being sought, t, is a member of U. If t is instead a key value, we consider U to be the set of potential key values, $k \in U$, and the collection C may contain more complex elements. Note that duplicate values may exist within C, so it cannot be treated as a set (which only supports unique membership).

When the collection C allows the indexing of arbitrary elements, we refer to the collection as an array A with the notation $A[i]$ representing the ith element of A. By convention, we use the value null to represent an element not in U; such a value is useful when a search is asked to return a specific element in a collection but that element is not present. In general, we assume it is impossible to search for null in a collection.

Sequential Search

Sequential Search, also called linear search, is the simplest of all searching algorithms. It is a brute-force approach to locate a single target value, t, in a collection, C. It finds t by starting at the first element of the collection and examining each subsequent element until it runs out of elements or it finds a matching element.

There must be some way to obtain each element from the collection being searched; the order is not important. Often the elements of a collection C can be accessed only with a read-only *iterator* that retrieves each element from C, as, for example, a database cursor in response to an SQL query. Both modes of access are shown here.

Input/Output

The input consists of a nonempty collection, C, of $n > 0$ elements and a target value, t, that is sought. The search will return true if C contains t and false otherwise.

Sequential Search Summary

Best: O(*1*)   Average, Worst: O(*n*)

```
search (A,t)
  for i=0 to n-1 do ❶
    if A[i] = t then
      return true
  return false
end

search (C,t)
  iter = C.begin()
  while iter ≠ C.end() do ❷
    e = iter.next() ❸
    if e = t then
      return true
  return false
end
```

❶ Access each element in order, from position 0 to *n* – *1*.

❷ Iterator continues until it is exhausted of elements.

❸ Each element is retrieved one by one from an *iterator*.

Context

You frequently need to locate an element in a collection that may or may not be ordered. With no further knowledge about the information that might be in the collection, **Sequential Search** gets the job done in a brute-force manner. It is the only search algorithm you can use if the collection is accessible only through an iterator.

If the collection is unordered and stored as a linked list, inserting an element is a constant time operation (simply append it to the end of the list). Frequent insertions into an array-based collection require dynamic array management, which is either provided by the underlying programming language or requires specific attention by the programmer. In both cases, the expected time to find an element is O(*n*); thus, removing an element takes at least O(*n*).

Sequential Search places the fewest restrictions on the type of elements you can search. The only requirement is the presence of a match function to determine whether the target element being searched for matches an element in the collection; often this functionality is delegated to the elements themselves.

Solution

Often the implementation of **Sequential Search** is trivial. The Python code in Example 5-1 searches sequentially through a collection.

Example 5-1. Sequential Search in Python

```python
def sequentialSearch (collection, t):
  for e in collection:
    if e == t:
      return True
  return False
```

The code is disarmingly simple. The function receives a collection and the target item *t* being sought. The collection can be a list or any other *iterable* Python object. Elements involved in the search must support the == operator. This same example written in Java is shown in Example 5-2. The SequentialSearch generic class has a type parameter, T, which specifies the elements in the collection; T must provide a valid equals (Object o) method for this code to work properly.

Example 5-2. Sequential Search in Java

```java
public class SequentialSearch<T> {

  /** Apply brute-force Sequential Search to search indexed
   *  collection (of type T) for the given target item. */
  public boolean search (T[] collection, T t) {
    for (T item : collection) {
      if (item.equals (t)) {
        return true;
      }
    }
    return false;
  }

  /** Apply brute-force Sequential Search to search iterable
   * collection (of type T) for the given target item. */
  public boolean search (Iterable<T> collection, T t) {
    Iterator<T> iter = collection.iterator();
    while (iter.hasNext()) {
      if (iter.next().equals (t)) {
        return true;
      }
    }
    return false;
  }
}
```

Analysis

If the item being sought belongs to the collection and is equally likely to be found at any of its indexed locations (alternatively, if it is equally likely to be emitted by an iterator at any position), on average **Sequential Search** probes $n/2 + 1/2$ elements (as presented in Chapter 2). That is, you will inspect about half the elements in the collection for each item you find, resulting in $O(n)$ performance. The best case is when the item being sought is the first element in the collection, resulting in O(*1*) performance. This algorithm exhibits linear growth in the average and worst cases. If you double the size of the collection, this should approximately double the amount of time spent searching.

To show **Sequential Search** in action, we construct an ordered collection of the *n* integers in the range [1, *n*]. Although the collection is ordered, this information is not used by the searching code. We ran a suite of 100 trials; in each trial we execute 1,000 queries for a random target *t* that would be present in the collection with probability *p*. Thus, of these 1,000 queries, *p**1,000 are guaranteed to find *t* in the collection (for *p* = 0.0, the target *t* is a negative number). We aggregated the time to execute these queries and discarded the best- and worst-performing trials. Table 5-1 shows the average of the remaining 98 trials at four specific *p* values. Note how the execution time approximately doubles as the size of the collection doubles. You should also observe that for each collection size *n*, the worst performance occurs in the final column where the target *t* does not exist in the collection.

Table 5-1. Sequential Search performance (in seconds)

n	p = 1.0	p = 0.5	p = 0.25	p = 0.0
4,096	0.0057	0.0087	0.0101	0.0116
8,192	0.0114	0.0173	0.0202	0.0232
16,384	0.0229	0.0347	0.0405	0.0464
32,768	0.0462	0.0697	0.0812	0.0926
65,536	0.0927	0.1391	0.1620	0.1853
131,072	0.1860	0.2786	0.3245	0.3705

Binary Search

Binary Search delivers better performance than **Sequential Search** because it starts with a collection whose elements are already sorted. **Binary Search** divides the sorted collection in half until the sought-for item is found, or until it is determined that the item does not exist in the collection.

Input/Output

The input to **Binary Search** is an indexed collection *A* whose elements are totally ordered, which means that given two index positions, *i* and *j*, *A*[*i*] < *A*[*j*] if and only if *i* < *j*. We construct a data structure that holds the elements (or pointers to the elements) and preserves the ordering of the keys. The output to **Binary Search** is either true or false.

Context

When searching through the ordered collection, a logarithmic number of probes is necessary in the worst case.

Different types of data structures support binary searching. If the collection never changes, the elements should be placed into an array. This makes it easy to navigate through the collection. However, if you need to add or remove elements from the collection, this approach becomes unwieldy. There are several structures we can use; one of the best known is the binary search tree, discussed later in this chapter.

Binary Search Summary

Best: O(*1*)   Average, Worst: O(*log n*)

```
search (A,t)
  low = 0
  high = n-1
  while low ≤ high do  ❶
    mid = (low + high)/2  ❷
    if t < A[mid] then
      high = mid - 1
    else if t > A[mid] then
      low = mid + 1
    else
      return true
  return false  ❸
end
```

❶   Repeat while there is a range to be searched.

❷   Midpoint computed using integer arithmetic.

❸   "Variations" on page 99 discusses how to support a "search-or-insert" operation based on final value of mid at this point.

Solution

Given an ordered collection of elements as an array, the Java code in Example 5-3 shows a parameterized implementation of **Binary Search** for any base type T. Java provides the java.util.Comparable<T> interface that contains the compareTo method. Any class that correctly implements this interface guarantees a total ordering of its instances.

Example 5-3. Binary Search implementation in Java

```
/**
 * Binary Search given a presorted array of the parameterized type.
 *
```

```
 * @param T    elements of the collection being searched are of this type.
 *              The parameter T must implement Comparable.
 */
public class BinarySearch<T extends Comparable<T>> {

  /** Search collection for non-null target; return true on success. */
  public boolean search(T[] collection, T target) {
    if (target == null) { return false; }

    int low = 0, high = collection.length - 1;
    while (low <= high) {
      int mid = (low + high)/2;
      int rc = target.compareTo (collection[mid]);
      if (rc < 0) {          // target is less than collection[i]
        high = mid - 1;
      } else if (rc > 0) {   // target is greater than collection[i]
        low = mid + 1;
      } else {               // item has been found
        return true;
      }
    }

    return false;
  }
}
```

Three variables are used in the implementation: low, high, and mid. low is the lowest index of the current subarray being searched, high is its upper index, and mid is its midpoint. The performance of this code depends on the number of times the while loop executes.

Binary Search adds a small amount of complexity for large performance gains. The complexity can increase when the collection is not stored in a simple in-memory data structure, such as an array. A large collection might need to be kept in secondary storage, such as a file on a disk. In such a case, the ith element is accessed by its offset location within the file. Using secondary storage, the time required to search for an element is dominated by the costs to access the storage; other solutions related to **Binary Search** may be appropriate.

Analysis

Binary Search divides the problem size approximately in half every time it executes the loop. The maximum number of times the collection of size n is cut in half is $1 + \lfloor log\,(n) \rfloor$. If we use a single operation to determine whether two items are equal, lesser than, or greater than (as is made possible by the Comparable interface), only $1 + \lfloor log\,(n) \rfloor$ comparisons are needed, resulting in a classification of O($log\,n$).

We ran 100 trials of 524,288 searches for an item stored in a collection in memory of size n (ranging in size from 4,096 to 524,288) with probability p (sampled at 1.0,

0.5, and 0.0) of finding each item. After removing the best and worst performers for each trial, Table 5-2 shows the average performance for the remaining 98 trials.

Table 5-2. In-memory execution of 524,288 searches using Binary Search compared to Sequential Search (in seconds)

n	Sequential Search time			Binary Search time		
	p = 1.0	p = 0.5	p = 0.0	p = 1.0	p = 0.5	p = 0.0
4,096	3.0237	4.5324	6.0414	0.0379	0.0294	0.0208
8,192	6.0405	9.0587	12.0762	0.0410	0.0318	0.0225
16,384	12.0742	18.1086	24.1426	0.0441	0.0342	0.0243
32,768	24.1466	36.2124	48.2805	0.0473	0.0366	0.0261
65,536	48.2762	72.4129	96.5523	0.0508	0.0395	0.0282
131,072	*	*	*	0.0553	0.0427	0.0300
262,144	*	*	*	0.0617	0.0473	0.0328
524,288	*	*	*	0.0679	0.0516	0.0355

These trials were designed to ensure that when $p = 1.0$, there is an equal probability of searching for any element in the collection; if this were not the case, the results could be skewed. For both **Sequential Search** and **Binary Search**, the input is an array of sorted integers in the range $[0, n)$. To produce 524,288 search items known to be in the collection ($p = 1.0$), we cycle through the n numbers 524,288/n times.

Table 5-3 shows the times for performing 524,288 searches on a collection stored on a local disk. Either the searched-for item always exists in the collection (i.e., $p = 1.0$), or it never does—that is, we search for –1 in the collection $[0, n)$. The data is simply a file of ascending integers, where each integer is packed into four bytes. The dominance of disk access is clear because the results in Table 5-3 are nearly 400 times slower than those in Table 5-2. Note how the performance of the search increases by a fixed amount as n doubles in size, a clear indication that the performance of **Binary Search** is O($log\ n$).

Table 5-3. Secondary-storage Binary Search performance for 524,288 searches (in seconds)

n	p = 1.0	p = 0.0
4,096	1.2286	1.2954
8,192	1.3287	1.4015
16,384	1.4417	1.5080
32,768	6.7070	1.6170
65,536	13.2027	12.0399

n	p = 1.0	p = 0.0
131,072	19.2609	17.2848
262,144	24.9942	22.7568
524,288	30.3821	28.0204

Variations

To support a "search-or-insert" operation, observe that all valid array indices are non-negative. The Python variation in Example 5-4 shows a bs_contains method that returns a negative number p if searching for a target element not contained in the ordered array. The value $-(p + 1)$ is the index position where *target* should be inserted, as shown in bs_insert. Naturally this will bump up all the higher indexed values to make room for the new element.

Example 5-4. Python search-or-insert variation

```
def bs_contains (ordered, target):
  """Return index of target in ordered or -(p+1) where to insert it."""
  low = 0
  high = len(ordered)-1
  while low <= high:
    mid = (low + high) // 2
    if target < ordered[mid]:
      high = mid-1
    elif target > ordered[mid]:
      low = mid+1
    else:
      return mid

  return -(low + 1)

def bs_insert (ordered, target):
  """Inserts target into proper location if not present."""
  idx = bs_contains (ordered, target)
  if idx < 0:
    ordered.insert (-(idx + 1), target)
```

Inserting into or deleting from an ordered array becomes inefficient as the size of the array grows, because every array entry must contain a valid element. Therefore, inserting involves extending the array (physically or logically) and pushing, on average, half of the elements ahead one index position. Deletion requires shrinking the array and moving half of the elements one index position lower.

Hash-Based Search

The previous sections on searching are appropriate when there are a small number of elements (**Sequential Search**) or the collection is already ordered (**Binary**

Search). We need more powerful techniques for searching larger collections that are not necessarily ordered. One of the most common approaches is to use a *hash function* to transform one or more characteristics of the searched-for item into an index into a hash table. **Hash-Based Search** has better average-case performance than the other search algorithms described in this chapter. Many books on algorithms discuss **Hash-Based Search** under the topic of *hash tables* (Cormen et al., 2009); you may also find this topic in books on data structures that describe hash tables.

In **Hash-Based Search** the n elements of a collection C are first loaded into a hash table H with b bins structured as an array. This *preprocessing step* has $O(n)$ performance, but improves the performance of future searches. The concept of a *hash function* makes this possible.

A *hash function* is a deterministic function that maps each element C_i to an integer value h_i. For a moment, let's assume that $0 \le h_i < b$. When loading the elements into a hash table, element C_i is inserted into the bin $H[h_i]$. Once all elements have been inserted, searching for an item t becomes a search for t within $H[hash(t)]$.

The *hash function* guarantees only that if two elements C_i and C_j are equal, $hash(C_i)$ = $hash(C_j)$. It can happen that multiple elements in C have the same hash value; this is known as a *collision* and the hash table needs a strategy to deal with these situations. The most common solution is to store a linked list at each hash index (even though many of these linked lists may contain only one element), so all colliding values can be stored in the hash table. The linked lists have to be searched linearly, but this will be quick because each is likely to store at most a few elements. The following pseudocode describes a linked list solution to collisions.

The general pattern for **Hash-Based Search** is shown in Figure 5-1 with a small example. The components are:

- A set U that defines the set of possible hash values. Each element $e \in C$ maps to a hash value $h \in U$

- A hash table, H, containing b bins that store the n elements from the original collection C

- The hash function, *hash*, which computes an integer value h for every element e, where $0 \le h < b$

This information is stored in memory using arrays and linked lists.

Hash-Based Search raises two main concerns: the design of the hash function and how to handle collisions. A poorly chosen hash function can leave keys poorly distributed in the primary storage, with two consequences: (a) many bins in the hash table may be unused, wasting space, and (b) there will be collisions that force many keys into the same bin, which worsens search performance.

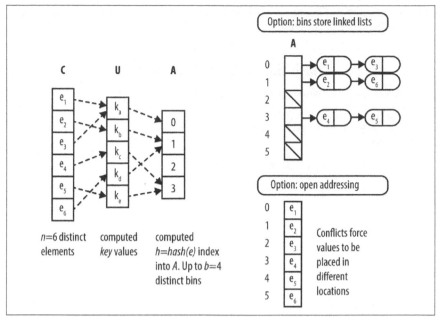

Figure 5-1. General approach to hashing

Input/Output

Unlike **Binary Search**, the original collection *C* does not need to be ordered for **Hash-Based Search**. Indeed, even if the elements in *C* were ordered in some way, the hashing method that inserts elements into the hash table *H* does not attempt to replicate this ordering within *H*.

The input to **Hash-Based Search** is the computed hash table, *H*, and the target element *t* being sought. The algorithm returns true if *t* exists in the linked list stored by *H*[*h*] where *h* = *hash*(*t*). If *t* does not exist within the linked list stored by *H*[*h*], false is returned to indicate *t* is not present in *H* (and thus, does not exist in *C*).

Context

Assume you had an array of 213,557 sorted English words (such as found in the code repository for this book). We know from our discussion on **Binary Search** that we can expect about 18 string comparisons on average to locate a word in this array (since *log* (213557) = 17.70). With **Hash-Based Search** the number of string comparisons is based on the length of the linked lists rather than the size of the collection.

We first need to define the *hash* function. One goal is to produce as many different values as possible, but not all values need to be unique. Hashing has been studied for decades, and numerous papers describe effective hash functions, but they can be used for much more than searching. For example, special hash functions are essential for cryptography. For searching, a hash function should have good distribution and should be quick to compute with respect to machine cycles.

Hash-Based Search Summary

Best, Average: O(*1*)   Worst: O(*n*)

```
loadTable (size, C)
  H = new array of given size
  foreach e in C do
    h = hash(e)
    if H[h] is empty then ❶
      H[h] = new Linked List
    add e to H[h]
  return A
end

search (H, t)
  h = hash(t)
  list = H[h]
  if list is empty then
    return false
  if list contains t then ❷
    return true
  return false
end
```

❶   Create linked lists when e is inserted into empty bin.

❷   Use **Sequential Search** on small lists.

A popular technique is to produce a value based on each character from the original string:

$$hashCode(s) = s[0]*31^{(len-1)} + s[1]*31^{(len-2)} + \ldots + s[len - 1]$$

where $s[i]$ is the ith character (as an ASCII value between 0 and 255) and *len* is the length of the string *s*. Computing this function is simple, as shown in the Java code in Example 5-5 (adapted from the Open JDK source code (*http://openjdk.java.net*)), where chars is the array of characters that defines a string. By our definition, the hashCode() method for the java.lang.String class is not yet a *hash* function because its computed value is not guaranteed to be in the range [0, *b*).

Example 5-5. Sample Java hashCode

```
public int hashCode() {
  int h = hash;
  if (h == 0) {
```

```
    for (int i = 0; i < chars.length; i++) {
        h = 31*h + chars[i];
    }
    hash = h;
    }
    return h;
}
```

For efficiency, this hashCode method caches the value of the computed hash to avoid recomputation (i.e., it computes the value only if hash is 0). Observe that this function returns very large integers and sometimes negative values because the int type in Java can store only 32 bits of information. To compute the integer bin for a given element, define *hash(s)* as:

$$hash(s) = abs(hashCode(s)) \% b$$

where *abs* is the absolute value function and % is the modulo operator that returns the remainder when dividing by *b*. Doing so ensures the computed integer is in the range [0, *b*).

Choosing the hashing function is just the first decision to make when implementing **Hash-Based Search**. Storage space poses another design issue. The primary storage, *H*, must be large enough to reduce the size of the linked lists storing the elements in each bin. You might think that *H* could contain *b* = *n* bins, where the hash function is a one-to-one mapping from the set of strings in the collection onto the integers [0, *n*), but this is not easy to accomplish! Instead, we try to define a hash table that will contain as few empty bins as possible. If our *hash* function distributes the keys evenly, we can achieve reasonable success by selecting an array size approximately as large as the collection.

The size of *H* is typically chosen to be a prime number to ensure that using the % modulo operator efficiently distributes the computed bin numbers. A good choice in practice is $2^k - 1$, even though this value isn't always prime.

The elements stored in the hash table have a direct effect on memory. Since each bin stores elements in a linked list, the elements of the list are pointers to objects on the heap. Each list has overhead storage that contains pointers to the first and last elements of the list and, if you use the LinkedList class from the Java JDK, a significant amount of additional fields. We could write a much simpler linked list class that provides only the necessary capabilities, but this certainly adds additional cost to the implementation of **Hash-Based Search**.

The advanced reader should, at this point, question the use of a basic hash function and hash table for this problem. When the word list is fixed and not likely to change, we can do better by creating a *perfect hash function*. A perfect hash function is one that guarantees no collisions for a specific set of keys; this option is discussed in "Variations" on page 109. Let's first try to solve the problem without one.

For our first try at this problem, we choose a primary hash table H that will hold $b = 2^{18} - 1 = 262{,}143$ elements. Our word list contains 213,557 words. If our hash function perfectly distributes the strings, there will be no collisions and only about 40,000 open bins. This, however, is not the case. Table 5-4 shows the distribution of the hash values for the Java String class on our word list with a table of 262,143 bins. Recall that $hash(s) = abs(hashCode(s))\%b$. As you can see, no bin contains more than seven strings; for nonempty bins, the average number of strings per bin is approximately 1.46. Each row shows the number of bins used and how many words hash to those bins. Almost half of the table bins (116,186) have no strings that hash to them. So this hashing function wastes about 500KB of memory (assuming the size of a pointer is four bytes). You may be surprised that this is really a good hashing function and that finding one with better distribution will require a more complex scheme.

For the record, there were only five pairs of strings with identical hashCode values (e.g., both "hypoplankton" and "unheavenly" have a computed hashCode value of 427,589,249)!

Table 5-4. Hash distribution using Java String.hashCode() method as key with b = 262,143 bins

Number of items in bin	Number of bins
0	116,186
1	94,319
2	38,637
3	10,517
4	2,066
5	362
6	53
7	3

If you use the LinkedList class, each nonempty element of H will require 12 bytes of memory, assuming the size of a pointer is four bytes. Each string element is incorporated into a ListElement that requires an additional 12 bytes. For the previous example of 213,557 words, we require 5,005,488 bytes of memory beyond the actual string storage. The breakdown of this memory usage is:

- Size of the primary table: 1,048,572 bytes
- Size of 116,186 linked lists: 1,394,232 bytes
- Size of 213,557 list elements: 2,562,684 bytes

Storing the strings also has an overhead when using the JDK String class. Each string has 12 bytes of overhead. We can therefore add 213,557*12 = 2,562,684 additional bytes to our overhead. So the algorithm chosen in the example requires 7,568,172 bytes of memory. The actual number of characters in the strings in the word list we used in the example is only 2,099,075, so it requires approximately 3.6 times the space required for the characters in the strings.

Most of this overhead is the price of using the classes in the JDK. The engineering trade-off must weigh the simplicity and reuse of the classes compared to a more complex implementation that reduces the memory usage. When memory is at a premium, you can use one of several variations discussed later to optimize memory usage. If, however, you have available memory, a reasonable hash function that does not produce too many collisions, and a ready-to-use linked list implementation, the JDK solution is usually acceptable.

The major force affecting the implementation is whether the collection is static or dynamic. In our example, the word list is fixed and known in advance. If, however, we have a dynamic collection that requires many additions and deletions of elements, we must choose a data structure for the hash table that optimizes these operations. Our collision handling in the example works quite well because inserting an item into a linked list can be done in constant time, and deleting an item is proportional to the length of the list. If the hash function distributes the elements evenly, the individual lists are relatively short.

Solution

In addition to the hash function, the solution for **Hash-Based Search** contains two parts. The first is to create the hash table. The code in Example 5-6 shows how to use linked lists to hold the elements that hash into a specific table element. The input elements from collection *C* are retrieved using an Iterator.

Example 5-6. Loading the hash table

```
public void load (Iterator<V> it) {
  table = (LinkedList<V>[]) new LinkedList[tableSize];

  // Pull each value from the iterator and find desired bin h.
  // Add to existing list or create new one into which value is added.
  while (it.hasNext()) {
    V v = it.next();

    int h = hashMethod.hash (v);
    if (table[h] == null) {
      table[h] = new LinkedList<V>();
    }
    table[h].add(v);
    count++;
  }
}
```

Note that listTable is composed of tableSize bins, each of which is of type LinkedList<V> to store the elements.

Searching the table for elements now becomes trivial. The code in Example 5-7 does the job. Once the hash function returns an index into the hash table, we look to see whether the table bin is empty. If it's empty, we return false, indicating the searched-for string is not in the collection. Otherwise, we search the linked list for that bin to determine the presence or absence of the searched-for string.

Example 5-7. Searching for an element

```
public boolean search (V v) {
    int h = hashMethod.hash (v);
    LinkedList<V> list = (LinkedList<V>) listTable[h];
    if (list == null) { return false; }
    return list.contains (v);
}

int hash(V v) {
    int h = v.hashCode();
    if (h < 0) { h = 0 - h; }
    return h % tableSize;
}
```

Note that the hash function ensures the hash index is in the range [0, *tableSize*). With the hashCode function for the String class, the hash function must account for the possibility that the integer arithmetic in hashCode has overflowed and returned a negative number. This is necessary because the modulo operator (%) returns a negative number if given a negative value (i.e., the Java expression –5%3 is equal to the value –2). For example, using the JDK hashCode method for String objects, the string "aaaaaa" returns the value –1,425,372,064.

Analysis

As long as the hash function distributes the elements in the collection fairly evenly, **Hash-Based Search** has excellent performance. The average time required to search for an element is constant, or O(*1*). The search consists of a single look-up in *H* followed by a linear search through a short list of collisions. The components to searching for an element in a hash table are:

- Computing the hash value
- Accessing the item in the table indexed by the hash value
- Finding the specified item in the presence of collisions

All **Hash-Based Search** algorithms share the first two components; different behaviors stem from variations in collision handling.

The cost of computing the hash value must be bounded by a fixed, constant upper bound. In our word list example, computing the hash value was proportional to the length of the string. If T_k is the time it takes to compute the hash value for the longest string, it will require $\leq T_k$ to compute any hash value. Computing the hash value is therefore considered a constant time operation.

The second part of the algorithm also performs in constant time. If the table is stored on secondary storage, there may be a variation that depends on the position of the element and the time required to position the device, but this has a constant upper bound.

If we can show that the third part of the computation also has a constant upper bound, it will prove the overall time performance of **Hash-Based Search** is constant. For a hash table, define the *load factor* α to be the average number of elements in a linked list for some bin $H[h]$. More precisely, $\alpha = n/b$, where b is the number of bins in the hash table and n is the number of elements stored in the hash table. Table 5-5 shows the actual load factor in the hash tables we create as b increases. Note how the maximum length of the element linked lists drops while the number of bins containing a unique element rapidly increases once b is sufficiently large. In the final row, 81% of the elements are hashed to a unique bin and the average number of elements in a bin becomes just a single digit. Regardless of the initial number of elements, you can choose a sufficiently large b value to ensure there will be a small, fixed number of elements (on average) in every bin. This means that searching for an element in a hash table is no longer dependent on the number of elements in the hash table, but rather is a fixed cost, producing amortized O(1) performance.

Searching

Table 5-5. Statistics of hash tables created by example code

b	Load factor α	Min length of linked list	Max length of linked list	Number of unique bins
4,095	52.15	27	82	0
8,191	26.07	9	46	0
16,383	13.04	2	28	0
32,767	6.52	0	19	349
65,535	3.26	0	13	8,190
131,071	1.63	0	10	41,858
262,143	0.815	0	7	94,319
524,287	0.41	0	7	142,530
1,048,575	0.20	0	5	173,912

Table 5-6 compares the performance of the code from Example 5-7 with the JDK class `java.util.Hashtable` on hash tables of different sizes. For the tests labeled $p = 1.0$, each of the 213,557 words is used as the target item to ensure the word exists in the hash table. For the tests labeled $p = 0.0$, each of these words has its last character replaced with a "*" to ensure the word does not exist in the hash table. Also note that we keep the size of the search words for these two cases the same to ensure the cost for computing the hash is identical.

We ran each test 100 times and discarded the best- and worst-performing trials. The average of the remaining 98 trials is shown in Table 5-6. To help understand these results, the statistics on the hash tables we created are shown in Table 5-5.

Table 5-6. Search time (in milliseconds) for various hash table sizes

b	Our hash table shown in Example 5-7		java.util.Hashtable with default capacity	
	p = 1.0	p = 0.0	p = 1.0	p = 0.0
4,095	200.53	373.24	82.11	38.37
8,191	140.47	234.68	71.45	28.44
16,383	109.61	160.48	70.64	28.66
32,767	91.56	112.89	71.15	28.33
65,535	80.96	84.38	70.36	28.33
131,071	75.47	60.17	71.24	28.28
262,143	74.09	43.18	70.06	28.43
524,287	75.00	33.05	69.33	28.26
1,048,575	76.68	29.02	72.24	27.37

As the load factor goes down, the average length of each element-linked list also goes down, leading to improved performance. Indeed, by the time $b = 1,045,875$ no linked list contains more than five elements. Because a hash table can typically grow large enough to ensure all linked lists of elements are small, its search performance is considered to be O(*1*). However, this is contingent (as always) on having sufficient memory and a suitable hash function to disperse the elements throughout the bins of the hash table.

The performance of the existing java.util.Hashtable class outperforms our example code, but the savings are reduced as the size of the hash table grows. The reason is that java.util.Hashtable contains optimized list classes that efficiently manage the element chains. In addition, java.util.Hashtable automatically "rehashes" the entire hash table when the load factor is too high; the rehash strategy is discussed in "Variations" on page 109. The implementation increases the cost of building the hash table, but improves search performance. If we prevent the "rehash" capability, search performance in java.util.Hashtable is nearly the same as our implementation.

Table 5-7 shows the number of times rehash is invoked when building the java.util.Hashtable hash table and the total time (in milliseconds) required to build the hash table. We constructed the hash tables from the word list described earlier; after running 100 trials, the best- and worst-performing timings were discarded and the table contains the average of the remaining 98 trials. The java.util.Hashtable class performs extra computation while the hash table is being constructed to improve the performance of searches (a common trade-off). Columns 3 and 5 of Table 5-7 show a noticeable cost penalty when a rehash occurs. Also note that in the last two rows, the hash tables do not rehash themselves, so the results in columns 3, 5, and 7 are nearly identical. Rehashing while building the hash table improves the overall performance by reducing the average length of the element chains.

Table 5-7. Comparable times (in milliseconds) to build hash tables

b	Our hash table	JDK hash table ($\alpha = .75$)		JDK hash table ($\alpha = 4.0$)		JDK hash table ($\alpha = n/b$) no rehash
	Build Time	Build Time	#Rehash	Build Time	#Rehash	Build Time
4,095	403.61	42.44	7	35.30	4	104.41
8,191	222.39	41.96	6	35.49	3	70.74
16,383	135.26	41.99	5	34.90	2	50.90
32,767	92.80	41.28	4	33.62	1	36.34
65,535	66.74	41.34	3	29.16	0	28.82
131,071	47.53	39.61	2	23.60	0	22.91
262,143	36.27	36.06	1	21.14	0	21.06
524,287	31.60	21.37	0	22.51	0	22.37
1,048,575	31.67	25.46	0	26.91	0	27.12

Variations

One popular variation of **Hash-Based Search** modifies the handling of collisions by restricting each bin to contain a single element. Instead of creating a linked list to hold all elements that hash to some bin in the hash table, it uses the *open addressing* technique to store colliding items *in some other empty bin in the hash table H*. This approach is shown in Figure 5-2. With open addressing, the hash table reduces storage overhead by eliminating all linked lists.

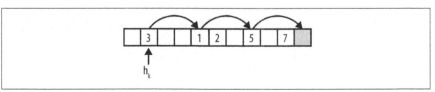

Figure 5-2. Open addressing

To insert an element using open addressing, compute the desired bin $h_k = hash(e)$ that should contain e. If $H[h_k]$ is empty, assign $H[h_k] = e$ just as in the standard algorithm. Otherwise *probe* through H using a *probing strategy* and place e in the first discovered empty bin:

Linear probing
> Repeatedly search other bins $h_k = (h_k + c*i)$ % b where c is an integer offset and i is the number of successive probes into H; often, $c = 1$. Clusters of elements may appear in H using this strategy.

Quadratic probing
> Repeatedly search other bins $h_k = (h_k + c_1*i + c_2*i^2)$ % b where c_1 and c_2 are constants. This approach tends to break up clusters of elements. Useful values in practice are $c_1 = c_2 = 1/2$.

Double hashing
> Like linear probing except that c is not a constant but is determined by a second hash function; this extra computation is intended to reduce the likelihood of clustering.

In all cases, if no empty bin is found after b probe attempts, the insert request must fail.

Figure 5-2 shows a sample hash table with $b = 11$ bins using linear probing with $c = 3$. The load factor for the hash table is $\alpha = 0.45$ because it contains five elements. This figure shows the behavior when attempting to add element e, which hashes to $h_k = 1$. The bin $H[1]$ is already occupied (by the value 3) so it proceeds to probe other potential bins. After $i = 3$ iterations it finds an empty bin and inserts e into $H[10]$.

Assuming we only search through b potential bins, the worst-case performance of insert is $O(b)$ but with a low-enough load factor and no clustering, it should require only a fixed number of probes. Figure 5-3 shows the expected number of probes for a search; see (Knuth, 1997) for details.

$$\frac{1 + \left(\frac{1}{1-\alpha}\right)}{2}$$

$$\frac{1 + \left(\frac{1}{1-\alpha}\right)^2}{2}$$

Successful Search   Unsuccessful Search

Figure 5-3. The expected number of probes for a search

It is a problem to remove elements from a hash table that uses open addressing. Let's assume in Figure 5-2 that the values 3, 1, and 5 all hash to $h_k = 1$ and that they were inserted into the hash table in this order. Searching for the value 5 will succeed because you will make three probes of the hash table and ultimately locate it in position $H[7]$. If you deleted value 1 from the hash table and cleared bin $H[4]$ you would no longer be able to locate value 5 because the search probes stop at the first empty bin located. To support deletions with open addressing you would need to *mark* a bin as deleted and adjust the search function accordingly.

The code for open addressing is shown in Example 5-8. The class assumes the user will provide a hash function that produces a valid index in the range $[0, b)$ and a probe function for open addressing; plausible alternatives are provided by default using Python's built-in hash method. This implementation allows elements to be deleted and it stores a deleted list to ensure the open addressing chains do not break. The following implementation follows *set* semantics for a collection, and only allows for unique membership in the hash table.

Example 5-8. Python implementation of open addressing hash table

```python
class Hashtable:
    def __init__(self, b=1009, hashFunction=None, probeFunction=None):
        """Initialize a hash table with b bins, given hash function, and
            probe function."""
        self.b = b
        self.bins = [None] * b
        self.deleted = [False] * b

        if hashFunction:
            self.hashFunction = hashFunction
        else:
            self.hashFunction = lambda value, size: hash(value) % size

        if probeFunction:
            self.probeFunction = probeFunction
        else:
            self.probeFunction = lambda hk, size, i : (hk + 37) % size

    def add (self, value):
        """
        Add element into hashtable returning -self.b on failure after
        self.b tries. Returns number of probes on success.

        Add into bins that have been marked for deletion and properly
        deal with formerly deleted entries.
        """
        hk = self.hashFunction (value, self.b)

        ctr = 1
        while ctr <= self.b:
            if self.bins[hk] is None or self.deleted[hk]:
```

```
      self.bins[hk] = value
      self.deleted[hk] = False
      return ctr

   # already present? Leave now
   if self.bins[hk] == value and not self.deleted[hk]:
     return ctr

   hk = self.probeFunction (hk, self.b, ctr)
   ctr += 1

 return -self.b
```

The code in Example 5-8 shows how open addressing adds elements into empty bins or bins marked as deleted. It maintains a counter that ensures the worst-case performance is O(*b*). The caller can determine that add was successful if the function returns a positive number; if probeFunction is unable to locate an empty bin in *b* tries, then a negative number is returned. The delete code in Example 5-9 is nearly identical to the code to check whether the hash table contains a value; specifically, the contains method (not reproduced here) omits the code that marks self.deleted[hk] = True. Observe how this code uses the probeFunction to identify the next bin to investigate.

Example 5-9. Open addressing delete method

```
def delete (self, value):
  """Delete value from hash table without breaking existing chains."""
  hk = self.hashFunction (value, self.b)

  ctr = 1
  while ctr <= self.b:
    if self.bins[hk] is None:
      return -ctr

    if self.bins[hk] == value and not self.deleted[hk]:
      self.deleted[hk] = True
      return ctr

    hk = self.probeFunction (hk, self.b, ctr)
    ctr += 1

  return -self.b
```

Let's review the performance of open addressing by considering how many probes it takes to locate an element in the hash table. Figure 5-4 shows the results for both successful and unsuccessful searches, using the same list of 213,557 words as before. As the number of bins increases—from 224,234 (or 95.2% full) to 639,757 (or 33.4% full)—you can see how the number of probes decreases dramatically. The top half of this figure shows the average (and worst) number of probes for a successful search while the bottom presents the same information for unsuccessful searches. In brief, open addressing reduces the overall storage used but requires noticeably more probes in the worst case. A second implication is that linear probing leads to more probes due to clustering.

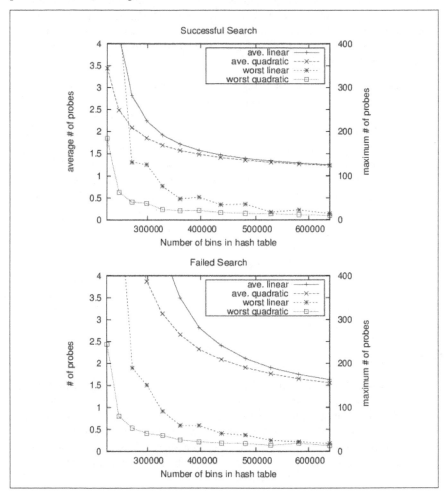

Figure 5-4. Performance of open addressing

Computing the load factor for a hash table describes the expected performance for searching and insertions. If the load factor is too high, the number of probes to locate an item becomes excessive, whether in a bucket's linked list or a chain of bins in open addressing. A hash table can increase the number of bins and reconstitute itself using a process known as "rehashing," an infrequent operation that reduces the load factor, although it is a costly $O(n)$ operation. The typical way to do this is to double the number of bins and add one (because hash tables usually contain an odd number of bins). Once more bins are available, all existing elements in the hash table are rehashed and inserted in the new structure. This expensive operation reduces the overall cost of future searches, but it must be run infrequently; otherwise, you will not observe the amortized O(1) performance of the hash tables.

A hash table should rehash its contents when it detects uneven distribution of elements. This can be done by setting a threshold value that will trigger a rehash when the load factor for the hash table exceeds that value. The default threshold load factor for the `java.util.Hashtable` class is 0.75; if the threshold is large enough, the hash table will never rehash.

These examples use a fixed set of strings for the hash table. When confronted with this special case, it is possible to achieve optimal performance by using *perfect hashing*, which uses two hash functions. A standard *hash()* function indexes into the primary table, H. Each bin, $H[i]$, then points to a smaller secondary hash table, S_i, that has an associated hash function $hash_i$. If there are k keys that hash to bin $H[i]$, S_i will contain k^2 bins. This seems like a lot of wasted memory, but judicious choice of the initial hash function can reduce this to an amount similar to previous variations. The selection of appropriate hash functions guarantees there are no collisions in the secondary tables. This means we have an algorithm with constant O(1) performance in every case.

Details on the analysis of perfect hashing can be found in (Cormen et al., 2009). Doug Schmidt (1990) has written an excellent paper on perfect hashing generation and there are freely available perfect hash function generators in various programming languages. GPERF for C and C++ can be downloaded from *http://www.gnu.org/software/gperf*, and JPERF for Java can be downloaded from *http://www.anarres.org/projects/jperf*.

Bloom Filter

Hash-Based Search stores the full set of values from a collection C in a hash table H, whether in linked lists or using open addressing. In both cases, as more elements are added to the hash table, the time to locate an element increases unless you also increase the amount of storage (in this case, the number of bins). Indeed, this is the behavior expected of all other algorithms in this chapter and we only seek a reasonable trade-off in the amount of space required to reduce the number of comparisons when looking for an element in the collection.

A **Bloom Filter** provides an alternative *bit array* structure B that ensures *constant performance* when adding elements from C into B or checking whether an element *has not been added* to B; amazingly, this behavior is independent of the number of items already added to B. There is a catch, however; with a **Bloom Filter**, checking whether an element is in B might return a *false positive* even though the element does not exist in C. The **Bloom Filter** can accurately determine when an element has not been added to B, so it never returns a *false negative*.

In Figure 5-5, two values, u and v, have been inserted into the bit array, B. The table at the top of the figure shows the bit positions computed by $k = 3$ hash functions. As you can see, the **Bloom Filter** can quickly demonstrate that a third value w has not been inserted into B, because one of its k computed bit values is zero (bit 6 in this case). However for value x, it returns a *false positive* since that value was not inserted, yet all k of its computed bit values are one.

Bloom Filter Summary

Best, Average, Worst: O(k)

```
create(m)
  return bit array of m bits ❶
end

add (bits,value)
  foreach hashFunction hf ❷
    setbit = 1 << hf(value) ❸
    bits |= setbit ❹
end

search (bits,value)
  foreach hashFunction hf
    checkbit = 1 << hf(value)
    if checkbit | bits = 0 then ❺
      return false

  return true ❻
end
```

❶ Storage is fixed in advance to m bits.

❷ There are k hash functions that compute (potentially) different bit positions.

❸ The << left shift operator efficiently computes $2^{hf(value)}$.

❹ Set k bits when inserting value.

❺ When searching for a value, if a computed bit is zero then that value can't be present.

❻ It may yet be the case that all bits are set but value was never added: *false positive*.

Input/Output

A **Bloom Filter** processes values much like **Hash-Based Search**. The algorithm starts with a bit array of *m* bits, all set to zero. There are *k* hash functions that compute (potentially different) bit positions within this bit array when values are inserted.

The **Bloom Filter** returns `false` when it can demonstrate that a target element *t* has not yet been inserted into the bit array, and by extension does not exist in the collection *C*. The algorithm may return `true` as a *false positive* if the target element *t* was not inserted into the bit array.

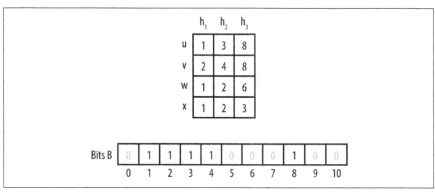

Figure 5-5. Bloom Filter example

Context

A **Bloom Filter** demonstrates efficient memory usage but it is only useful when *false positives* can be tolerated. Use a **Bloom Filter** to reduce the number of expensive searches by filtering out those that are guaranteed to fail—for example, use a **Bloom Filter** to confirm whether to conduct an expensive search over disk-based storage.

Solution

A **Bloom Filter** needs *m* bits of storage. The implementation in Example 5-10 uses Python's ability to work with arbitrarily large "bignum" values.

Example 5-10. Python Bloom Filter

```python
class bloomFilter:
  def __init__(self, size = 1000, hashFunctions=None):
    """
    Construct a bloom filter with size bits (default: 1000) and the
    associated hash functions.
    """
    self.bits = 0
    self.size = size
```

```
if hashFunctions is None:
    self.k = 1
    self.hashFunctions = [lambda e, size : hash(e) % size]
else:
    self.k = len(hashFunctions)
    self.hashFunctions = hashFunctions


def add (self, value):
    """Insert value into the bloom filter."""
    for hf in self.hashFunctions:
        self.bits |= 1 << hf (value, self.size)

def __contains__ (self, value):
    """
    Determine whether value is present. A false positive might be
    returned even if the element is not present. However, a false
    negative will never be returned (i.e., if the element is
    present, then it will return True).
    """
    for hf in self.hashFunctions:
        if self.bits & 1 << hf (value, self.size) == 0:
            return False

    # might be present
    return True
```

This implementation assumes the existence of k hash functions, each of which takes the value to be inserted and the size of the bit array. Whenever a value is added, k bits are set in the bit array, based on the individual bit positions computed by the hash functions. This code uses the bitwise shift operator << to shift a 1 to the appropriate bit position, and the bitwise **or** operator (|) to set that bit value. To determine whether a value has been added, check the same k bits from these hash functions using the bitwise **and** operator (&); if any bit position is set to 0, you know the value could not have been added, so it returns False. However, if these k bit positions are all set to 1, you can only state that the value "might" have been added.

Analysis

The total storage required for a **Bloom Filter** is fixed to be m bits, and this won't increase regardless of the number of values stored. Additionally, the algorithm only requires a fixed number of k probes, so each insertion and search can be processed in $O(k)$ time, which is considered constant. It is for these reasons that we present this algorithm as a counterpoint to the other algorithms in this chapter. It is challenging to design effective hash functions to truly distribute the computed bits for the values to be inserted into the bit array. While the size of the bit array is constant, it may need to be quite large to reduce the false positive rate. Finally, there is no ability to remove an element from the filter since that would potentially disrupt the processing of other values.

The only reason to use a **Bloom Filter** is that it has a predicable false positive rate, p^k, assuming the k hash functions are uniformly random (Bloom, 1970). A reasonably accurate computation for p^k is:

$$p^k = \frac{\left(1 - \left(1 - \frac{1}{m}\right)^{kn}\right)^k}{2}$$

where n is the number of values already added (Bose et al., 2008). We empirically computed the false positive rate as follows:

1. Randomly remove 2,135 words from the list of 213,557 words (1% of the full list) and insert the remaining 211,422 words into a **Bloom Filter**.

2. Count the false positives when searching for the missing 2,135 words.

3. Count the false positives when searching for 2,135 random strings (of between 2 and 10 lowercase letters).

We ran trials for m with values of 100,000 to 2,000,000 (steps of 10,000). We used $k = 3$ hash functions. The results are found in Figure 5-6.

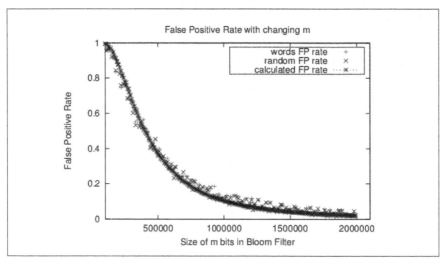

Figure 5-6. Bloom Filter example

If you know in advance that you want your false positive rate to be smaller than some small value, you need to set k and m after estimating the number of elements n to insert. The literature suggests trying to ensure $1 - (1 - 1/m)^{kn}$ is close to 1/2. For example, to ensure a *false positive* rate of smaller than 10% for the word list, be sure to set m to at least 1,120,000 or a total of 131,250 bytes.

Binary Search Tree

Binary searching on an array in memory is efficient, as we have already seen. However, using ordered arrays becomes drastically less effective when the underlying collection changes frequently. With a dynamic collection, we must adopt a different data structure to maintain acceptable search performance. **Hash-Based Search** can handle dynamic collections, but we might select a hash table size that is much too small for effective resource usage; we often have no *a priori* knowledge of the number of elements to store so it is hard to select the proper size of the hash table. Hash tables do not allow you to iterate over their elements in sorted order.

An alternate strategy is to use a *search tree* to store dynamic sets. Search trees perform well both in memory and in secondary storage and make it possible to return ordered ranges of elements together, something hash tables are unable to accomplish. The most common type of search tree is the *binary search tree (BST)*, which is composed of *nodes* as shown in Figure 5-7. Each node contains a single value in the collection and stores references to potentially two child nodes, *left* and *right*.

Use a binary search tree when:

- You must traverse the data in ascending (or descending) order
- The data set size is unknown, and the implementation must be able to handle any possible size that will fit in memory
- The data set is highly dynamic, and there will be many insertions and deletions during the collection's lifetime

Input/Output

The input and output to algorithms using search trees is the same as for **Binary Search**. Each element e from a collection C to be stored in the binary search tree needs to have one or more properties that can be used as a key k; these keys determine the universe U and must be fully ordered. That is, given two key values k_i and k_j, either k_i equals k_j, $k_i > k_j$, or $k_i < k_j$.

When the values in the collections are primitive types (such as strings or integers), the values themselves can be the key values. Otherwise, they are references to the structures that contain the values.

Context

A BST is a nonempty collection of nodes containing ordered values known as *keys*. The top *root* node is the ancestor of all other nodes in the BST. Each node n may potentially refer to two binary nodes, n_{left} and n_{right}, each the root of BSTs *left* and *right*. A BST ensures the *binary search tree property*, namely, that if k is the key for node n, then all keys in *left* $\leq k$ and all the keys in *right* $\geq k$. If both n_{left} and n_{right} are **null**, then n is a *leaf node*. Figure 5-7 shows a small example of a BST where each node contains an integer value. The root contains the value 7 and there are four leaf nodes containing values 1, 6, 10, and 17. An interior node, such as 5, has both a parent node and some children nodes. You can see that finding a key in the tree in Figure 5-7 requires examining at most four nodes, starting with the root.

A BST might not be *balanced*; as elements are added, some branches may end up relatively short while others become longer. This produces suboptimal search times on the longer branches. In the worst case, the structure of a BST might *degenerate* and take on the basic properties of a list. Consider the same values for Figure 5-7 arranged as shown in Figure 5-8. Although the structure fits the strict definition of a BST, the structure is effectively a linked list because the right subtree of each node is empty.

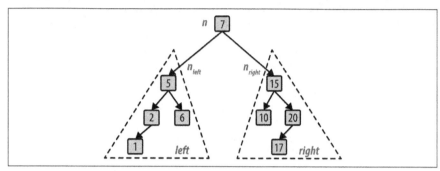

Figure 5-7. A simple binary search tree

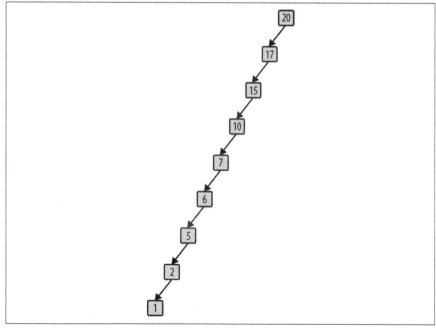

Figure 5-8. A degenerate binary search tree

You must balance the tree to avoid a skewed tree that has a few branches that are much longer than the other branches. We present a full solution for a balanced AVL tree supporting insertion and deletion of values.

Solution

The initial Python structure is shown in Example 5-11 together with the add methods necessary to add values to the BST. The methods are recursive, going down a branch from the root until an empty place for the new node is found at the right position.

Example 5-11. Python Binary Search Tree class definition

```python
class BinaryNode:
  def __init__(self, value = None):
    """Create binary node."""
    self.value = value
    self.left = None
    self.right = None

  def add (self, val):
    """Adds a new node to BST with given value."""
    if val <= self.value:
      if self.left:
        self.left.add (val)
      else:
        self.left = BinaryNode(val)
    else:
      if self.right:
        self.right.add(val)
      else:
        self.right = BinaryNode(val)

class BinaryTree:
  def __init__(self):
    """Create empty BST."""
    self.root = None

  def add (self, value):
    """Insert value into proper location in BST."""
    if self.root is None:
      self.root = BinaryNode(value)
    else:
      self.root.add (value)
```

Adding a value to an empty BST creates the root node; thereafter, the inserted values are placed into new BinaryNode objects at the appropriate place in the BST. There can be two or more nodes in the BST with the same *value*, but if you want to restrict the tree to conform to set-based semantics (such as defined in the Java Collections Framework) you can modify the code to prevent the insertion of duplicate keys. For now, assume that duplicate keys may exist in the BST.

With this structure in place, the nonrecursive `contains(value)` method in the `BinaryTree` class, shown in Example 5-12, searches for a target value within the BST. Rather than perform a recursive function call, this simply traverses `left` or `right` pointers until it finds the target or determines that the target does not exist in the BST.

Example 5-12. BinaryTree contains method

```
def __contains__ (self, target):
  """Check whether BST contains target value."""
  node = self.root
  while node:
    if target < node.value:
      node = node.left
    ielif target > node.value:
      node = node.right
    else:
      node = node.right
  return true
```

The efficiency of this implementation depends on whether the BST is *balanced*. For a balanced tree, the size of the collection being searched is cut in half with each pass through the `while` loop, resulting in O(*log n*) behavior. However, for a degenerate binary tree such as shown in Figure 5-8, the performance is O(*n*). To preserve optimal performance, you need to balance a BST after each addition (and deletion).

AVL trees (named after their inventors, Adelson-Velskii and Landis) were the first *self-balancing* BST, invented in 1962. Let's define the concept of an AVL node's *height*. The height of a leaf node is 0, because it has no children. The height of a nonleaf node is 1 greater than the maximum of the height values of its two children nodes. For consistency, the height of a nonexistent child node is –1.

An AVL tree guarantees the *AVL property* at every node, namely, that the *height difference* for any node is –1, 0, or 1. The *height difference* is defined as *height(left)* – *height(right)*—that is, the height of the left subtree minus the height of the right subtree. An AVL tree must enforce this property whenever a value is inserted or removed from the tree. Doing so requires two helper methods: `computeHeight` to compute the height of a node and `heightDifference` to compute the height difference. Each node in the AVL tree stores its *height* value, which increases the overall storage requirements.

Figure 5-9 demonstrates what happens when you insert the values 50, 30, and 10 into a BST in that order. As shown, the resulting tree no longer satisfies the *AVL property* because the height of the root's left subtree is 1 while the height of its nonexisting right subtree is –1, resulting in a height difference of 2. Imagine "grabbing" the 30 node in the original tree and rotating the tree to the right (or clockwise), and pivoting around the 30 node to make 30 the root, thereby creating a balanced tree (shown in Figure 5-10). In doing so, only the height of the 50 node has changed (dropping from 2 to 0) and the *AVL property* is restored.

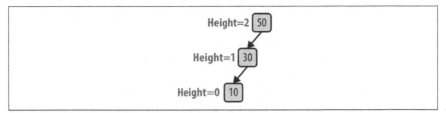

Figure 5-9. Unbalanced AVL tree

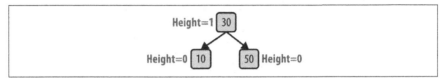

Figure 5-10. Balanced AVL tree

This *rotate right* operation alters the structure of a subtree within an unbalanced BST; as you can imagine, there is a similar *rotate left* operation.

What if this tree had other nodes, each of which were balanced and satisfied the *AVL property*? In Figure 5-11, each of the shaded triangles represents a potential subtree of the original tree; each is labeled by its position, so **30R** is the subtree representing the right subtree of node **30**. The root is the only node that doesn't support the *AVL property*. The various heights in the tree are computed assuming the node **10** has some height *k*.

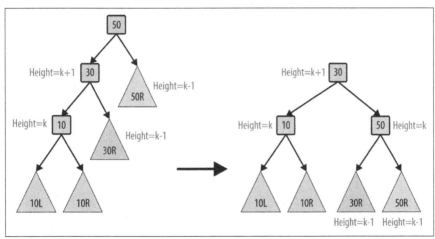

Figure 5-11. Balanced AVL tree with subtrees

The modified BST still guarantees the *binary search property*. All of the key values in the subtree **30R** are greater than or equal to 30. The other subtrees have not changed positions relative to each other, so they continue to guarantee the *binary search property*. Finally, the value 30 is smaller than 50, so the new root node is valid.

Consider adding three values to an empty AVL tree; Figure 5-12 shows the four different insert orders that result in an unbalanced tree. In the **Left-Left** case you perform a *rotate right* operation to rebalance the tree; similarly, in the **Right-Right** case you perform a *rotate left* operation. However, in the **Left-Right** case, you cannot simply *rotate right* because the "middle" node, **10**, cannot become the root of the tree; its value is smaller than both of the other two values.

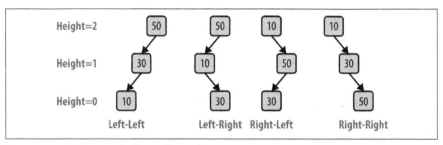

Figure 5-12. Four unbalanced scenarios

Fortunately, you can resolve the issue by first completing a *rotate left* on the child node **10** to convert the tree into a **Left-Left** case; then you'll be able to perform the *rotate right* step as described earlier. Figure 5-13 demonstrates this situation on a larger tree. After the *rotate left* operation, the tree is identical to the earlier tree on which the *rotate right* operation was described. A similar argument explains how to handle the **Right-Left** case.

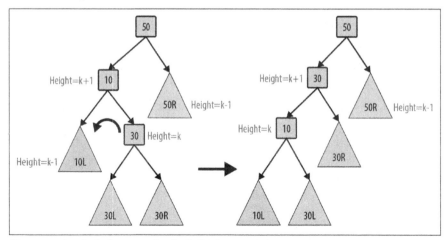

Figure 5-13. Rebalancing the Left-Right scenario

The recursive add operation shown in Example 5-13 has the same structure as Example 5-11 and the difference is that it may need to rebalance the tree once the value is inserted as a newly added leaf node. The BinaryNode add operation adds the new value to the BST rooted at that node and returns a BinaryNode object, *which is to become the new root of that BST*. This happens because a rotation operation moves a new node to be the root of that BST. Because BSTs are recursive structures, you should realize that the rotation can happen at any point. It is for this reason that the recursive invocation within add has the form self.left = self.addToSubTree (self.left, val). After adding val to the subtree rooted at self.left, that subtree might have rebalanced to have a new node to be its root, and that new node must now become the left child of self. The final act of add is to compute its height to allow the recursion to propagate back up to the original root of the tree.

Example 5-13. add methods in BinaryTree and BinaryNode

```
class BinaryTree:

  def add (self, value):
    """Insert value into proper location in Binary Tree."""
    if self.root is None:
      self.root = BinaryNode(value)
    else:
      self.root = self.root.add (value)

class BinaryNode:
  def __init__(self, value = None):
    """Create binary node."""
    self.value  = value
    self.left   = None
    self.right  = None
    self.height = 0

  def computeHeight (self):
    """Compute height of node in BST from children."""
    height = -1
    if self.left:
      height = max(height, self.left.height)
    if self.right:
      height = max(height, self.right.height)

    self.height = height + 1

  def heightDifference(self):
    """Compute height difference of node's children in BST."""
    leftTarget = 0
    rightTarget = 0
    if self.left:
      leftTarget = 1 + self.left.height
    if self.right:
      rightTarget = 1 + self.right.height
```

```
      return leftTarget - rightTarget

  def add (self, val):
    """Adds a new node to BST with value and rebalance as needed."""
    newRoot = self
    if val <= self.value:
      self.left = self.addToSubTree (self.left, val)
      if self.heightDifference() == 2:
        if val <= self.left.value:
          newRoot = self.rotateRight()
        else:
          newRoot = self.rotateLeftRight()
    else:
      self.right = self.addToSubTree (self.right, val)
      if self.heightDifference() == -2:
        if val > self.right.value:
          newRoot = self.rotateLeft()
        else:
          newRoot = self.rotateRightLeft()

    newRoot.computeHeight()
    return newRoot

  def addToSubTree (self, parent, val):
    """Add val to parent subtree (if exists) and return root in case it
    has changed because of rotation."""
    if parent is None:
      return BinaryNode(val)

    parent = parent.add (val)
    return parent
```

The compact implementation of add shown in Example 5-13 has an elegant behavior: a form of recursion that makes a choice between two possible recursive functions at each iteration. The method recursively traverses the tree, heading *left* or *right* as circumstances require, until addToSubTree eventually is asked to add val to an empty subtree (i.e., when parent is None). This terminates the recursion and ensures the newly added value is always a leaf node in the BST. Once this action is completed, each subsequent recursive call ends and add determines whether any rotation is needed to maintain the *AVL property*. These rotations start deep in the tree (i.e., nearest to the leaves) and work their way back to the root. Because the tree is balanced, the number of rotations is bounded by O($log\ n$). Each rotation method has a fixed number of steps to perform; thus the extra cost for maintaining the *AVL property* is bounded by O($log\ n$). Example 5-14 contains the rotateRight and rotateRightLeft operations.

Example 5-14. rotateRight and rotateRightLeft methods

```python
def rotateRight (self):
    """Perform right rotation around given node."""
    newRoot = self.left
    grandson = newRoot.right
    self.left = grandson
    newRoot.right = self

    self.computeHeight()
    return newRoot

def rotateRightLeft (self):
    """Perform right, then left rotation around given node."""
    child = self.right
    newRoot = child.left
    grand1 = newRoot.left
    grand2 = newRoot.right
    child.left = grand2
    self.right = grand1

    newRoot.left = self
    newRoot.right = child

    child.computeHeight()
    self.computeHeight()
    return newRoot
```

For completeness, Example 5-15 lists the rotateLeft and rotateLeftRight methods.

Example 5-15. rotateLeft and rotateLeftRight methods

```python
def rotateLeft (self):
    """Perform left rotation around given node."""
    newRoot = self.right
    grandson = newRoot.left
    self.right = grandson
    newRoot.left = self

    self.computeHeight()
    return newRoot

def rotateLeftRight (self):
    """Perform left, then right rotation around given node."""
    child = self.left
    newRoot = child.right
    grand1 = newRoot.left
    grand2 = newRoot.right
    child.right = grand1
    self.left = grand2
```

```
newRoot.left = child
newRoot.right = self

child.computeHeight()
self.computeHeight()
return newRoot
```

To complete the dynamic behavior of the BST, we need to be able to remove elements efficiently. When removing a value from the BST, it is critical to maintain the
binary search tree property. If the **target** node containing the value to be removed
has no left child, you can simply "lift" up its right child node to take its place. Otherwise, find the node with the largest value in the tree rooted at the left child. You
can swap that largest value into the **target** node. Note that the largest value in the
left subtree has no right child, so you can easily remove it by moving up its left
child, should it have one, as shown in Figure 5-14. Example 5-16 shows the necessary methods.

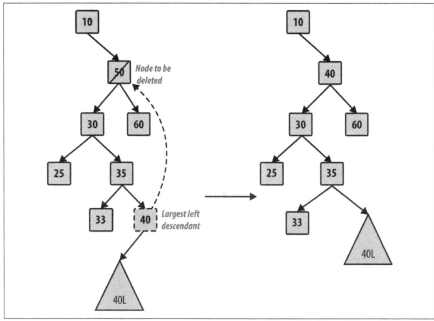

Figure 5-14. Locating largest descendant in left subtree

Example 5-16. BinaryNode remove and removeFromParent methods

```
def removeFromParent (self, parent, val):
    """ Helper method for remove. Ensures proper behavior when
    removing node that has children."""
    if parent:
        return parent.remove (val)
```

```
    return None

def remove (self, val):
    """
    Remove val from Binary Tree. Works in conjunction with
    remove method in Binary Tree.
    """
    newRoot = self
    if val == self.value:
      if self.left is None:
        return self.right

      child = self.left
      while child.right:
        child = child.right

      childKey = child.value;
      self.left = self.removeFromParent (self.left, childKey)
      self.value = childKey;

      if self.heightDifference() == -2:
        if self.right.heightDifference() <= 0:
          newRoot = self.rotateLeft()
        else:
          newRoot = self.rotateRightLeft()
    elif val < self.value:
      self.left = self.removeFromParent (self.left, val)
      if self.heightDifference() == -2:
        if self.right.heightDifference() <= 0:
          newRoot = self.rotateLeft()
        else:
          newRoot = self.rotateRightLeft()
    else:
      self.right = self.removeFromParent (self.right, val)
      if self.heightDifference() == 2:
        if self.left.heightDifference() >= 0:
          newRoot = self.rotateRight()
        else:
          newRoot = self.rotateLeftRight()

    newRoot.computeHeight()
    return newRoot
```

The remove code has a structure similar to add. Once the recursive call locates the target node that contains the value to be removed, it checks to see whether there is a larger descendant in the left subtree to be swapped. As each recursive call returns, observe how it checks whether any rotation is needed. Because the depth of the tree is bounded by O(*log n*), and each rotation method executes a constant time, the total execution time for remove is bounded by O(*log n*).

The final logic we expect in a BST is the ability to iterate over its contents in sorted order; this capability is simply not possible with hash tables. Example 5-17 contains the necessary changes to `BinaryTree` and `BinaryNode`.

Example 5-17. Support for in-order traversal

```
class BinaryTree:
  def __iter__(self):
    """In order traversal of elements in the tree."""
    if self.root:
      return self.root.inorder()

class BinaryNode:
  def inorder(self):
    """In order traversal of tree rooted at given node."""
    if self.left:
      for n in self.left.inorder():
        yield n

    yield self.value

    if self.right:
      for n in self.right.inorder():
        yield n
```

With this implementation in place, you can print out the values of a `BinaryTree` in sorted order. The code fragment in Example 5-18 adds 10 integers (in reverse order) to an empty `BinaryTree` and prints them out in sorted order:

Example 5-18. Iterating over the values in a BinaryTree

```
bt = BinaryTree()
for i in range(10, 0, -1):
  bt.add(i)
for v in bt:
  print (v)
```

Analysis

The average-case performance of search in a balanced AVL tree is the same as a **Binary Search** (i.e., O(*log n*)). Note that no rotations ever occur during a search.

Self-balancing binary trees require more complicated code to insert and remove than simple binary search trees. If you review the rotation methods, you will see that they each have a fixed number of operations, so these can be treated as behaving in constant time. The height of a balanced AVL will always be on the order of O(*log n*) because of the rotations; thus there will never be more than O(*log n*) rotations performed when adding or removing an item. We can then be confident that insertions and deletions can be performed in O(*log n*) time. The trade-off is usually worth it in terms of runtime performance gains. AVL trees store additional *height* information with each node, increasing storage requirements.

Variations

One natural extension for a binary tree is an *n*-way tree, where each node has more than one value, and correspondingly, more than two children. A common version of such trees is called the B-Tree, which performs very well when implementing relational databases. A complete analysis of B-Trees can be found in (Cormen et al., 2009) and there are helpful online B-Tree tutorials (*http://www.bluerwhite.org/btree*) with examples.

Another common self-balancing binary tree is the *red–black tree*. Red–black trees are approximately balanced and guarantee that no branch has a height more than twice that of any other branch in the tree. This relaxed guarantee improves the performance of insert and delete by reducing the number of rotations needed. We provide an implementation in the `algs.model.tree.BalancedTree` class found in the repository. Further details can be found in (Cormen et al., 2009).

References

Adel'son-Vel'skii, G. M. and E. Landis, "An algorithm for the organization of information," *Soviet Mathematics Doklady*, 3: 1259–1263, 1962.

Bloom, B., "Space/time trade-offs in hash coding with allowable errors," *Communications of the ACM*, 13(7): 422–426, 1970, *http://dx.doi.org/10.1145/362686.362692*.

Bose, P., H. Guo, E. Kranakis, A. Maheshwari, P. Morin, J. Morrison, M. Smid, and Y. Tang, "On the false-positive rate of Bloom filters," *Information Processing Letters* 108: 210–213, 2008, *http://dx.doi.org/10.1016/j.ipl.2008.05.018*.

Cormen, T. H., C. Leiserson, R. Rivest, and C. Stein, *Introduction to Algorithms*. Third Edition. MIT Press, 2009.

Hester, J. H. and D. Hirschberg, "Self-organizing linear search," *ACM Computing Surveys*, 17(3): 295–311, 1985, *http://dx.doi.org/10.1145/5505.5507*.

Knuth, D. E., *The Art of Computer Programming, Volume 3: Sorting and Searching*. Second Edition. Addison-Wesley, 1998.

Schmidt, D., "GPERF: A Perfect Hash Function Generator," C++ Report, SIGS, 10(10), 1998, *http://www.cs.wustl.edu/~schmidt/PDF/gperf.pdf*.

6

Graph Algorithms

Graphs are fundamental structures that represent complex structured information. The images in Figure 6-1 are all sample graphs.

In this chapter, we investigate common ways to represent graphs and associated algorithms that frequently occur. Inherently, a graph contains a set of elements, known as *vertices*, and relationships between pairs of these elements, known as *edges*. We use these terms consistently in this chapter; other descriptions might use the terms "node" and "link" to represent the same information. We consider only simple graphs that avoid (a) self-edges from a vertex to itself, and (b) multiple edges between the same pair of vertices.

Given the structure defined by the edges in a graph, many problems can be stated in terms of *paths* from a source vertex to a destination vertex in the graph constructed using the existing edges in the graph. Sometimes an edge has an associated numeric value known as its *weight*; sometimes an edge is *directed* with a specific orientation (like a one-way street). In the **Single-Source Shortest Path** algorithm, one is given a specific vertex, s, and asked to compute the shortest path (by sum of edge weights) to all other vertices in the graph. The **All-Pairs Shortest Path** problem requires that the shortest path be computed for all pairs (u, v) of vertices in the graph.

Some problems seek a deeper understanding of the underlying graph structure. For example, the minimum spanning tree (MST) of an undirected, weighted graph is a subset of that graph's edges such that (a) the original set of vertices is still connected in the MST, and (b) the sum total of the weights of the edges in the MST is minimum. We show how to efficiently solve this problem using **Prim's Algorithm**.

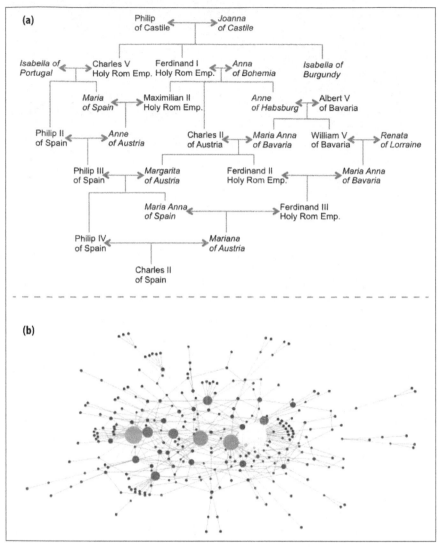

Figure 6-1. (a) The genealogy of Charles II of Spain (1661–1700); (b) a molecular network related to liver cancer

Graphs

A graph G = (V, E) is defined by a set of vertices, V, and a set of edges, E, over pairs of these vertices. There are three common types of graphs:

Undirected, unweighted graphs
> These model relationships between vertices (u, v) without regard for the direction of the relationship. These graphs are useful for capturing symmetric infor-

mation. For example, in a graph modeling a social network, if *Alice* is a friend of *Bob*, then *Bob* is a friend of *Alice*.

Directed graphs

These model relationships between vertices (u, v) that are distinct from the relationship between (v, u), which may or may not exist. For example, a program to provide driving directions must store information on one-way streets to avoid giving illegal directions.

Weighted graphs

These model relationships where there is a numeric value known as a *weight* associated with the relationship between vertices (u, v). Sometimes these values can store arbitrary non-numeric information. For example, the edge between towns A and B could store the mileage between the towns, the estimated traveling time in minutes, or the name of the street or highway connecting the towns.

The most highly structured of the graphs—a directed, weighted graph—defines a nonempty set of vertices $\{v_0, v_1, ..., v_{n-1}\}$, a set of directed edges between pairs of distinct vertices (such that every pair has at most one edge between them in each direction), and a positive weight associated with each edge. In many applications, the weight is considered to be a distance or cost. For some applications, we may want to relax the restriction that the weight must be positive (e.g., a negative weight could reflect a loss, not a profit), but we will be careful to declare when this happens.

Consider the directed, weighted graph in Figure 6-2, which is composed of six vertices and five edges. We could store the graph using adjacency lists, as shown in Figure 6-3, where each vertex v_i maintains a linked list of nodes, each of which stores the weight of the edge leading to an adjacent vertex of v_i. Thus, the base structure is a one-dimensional array of vertices in the graph.

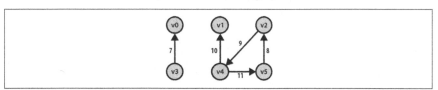

Figure 6-2. Sample directed, weighted graph

Figure 6-4 shows how to store the directed, weighted graph as an *n*-by-*n* adjacency matrix A of integers, indexed in both dimensions by the vertices. The entry $A[i][j]$ stores the weight of the edge from v_i to v_j; when there is no edge from v_i to v_j, $A[i][j]$ is set to some special value, such as 0, –1 or even –∞. We can use adjacency lists and matrices to store unweighted graphs as well (perhaps using the value 1 to represent an edge). With an adjacency matrix, checking whether an edge (v_i, v_j) exists takes constant time, but with an adjacency list, it depends on the number of edges in the list for v_i. In contrast, with an adjacency matrix, you need more space and you lose the ability to identify all incident edges to a vertex *in time proportional to the number of those edges*; instead, you must check all possible edges, which becomes significantly more expensive when the number of vertices becomes large. You should use an adjacency matrix representation when working with *dense graphs* in which nearly every possible edge exists.

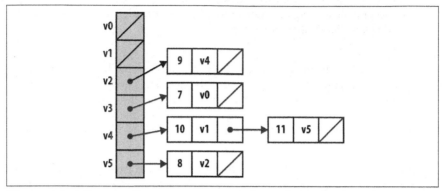

Figure 6-3. Adjacency list representation of directed, weighted graph

We use the notation $<v_0, v_1, ..., v_{k-1}>$ to describe a path of k vertices in a graph that traverses $k - 1$ edges (v_i, v_{i+1}) for $0 \leq i < k - 1$; paths in a directed graph honor the direction of the edge. In Figure 6-2, the path $<v_4, v_5, v_2, v_4, v_1>$ is valid. In this graph there is a *cycle*, which is a path of vertices that includes the same vertex multiple times. A cycle is typically represented in its most minimal form. If a path exists between any two pairs of vertices in a graph, then that graph is *connected*.

	v0	v1	v2	v3	v4	v5
v0	0	0	0	0	0	0
v1	0	0	0	0	0	0
v2	0	0	0	0	9	0
v3	7	0	0	0	0	0
v4	0	10	0	0	0	11
v5	0	0	8	0	0	0

Figure 6-4. Adjacency matrix representation of directed, weighted graph

When using an adjacency list to store an undirected graph, the same edge (u, v) appears twice: once in the linked list of neighbor vertices for u and once for v. Thus, undirected graphs may require up to twice as much storage in an adjacency list as a directed graph with the same number of vertices and edges. Doing so lets you locate the neighbors for a vertex u in time proportional to the number of actual neighbors.

When using an adjacency matrix to store an undirected graph, entry $A[i][j] = A[j][i]$.

Data Structure Design

We implement a C++ Graph class to store a directed (or undirected) graph using an adjacency list representation implemented with core classes from the C++ Standard Template Library (STL). Specifically, it stores the information as an array of list objects, with one list for each vertex. For each vertex u there is a list of Integer Pair objects representing the edge (u, v) of weight w.

The operations on graphs are subdivided into several categories:

Create

A graph can be initially constructed from a set of n vertices, and it may be directed or undirected. When a graph is undirected, adding edge (u, v) also adds edge (v, u).

Inspect

We can determine whether a graph is directed, find all incident edges to a given vertex, determine whether a specific edge exists, and determine the weight associated with an edge. We can also construct an iterator that returns the neighboring edges (and their weights) for any vertex in a graph.

Update

We can add edges to (or remove edges from) a graph. It is also possible to add a vertex to (or remove a vertex from) a graph, but algorithms in this chapter do not need to add or remove vertices.

We begin by discussing ways to explore a graph. Two common search strategies are **Depth-First Search** and **Breadth-First Search**.

Depth-First Search

Consider the maze shown on the left in Figure 6-5. After some practice, a child can rapidly find the path that stretches from the start box labeled s to the target box labeled t. One way to solve this problem is to make as much forward progress as possible and randomly select a direction whenever a choice is possible, marking where you have come from. If you ever reach a dead end or you revisit a location you have already seen, then backtrack until an untraveled branch is found and set off in that direction. The numbers on the right side of Figure 6-5 reflect the branching points of one such solution; in fact, every square in the maze is visited in this solution.

We can represent the maze in Figure 6-5 by creating a graph consisting of vertices and edges. A vertex is created for each branching point in the maze (labeled by numbers on the right in Figure 6-5) as well as "dead ends." An edge exists only if there is a direct path in the maze between the two vertices where no choice in direction can be made. The undirected graph representation of the maze from Figure 6-5 is shown in Figure 6-6; each vertex has a unique identifier.

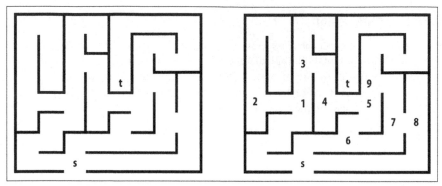

Figure 6-5. A small maze to get from s to t

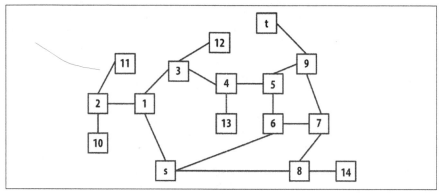

Figure 6-6. Graph representation of maze from Figure 6-5

To solve the maze, we need only find a path in the graph $G = (V, E)$ of Figure 6-5 from the start vertex, s, to the target vertex, t. In this example, all edges are undirected, but we could easily consider directed edges if the maze imposed such restrictions.

The heart of **Depth-First Search** is a recursive dfsVisit(u) operation that visits a vertex u that has not yet been visited. dfsVisit(u) records its progress by coloring vertices one of three colors:

White
> Vertex has not yet been visited.

Gray
> Vertex has been visited, but it may have an adjacent vertex that has not yet been visited.

Black

Vertex has been visited and so have all of its adjacent vertices.

Depth-First Search Summary

Best, Average, Worst: O($V+E$)

```
depthFirstSearch (G,s)
  foreach v in V do
    pred[v] = -1
    color[v] = White ❶
  dfsVisit(s)
end

dfsVisit(u)
  color[u] = Gray
  foreach neighbor v of u do
    if color[v] = White then ❷
      pred[v] = u
      dfsVisit(v)
  color[u] = Black ❸
end
```

❶ Initially all vertices are marked as not visited.

❷ Find unvisited neighbor and head in that direction.

❸ Once all neighbors are visited, this vertex is done.

Initially, each vertex is colored white to represent that it has not yet been visited, and **Depth-First Search** invokes dfsVisit on the source vertex, *s*. dfsVisit(u) colors *u* gray before recursively invoking dfsVisit on all adjacent vertices of *u* that have not yet been visited (i.e., they are colored white). Once these recursive calls have completed, *u* can be colored black, and the function returns. When the recursive dfsVisit function returns, **Depth-First Search** backtracks to an earlier vertex in the search (indeed, to a vertex that is colored gray), which may have an unvisited adjacent vertex that must be explored. Figure 6-7 contains an example showing the partial progress on a small graph.

For both directed and undirected graphs, **Depth-First Search** investigates the graph from *s* until all vertices reachable from *s* are visited. During its execution, **Depth-First Search** traverses the edges of the graph, computing information that reveals the inherent, complex structure of the graph. For each vertex, **Depth-First Search** records pred[v], the predecessor vertex to *v* that can be used to recover a path from the source vertex *s* to the vertex *v*.

This computed information is useful to a variety of algorithms built on **Depth-First Search**, including topological sort and identifying strongly connected components.

Graph Algorithms

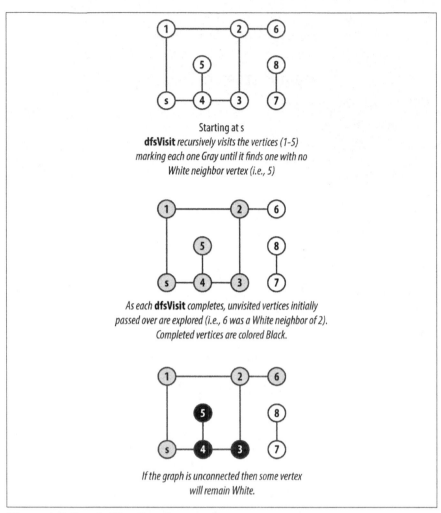

Figure 6-7. Depth-First Search example

Given the graph in Figure 6-6 and assuming the neighbors of a vertex are listed in increasing numerical order, the information computed during the search is shown in Figure 6-8. The coloring of the vertices of the graph shows the snapshot just after the fifth vertex (in this case, vertex 13) is colored black. Some parts of the graph (i.e., the vertices colored black) have been fully searched and will not be revisited. Note that white vertices have not been visited yet and gray vertices are currently being recursively visited by dfsVisit.

Depth-First Search has no global awareness of the graph, and so it will blindly search the vertices <5, 6, 7, 8>, even though these are in the wrong direction from the target, *t*. Once **Depth-First Search** completes, the pred[] values can be used to generate a path from the original source vertex, *s*, to each vertex in the graph.

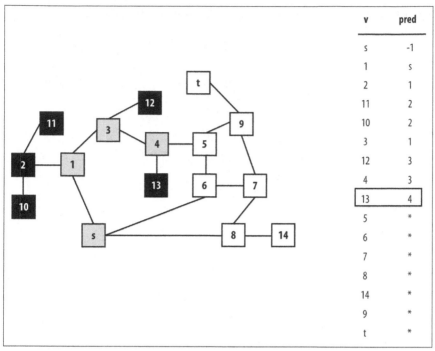

v	pred
s	-1
1	s
2	1
11	2
10	2
3	1
12	3
4	3
13	4
5	*
6	*
7	*
8	*
14	*
9	*
t	*

Figure 6-8. Computed pred for a sample undirected graph; snapshot taken after five vertices are colored black

Note that this path may not be the shortest possible path; when **Depth-First Search** completes, the path from s to t has seven vertices <s, 1, 3, 4, 5, 9, t>, while a shorter path of five vertices exists <s, 6, 5, 9, t>. Here the notion of a "shortest path" refers to the number of decision points between s and t.

Input/Output

The input is a graph $G = (V, E)$ and a source vertex $s \in V$ representing the start location.

Depth-First Search produces the pred[v] array that records the predecessor vertex of v based on the depth-first search ordering.

Context

Depth-First Search only needs to store a color (either white, gray, or black) with each vertex as it traverses the graph. Thus, **Depth-First Search** requires only O(n) overhead in storing information while it explores the graph starting from s.

Depth-First Search can store its processing information in arrays separately from the graph. **Depth-First Search** only requires that it can iterate over the vertices in a graph that are adjacent to a given vertex. This feature makes it easy to perform

Depth-First Search on complex information, since the dfsVisit function accesses the original graph as a read-only structure.

Solution

Example 6-1 contains a sample C++ solution. Note that vertex color information is used only within the dfsVisit methods.

Example 6-1. Depth-First Search implementation

```
// visit a vertex, u, in the graph and update information
void dfsVisit (Graph const &graph, int u,                    /* in */
          vector<int> &pred, vector<vertexColor> &color) {  /* out */
  color[u] = Gray;

  // process all neighbors of u.
  for (VertexList::const_iterator ci = graph.begin (u);
       ci != graph.end (u); ++ci) {
    int v = ci->first;

    // Explore unvisited vertices immediately and record pred[].
    // Once recursive call ends, backtrack to adjacent vertices.
    if (color[v] == White) {
      pred[v] = u;
      dfsVisit (graph, v, pred, color);
    }
  }

  color[u] = Black;  // our neighbors are complete; now so are we.
}

/**
 * Perform Depth-First Search starting from vertex s, and compute
 * pred[u], the predecessor vertex to u in resulting depth-first
 * search forest.
 */
void dfsSearch (Graph const &graph, int s,    /* in */
          vector<int> &pred) {                /* out */
  // initialize pred[] array and mark all vertices White
  // to signify unvisited.
  const int n = graph.numVertices();
  vector<vertexColor> color (n, White);
  pred.assign(n, -1);

  // Search starting at the source vertex.
  dfsVisit (graph, s, pred, color);
}
```

Analysis

The recursive dfsVisit function is called once for each vertex in the graph. Within dfsVisit, every neighboring vertex must be checked; for directed graphs, edges are traversed once, whereas in undirected graphs they are traversed once and are seen one other time. In any event, the total performance cost is O($V + E$).

Variations

If the original graph is unconnected, then there may be no path between s and some vertices; these vertices will remain unvisited. Some variations ensure all vertices are processed by conducting additional dfsVisit executions on the unvisited vertices in the dfsSearch method. If this is done, pred[] values record a depth-first forest of depth-first tree search results. To find the roots of the trees in this forest, scan pred[] to find vertices r whose pred[r] value is –1.

Breadth-First Search

Breadth-First Search takes a different approach from **Depth-First Search** when searching a graph. **Breadth-First Search** systematically visits all vertices in the graph $G = (V, E)$ that are k edges away from the source vertex s before visiting any vertex that is $k + 1$ edges away. This process repeats until no more vertices are reachable from s. **Breadth-First Search** does not visit vertices in G that are not reachable from s. The algorithm works for undirected as well as directed graphs.

Breadth-First Search is guaranteed to find the shortest path in the graph from vertex s to a desired *target* vertex, although it may evaluate a rather large number of nodes as it operates. **Depth-First Search** tries to make as much progress as possible, and may locate a path more quickly, which may not be the shortest path.

Figure 6-9 shows the partial progress of **Breadth-First-Search** on the same small graph from Figure 6-7. First observe that the gray vertices in the graph are exactly the ones contained within the queue. Each time through the loop a vertex is removed from the queue and unvisited neighbors are added.

Breadth-First Search makes its progress without requiring any backtracking. It records its progress by coloring vertices white, gray, or black, as **Depth-First Search** did. Indeed, the same colors and definitions apply. To compare directly with **Depth-First Search**, we can take a snapshot of **Breadth-First Search** executing on the same graph used earlier in Figure 6-6 after it colors its fifth vertex black (vertex 2) as shown in Figure 6-10. At the point shown in the figure, the search has colored black the source vertex s, vertices that are one edge away from s—{ 1, 6, and 8 }—and vertex 2, which is two edges away from s.

The remaining vertices two edges away from s—{ 3, 5, 7, 14 }—are all in the queue Q waiting to be processed. Some vertices three edges away from s have also been visited—{10,11}—and are at the tail of the queue. Note that all vertices within the queue are colored gray, reflecting their active status.

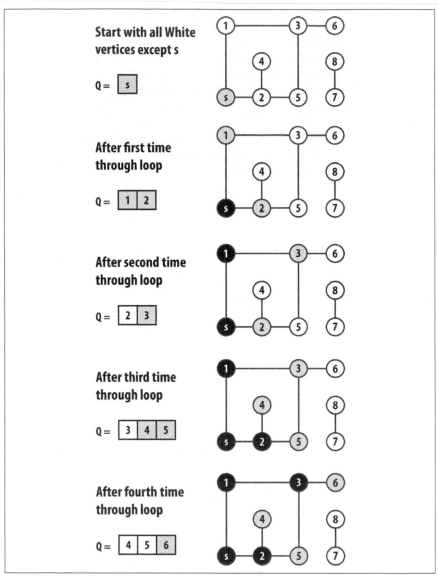

Figure 6-9. Breadth-First Search example

Input/Output

The input is a graph $G = (V, E)$ and a source vertex $s \in V$ representing the start location.

Breadth-First Search produces two computed arrays. dist[v] records the number of edges in a shortest path from *s* to *v*. pred[v] records the predecessor vertex of *v* based on the breadth-first search ordering. The pred[] values record the breadth-first tree search result; if the original graph is unconnected, then all vertices *w* unreachable from *s* have a pred[w] value of –1.

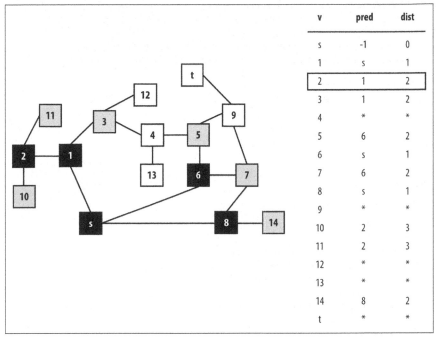

v	pred	dist
s	-1	0
1	s	1
2	1	2
3	1	2
4	*	*
5	6	2
6	s	1
7	6	2
8	s	1
9	*	*
10	2	3
11	2	3
12	*	*
13	*	*
14	8	2
t	*	*

Figure 6-10. Breadth-First Search progress on graph after five vertices are colored black

Context

Breadth-First Search stores the vertices being processed in a queue, thus there is O(*V*) storage. **Breadth-First Search** is guaranteed to find a shortest path (there may be ties) in graphs whose vertices are generated "on the fly" (as will be seen in Chapter 7). Indeed, all paths in the generated breadth-first tree are shortest paths from *s* in terms of edge count.

Solution

A sample C++ solution is shown in Example 6-2. **Breadth-First Search** stores its state in a queue, and therefore there are no recursive function calls.

Example 6-2. Breadth-First Search implementation

```
/**
 * Perform breadth-first search on graph from vertex s, and compute BFS
 * distance and pred vertex for all vertices in the graph.
 */
void bfsSearch (Graph const &graph, int s,                    /* in */
                vector<int> &dist, vector<int> &pred)  /* out */
{
  // initialize dist and pred to mark vertices as unvisited. Begin at s
  // and mark as Gray since we haven't yet visited its neighbors.
  const int n = graph.numVertices();
  pred.assign(n, -1);
  dist.assign(n, numeric_limits<int>::max());
  vector<vertexColor> color (n, White);

  dist[s] = 0;
  color[s] = Gray;

  queue<int> q;
  q.push(s);
  while (!q.empty()) {
    int u = q.front();

    // Explore neighbors of u to expand the search horizon
    for (VertexList::const_iterator ci = graph.begin (u);
         ci != graph.end (u); ++ci) {
      int v = ci->first;
      if (color[v] == White) {
        dist[v] = dist[u]+1;
        pred[v] = u;
        color[v] = Gray;
        q.push(v);
      }
    }

    q.pop();
    color[u] = Black;
  }
}
```

Analysis

During initialization, **Breadth-First Search** updates information for all vertices, with performance $O(V)$. When a vertex is first visited (and colored gray), it is inserted into the queue, and no vertex is added twice. Since the queue can add and remove elements in constant time, the cost of managing the queue is $O(V)$. Finally, each vertex is dequeued exactly once and its adjacent vertices are traversed exactly once. The sum total of the edge loops, therefore, is bounded by the total number of edges, or $O(E)$. Thus, the total performance is $O(V + E)$.

Breadth-First Search Summary

Best, Average, Worst: O(*V*+*E*)

```
breadthFirstSearch (G, s)
  foreach v in V do
    pred[v] = -1
    dist[v] = ∞
    color[v] = White ❶
  color[s] = Gray
  dist[s] = 0
  Q = empty Queue ❷
  enqueue (Q, s)

  while Q is not empty do
    u = head(Q)
    foreach neighbor v of u do
      if color[v] = White then
        dist[v] = dist[u] + 1
        pred[v] = u
        color[v] = Gray
        enqueue (Q, v)
    dequeue (Q)
    color[u] = Black ❸
  end
```

❶   Initially all vertices are marked as not visited.

❷   Queue maintains collection of gray nodes that are visited.

❸   Once all neighbors are visited, this vertex is done.

Single-Source Shortest Path

Suppose you want to fly a private plane on the shortest path from St. Johnsbury, VT, to Waco, TX. Assume you know the distances between the airports for all pairs of cities and towns that are reachable from each other in one nonstop flight of your plane. The best-known algorithm to solve this problem, **Dijkstra's Algorithm**, finds the shortest path from St. Johnsbury to all other airports, although the search may be halted once the shortest path to Waco is known.

In this example, we minimize the distance traversed. In other applications we might replace distance with time (e.g., deliver a packet over a network as quickly as possible) or with cost (e.g., find the cheapest way to fly from St. Johnsbury to Waco). Solutions to these problems also correspond to shortest paths.

Dijkstra's Algorithm relies on a data structure known as a *priority queue* (PQ). A PQ maintains a collection of items, each of which has an associated integer *priority* that represents the importance of an item. A PQ allows one to insert an item, *x*, with its associated priority, *p*. Lower values of *p* represent items of higher importance. The fundamental operation of a PQ is *getMin*, which returns the item in PQ whose priority value is lowest (or in other words, is the most important item). Another operation, *decreasePriority*, may be provided by a PQ that allows us to locate a specific item in the PQ and reduce its associated *priority* value (which increases its importance) while leaving the item in the PQ.

Dijkstra's Algorithm Summary

Best, Average, Worst: O(($V+E$)*$log\ V$)

```
singleSourceShortest (G, s)
  PQ = empty Priority Queue
  foreach v in V do
    dist[v] = ∞  ❶
    pred[v] = -1

  dist[s] = 0
  foreach v in V do  ❷
    insert (v, dist[v]) into PQ

  while PQ is not empty do
    u = getMin(PQ)  ❸
    foreach neighbor v of u do
      w = weight of edge (u, v)
      newLen = dist[u] + w
      if newLen < dist[v] then  ❹
        decreasePriority (PQ, v, newLen)
        dist[v] = newLen
        pred[v] = u
  end
```

❶ Initially all vertices are considered to be unreachable.

❷ Populate PQ with vertices by shortest path distance.

❸ Remove vertex that has shortest distance to source.

❹ If discovered a shorter path from *s* to *v*, record and update PQ.

The source vertex, *s*, is known in advance and dist[v] is set to ∞ for all vertices other than *s*, whose dist[s] = 0. These vertices are all inserted into the priority queue, PQ, with priority equal to dist[v]; thus *s* will be the first vertex removed from PQ. At each iteration, **Dijkstra's Algorithm** removes a vertex from PQ that is closest to *s* of all remaining unvisited vertices in PQ. The vertices in PQ are potentially updated to reflect a closer distance, given the visited vertices seen so far, as shown in Figure 6-11. After *V* iterations, dist[v] contains the shortest distance from *s* to all vertices *v* ∈ *V*.

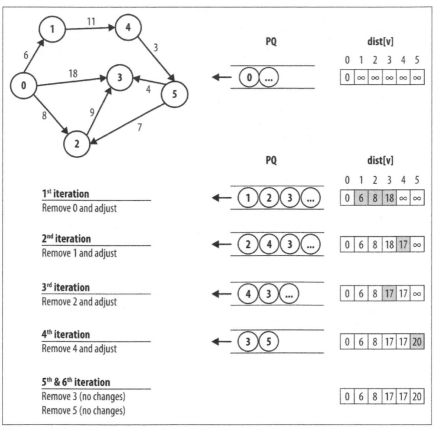

Figure 6-11. Dijkstra's Algorithm example

Dijkstra's Algorithm conceptually operates in a greedy fashion by expanding a set of vertices, S, for which the shortest path from a designated source vertex, s, to every vertex $v \in S$ is known, *but only using paths that include vertices in S*. Initially, S equals the set {s}. To expand S, as shown in Figure 6-12, **Dijkstra's Algorithm** finds the vertex $v \in V - S$ (i.e., the vertices outside the shaded region) whose distance to s is smallest, and follows v's edges to see whether a shorter path exists to some other vertex. After processing v_2, for example, the algorithm determines that the distance from s to v_3 containing only vertices in S is really 17 through the path $<s, v_2, v_3>$. Once S equals V, the algorithm completes and the final result is depicted in Figure 6-12.

Input/Output

The input is a directed, weighted graph $G = (V, E)$ and a source vertex $s \in V$. Each edge $e = (u, v)$ has an associated non-negative weight in the graph.

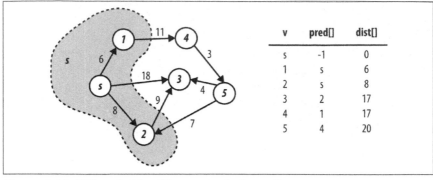

v	pred[]	dist[]
s	-1	0
1	s	6
2	s	8
3	2	17
4	1	17
5	4	20

Figure 6-12. Dijkstra's Algorithm expands the set S

Dijkstra's Algorithm produces two computed arrays. The primary result is the array dist[] of values representing the distance from source vertex *s* to each vertex in the graph. The secondary result is the array pred[] that can be used to rediscover the actual shortest paths from vertex *s* to each vertex in the graph.

The edge weights are non-negative (i.e., greater than or equal zero); if this assumption is not true, then dist[] may contain invalid results. Even worse, **Dijkstra's Algorithm** will loop forever if a cycle exists whose sum of all weights is less than zero.

Solution

As **Dijkstra's Algorithm** executes, dist[v] represents the maximum length of the shortest path found from the source *s* to *v* using only vertices visited within the set *S*. Also, for each *v* ∈ *S*, dist[v] is correct. Fortunately, **Dijkstra's Algorithm** does not need to create and maintain the set *S*. It initially constructs a set containing the vertices in *V*, and then it removes vertices one at a time from the set to compute proper dist[v] values; for convenience, we continue to refer to this ever-shrinking set as *V-S*. **Dijkstra's Algorithm** terminates when all vertices are either visited or are shown to not be reachable from the source vertex *s*.

In the C++ solution shown in Example 6-3, a *binary heap* stores the vertices in the set *V-S* as a priority queue because, in constant time, we can locate the vertex with *smallest priority* (i.e., the vertex's distance from *s*). Additionally, when a shorter path from *s* to *v* is found, dist[v] is decreased, requiring the heap to be modified. Fortunately, the *decreasePriority* operation (in a binary heap, it is known as decreaseKey) can be performed in O(*log q*) time in the worst case, where *q* is the number of vertices in the binary heap, which will always be less than or equal to the number of vertices, *V*.

Example 6-3. Dijkstra's Algorithm implementation

```
/** Given directed, weighted graph, compute shortest distance to
 * vertices and record predecessor links for all vertices. */
void singleSourceShortest (Graph const &g, int s,    /* in */
                          vector<int> &dist,        /* out */
                          vector<int> &pred) {      /* out */
  // initialize dist[] and pred[] arrays. Start with vertex s by
  // setting dist[] to 0. Priority Queue PQ contains all v in G.
  const int n = g.numVertices();
  pred.assign (n, -1);
  dist.assign (n, numeric_limits<int>::max());
  dist[s] = 0;
  BinaryHeap pq(n);
  for (int u = 0; u < n; u++) { pq.insert (u, dist[u]); }

  // find vertex in ever shrinking set, V-S, whose dist[] is smallest.
  // Recompute potential new paths to update all shortest paths
  while (!pq.isEmpty()) {
    int u = pq.smallest();

    // For neighbors of u, see if newLen (best path from s->u + weight
    // of edge u->v) is better than best path from s->v. If so, update
    // in dist[v] and readjust binary heap accordingly. Compute using
    // longs to avoid overflow error.
    for (VertexList::const_iterator ci = g.begin (u);
         ci != g.end (u); ++ci) {
      int v = ci->first;
      long newLen = dist[u];
      newLen += ci->second;
      if (newLen < dist[v]) {
        pq.decreaseKey (v, newLen);
        dist[v] = newLen;
        pred[v] = u;
      }
    }
  }
}
```

Arithmetic error may occur if the sum of the individual edge weights exceeds `numeric_limits<int>::max()` (although individual values do not). To avoid this situation, compute `newLen` using a long data type.

Analysis

In the implementation of **Dijkstra's Algorithm** in Example 6-3, the for loop that constructs the initial priority queue performs the insert operation V times, resulting in performance $O(V \log V)$. In the remaining while loop, each edge is visited once, and thus `decreaseKey` is called no more than E times, which contributes $O(E \log V)$ time. Thus, the overall performance is $O((V + E) \log V)$.

Dijkstra's Algorithm for Dense Graphs

There is a version of **Dijkstra's Algorithm** suitable for dense graphs represented using an adjacency matrix. The C++ implementation found in Example 6-4 no longer needs a priority queue and it is optimized to use a two dimensional array to contain the adjacency matrix. The efficiency of this version is determined by considering how fast the smallest dist[] value in $V - S$ can be retrieved. The while loop is executed V times, since S grows one vertex at a time. Finding the smallest dist[u] in $V - S$ inspects all V vertices. Note that each edge is inspected exactly once in the inner loop within the while loop. Since E can never be larger than V^2, the total running time of this version is O (V^2).

Dijkstra's Algorithm for Dense Graphs Summary

Best, Average, Worst: $O(V^2 + E)$

```
singleSourceShortest (G, s)
  foreach v in V do
    dist[v] = ∞  ❶
    pred[v] = -1
    visited[v] = false
  dist[s] = 0

  while some unvisited vertex v has dist[v] < ∞ do  ❷
    u = find dist[u] that is smallest of unvisited vertices  ❸
    if dist[u] = ∞ then return
    visited[u] = true

    foreach neighbor v of u do
      w = weight of edge (u, v)
      newLen = dist[u] + w
      if newLen < dist[v] then  ❹
        dist[v] = newLen
        pred[v] = u
end
```

❶ Initially all vertices are considered to be unreachable.

❷ Stop if all unvisited vertices v have dist[v] = ∞.

❸ Find the vertex that has the shortest distance to source.

❹ If a shorter path is discovered from s to v, record new length.

Because of the adjacency matrix structure, this variation no longer needs a priority queue; instead, at each iteration it selects the unvisited vertex with smallest dist[] value. Figure 6-13 demonstrates the execution on a small graph.

Example 6-4. Optimized Dijkstra's Algorithm for dense graphs

```
/** Given int[][] of edge weights as adjacency matrix, compute shortest
 * distance to all vertices in graph (dist) and record predecessor
 * links for all vertices (pred) */
void singleSourceShortestDense (int n, int ** const weight, int s, /* in */
                                int *dist, int *pred) {          /* out */
  // initialize dist[] and pred[] arrays. Start with vertex s by setting
  // dist[] to 0. All vertices are unvisited.
  bool *visited = new bool[n];
  for (int v = 0; v < n; v++) {
    dist[v] = numeric_limits<int>::max();
    pred[v] = -1;
    visited[v] = false;
  }
  dist[s] = 0;

  // find shortest distance from s to unvisited vertices.  Recompute
  // potential new paths to update all shortest paths.
  while (true) {
    int u = -1;
    int sd = numeric_limits<int>::max();
    for (int i = 0; i < n; i++) {
      if (!visited[i] && dist[i] < sd) {
        sd = dist[i];
        u = i;
      }
    }
    if (u == -1) { break; } // exit if no new paths found

    // For neighbors of u, see if best path-length from s->u + weight of
    // edge u->v is better than best path from s->v. Compute using longs.
    visited[u] = true;
    for (int v = 0; v < n; v++) {
      int w = weight[u][v];
      if (v == u) continue;

      long newLen = dist[u];
      newLen += w;
      if (newLen < dist[v]) {
        dist[v] = newLen;
        pred[v] = u;
      }
    }
  }
  delete [] visited;
}
```

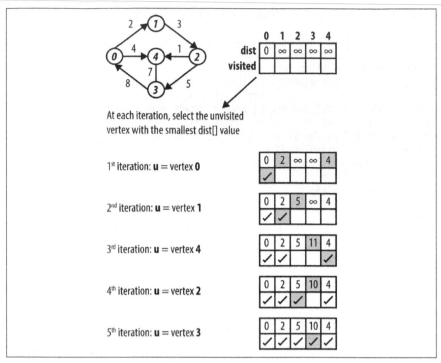

Figure 6-13. Dijkstra's Algorithm dense graph example

Variations

We may seek the most reliable path to send a message from one point to another through a network where we know the probability that any leg of a transmission delivers the message correctly. The probability of any path (i.e., a sequence of legs) delivering a message correctly is the product of all the probabilities along the path. Using the same technique that makes multiplication possible on a slide rule, we can replace the probability on each edge with the negative value of the logarithm of the probability. The shortest path in this new graph corresponds to the most reliable path in the original graph.

Dijkstra's Algorithm cannot be used when edge weights are negative. However, **Bellman–Ford** can be used as long as there is no cycle whose edge weights sum to a value less than zero. The concept of "shortest path" is meaningless when such a cycle exists. Although the sample graph in Figure 6-14 contains a cycle involving vertices {1,3,2}, the edge weights are positive, so **Bellman–Ford** will work.

A C++ implementation of Bellman-Ford is shown in Example 6-5.

Bellman–Ford Summary

Best, Average, Worst: O(*V*E*)

```
singleSourceShortest (G, s)
  foreach v in V do
    dist[v] = ∞ ❶
    pred[v] = -1
  dist[s] = 0

  for i = 1 to n do
    foreach edge (u,v) in E do
      newLen = dist[u] + weight of edge (u,v)
      if newLen < dist[v] then ❷
        if i = n then report "Negative Cycle"
        dist[v] = newLen
        pred[v] = u
end
```

❶ Initially all vertices are considered to be unreachable.

❷ If a shorter path is discovered from *s* to *v*, record new length.

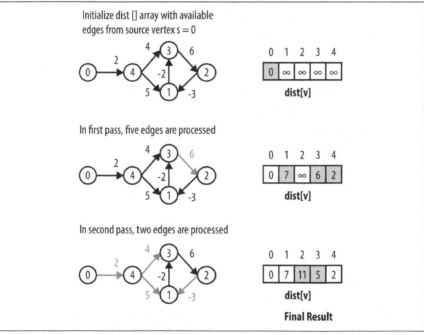

Figure 6-14. Bellman–Ford example

Example 6-5. Bellman–Ford algorithm for single-source shortest path

```
/**
 * Given directed, weighted graph, compute shortest distance to vertices
 * in graph (dist) and record predecessor links for all vertices (pred) to
 * be able to re-create these paths. Graph weights can be negative so long
 * as there are no negative cycles.
 */
void singleSourceShortest (Graph const &graph, int s,             /* in */
                           vector<int> &dist, vector<int> &pred) { /* out */
  // initialize dist[] and pred[] arrays.
  const int n = graph.numVertices();
  pred.assign (n, -1);
  dist.assign (n, numeric_limits<int>::max());
  dist[s] = 0;

  // After n-1 times we can be guaranteed distances from s to all
  // vertices are properly computed to be shortest. So on the nth
  // pass, a change to any value guarantees there is a negative cycle.
  // Leave early if no changes are made.
  for (int i = 1; i <= n; i++) {
    bool failOnUpdate = (i == n);
    bool leaveEarly = true;

    // Process each vertex, u, and its respective edges to see if
    // some edge (u,v) realizes a shorter distance from s->v by going
    // through s->u->v. Use longs to prevent overflow.
    for (int u = 0; u < n; u++) {
      for (VertexList::const_iterator ci = graph.begin (u);
           ci != graph.end (u); ++ci) {
        int v = ci->first;
        long newLen = dist[u];
        newLen += ci->second;
        if (newLen < dist[v]) {
          if (failOnUpdate) { throw "Graph has negative cycle"; }
          dist[v] = newLen;
          pred[v] = u;
          leaveEarly = false;
        }
      }
    }
    if (leaveEarly) { break; }
  }
}
```

Intuitively **Bellman–Ford** operates by making n sweeps over a graph that check to see if any edge (u, v) is able to improve on the computation for dist[v] given dist[u] and the weight of the edge over (u, v). At least $n - 1$ sweeps are needed, for example, in the extreme case that the shortest path from s to some vertex v goes through all vertices in the graph. Another reason to use $n - 1$ sweeps is that the edges can be visited in an arbitrary order, and this ensures all reduced paths have been found.

Bellman–Ford is thwarted only when there exists a negative cycle of directed edges whose total sum is less than zero. To detect such a negative cycle, we execute the primary processing loop n times (one more than necessary), and if there is an adjustment to some dist[] value, a negative cycle exists. The performance of **Bellman–Ford** is $O(V*E)$, as clearly seen by the nested for loops.

Comparing Single-Source Shortest-Path Options

The following summarizes the expected performance of the three algorithms by computing a rough cost estimate:

- **Bellman–Ford**: $O(V*E)$
- **Dijkstra's Algorithm** for dense graphs: $O(V^2 + E)$
- **Dijkstra's Algorithm** with priority queue: $O((V + E)*log\ V)$

We compare these algorithms under different scenarios. Naturally, to select the one that best fits your data, you should benchmark the implementations as we have done. In the following tables, we execute the algorithms 10 times and discard the best- and worst-performing runs; the tables show the average of the remaining eight runs.

Benchmark Data

It is difficult to generate random graphs. In Table 6-1, we show the performance on generated graphs with $|V| = k^2 + 2$ vertices and $|E| = k^3 - k^2 + 2k$ edges in a highly stylized graph construction (for details, see the code implementation in the repository). Note that the number of edges is roughly $n^{1.5}$ where n is the number of vertices in V. The best performance comes from using the priority queue implementation of **Dijkstra's Algorithm** but **Bellman–Ford** is not far behind. Note how the variations optimized for dense graphs perform poorly.

Table 6-1. Time (in seconds) to compute single-source shortest path on benchmark graphs

V	E	Dijkstra's Algorithm with PQ	Optimized Dijsktra's Algorithm for DG	Bellman–Ford
6	8	0.000002	0.000002	0.000001
18	56	0.000004	0.000003	0.000001
66	464	0.000012	0.000018	0.000005
258	3,872	0.00006	0.000195	0.000041
1,026	31,808	0.000338	0.0030	0.000287

V	E	Dijkstra's Algorithm with PQ	Optimized Dijkstra's Algorithm for DG	Bellman–Ford
4,098	258,176	0.0043	0.0484	0.0076
16,386	2,081,024	0.0300	0.7738	0.0535

Dense Graphs

For dense graphs, E is on the order of $O(V^2)$; for example, in a complete graph of n = $|V|$ vertices that contains an edge for every pair of vertices, there are $n*(n - 1)/2$ edges. Using **Bellman–Ford** on such dense graphs is not recommended, since its performance degenerates to $O(V^3)$. The set of dense graphs reported in Table 6-2 is taken from a set of publicly available data sets (*http://www.iwr.uni-heidelberg.de/groups/comopt/software/TSPLIB95/*) used by researchers investigating the Traveling Salesman Problem (TSP). We executed 100 trials and discarded the best and worst performances; the table contains the average of the remaining 98 trials. Although there is little difference between the priority queue and dense versions of **Dijsktra's Algorithm**, there is a vast improvement in the optimized **Dijsktra's Algorithm**, as shown in the table. In the final column we show the performance time for **Bellman–Ford** for the same problems, but these results are the averages of only five executions because the performance degrades so sharply. The lesson to draw from the last column is that the absolute performance of **Bellman–Ford** on sparse graphs seems to be quite reasonable, but when compared relatively to its peers on dense graphs, we see clearly that it is the wrong algorithm to use (unless there are edges with negative weights, in which case this algorithm must be used).

Table 6-2. Time (in seconds) to compute single-source shortest path on dense graphs

V	E	Dijkstra's Algorithm with PQ	Optimized Dijkstra's Algorithm for DG	Bellman–Ford
980	479,710	0.0681	0.0050	0.1730
1,621	1,313,010	0.2087	0.0146	0.5090
6,117	18,705,786	3.9399	0.2056	39.6780
7,663	29,356,953	7.6723	0.3295	40.5585
9,847	48,476,781	13.1831	0.5381	78.4154
9,882	48,822,021	13.3724	0.5413	42.1146

Sparse graphs

Large graphs are frequently sparse, and the results in Table 6-3 confirm that one should use the **Dijsktra's Algorithm** with a priority queue rather than the implementation crafted for dense graphs; note how the implementation for dense graphs is noticeably slower. The rows in the table are sorted by the number of edges in the sparse graphs, since that appears to be the determining cost factor in the results.

Table 6-3. Time (in seconds) to compute single-source shortest path on large sparse graphs

V	E	Density	Dijkstra's Algorithm with PQ	Optimized Dijkstra's Algorithm for DG
3,403	137,845	2.4%	0.0102	0.0333
3,243	294,276	5.6%	0.0226	0.0305
19,780	674,195	0.34%	0.0515	1.1329

All-Pairs Shortest Path

Instead of finding the shortest path from a single source, we often seek the shortest path between any two vertices (v_i, v_j); there may be several paths with the same total distance. The fastest solution to this problem uses the Dynamic Programming technique introduced in Chapter 3.

There are two interesting features of dynamic programming:

- It stores the solution to small, constrained versions of the problem.
- Although we seek an optimal answer to a problem, it is easier to compute the *value* of an optimal answer rather than the answer itself. In our case, we compute, for each pair of vertices (v_i, v_j), the length of a shortest path from v_i to v_j and perform additional computation to recover the actual path. In the following pseudocode, k, u, and v each represent a potential vertex of G.

Floyd–Warshall computes an *n*-by-*n* matrix dist such that for all pairs of vertices (v_i, v_j), dist[i][j] contains the length of a shortest path from v_i to v_j.

Figure 6-15 demonstrates an example of **Floyd-Warshall** on the sample graph from Figure 6-13. As you can confirm, the first row of the computed matrix is the same as the computed vector from Figure 6-13. **Floyd-Warshall** computes the shortest path between all pairs of vertices.

Input/Output

The input is a directed, weighted graph $G = (V, E)$. Each edge $e = (u, v)$ has an associated positive (i.e., greater than zero) weight in the graph.

Floyd–Warshall computes a matrix dist[][] representing the shortest distance from each vertex u to every vertex in the graph (including itself). Note that if dist[u][v] is ∞, then there is no path from u to v. The actual shortest path between any two vertices can be computed from a second matrix, pred[][], also computed by the algorithm.

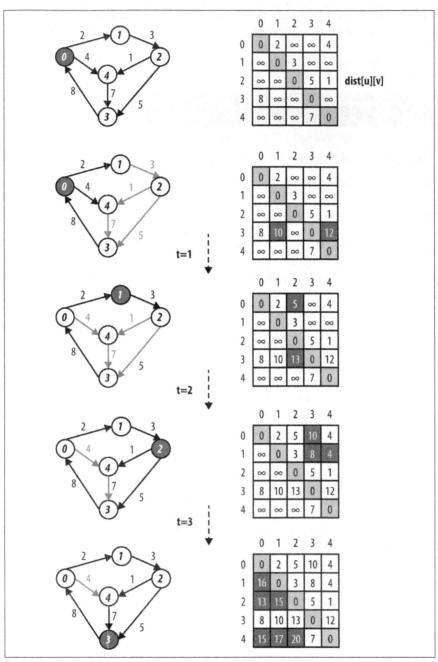

Figure 6-15. Floyd–Warshall example

Floyd–Warshall Summary

Best, Average, Worst: $O(V^3)$

```
allPairsShortestPath (G)
  foreach u in V do
    foreach v in V do
      dist[u][v] = ∞  ❶
      pred[u][v] = -1
    dist[u][u] = 0
    foreach neighbor v of u do
      dist[u][v] = weight of edge (u,v)
      pred[u][v] = u

  foreach k in V do
    foreach u in V do
      foreach v in V do
        newLen = dist[u][k] + dist[k][v]
        if newLen < dist[u][v] then  ❷
          dist[u][v] = newLen
          pred[u][v] = pred[k][v]  ❸
  end
```

❶   Initially all vertices are considered to be unreachable.

❷   If a shorter path is discovered from *s* to *v* record new length.

❸   Record the new predecessor link.

Solution

A Dynamic Programming approach computes, in order, the results of simpler sub-problems. Consider the edges of *G*: these represent the length of the shortest path between any two vertices *u* and *v* that **does not include any other vertex**. Thus, the dist[u][v] matrix is set initially to ∞ and dist[u][u] is set to zero (to confirm that there is no cost for the path from a vertex *u* to itself). Finally, dist[u][v] is set to the weight of every edge $(u, v) \in E$. At this point, the dist matrix contains the best computed shortest path (so far) for each pair of vertices, (u, v).

Now consider the next larger subproblem, namely, computing the length of the shortest path between any two vertices *u* and *v* that **might also include** v_1. Dynamic Programming will check each pair of vertices (u, v) to check whether the path $\{u, v_1, v\}$ has a total distance smaller than the best score. In some cases, dist[u][v] is still ∞ because there was no information on any path between *u* and *v*. At other times, the sum of the paths from *u* to v_1 and then from v_1 to *v* is better than the current distance, and the algorithm records that total in dist[u][v]. The next larger subproblem tries to compute the length of the shortest path between any two vertices *u* and *v* that **might also include** v_1 or v_2. Eventually the algorithm increases these subproblems until the result is a dist[u][v] matrix that contains the shortest path between any two vertices *u* and *v* that might also include any vertex in the graph.

Floyd–Warshall computes the key optimization check whether dist[u][k] + dist[k][v] < dist[u][v]. Note that the algorithm also computes a pred[u][v] matrix that "remembers" that the newly computed shorted path from *u* to *v* must go through vertex *k*. The surprisingly brief solution is shown in Example 6-6.

Example 6-6. Floyd–Warshall algorithm for computing all-pairs shortest path

```
void allPairsShortest (Graph const &graph,      /* in */
        vector< vector<int> > &dist,            /* out */
        vector< vector<int> > &pred) {          /* out */
  int n = graph.numVertices();

  // Initialize dist[][] with 0 on diagonals, INFINITY where no edge
  // exists, and the weight of edge (u,v) placed in dist[u][v]. pred
  // initialized in corresponding way.
  for (int u = 0; u < n; u++) {
    dist[u].assign (n, numeric_limits<int>::max());
    pred[u].assign (n, -1);
    dist[u][u] = 0;
    for (VertexList::const_iterator ci = graph.begin (u);
        ci != graph.end (u); ++ci) {
      int v = ci->first;
      dist[u][v] = ci->second;
      pred[u][v] = u;
    }
  }

  for (int k = 0; k < n; k++) {
    for (int i = 0; i < n; i++) {
      if (dist[i][k] == numeric_limits<int>::max()) { continue; }

      // If an edge is found to reduce distance, update dist[][].
      // Compute using longs to avoid overflow of Infinity distance.
      for (int j = 0; j < n; j++) {
        long newLen = dist[i][k];
        newLen += dist[k][j];

        if (newLen < dist[i][j]) {
          dist[i][j] = newLen;
          pred[i][j] = pred[k][j];
        }
      }
    }
  }
}
```

The function shown in Example 6-7 constructs an actual shortest path (there may be more than one) from a given s to t. It works by recovering predecessor information from the pred matrix.

Example 6-7. Code to recover shortest path from computed pred[][]

```
/** Output path as list of vertices from s to t given the pred results
 * from an allPairsShortest execution. Note that s and t must be valid
 * integer vertex identifiers. If no path is found between s and t, then
 * an empty path is returned.  */
void constructShortestPath (int s, int t,        /* in */
          vector< vector<int> > const &pred,     /* in */
          list<int> &path) {                     /* out */
  path.clear();
  if (t < 0 || t >= (int) pred.size() || s < 0 || s >= (int) pred.size()) {
    return;
  }

  // construct path until we hit source 's' or -1 if there is no path.
  path.push_front (t);
  while (t != s) {
    t = pred[s][t];
    if (t == -1) { path.clear (); return; }

    path.push_front (t);
  }
}
```

Analysis

The time taken by **Floyd–Warshall** is dictated by the number of times the minimization function is computed, which is $O(V^3)$, as can be seen from the three nested for loops. The constructShortestPath function in Example 6-7 executes in $O(E)$ since the shortest path might include every edge in the graph.

Minimum Spanning Tree Algorithms

Given an undirected, connected graph $G = (V, E)$, we might be concerned with finding a subset ST of edges from E that "span" the graph because it connects all vertices. If we further require that the total weight of the edges in ST is the minimal across all possible spanning trees, then we are interested in finding a minimum spanning tree (MST).

Prim's Algorithm shows how to construct an MST from such a graph by using a Greedy approach in which each step of the algorithm makes forward progress toward a solution without reversing earlier decisions. **Prim's Algorithm** grows a spanning tree T one edge at a time until an MST results (and the resulting spanning tree is provably minimum). It randomly selects a start vertex $s \in v$ to belong to a growing set S and ensures that T forms a tree of edges in S. **Prim's Algorithm** is greedy in that it incrementally adds edges to T until an MST is computed. The intuition behind the algorithm is that the edge (u, v) with lowest weight between $u \in S$ and $v \in V\text{-}S$ must belong to the MST. When such an edge (u, v) with lowest weight is found, it is added to T and the vertex v is added to S.

The algorithm uses a priority queue to store the vertices $v \in V - S$ with an associated *priority key* equal to the lowest weight of some edge (u, v) where $u \in S$. This key value reflects the priority of the element within the priority queue; smaller values are of higher importance.

Prim's Algorithm Summary

Best, Average, Worst: $O((V + E)\text{*}log\ V)$

```
computeMST (G)
  foreach v in V do
    key[v] = ∞  ❶
    pred[v] = -1
  key[0] = 0
  PQ = empty Priority Queue
  foreach v in V do
    insert (v, key[v]) into PQ

  while PQ is not empty do
    u = getMin(PQ)  ❷
    foreach edge(u,v) in E do
      if PQ contains v then
        w = weight of edge (u,v)
        if w < key[v] then  ❸
          pred[v] = u
          key[v] = w
          decreasePriority (PQ, v, w)
  end
```

❶ Initially all vertices are considered to be unreachable.

❷ Find vertex in V with lowest computed distance.

❸ Revise cost estimates for v and record MST edge in *pred*[v].

Figure 6-16 demonstrates the behavior of **Prim's Algorithm** on a small undirected graph. The priority queue is ordered based on the distance from the vertices in the queue to any vertex already contained in the MST.

Input/Output

The input is an undirected graph $G = (V, E)$.

The output is an MST encoded in the pred[] array. The *root* of the MST is the vertex whose pred[v] = −1.

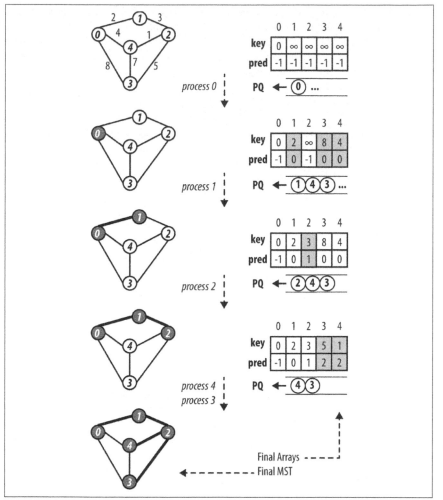

Figure 6-16. Prim's Algorithm example

Solution

The C++ solution shown in Example 6-8 relies on a binary heap to provide the implementation of the priority queue that is central to **Prim's Algorithm**. Ordinarily, using a binary heap would be inefficient because of the check in the main loop for whether a particular vertex is a member of the priority queue (an operation not supported by binary heaps). However, the algorithm ensures each vertex is removed from the priority queue only after being processed by the program, thus it maintains a status array inQueue[] that is updated whenever a vertex is extracted from the priority queue. In another implementation optimization, it maintains an external array key[] recording the current priority key for each vertex in the queue, which again eliminates the need to search the priority queue for a given vertex.

Prim's Algorithm randomly selects one of the vertices to be the starting vertex, *s*. When the minimum vertex, *u*, is removed from the priority queue PQ and "added" to the visited set *S*, the algorithm uses existing edges between *S* and the growing spanning tree *T* to reorder the elements in PQ. Recall that the *decreasePriority* operation moves an element closer to the front of PQ.

Example 6-8. Prim's Algorithm implementation with binary heap

```
/** Given undirected graph, compute MST starting from a randomly
 * selected vertex. Encoding of MST is done using 'pred' entries. */
void mst_prim (Graph const &graph, vector<int> &pred) {
  // initialize pred[] and key[] arrays. Start with arbitrary
  // vertex s=0. Priority Queue PQ contains all v in G.
  const int n = graph.numVertices();
  pred.assign (n, -1);
  vector<int> key(n, numeric_limits<int>::max());
  key[0] = 0;
  BinaryHeap pq(n);
  vector<bool> inQueue(n, true);
  for (int v = 0; v < n; v++) {
    pq.insert (v, key[v]);
  }

  while (!pq.isEmpty()) {
    int u = pq.smallest();
    inQueue[u] = false;

    // Process all neighbors of u to find if any edge beats best distance
    for (VertexList::const_iterator ci = graph.begin (u);
         ci != graph.end (u); ++ci) {
      int v = ci->first;
      if (inQueue[v]) {
        int w = ci->second;
        if (w < key[v]) {
          pred[v] = u;
          key[v] = w;
          pq.decreaseKey (v, w);
        }
      }
    }
  }
}
```

Analysis

The initialization phase of **Prim's Algorithm** inserts each vertex into the priority queue (implemented by a binary heap) for a total cost of O(*V log V*). The decrease Key operation in **Prim's Algorithm** requires O(*log q*) performance, where *q* is the number of elements in the queue, which will always be less than *V*. It can be called at most 2*E times since each vertex is removed once from the priority queue and each undirected edge in the graph is visited exactly twice. Thus, the total performance is $O((V + 2*E)*log\ V)$ or $O((V + E)*log\ V)$.

Variations

Kruskal's Algorithm is an alternative to **Prim's Algorithm**. It uses a "disjoint-set" data structure to build up the minimum spanning tree by processing all edges in the graph in order of weight, starting with the edge with the smallest weight and ending with the edge with the largest weight. **Kruskal's Algorithm** can be implemented in $O(E\ log\ V)$. Details on this algorithm can be found in (Cormen et al., 2009).

Final Thoughts on Graphs

In this chapter, we have seen that the algorithms behave differently based on whether a graph is sparse or dense. We will now explore this concept further to analyze the break-even point between sparse and dense graphs and understand the impact on storage requirements.

Storage Issues

When using a two-dimensional adjacency matrix to represent potential relationships among n elements in a set, the matrix requires n^2 elements of storage, yet there are times when the number of relationships is much smaller. In these cases—known as *sparse* graphs—it may be impossible to store large graphs with more than several thousand vertices because of the limitations of computer memory. Additionally, traversing through large matrices to locate the few edges in sparse graphs becomes costly, and this storage representation prevents efficient algorithms from achieving their true potential.

The adjacency representations discussed in this chapter contain the same information. Suppose, however, you were writing a program to compute the cheapest flights between any pair of cities in the world that are served by commercial flights. The weight of an edge would correspond to the cost of the cheapest direct flight between that pair of cities (assuming airlines do not provide incentives by bundling flights). In 2012, Airports Council International (ACI) reported a total of 1,598 airports worldwide in 159 countries, resulting in a two-dimensional matrix with 2,553,604 entries. The question "how many of these entries has a value?" is dependent on the number of direct flights. ACI reported 79 million "aircraft movements" in 2012, roughly translating to a daily average of 215,887 flights. Even if all of these flights represented an actual direct flight between two unique airports (clearly the number of direct flights will be much smaller), this means the matrix is 92% empty—a good example of a sparse matrix!

Graph Analysis

When applying the algorithms in this chapter, the essential factor that determines whether to use an adjacency list or adjacency matrix is whether the graph is sparse. We compute the performance of each algorithm in terms of the number of vertices in the graph, V, and the number of edges in the graph, E. As is common in the literature on algorithms, we simplify the presentation of the formulas that represent best, average, and worst case by using V and E within the big-O notation. Thus, $O(V)$ means a computation requires a number of steps that is directly proportional to the number of vertices in the graph. However, the density of the edges in the graph will also be relevant. Thus, $O(E)$ for a sparse graph is on the order of $O(V)$, whereas for a dense graph it is closer to $O(V^2)$.

As we will see, the performance of some algorithms depends on the structure of the graph; one variation might execute in $O((V + E)^*log\ V)$ time, while another executes in $O(V^2 + E)$ time. Which one is more efficient? Table 6-4 shows that the answer depends on whether the graph G is sparse or dense. For sparse graphs, $O((V + E)^*log\ V)$ is more efficient, whereas for dense graphs $O(V^2 + E)$ is more efficient. The table entry labeled "Break-even graph" identifies the type of graphs for which the expected performance is the same $O(V^2)$ for both sparse and dense graphs; in these graphs, the number of edges is on the order of $O(V^2/log\ v)$.

Table 6-4. Performance comparison of two algorithm variations

Graph type	$O((V + E)^*logV)$	Comparison	$O(V^2 + E)$
Sparse graph: $\|E\|$ is $O(V)$	$O(V\ log\ V)$	is smaller than	$O(V^2)$
Break-even graph: $\|E\|$ is $O(V^2/\log\ V)$	$O(V^2 + V\ log\ v) = O(V^2)$	is equivalent to	$O(V^2 + V^2/log\ V) = O(V^2)$
Dense graph: $\|E\|$ is $O(V^2)$	$O(V^2\ log\ V)$	is larger than	$O(V^2)$

References

Cormen, T. H., C. Leiserson, R. Rivest, and C. Stein, *Introduction to Algorithms*. Third Edition. MIT Press, 2009.

7

Path Finding in AI

To solve a problem when there is no clear computation for a valid solution, we turn to path finding. This chapter covers two related path-finding approaches: one using *game trees* for two-player games and the other using *search trees* for single-player games. These approaches rely on a common structure, namely a state tree whose root node represents the initial state and edges represent potential moves that transform the state into a new state. The searches are challenging because the underlying structure is not computed in its entirety due to the explosion of the number of states. In a game of checkers, for example, there are roughly $5*10^{20}$ different board configurations (Schaeffer, 2007). Thus, the trees over which the search proceeds are constructed on demand as needed. The two path-finding approaches are characterized as follows:

Game tree
> Two players take turns alternating moves that modify the game state from its initial state. There are many states in which either player can win the game. There may also be some "draw" states in which no one wins. A path-finding algorithm maximizes the chance that a player will win or force a draw.

Search tree
> A single player starts from an initial board state and makes valid moves until the desired goal state is reached. A path-finding algorithm identifies the exact sequence of moves that will transform the initial state into the goal state.

Game Trees

The game of tic-tac-toe is played on a 3×3 board where players take turns placing X and O marks on the board. The first player to place three of his marks in a row wins; the game is a draw if no spaces remain and no player has won. In tic-tac-toe there are only 765 unique positions (ignoring reflections and rotations of the board state) and a calculated 26,830 possible games that can be played (Schaeffer, 2002). To see some of the potential games, construct a *game tree*, as shown partially in Figure 7-1, and find a path from player O's current game state (represented as the top node in this tree) to some future game state that ensures either a victory or a draw for player O.

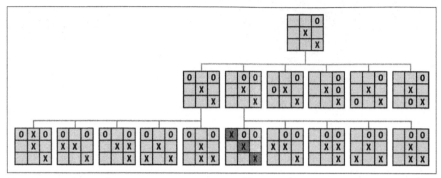

Figure 7-1. Partial game tree given an initial tic-tac-toe game state

A game tree is also known as an AND/OR tree since it is formed by two different types of nodes. The top node is an OR node, because the goal is for player O to select just one of the six available moves in the middle tier. The middle-tier nodes are AND nodes, because the goal (from O's perspective) is to ensure all counter-moves by X (shown as children nodes in the bottom tier) will still lead to either a victory or a draw for O. The game tree in Figure 7-1 is only partially expanded because there are actually 30 different game states in the bottom tier.

In a sophisticated game, the game tree may never be computed fully because of its size. The goal of a path-finding algorithm is to determine from a game state the player's move that maximizes (or even guarantees) his chance of winning the game. We thus transform an intelligent set of player decisions into a *path-finding problem* over the game tree. This approach works for games with small game trees, but it can also scale to solve more complex problems.

The American game of checkers is played on an 8×8 board with an initial set of 24 pieces (12 red and 12 black). For decades, researchers attempted to determine whether the opening player could force a draw or a win. Although it is difficult to compute exactly, the size of the game tree must be incredibly large. After nearly 18 years of computations (sometimes on as many as 200 computers), researchers at the University of Alberta, Canada, demonstrated that perfect play by both players leads to a draw (Schaeffer, 2007).

Path finding in artificial intelligence (AI) provides specific algorithms to tackle incredibly complex problems if they can be translated into a combinatorial game of alternating players. Early researchers in AI (Shannon, 1950) considered the challenge of building a chess-playing machine and developed two types of approaches for search problems that continue to define the state of the practice today:

Type A

Consider the various allowed moves for both players a fixed set of turns into the future, and determine the most favorable position that results for the original player. Then, select the initial move that makes progress in that direction.

Type B

Add some adaptive decision based on knowledge of the game rather than static evaluation functions. More explicitly, (a) evaluate promising positions as far ahead as necessary to find a stable position where the board evaluation truly reflects the strength of the resulting position, and (b) select appropriate available moves. This approach tries to prevent pointless possibilities from consuming precious time.

In this chapter, we describe the family of Type A algorithms that provides a general-purpose approach for searching a game tree to find the best move for a player in a two-player game. These algorithms include **Minimax**, **AlphaBeta**, and **NegMax**.

The algorithms discussed in this chapter become unnecessarily complicated if the underlying information is poorly modeled. Many of the examples in textbooks or on the Internet naturally describe these algorithms in the context of a particular game. However, it may be difficult to separate the arbitrary way in which the game is represented from the essential elements of these algorithms. For this reason, we intentionally designed a set of object-oriented interfaces to maintain a clean separation between the algorithms and the games. We'll now briefly summarize the core interfaces in our implementation of game trees, which are illustrated in Figure 7-2.

The IGameState interface abstracts the essential concepts needed to conduct searches over a game state. It defines how to:

Interpret the game state

isDraw() determines whether the game concludes with neither player winning; isWin() determines whether the game is won.

Manage the game state

copy() returns an identical copy of the game state so moves can be applied without updating the original game state; equivalent(IGameState) determines whether two game state positions are equal.

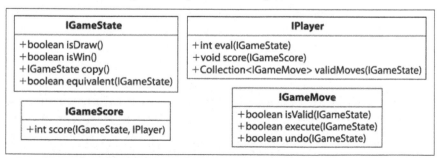

Figure 7-2. Core interfaces for game-tree algorithms

The IPlayer interface abstracts the abilities of a player to manipulate the game state. It defines how to:

Evaluate a board
> eval(IGameState) returns an integer evaluating the game state from the player's perspective; score(IGameScore) sets the scoring computation the player uses to evaluate a game state.

Generate valid moves
> validMoves(IGameState) returns a collection of available moves given the game state.

The IGameMove interface defines how moves manipulate the game state. The move classes are problem-specific, and the search algorithm need not be aware of their specific implementation. IGameScore defines the interface for scoring states.

From a programming perspective, the heart of the path-finding algorithm for a game tree is an implementation of the IEvaluation interface shown in Example 7-1.

Example 7-1. Common interface for game-tree path finding

```
/**
 * For game state, player and opponent, return the best move
 * for player. If no move is even available, null is returned.
 */
public interface IEvaluation {
  IGameMove bestMove(IGameState state, IPlayer player, IPlayer opponent);
}
```

Given a node representing the current game state, the algorithm computes the best move for a player assuming the opponent will play a perfect game in return.

Static Evaluation Functions

There are several ways to add intelligence to the search (Barr and Feigenbaum, 1981):

Select the order and number of allowed moves to be applied
> When considering available moves at a game state, we should first evaluate the moves that are likely to lead to a successful outcome. In addition, we might discard specific moves that do not seem to lead to a successful outcome.

Select game states to "prune" from the search tree
> As the search progresses, new knowledge may be discovered that can be used to eliminate game states that had (at one time) been selected to be part of the search.

The most common approach is to define *static evaluation functions* to evaluate the game state at intermediate points in the computation, and then order the set of

---

available moves so that moves with a higher probability of leading to a solution are tried first. However, poor evaluation functions can prevent path-finding algorithms from selecting the best moves to make. As the saying goes, "garbage in, garbage out."

A static evaluation function must take into account various features of the game-tree position to return an integer score that reflects the relative strength of the position from a player's perspective. For example, the first successful program to play checkers, developed by Arthur Samuel (1959), evaluated board positions by considering two dozen features of a game, such as the "piece advantage feature" (comparing the number of pieces a player has versus her opponent) and a "winning trade feature" (trading pieces when winning but not when losing). Clearly, a more accurate evaluation function makes the game-solving engine a better player.

In this chapter, we use the BoardEvaluation scoring function for tic-tac-toe, which was defined by Nil Nilsson (1971). Let $nc(gs, p)$ be the number of rows, columns, or diagonals on a tic-tac-toe game state, gs, in which player p may still get three in a row. We then define $score(gs, p)$ to be:

- $+\infty$ if player p has won the game in game state gs
- $-\infty$ if the opponent of player p has won the game in game state gs
- $nc(gs, p) - nc(gs, opponent)$ if neither player has won the game in game state gs

Instead of restricting the evaluation to the current game state, an evaluation function could temporarily expand that state a fixed number of moves and select the move that may ultimately lead to a game state with maximum benefit to the player. This is frowned upon in practice because of (a) the cost in performing the operations, and (b) the sharing of code logic between the evaluation function and the search function, which breaks the clean separation between them.

Path-Finding Concepts

The following concepts apply to both two-player game trees and single-player search trees.

Representing State

Each node in a game or search tree contains all state information known at that position in the game. For example, in chess, the king can "castle" with the rook only if (a) neither piece has yet moved, (b) the intervening squares are empty and not currently attacked by an enemy piece, and (c) the king is not currently in check. Note that (b) and (c) can be computed directly from the board state and therefore do not need to be stored; however, the board state must separately store whether the king or rooks have moved.

For games with exponentially large trees, the state must be stored as compactly as possible. If symmetries exist in the state, such as with Connect Four, Othello, or the 15-puzzle, the tree can be greatly reduced by eliminating identical states that may simply be rotated or reflected. More complex representations called *bitboards* have been used for chess, checkers, or Othello to manage the incredibly large number of states with impressive efficiency gains (Pepicelli, 2005).

Calculating Available Moves

To find the best move, it must be possible at each state to compute the available moves allowed to the player making the move. The term *branching factor* refers to the total number of moves that are allowed at any individual state. The original 3×3 Rubik's Cube has (on average) a branching factor of 13.5 (Korf, 1985). The popular children's game Connect Four has a branching factor of 7 for most of the game. Checkers is more complicated because of the rule that a player must capture a piece if that move is available. Based on analyzing a large number of checkers databases, the branching factor for capture positions is 1.20, whereas for noncapture positions it is 7.94; Schaeffer (2008) computes the average branching factor in Checkers to be 6.14. The game of Go has an initial branching factor of 361 because it is played on a 19×19 board.

Algorithms are sensitive to the order by which the available moves are attempted. When the branching factor for a game is high but the moves are not properly ordered based on some evaluative measure of success, blindly searching a tree is inefficient.

Maximum Expansion Depth

Because of limited memory resources, some search algorithms limit the extent to which they expand the search and game trees. This approach has its weaknesses in games where a sequence of moves forms a calculated strategy. In chess, for example, a piece is often sacrificed for a potential advantage; if the sacrifice occurs at the edge of the maximum expansion, the advantageous game state would not be found. A fixed expansion depth leaves a "horizon" beyond which the search cannot see, often to the detriment of the success of the search. For single-player games, fixing the maximum depth means the algorithm will not find the solution that lies just beyond the horizon.

Minimax

Given a specific position in a game tree from the perspective of an initial player, a search program must find a move that leads to the greatest chance of victory (or at least a draw). Instead of considering only the current game state and the available moves at that state, the program must consider any countermoves that its opponent will make after it makes each move. The program assumes there is an evaluation function score(state, player) that returns an integer representing the score of the game state from player's perspective; lower integer numbers (which may be negative) reflect weaker positions.

The game tree is expanded by considering future game states after a sequence of n moves have been made. Each level of the tree alternates between *MAX* levels (where

---

the goal is to benefit the original player by maximizing the evaluated score of a game state) and *MIN* levels (where the goal is to benefit the opponent by minimizing the evaluated score of a game state). At alternating levels, then, the program selects a move that maximizes `score(state, initial)`, but when the opponent is making its move, the program assumes the opponent will select a move that minimizes `score(state, initial)`.

Of course, the program can look ahead only a finite number of moves because the game tree is potentially infinite. The number of moves chosen to look ahead is called the *ply*. The trade-off is to select a suitable ply that leads to a search exploration that completes in reasonable time.

The following pseudocode illustrates the **Minimax** algorithm.

Minimax Summary

Best, Average, Worst: $O(b^{ply})$

```
bestmove (s, player, opponent)
  original = player ❶
  [move, score] = minimax (s, ply, player, opponent)
  return move
end

minimax (s, ply, player, opponent)
  best = [null, null]
  if ply is 0 or there are no valid moves then ❷
    score = evaluate s for original player
    return [null, score]

  foreach valid move m for player in state s do
    execute move m on s
    [move, score] = minimax(s, ply-1, opponent, player) ❸
    undo move m on s
    if player is original then ❹
      if score > best.score then best = [m, score]
    else
      if score < best.score then best = [m, score]
  return best
end
```

❶ Remember original player since evaluation is always from that player's perspective.

❷ If no more moves remain, player might have won (or lost), which is equivalent to reaching target ply depth.

❸ With each recursive call, swap player and opponent to reflect alternating turns.

❹ Successive levels alternate between MAX or MIN.

Figure 7-3 shows an evaluation of a move using **Minimax** with ply depth of 3. The bottom row of the game tree contains the five possible game states that result after the player makes a move, the opponent responds, and then the player makes a move. Each of these game states is evaluated from the point of view of the original player, and the integer rating is shown in each node. The *MAX* second row from the bottom contains internal nodes whose scores are the maximum of their respective children. From the point of view of the original player, these represent the best scores he can attain. However, the *MIN* third row from the bottom represents the worst positions the opponent can force on the player, thus its scores are the minimum of its children. As you can see, each level alternates between selecting the maximum and minimum of its children. The final score demonstrates that the original player can force the opponent into a game state that evaluates to *3*.

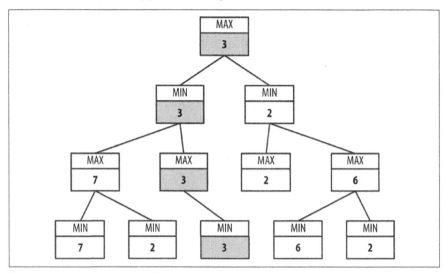

Figure 7-3. Minimax sample game tree

Input/Output

Minimax looks ahead a fixed number of moves, which is called the *ply depth*.

Minimax returns a move from among the valid moves that leads to the best future game state for a specific player, as determined by the evaluation function.

Context

Evaluating the game state is complex, and we must resort to heuristic evaluations to determine the better game state. Indeed, developing effective evaluation functions for games such as chess, checkers, or Othello is the greatest challenge in designing intelligent programs. We assume these evaluation functions are available.

The size of the game tree is determined by the number of available moves, *b*, at each game state. For most games, we can only estimate the value of *b*. For tic-tac-toe (and other games such as Nine Men's Morris) there are *b* available moves in the initial empty game state, and each move takes away a potential move from the opponent. If the ply depth is *d*, the number of game states checked for tic-tac-toe is

$$\sum_{i=1}^{d} \frac{b!}{(b-i)!}$$

where $b!$ is the factorial of *b*. To give an example of the scale involved, **Minimax** evaluates 187,300 states when $b = 10$ and $d = 6$.

During the recursive invocation within **Minimax**, the score(state, player) evaluation function must be consistently applied using the *original player* for whom a move is being calculated. This coordinates the minimum and maximum recursive evaluations.

Solution

The helper class MoveEvaluation pairs together an IMove and an int evaluation to be associated with that move. **Minimax** explores to a fixed ply depth, or when a game state has no valid moves for a player. The Java code in Example 7-2 returns the best move for a player in a given game state.

Example 7-2. Minimax implementation

```
public class MinimaxEvaluation implements IEvaluation {
  IGameState state;      /** State to be modified during search. */
  int ply;               /** Ply depth. How far to continue search. */
  IPlayer original;      /** Evaluate all states from this perspective. */

  public MinimaxEvaluation (int ply) {
    this.ply = ply;
  }

  public IGameMove bestMove (IGameState s,
                             IPlayer player, IPlayer opponent) {
    this.original = player;
    this.state = s.copy();

    MoveEvaluation me = minimax(ply, IComparator.MAX,
                                player, opponent);
    return me.move;
  }

  MoveEvaluation minimax (int ply, IComparator comp,
                          IPlayer player, IPlayer opponent) {

    // If no allowed moves or a leaf node, return game state score.
    Iterator<IGameMove> it = player.validMoves (state).iterator();
    if (ply == 0 || !it.hasNext()) {
```

```
      return new MoveEvaluation (original.eval (state));
    }

    // Try to improve on this lower bound (based on selector).
    MoveEvaluation best = new MoveEvaluation (comp.initialValue());

    // Generate game states resulting from valid moves for player
    while (it.hasNext()) {
      IGameMove move = it.next();
      move.execute(state);

      // Recursively evaluate position. Compute Minimax and swap
      // player and opponent, synchronously with MIN and MAX.
      MoveEvaluation me = minimax (ply-1, comp.opposite(),
                                   opponent, player);
      move.undo(state);

      // Select maximum (minimum) of children if we are MAX (MIN)
      if (comp.compare (best.score, me.score) < 0) {
        best = new MoveEvaluation (move, me.score);
      }
    }
    return best;
  }
}
```

The *MAX* and *MIN* selectors evaluate scores to properly select the maximum or minimum score as desired. This implementation is simplified by defining an IComparator interface, shown in Figure 7-4, that defines *MAX* and *MIN* and consolidates how they select the best move from their perspective. Switching between the *MAX* and *MIN* selector is done using the opposite() method. The worst score for each of these comparators is returned by initialValue().

Minimax can rapidly become overwhelmed by the sheer number of game states generated during the recursive search. In chess, where the average number of moves on a board is 30 (Laramée, 2000), looking ahead just five moves (i.e., $b = 30$, $d = 5$) requires evaluating up to 25,137,931 board positions, as determined by the expression:

$$\sum_{i=0}^{d} b^i$$

Minimax can take advantage of symmetries in the game state, such as rotations or reflections of the board, by caching past states viewed (and their respective scores), but the savings are game-specific.

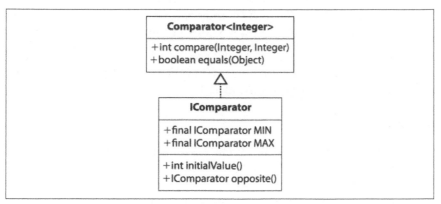

Figure 7-4. IComparator interface abstracts MAX and MIN operators

Figure 7-5 contains a two-ply exploration of an initial tic-tac-toe game state for player O using **Minimax**. The alternating levels of *MAX* and *MIN* show how the first move from the left—placing an O in the upper-left corner—is the only move that averts an immediate loss. Note that all possible game states are expanded, even when it becomes clear the opponent X can secure a win if O makes a poor move choice.

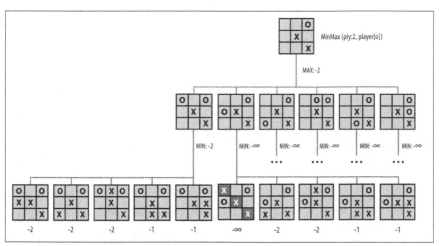

Figure 7-5. Sample Minimax exploration

Analysis

When there is a fixed number b of moves at each game state (or even when the number of available moves reduces by one with each level), the total number of game states searched in a d-ply **Minimax** is $O(b^d)$, demonstrating exponential growth. The ply-depth restriction can be eliminated if the game tree is small enough to be completely evaluated in an acceptable amount of time.

Given the results of Figure 7-5, is there some way to eliminate exploring useless game states? Because we assume the player and opponent make no mistakes, we need to find a way to stop expanding the game tree once the algorithm determines that an entire subtree is worthless to explore further. **AlphaBeta** properly implements this capability; we first explain how to simplify the alternating *MAX* and *MIN* levels of the game tree with the **NegMax** algorithm.

NegMax

NegMax replaces the alternative *MAX* and *MIN* levels of **Minimax** with a single approach used at each level of the game tree. It also forms the basis of the **Alpha-Beta** algorithm presented next.

In **Minimax**, the game state is always evaluated from the perspective of the player making the initial move (which requires the evaluation function to store this information). The game tree is thus composed of alternating levels that maximize the score of children nodes (when the original player) or minimize the score of children nodes (when the opponent). Instead, **NegMax** consistently seeks the move that produces the maximum of the negative values of a state's children nodes.

NegMax Summary

Best, Average, Worst: $O(b^{ply})$

```
bestmove (s, player, opponent)
  [move, score] = negmax (s, ply, player, opponent)
  return move
end

negmax (s, ply, player, opponent)
  best = [null, null]
  if ply is 0 or there are no valid moves then
    score = evaluate s for player
    return [null, score]

  foreach valid move m for player in state s do
    execute move m on s
    [move, score] = negmax (s, ply-1, opponent, player) ❶
    undo move m on s
    if -score > best.score then best = [m, -score] ❷
  return best
end
```

❶   **NegMax** swaps players with each successive level.

❷   Choose largest of the negative scores of its children.

Intuitively, after a player has made its move, the opponent will try to make its best move; thus, to find the best move for a player, select the one that restricts the oppo-

---

nent from scoring too highly. If you compare the pseudocode examples, you will see that **Minimax** and **NegMax** produce two game trees with identical structure; the only difference is how the game states are scored.

The structure of the **NegMax** game tree is identical to the **Minimax** game tree because it finds the exact same move; the only difference is that the values in levels previously labeled as *MIN* are negated in **NegMax**. If you compare the tree in Figure 7-6 with Figure 7-3, you see this behavior.

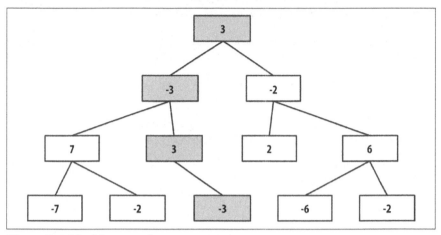

Figure 7-6. NegMax sample game tree

Solution

In Example 7-3, note that the score for each MoveEvaluation is simply the evaluation of the game state from the perspective of the player making that move. Reorienting each evaluation toward the player making the move simplifies the algorithm implementation.

Example 7-3. NegMax implementation

```
public class NegMaxEvaluation implements IEvaluation {
  IGameState state;        /** State to be modified during search. */
  int ply;                 /** Ply depth. How far to continue search. */
  public NegMaxEvaluation (int ply) {
    this.ply = ply;
  }

  public IGameMove bestMove (IGameState s, IPlayer player, IPlayer opponent)
  {
    state = s.copy();
    MoveEvaluation me = negmax (ply, player, opponent);
    return me.move;
  }
}
```

```
public MoveEvaluation negmax (int ply, IPlayer player, IPlayer opponent)
{
    // If no allowed moves or a leaf node, return board state score.
    Iterator<IGameMove> it = player.validMoves (state).iterator();
    if (ply == 0 || !it.hasNext()) {
        return new MoveEvaluation (player.eval (state));
    }

    // Try to improve on this lower-bound move.
    MoveEvaluation best = new MoveEvaluation (MoveEvaluation.minimum());

    // get moves for this player and generate the boards that result from
    // these moves. Select maximum of the negative scores of children.
    while (it.hasNext()) {
      IGameMove move = it.next();
      move.execute (state);

      // Recursively evaluate position using consistent negmax.
      MoveEvaluation me = negmax (ply-1, opponent, player);
      move.undo (state);
      if (-me.score > best.score) {
        best = new MoveEvaluation (move, -me.score);
      }
    }
    return best;
  }
}
```

NegMax is useful because it prepares a simple foundation on which to extend to **AlphaBeta**. Because board scores are routinely negated in this algorithm, we must carefully choose values that represent winning and losing states. Specifically, the minimum value must be the negated value of the maximum value. Note that Integer.MIN_VALUE (defined in Java as 0x80000000 or −2,147,483,648) is not the negated value of Integer.MAX_VALUE (in Java, defined as 0x7fffffff or 2,147,483,647). For this reason, we use Integer.MIN_VALUE+1 as the minimum value, which is retrieved by the static function MoveEvaluation.minimum(). For completeness, we provide MoveEvaluation.maximum() as well.

Figure 7-7 contains a two-ply exploration of an initial tic-tac-toe game state for player O using **NegMax**. **NegMax** expands all possible game states, even when it becomes clear the opponent X can secure a win if O makes a poor move. The scores associated with each of the leaf game states are evaluated from that player's perspective (in this case, the original player O). The score for the initial game state is −2, because that is the "maximum of the negative scores of its children."

Analysis

The number of states explored by **NegMax** is the same as **Minimax**, on the order of b^d for a d-ply search with fixed number b of moves at each game state. In all other respects, it performs identically to **Minimax**.

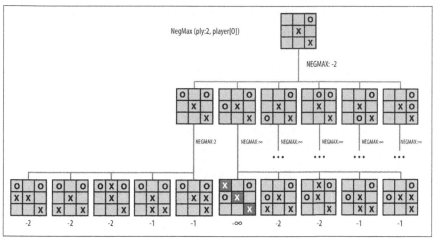

Figure 7-7. Sample NegMax exploration

AlphaBeta

Minimax evaluates a player's best move when considering the opponent's counter-moves, but this information is not used while the game tree is generated! Consider the BoardEvaluation scoring function introduced earlier. Recall Figure 7-5, which shows the partial expansion of the game tree from an initial game state after X has made two moves and O has made just one move.

Note how **Minimax** plods along even though each subsequent search reveals a losing board if X is able to complete the diagonal. A total of 36 nodes are evaluated. **Minimax** takes no advantage of the fact that the original decision for O to play in the upper-left corner prevented X from scoring an immediate victory. **AlphaBeta** defines a consistent strategy to prune unproductive searches from the search tree.

After evaluating the sub game tree rooted at (1) in Figure 7-8, **AlphaBeta** knows that if this move is made the opponent cannot force a worse position than -3, which means the best the player can do is score a 3. When **AlphaBeta** gets to the game state (2), the first child game state (3) evaluates to 2. This means that if the move for (2) is selected, the opponent can force the player into a game state that is less than the best move found so far (i.e., 3). There is no need to check the sibling subtree rooted at (4), so it is pruned away.

Using **AlphaBeta**, the equivalent expansion of the game tree is shown in Figure 7-9.

As **AlphaBeta** searches for the best move in Figure 7-9, it remembers that X can score no higher than 2 if O plays in the upper-left corner. For each subsequent other move for O, **AlphaBeta** determines that X has at least one countermove that outperforms the first move for O (indeed, in all cases X can win). Thus, the game tree expands only 16 nodes, a savings of more than 50% from **Minimax**. **AlphaBeta** selects the same move that **Minimax** would have selected, with potentially significant performance savings.

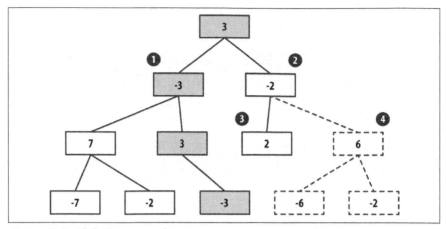

Figure 7-8. AlphaBeta sample game tree

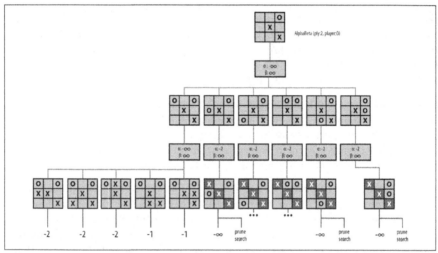

Figure 7-9. AlphaBeta two-ply search

AlphaBeta recursively searches through the game tree and maintains two values, α and β, which define a "window of opportunity" for a player as long as $\alpha < \beta$. The value α represents the lower bound of the game states found for the player so far (or $-\infty$ if none have been found) and declares that the player has found a move to ensure it can score at least that value. Higher values of α mean the player is doing well; when $\alpha = +\infty$, the player has won and the search can terminate.

The value β represents the upper bound of game states so far (or $+\infty$ if none have been found) and declares the maximum value the player can achieve. When β drops lower and lower, the opponent is doing better at restricting the player's options. Since **AlphaBeta** has a maximum ply depth beyond which it will not search, any decisions it makes are limited to this scope.

AlphaBeta Summary

Best, Average: $O(b^{ply/2})$ **Worst:** $O(b^{ply})$

```
bestmove (s, player, opponent)
  [move, score] = alphaBeta (s, ply, player, opponent, -∞, ∞)  ❶
  return move
end

alphaBeta (s, ply, player, opponent, low, high)
  best = [null, null]
  if ply is 0 or there are no valid moves then  ❷
    score = evaluate s for player
    return [null, score]

  foreach valid move m for player in state s do
    execute move m on s
    [move, score] = alphaBeta (s, ply-1, opponent, player, -high, -low)
    undo move m on s
    if -score > best.score then
      low = -score
      best = [m, -low]
    if low ≥ high then return best  ❸
  return best
end
```

❶ At start, worst player can do is lose (*low* = –∞). Best player can do is win (*high* = +∞).

❷ **AlphaBeta** evaluates leaf nodes as in **NegMax**.

❸ Stop exploring sibling nodes when worst score possible by opponent equals or exceeds our maximum threshold.

The game tree in Figure 7-9 shows the [α, β] values as **AlphaBeta** executes; initially they are [–∞, ∞]. With a two-ply search, **AlphaBeta** is trying to find the best move for O when considering just the immediate countermove for X.

Because **AlphaBeta** is recursive, we can retrace its progress by considering a traversal of the game tree. The first move **AlphaBeta** considers is for O to play in the upper-left corner. After all five of X's countermoves are evaluated, it is evident that X can ensure only a score of –2 for itself (using the static evaluation BoardEvaluation for tic-tac-toe). When **AlphaBeta** considers the second move for O (playing in the middle of the left column), its [α, β] values are now [–2, ∞], which means "the worst that O can end up with so far is a state whose score is –2, and the best that O can do is still win the game." When the first countermove for X is evaluated, **AlphaBeta** detects that X has won, which falls outside of this "window of opportunity," so further countermoves by X no longer need to be considered.

To explain how **AlphaBeta** prunes the game tree to eliminate nonproductive nodes, Figure 7-10 presents a three-ply search of Figure 7-5 that expands 66 nodes (whereas the corresponding **Minimax** game tree would require 156 nodes).

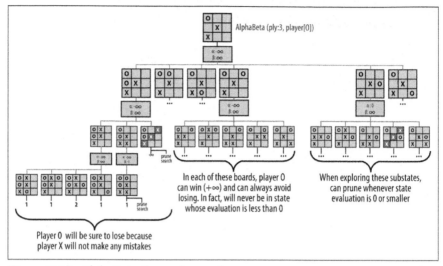

Figure 7-10. AlphaBeta three-ply search

At the initial node *n* in the game tree, player O must consider one of six potential moves. Pruning can occur on either the player's turn or the opponent's turn. In the search shown in Figure 7-10, there are two such examples:

Player's turn

Assume O plays in the middle of the left column and X responds by playing in the middle of the top row (this is the leftmost grandchild of the root node in the search tree). From O's perspective, the best score that O can force is −1 (note that in the diagram the scores are shown as 1 because **AlphaBeta** uses the same scoring mechanism used by **NegMax**). This value is remembered when it tries to determine what O can achieve if X had instead countered by playing in the middle of the bottom row. Note that [α, β] is now [−∞, −1]. **AlphaBeta** evaluates the result when O plays in the middle of the top row and computes the score 1. Because this value is greater than or equal to the −1 value, the remaining three potential moves for O in this level are ignored.

Opponent's turn

Assume O plays in the middle of the left column and X responds by playing in the upper-right corner, immediately winning the game. **AlphaBeta** can ignore X's two other potential moves, because O will prune the remaining nodes in the search subtree "rooted" in the decision to play in the middle of the left column.

The pruning of the search occurs when α ≥ β, or in other words, when the "window of opportunity" closes. When **AlphaBeta** is based on **Minimax**, there are two ways to prune the search, known as α-prune and β-prune; in the simpler **AlphaBeta** based on **NegMax**, these two cases are combined into the one discussed here. Because **AlphaBeta** is recursive, the range [α, β] represents the window of opportunity for the player, and the window of opportunity for the opponent is [–β, –α]. Within the recursive invocation of **AlphaBeta** the player and opponent are swapped, and the window is similarly swapped.

Solution

The **AlphaBeta** implementation in Example 7-4 augments **NegMax** by terminating early the evaluation of game states once it becomes clear that either the player can't guarantee a better position (an α-prune) or the opponent can't force a worse position (a β-prune).

Example 7-4. AlphaBeta implementation

```
public class AlphaBetaEvaluation implements IEvaluation {
  IGameState state;    /** State to be modified during search. */
  int ply;             /** Ply depth. How far to continue search. */

  public AlphaBetaEvaluation (int ply) { this.ply = ply; }
  public IGameMove bestMove (IGameState s,
                             IPlayer player, IPlayer opponent) {
    state = s.copy();
    MoveEvaluation me = alphabeta (ply, player, opponent,
                                   MoveEvaluation.minimum(),
                                   MoveEvaluation.maximum());
    return me.move;
  }

  MoveEvaluation alphabeta (int ply, IPlayer player, IPlayer opponent,
                            int alpha, int beta) {
    // If no moves, return board evaluation from player's perspective.
    Iterator<IGameMove> it = player.validMoves (state).iterator();
    if (ply == 0 || !it.hasNext()) {
      return new MoveEvaluation (player.eval (state));
    }
    // Select "maximum of negative value of children" that improves alpha
    MoveEvaluation best = new MoveEvaluation (alpha);
    while (it.hasNext()) {
      IGameMove move = it.next();

      move.execute (state);
      MoveEvaluation me = alphabeta (ply-1,opponent,player,-beta,-alpha);
      move.undo (state);
      // If improved upon alpha, keep track of this move.
      if (-me.score > alpha) {
        alpha = -me.score;
```

```
        best = new MoveEvaluation (move, alpha);
      }
      if (alpha >= beta) { return best; } // search no longer productive.
    }
    return best;
  }
}
```

The moves found will be exactly the same as those found by **Minimax**. But because many states are removed from the game tree as it is expanded, execution time is noticeably less for **AlphaBeta**.

Analysis

To measure the benefit of **AlphaBeta** over **NegMax**, we compare the size of their respective game trees. This task is complicated because **AlphaBeta** will show its most impressive savings if the opponent's best move is evaluated first whenever **AlphaBeta** executes. When there is a fixed number b of moves at each game state, the total number of potential game states to search in a d-ply **AlphaBeta** is on the order of b^d. If the moves are ordered by decreasing favorability (i.e., the best move first), we still have to evaluate all b children for the initiating player (because we are to choose his best move); however, in the best case we need to evaluate only the first move by the opponent. Note in Figure 7-9 that, because of move ordering, the prune occurs after several moves have been evaluated, so the move ordering for that game tree is not optimal.

In the best case, therefore, **AlphaBeta** evaluates b game states for the initial player on each level, but only one game state for the opponent. So, instead of expanding $b*b*b* \ldots *b*b$ (a total of d times) game states on the dth level of the game tree, **AlphaBeta** may require only $b*1*b*\ldots*b*1$ (a total of d times). The resulting number of game states is $b^{d/2}$, an impressive savings.

Instead of simply trying to minimize the number of game states, **AlphaBeta** could explore the same total number of game states as **Minimax**. This would extend the depth of the game tree to $2*d$, thus doubling how far ahead the algorithm can look.

To empirically evaluate **Minimax** and **AlphaBeta**, we construct a set of initial tic-tac-toe board states that are possible after k moves have been made. We then compute **Minimax** and **AlphaBeta** with a ply of $9 - k$, which ensures all possible moves are explored. The results are shown in Table 7-1. Observe the significant reduction of explored states using **AlphaBeta**.

Table 7-1. Statistics comparing Minimax versus AlphaBeta

Ply	Minimax states	AlphaBeta states	Aggregate reduction
6	549,864	112,086	80%
7	549,936	47,508	91%
8	549,945	27,565	95%

Individual comparisons show the dramatic improvement of **AlphaBeta**; some of these cases explain why **AlphaBeta** is so powerful. For the game state shown in Figure 7-11, **AlphaBeta** explores only 450 game states (instead of 8,232 for **Minimax**, a 94.5% reduction) to determine that player X should select the center square, after which a win is assured.

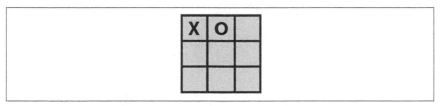

Figure 7-11. Sample tic-tac-toe board after two plays

However, the only way to achieve such deep reductions is if the available moves are ordered such that the best move appears first. Because our tic-tac-toe solution does not order moves in this fashion, some anomalies will result. For example, given the same board state rotated 180 degrees (Figure 7-12), **AlphaBeta** will explore 960 game states (an 88.3% reduction) because it expands the game tree using a different ordering of valid moves. For this reason, search algorithms often reorder moves using a static evaluation function to reduce the size of the game tree.

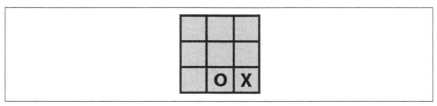

Figure 7-12. Sample tic-tac-toe board after two plays, rotated

Search Trees

Games that have just one player are similar to game trees, featuring an initial state (the top node in the search tree) and a sequence of moves that transforms the board state until a goal state is reached. A *search tree* represents the set of intermediate board states as a path-finding algorithm progresses. The computed structure is a tree because the algorithm ensures it does not visit a board state twice. The algorithm decides the order of board states to visit as it attempts to reach the goal.

We'll explore search trees using an 8-puzzle, which is played on a 3×3 grid containing eight square tiles numbered 1 to 8 and an empty space that contains no tile. A tile adjacent (either horizontally or vertically) to the empty space can be moved by sliding it into the empty space. The aim is to start from a shuffled initial state and move tiles to achieve the goal state. The eight-move solution in Figure 7-13 is recorded as the bold path from the initial node to the goal node.

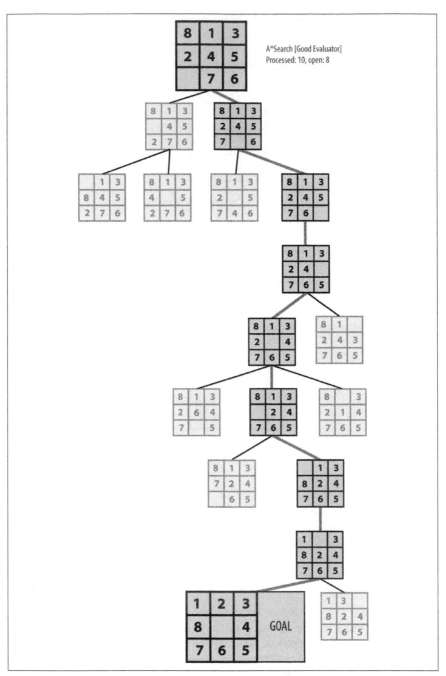

Figure 7-13. Sample 8-puzzle search

Search trees can rapidly explode to contain (potentially) billions or trillions of states. The algorithms in this chapter describe how to efficiently search through these trees more rapidly than using a blind search. To describe the inherent complexity of the problem, we introduce **Depth-First Search** and **Breadth-First Search** as two potential approaches to path-finding algorithms. We then present the powerful **A*Search** algorithm for finding a minimal-cost solution (under certain conditions). We'll now briefly summarize the core classes, illustrated in Figure 7-14, that will be used when discussing search tree algorithms.

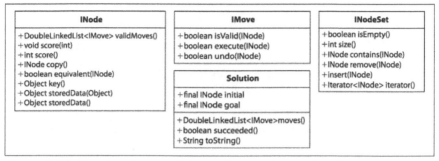

Figure 7-14. Core interfaces and classes for search-tree algorithms

The INode interface abstracts the essential concepts needed to conduct searches over a board state:

Generate valid moves
validMoves() returns a list of available moves for a board state.

Evaluate the board state
score(int) associates an integer score with the board state, representing the result of an evaluation function; score() returns the evaluation result previously associated with the board state.

Manage the board state
copy() returns an identical copy of the board state (except for the optional stored data); equivalent(INode) determines whether two board states are equal (sophisticated implementations may detect rotational symmetries in the board state or other means for equivalence). key() returns an object to support an equivalence check: if two board states have the same key() result, the board states are equivalent.

Managing optional board state data
storedData(Object o) associates the given object with the board state to be used by search algorithms; storedData() returns the optionally stored data that may be associated with the board state.

The INodeSet interface abstracts the underlying implementation of a set of INodes. Some algorithms require a queue of INode objects, some a stack, and others a balanced binary tree. Once properly constructed (using the StateStorageFactory

Path
Finding in
AI

class), the provided operations enable algorithms to manipulate the state of the INode set no matter the underlying data structure used. The IMove interface defines how moves can manipulate the board state; the specific move classes are problem-specific, and the search algorithm need not be aware of their specific implementation.

From a programming perspective, the heart of the path-finding algorithm for a search tree is the implementation of the ISearch interface shown in Example 7-5. Given such a solution, the moves that produced the solution can be extracted.

Example 7-5. Common interface for search-tree path finding

```
/**
 * Given an initial state, return a Solution to the final
 * state, or null if no such path can be found.
 */
public interface ISearch {
  Solution search (INode initial, INode goal);
}
```

Given a node representing the initial board state and a desired goal node, an ISearch implementation computes a path representing a solution, or returns null if no solution was found. To differentiate from game trees, we use the term *board state* when discussing search tree nodes.

Path-Length Heuristic Functions

A blind-search algorithm uses a fixed strategy rather than evaluating the board state. A *depth-first* blind search simply plays the game forward by arbitrarily choosing the next move from available choices in that board state, backtracking when it hits its maximum expansion depth. A *breadth-first* blind search methodically explores all possible solutions with k moves before first attempting any solution with $k + 1$ moves. Surely there must be a way to guide the search based on the characteristics of the board states being investigated, right?

The discussion of **A*Search** will show searches over the 8-puzzle using different *heuristic functions*. These heuristic functions do not play the game, rather they estimate the number of remaining moves to a goal state from a given board state and can be used to direct the path-finding search. For example, in the 8-puzzle, such a function would evaluate for each tile in the board state the number of moves to position it in its proper location in the goal state. Most of the difficulty in path finding is crafting effective heuristic functions.

Depth-First Search

Depth-First Search attempts to locate a path to the goal state by making as much forward progress as possible. Because some search trees explore a high number of board states, **Depth-First Search** is practical only if a maximum search depth is fixed in advance. Furthermore, loops must be avoided by remembering each state and ensuring it is visited only once.

Depth-First Search Summary

Best: $O(b^*d)$ **Average, Worst:** $O(b^d)$

```
search (initial, goal, maxDepth)
  if initial = goal then return "Solution"
  initial.depth = 0
  open = new Stack ❶
  closed = new Set
  insert (open, copy(initial))

  while open is not empty do
    n = pop (open) ❷
    insert (closed, n)
    foreach valid move m at n do
      nextState = state when playing m at n
      if closed doesn't contain nextState then
        nextState.depth = n.depth + 1 ❸
        if nextState = goal then return "Solution"
        if nextState.depth < maxDepth then
          insert (open, nextState) ❹

  return "No Solution"
end
```

❶ **Depth-First Search** uses a Stack to store open states to be visited.

❷ Pop the most recent state from the stack.

❸ **Depth-First Search** computes the depth to avoid exceeding *maxDepth*.

❹ Inserting the next state will be a push operation since *open* is a stack.

Depth-First Search maintains a stack of *open* board states that have yet to be visited and a set of *closed* board states that have been visited. At each iteration, **Depth-First Search** pops from the stack an unvisited board state and expands it to compute the set of successor board states given the available valid moves. The search terminates if the goal state is reached. Any successor board states that already exist within the *closed* set are discarded. The remaining unvisited board states are pushed onto the stack of *open* board states and the search continues.

Figure 7-15 shows the computed search tree for an initial 8-puzzle board state using a depth limit of 9. Note how a path of 8 moves is found to the solution (marked as GOAL) after some exploration to depth 9 in other areas of the tree. In all, 50 board states were processed and 4 remain to be explored (shown in light gray). Thus, we have solved the puzzle in this case, but we cannot be sure we have found the best (shortest) solution.

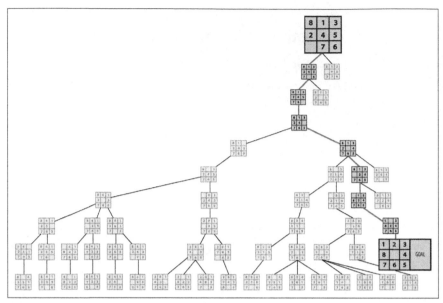

Figure 7-15. Sample Depth-First Search tree for 8-puzzle

Input/Output

The algorithm starts from an initial board state and seeks a goal state. It returns a sequence of moves that represents a path from the initial state to the goal state (or declares that no such solution was found).

Context

Depth-First Search is a blind search that is made practical by restricting the search to stop after a fixed depth bound, *maxDepth*, is reached, which helps manage memory resources.

Solution

Depth-First Search stores the set of *open* (i.e., yet to be visited) board states in a stack, and retrieves them one at a time for processing. In the implementation shown in Example 7-6, the *closed* set is stored in a hash table to efficiently determine when not to revisit a board state previously encountered within the search tree; the hash function used is based on the key computed for each INode object.

Each board state stores a reference, called a DepthTransition, that records (a) the move that generated it, (b) the previous state, and (c) the depth from the initial position. The algorithm generates copies of each board state, because the moves are applied directly to the boards and not undone. As soon as a node is identified as the goal, the search algorithm terminates (this is true for **Breadth-First Search** as well).

Example 7-6. Depth-First Search implementation

```
public Solution search(INode initial, INode goal) {
    // If initial is the goal, return now.
    if (initial.equals (goal)) { return new Solution (initial, goal); }

    INodeSet open = StateStorageFactory.create (OpenStateFactory.STACK);
    open.insert (initial.copy());

    // states we have already visited.
    INodeSet closed = StateStorageFactory.create (OpenStateFactory.HASH);
    while (!open.isEmpty()) {
        INode n = open.remove();
        closed.insert (n);

        DepthTransition trans = (DepthTransition) n.storedData();

        // All successor moves translate into appended OPEN states.
        DoubleLinkedList<IMove> moves = n.validMoves();
        for (Iterator<IMove> it = moves.iterator(); it.hasNext(); ) {
            IMove move = it.next();

            // Execute move on a copy since we maintain sets of board states.
            INode successor = n.copy();
            move.execute (successor);

            // If already visited, try another state.
            if (closed.contains (successor) != null) { continue; }

            int depth = 1;
            if (trans != null) { depth = trans.depth+1; }

            // Record previous move for solution trace. If solution, leave now,
            // otherwise add to the OPEN set if still within depth bound
            successor.storedData (new DepthTransition (move, n, depth));
            if (successor.equals (goal)) {
                return new Solution (initial, successor);
            }
            if (depth < depthBound) { open.insert (successor); }
        }
    }

    return new Solution (initial, goal, false);  // No solution
}
```

Board states are stored to avoid visiting the same state twice. We assume there is an efficient function to generate a unique key for a board state; we consider two board states to be equivalent if this function generates the same key value for the two states.

Analysis

Assume d is the maximum depth bound for **Depth-First Search** and define b to be the branching factor for the underlying search tree.

The performance of the algorithm is governed by problem-specific and generic characteristics. In general, the core operations provided by the *open* and *closed* sets may unexpectedly slow the algorithm down, because naïve implementations would require $O(n)$ performance to locate a board state within the set. The key operations include:

`open.remove()`
   Remove the next board state to evaluate.

`closed.insert(INode state)`
   Add board state to the *closed* set.

`closed.contains(INode state)`
   Determine whether board state already exists in *closed*.

`open.insert(INode state)`
   Add board state into the *open* set, to be visited later.

Because **Depth-First Search** uses a stack to store the *open* set, remove and insert operations are performed in constant time. Because *closed* is a hash table that stores the board states using key values (as provided by the board state class implementing INode) the lookup time is amortized to be constant.

The problem-specific characteristics that affect the performance are (a) the number of successor board states for an individual board state, and (b) the ordering of valid moves. Some games have a large number of potential moves at each board state, which means that many depth-first paths may be ill-advised. Also, the way that moves are ordered will affect the overall search. If any heuristic information is available, make sure that moves most likely leading to a solution appear earlier in the ordered list of valid moves.

We evaluate **Depth-First Search** using a set of three examples (N1, N2, and N3) to show how capricious the search is with seemingly slight differences in state. In each example, 10 tiles are moved from the goal state. Occasionally **Depth-First Search** penetrates quickly to locate a solution. In general, the size of the search tree grows exponentially based on the branching factor b. For the 8-puzzle, the *branching factor* is between 2 and 4, based on where the empty tile is located, with an average of 2.67. We make the following two observations:

An ill-chosen depth level may prevent a solution from being found
   For initial position N2 shown in Figure 7-16 and a depth of 25, no solution was found after searching 20,441 board states. How is this even possible? It's

because **Depth-First Search** will not visit the same board state twice. Specifically, the closest this particular search comes to finding the solution is on the 3,451ˢᵗ board state, which is inspected in the 25ᵗʰ level. That board is only three moves away from the solution! But because the board was visited just as the depth limit was reached, expansion stopped and the board was added to the *closed* set. If **Depth-First Search** later encountered this node again at an earlier level, it would not explore further because the node would be in the *closed* set.

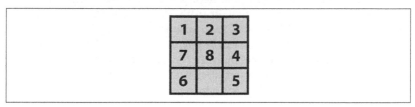

Figure 7-16. Initial position N2

It may seem better, therefore, to set the maximum depth level to be a high value; but as shown in Figure 7-17, this routinely leads to extremely large search trees and may not guarantee a solution will be found.

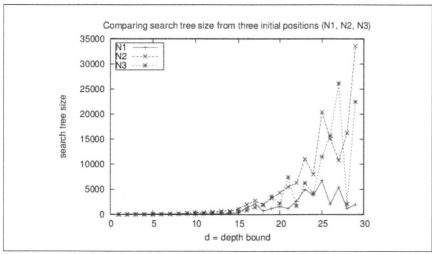

Figure 7-17. Search-tree size for Depth-First Search as depth increases

As the depth level increases, the solution found may be suboptimal
The discovered solutions grow as the depth limit increases, sometimes to two or three times larger than necessary.

Interestingly, given the example N1, an unbounded **Depth-First Search** actually finds a 30-move solution after processing only 30 board states, with 23 left in its *open* set to be processed. However, this fortunate series of events is not repeated for examples N2 and N3.

Breadth-First Search

Breadth-First Search attempts to locate a path by methodically evaluating board states closest to the initial board state. **Breadth-First Search** is guaranteed to find the shortest path to the goal state, if such a path exists.

The essential difference from **Depth-First Search** is that **Breadth-First Search** maintains a queue of open states that have yet to be visited, whereas **Depth-First Search** uses a stack. At each iteration, **Breadth-First Search** removes from the front of the queue an unvisited board state and expands it to compute the set of successor board states given the valid moves. If the goal state is reached, then the search terminates. Like **Depth-First Search**, this search makes sure not to visit the same state twice. Any successor board states that already exist within *closed* are discarded. The remaining unvisited board states are appended to the end of the queue of *open* board states, and the search continues.

Using the example from the 8-puzzle starting at Figure 7-18, the computed search tree is shown in Figure 7-19. Note how a solution is found with five moves after all paths with four moves are explored (and nearly all five-move solutions were inspected). The 20 light-gray board states in the figure are board states in the *open* queue waiting to be inspected. In total, 25 board states were processed.

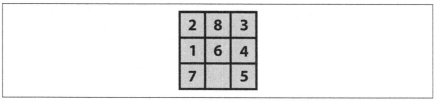

Figure 7-18. Starting board for Breadth-First Search

Input/Output

The algorithm starts from an initial board state and seeks a goal state. It returns a sequence of moves that represents a minimal-cost solution from the initial state to the goal state (or declares that no such solution was found given existing resources).

Context

A blind search is practical only if the predicted search space is within the memory space of the computer. Because **Breadth-First Search** methodically checks all shortest paths first, it may take quite a long time to locate paths that require a large number of moves. This algorithm may not be suitable if you need only some path from an initial state to the goal (i.e., if there is no need for it to be the shortest path).

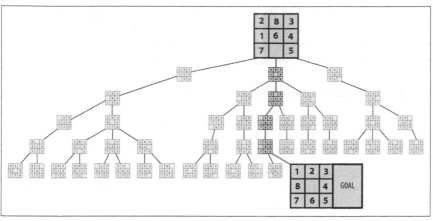

Figure 7-19. Sample Breadth-First Search tree for 8-puzzle

Breadth-First Search Summary

Best, Average, Worst: $O(b^d)$

```
search (initial, goal)
  if initial = goal then return "Solution"
  open = new Queue ❶
  closed = new Set
  insert (open, copy(initial))

  while open is not empty do
    n = head (open) ❷
    insert (closed, n)
    foreach valid move m at n do
      nextState = state when playing m at n
      if closed doesn't contain nextState then
        if nextState = goal then return "Solution"
        insert (open, nextState) ❸

  return "No Solution"
end
```

❶ **Breadth-First Search** uses a Queue to store open states to be visited.

❷ Remove the oldest state from the queue.

❸ Inserting the next state will be an append operation since *open* is a queue.

Solution

Breadth-First Search stores the set of *open* (i.e., yet to be visited) board states in a queue, and retrieves them one at a time for processing. The *closed* set is stored using a hash table. Each board state stores a back link, called a `Transition`, that records the move that generated it and a reference to the previous state. **Breadth-First Search** generates copies of each board state, because moves are applied directly to the boards and not undone. Example 7-7 shows the implementation.

Example 7-7. Breadth-First Search implementation

```
public Solution search (INode initial, INode goal) {
    // Return now if initial is the goal
    if (initial.equals (goal)) { return new Solution (initial, goal); }

    // Start from the initial state
    INodeSet open = StateStorageFactory.create (StateStorageFactory.QUEUE);
    open.insert (initial.copy());

    // states we have already visited.
    INodeSet closed = StateStorageFactory.create (StateStorageFactory.HASH);
    while (!open.isEmpty()) {
      INode n = open.remove();
      closed.insert (n);

      // All successor moves translate into appended OPEN states.
      DoubleLinkedList<IMove> moves = n.validMoves();
      for (Iterator<IMove> it = moves.iterator(); it.hasNext(); ) {
        IMove move = it.next();

        // make move on a copy
        INode successor = n.copy();
        move.execute (successor);

        // If already visited, search this state no more
        if (closed.contains (successor) != null) {
          continue;
        }

        // Record previous move for solution trace. If solution, leave
        // now, otherwise add to the OPEN set.
        successor.storedData (new Transition (move, n));
        if (successor.equals (goal)) {
          return new Solution (initial, successor);
        }
        open.insert (successor);
      }
    }
}
```

Analysis

As with **Depth-First Search**, the algorithm's performance is governed by problem-specific and generic characteristics. The same analysis regarding **Depth-First Search** applies here, and the only difference is the size of the set of open board states. **Breadth-First Search** must store on the order of b^d board states in *open*, where b is the branching factor for the board states and d is the depth of the solution found. This is much higher than **Depth-First Search**, which needs to store only about $b*d$ board states in *open* at any one time, based on the actively pursued board state at depth d. **Breadth-First Search** is guaranteed to find the solution with the least number of moves that transforms the initial board state to the goal board state.

Breadth-First Search only adds a board state to the *open* set if it does not already exist in the *closed* set. You can save additional space (at the expense of some extra processing) by only adding the board state if you first confirm that it is not already contained by the *open* set.

A*Search

Breadth-First Search finds an optimal solution (if one exists), but it may explore a tremendous number of nodes because it makes no attempt to intelligently select the order of moves to investigate. In contrast, **Depth-First Search** tries to rapidly find a path by making as much progress as possible when investigating moves; however, it must be bounded because otherwise it may fruitlessly search unproductive areas of the search tree. **A*Search** adds heuristic intelligence to guide its search rather than blindly following either of these fixed strategies.

A*Search is an iterative, ordered search that maintains a set of open board states to explore in an attempt to reach the goal state. At each search iteration, **A*Search** uses an evaluation function $f(n)$ to select a board state n from *open* whose $f(n)$ has the smallest value. $f(n)$ has the distinctive structure $f(n) = g(n) + h(n)$, where:

- $g(n)$ records the length of the shortest sequence of moves from the initial state to board state n; this value is recorded as the algorithm executes
- $h(n)$ estimates the length of the shortest sequence of moves from n to the goal state

Thus, $f(n)$ estimates the length of the shortest sequence of moves from initial state to goal state, passing through n. **A*Search** checks whether the goal state is reached only when a board state is removed from the *open* board states (differing from **Breadth-First Search** and **Depth-First Search**, which check when the successor board states are generated). This difference ensures the solution represents the shortest number of moves from the initial board state, as long as $h(n)$ never overestimates the distance to the goal state.

Having a low $f(n)$ score suggests the board state n is close to the final goal state. The most critical component of $f(n)$ is the heuristic evaluation that computes $h(n)$, because $g(n)$ can be computed on the fly by recording with each board state its depth from the initial state. If $h(n)$ is unable to accurately separate promising board states from unpromising board states, **A*Search** will perform no better than the blind searches already described. In particular, $h(n)$ must be *admissable*—that is, it must never *overstate* the actual minimum cost of reaching the goal state. If the estimate is too high, **A*Search** may not find the optimal solution. However, it is difficult to determine an effective $h(n)$ that is admissible and that can be computed effectively. There are numerous examples of inadmissible $h(n)$ that still lead to solutions that are practical without necessarily being optimal.

A*Search Summary

Best: $O(b^*d)$ **Average, Worst:** $O(b^d)$

```
search (initial, goal)
  initial.depth = 0
  open = new PriorityQueue ❶
  closed = new Set
  insert (open, copy(initial))

  while open is not empty do
    n = minimum (open)
    insert (closed, n)
    if n = goal then return "Solution"
    foreach valid move m at n do
      nextState = state when playing m at n
      if closed contains nextState then continue

      nextState.depth = n.depth + 1
      prior = state in open matching nextState ❷
      if no prior state or nextState.score < prior.score then
        if prior exists ❸
          remove (open, prior) ❹
        insert (open, nextState) ❺
  return "No Solution"
end
```

❶ **A*Search** stores open states in a priority queue by evaluated score.

❷ Must be able to rapidly locate matching node in *open*.

❸ If **A*Search** revisits a prior state in *open* that now has a lower score…

❹ …replace prior state in *open* with better scoring alternative.

❺ Since *open* is a priority queue, nextState is inserted based on its score.

Input/Output

The algorithm starts from an initial board state in a search tree and a goal state. It assumes the existence of an evaluation function $f(n)$ with admissible $h(n)$ function. It returns a sequence of moves that represents the solution that most closely approximates the minimal-cost solution from the initial state to the goal state (or declares that no such solution was found given existing resources).

Context

Using the example from the 8-puzzle starting at Figure 7-20, two computed search trees are shown in Figures 7-21 and 7-22. Figure 7-21 uses the GoodEvaluator $f(n)$ function proposed by Nilsson (1971). Figure 7-22 uses the WeakEvaluator $f(n)$ function also proposed by Nilsson. These evaluation functions will be described shortly. The light-gray board states depict the *open* set when the goal is found.

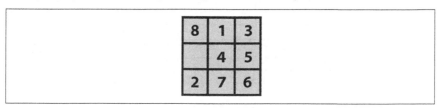

Figure 7-20. Starting board state for A*Search

Both GoodEvaluator and WeakEvaluator locate the same nine-move solution to the goal node (labeled GOAL) but GoodEvaluator is more efficient in its search. Let's review the $f(n)$ values associated with the nodes in both search trees to see why the WeakEvaluator search tree explores more nodes.

Observe that just two moves away from the initial state in the GoodEvaluator search tree, there is a clear path of nodes with ever-decreasing $f(n)$ values that lead to the goal node. In contrast, the WeakEvaluator search tree explores four moves away from the initial state before narrowing its search direction. WeakEvaluator fails to differentiate board states; indeed, note how its $f(n)$ value of the goal node is actually higher than the $f(n)$ values of the initial node and all three of its children nodes.

Solution

A*Search stores the *open* board states so it can both efficiently remove the board state whose evaluation function is smallest and determine whether a specific board state exists within *open*. Example 7-8 contains a sample Java implementation.

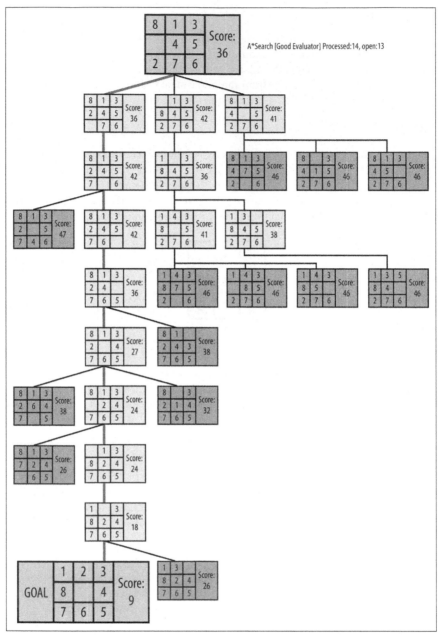

A*Search [Good Evaluator] Processed:14, open:13

Figure 7-21. Sample A*Search tree in 8-puzzle using GoodEvaluator

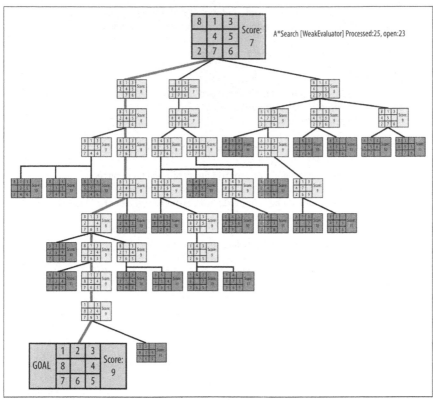

Figure 7-22. Sample A*Search tree in 8-puzzle using WeakEvaluator

Example 7-8. A*Search implementation

```
public Solution search (INode initial, INode goal) {
  // Start from the initial state
  int type = StateStorageFactory.PRIORITY_RETRIEVAL;
  INodeSet open = StateStorageFactory.create (type);
  INode copy = initial.copy();
  scoringFunction.score (copy);
  open.insert (copy);

  // Use Hashtable to store states we have already visited.
  INodeSet closed = StateStorageFactory.create (StateStorageFactory.HASH);
  while (!open.isEmpty()) {
    // Remove node with smallest evaluation function and mark closed.
    INode best = open.remove();

    // Return if goal state reached.
    if (best.equals (goal)) { return new Solution (initial, best); }
    closed.insert (best);
```

```
// Compute successor moves and update OPEN/CLOSED lists.
DepthTransition trans = (DepthTransition) best.storedData();
int depth = 1;
if (trans != null) { depth = trans.depth+1; }

for (IMove move : best.validMoves()) {
  // Make move and score the new board state.
  INode successor = best.copy();
  move.execute (successor);

  if (closed.contains(successor) != null) { continue; }

  // Record previous move for solution trace and compute
  // evaluation function to see if we have improved.
  successor.storedData (new DepthTransition (move, best, depth));
  scoringFunction.score (successor);

  // If not yet visited, or it has better score.
  INode exist = open.contains (successor);
  if (exist == null || successor.score() < exist.score()) {
    // remove old one, if one had existed, and insert better one
    if (exist != null) {
      open.remove (exist);
    }
    open.insert(successor);
  }
}
}

// No solution.
return new Solution (initial, goal, false);
}
```

As with **Breadth-First Search** and **Depth-First Search**, board states are entered into the *closed* set when processed. Each board state stores a reference, called a Depth Transition, that records (a) the move that generated it, (b) the previous state, and (c) the depth from the initial position. That last value, the depth, is used as the $g(n)$ component within the evaluation function. The algorithm generates copies of each board state, because the moves are applied directly to the boards and not undone.

Because **A*Search** incorporates heuristic information that includes a $g(n)$ computational component, there is one situation when **A*Search** may review a past decision on boards already visited. A board state to be inserted into the *open* set may have a lower evaluation score than an identical state that already appears in *open*. If so, **A*Search** removes the existing board in *open* with the higher score, since that state will not be part of the minimum-cost solution. Recall the situation in **Depth-First Search** where board states at the depth limit were found to be (as it turned out) only three moves away from the goal state (see "Analysis" on page 196). These board states were placed into the *closed* set, never to be processed again. **A*Search** avoids this mistake by continuing to evaluate the board state in *open* with the lowest evaluated score.

The success of **A*Search** is directly dependent on its heuristic function. The $h(n)$ component of $f(n)$ must be carefully designed, and this effort is more of a craft than a science. If $h(n)$ is always zero, **A*Search** is nothing more than **Breadth-First Search**. Furthermore, if $h(n)$ overestimates the cost of reaching the goal, **A*Search** may not be able to find the optimal solution, although it may be possible to return some solution, assuming $h(n)$ is not wildly off the mark. **A*Search** will find an optimal solution if its heuristic function $h(n)$ is admissible.

Much of the available **A*Search** literature describes highly specialized $h(n)$ functions for different domains, such as route finding on digital terrains (Wichmann and Wuensche, 2004) or project scheduling under limited resources (Hartmann, 1999). Pearl (1984) has written an extensive (and unfortunately out-of-print) reference for designing effective heuristics. Korf (2000) discusses how to design admissible $h(n)$ functions (defined in the following section). Michalewicz and Fogel (2004) provide a recent perspective on the use of heuristics in problem solving, not just for **A*Search**.

For the 8-puzzle, here are three admissible heuristic functions and one badly-defined function:

FairEvaluator
: $P(n)$, where $P(n)$ is the sum of the Manhattan distance that each tile is from its "home."

GoodEvaluator
: $P(n) + 3*S(n)$, where $P(n)$ is as above and $S(n)$ is a sequence score that checks the noncentral squares in turn, allotting 0 for every tile followed by its proper successor and 2 for every tile that is not; having a piece in the center scores 1.

WeakEvaluator
: Counts the number of misplaced tiles.

BadEvaluator
: Total the differences of opposite cells (across the center square) and compare against the ideal of 16.

To justify why the first three heuristic functions are admissible, consider WeakEvaluator, which simply returns a count from 0 to 8. Clearly this doesn't overestimate the number of moves but is a poor heuristic for discriminating among board states. FairEvaluator computes $P(n)$, the Manhattan distance that computes the distance between two tiles assuming you can only move horizontally or vertically; this accurately sums the distance of each initial tile to its ultimate destination. Naturally this underestimates the actual number of moves because in 8-puzzle you can only move tiles neighboring the empty tile. What is important is not to *overestimate* the number of moves. GoodEvaluator adds a separate count $3*S(n)$ that detects sequences and adds to the move total when more tiles are out of sequence. All three of these functions are admissible.

These functions evaluated the sample board state in Figure 7-23, with the results shown in Table 7-2. You can see that all admissible functions located a shortest 13-move solution while the nonadmissible heuristic function `BadEvaluator` found a 19-move solution with a much larger search tree.

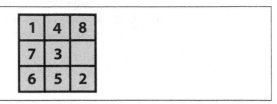

Figure 7-23. Sample board state for evaluation functions

Table 7-2. Comparing three admissible h(n) functions and one nonadmissible function

Measure name	Evaluation of h(n)	Statistics
GoodEvaluator	$13 + 3*11 = 46$	13-move solution closed:18 open: 15
FairEvaluator	13	13-move solution closed:28 open:21
WeakEvaluator	7	13-move solution closed: 171 open: 114
BadEvaluator	9	19-move solution closed: 1496 open: 767

Breadth-First Search and **Depth-First Search** inspect the *closed* set to see whether it contains a board state, so we used a hash table for efficiency. However, **A*Search** may need to reevaluate a board state that had previously been visited if its evaluated score function is lower than the current state. Therefore, a hash table is not appropriate because **A*Search** must be able to rapidly locate the board state in the *open* priority queue with the lowest evaluation score.

Note that **Breadth-First Search** and **Depth-First Search** retrieve the next board state from the open set in constant time because they use a queue and a stack, respectively. If we stored the *open* set as an ordered list, performance suffers because inserting a board state into the *open* set takes O(n). Nor can we use a binary heap to store the *open* set, because we don't know in advance how many board states are to be evaluated. Thus, we use a balanced binary tree, which offers O(*log n*) performance, where *n* is the size of the open set, when retrieving the lowest-cost board state and for inserting nodes into the *open* set.

Analysis

The computational behavior of **A*Search** is entirely dependent on the heuristic function. Russel and Norvig (2003) summarize the characteristics of effective heuristic functions. Barr and Feigenbaum (1981) present several alternatives to consider when one cannot efficiently compute an admissible $h(n)$ function. As the board states become more complex, heuristic functions become more important than ever—and more complicated to design. They must remain efficient to compute, or the entire search process is affected. However, even rough heuristic functions are capable of pruning the search space dramatically. For example, the 15-puzzle, the natural extension of the 8-puzzle, includes 15 tiles in a 4×4 board. It requires but a few minutes of work to create a 15-puzzle GoodEvaluator based on the logic of the 8-puzzle GoodEvaluator. With the goal state of Figure 7-24 (left) and an initial state of Figure 7-24 (right), **A*Search** rapidly locates a 15-move solution after processing 39 board states. When the search ends, 43 board states remain in the *open* set waiting to be explored.

With a 15-move limit, **Depth-First Search** fails to locate a solution after exploring 22,125 board states. After 172,567 board states (85,213 in the *closed* set and 87,354 remaining in the *open* set), **Breadth-First Search** runs out of memory when using 64MB of RAM to try the same task. Of course, you could add more memory or increase the depth limit, but this won't work in all cases since every problem is different.

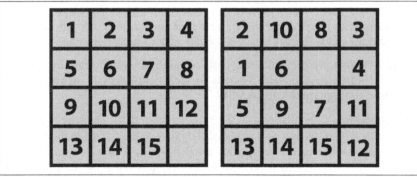

Figure 7-24. Goal for 15-puzzle (left) and sample starting board for 15-puzzle (right)

But do not be fooled by how easily **A*Search** solved this sample 15-puzzle; **A*Search** runs out of memory when attempting a more complicated initial board, such as Figure 7-25.

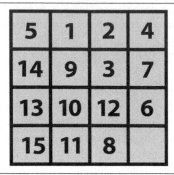

Figure 7-25. Complicated starting board for 15-puzzle

Clearly the rough evaluation function for the 15-puzzle is ineffective for the 15-puzzle, which has over 10^{25} possible states (Korf, 2000).

Variations

Instead of only searching forward from the initial state, Kaindl and Kain (1997) augment this search by simultaneously searching backward from the goal state. Initially discarded by early AI researchers as being unworkable, Kaindl and Kainz have presented powerful arguments that the approach should be reconsidered.

A common powerful alternative to **A*Search**, known as **IterativeDeepeningA*** (or IDA*), relies on a series of expanding depth-first searches with a fixed cost bound (Reinefeld, 1993). For each successive iteration, the bound is increased based on the results of the prior iteration. IDA* is more efficient than **Breadth-First Search** or **Depth-First Search** alone because each computed cost value is based on actual move sequences rather than heuristic estimates. Korf (2000) has described how powerful heuristics, coupled with IDA*, have been used to solve random instances of the 15-puzzle, evaluating more than 400 million board states during the search.

Although **A*Search** produces minimal-cost solutions, the search space may be too large for **A*Search** to complete. The major ideas that augment **A*Search** and address these very large problems include:

Iterative deepening
> This state search strategy uses repeated iterations of limited depth-first search, with each iteration increasing the depth limit. This approach can prioritize the nodes to be searched in successive iterations, thus reducing nonproductive searching and increasing the likelihood of rapidly converging on winning moves. Also, because the search space is fragmented into discrete intervals, real-time algorithms can search as much space as allowed within a time period and return a "best effort" result. The technique was first applied to **A*Search** by (Korf, 1985) to create IDA*.

Transposition tables

To avoid repeating computations that have already proved fruitless, we can hash game states and store in a transposition table the length of the path (from the source state) needed to reach each state. If the state appears later in the search, and its current depth is greater than what was discovered earlier, the search can be terminated. This approach can avoid searching entire subtrees that will ultimately prove to be unproductive.

Hierarchy

If the game state can be represented as a hierarchy, rather than as a flat model, techniques can be applied to restructure large search spaces into clusters, over which **A*Search** can be run. **Hierarchical Path-Finding A*** (HPA*) is an example of this approach (Botea et al., 2004).

Memory bound

Instead of restricting the search space by computation time, we could perform a "lossy" search and throw away various nodes as the search progresses, focusing on searches within areas that are deemed relevant. **Simplified Memory Bounded A*** (SMA*) is an example (Russell, 1992).

Reinefeld and Marsland (1994) summarize a variety of interesting extensions to **A*Search**. Much information on the use of **A*Search** in AI systems is available in textbooks and various online sources (Barr and Feigenbaum, 1981).

Comparing Search-Tree Algorithms

Breadth-First Search is guaranteed to find the solution with the least number of moves from the initial state, although it may evaluate a rather large number of potential move sequences as it operates. **Depth-First Search** tries to make as much progress as possible each time it searches, and may locate a solution rather quickly, but it also may waste a lot of time on searching parts of the search tree that seem to offer no hope for success. **A*Search**, when paired with an admissible heuristic function, takes the least time and finds the optimal solution, but finding an admissible function may be difficult.

It is thus worthwhile to compare **Depth-First Search**, **Breadth-First Search**, and **A*Search** directly. Using the 8-puzzle as our sample game, we created an initial state by randomly moving n tiles (ranging from 2 to 14); note that the same tile will not be moved twice in a row, because that would "undo" the move. Once n reached 32, the searches ran out of memory. For each board state, we execute **Breadth-First Search**, **Depth-First Search**(n), **Depth-First Search**($2*n$), and **A*Search**. Note that the parameters to **Depth-First Search** indicate the maximum allowed depth during the search. For each move size n:

- We total the number of board states in the *open* and *closed* lists. This reveals the efficiency of the algorithm in locating the solution. The columns marked with # contain the average of these totals over all runs. This analysis focuses on the number of states searched as the prime factor in determining search efficiency.

- We total the number of moves in the solution once found. This reveals the efficiency of the found solution paths. The columns whose names begin with *s* contain the average of these totals over all runs. The number in parentheses records the number of trials that failed to locate a solution within the given ply depth.

Table 7-3 contains the aggregate results of 1,000 trials, where *n* random moves were made (*n* = 2 through 14). Table 7-3 shows two statistics: (a) the average number of states of the generated search trees, and (b) the average number of moves of the identified solutions.

Table 7-3. Comparing search algorithms

n	#A*	#BFS	#DFS(n)	#DFS(2n)	sA*	sBFS	sDFS(n)	sDFS(2n)
2	4	4.5	3	6.4	2	2	2	2
3	6	13.3	7.1	27.3	3	3	3	3
4	8	25.7	12.4	68.3	4	4	4	5
5	10	46.4	21.1	184.9	5	5	5	5.8
6	11.5	77.6	31.8	321	6	6	6	9.4 (35)
7	13.8	137.9	56.4	767.2	6.8	6.8	6.9	9.7 (307)
8	16.4	216.8	84.7	1096.7	7.7	7.7	7.9 (36)	12.9 (221)
9	21	364.9	144	2520.5	8.7	8.6	8.8 (72)	13.1 (353)
10	24.7	571.6	210.5	3110.9	9.8	9.5	9.8 (249)	16.4 (295)
11	31.2	933.4	296.7	6983.3	10.7	10.4	10.6 (474)	17.4 (364)
12	39.7	1430	452	6196.2	11.7	11.3	11.7 (370)	20.8 (435)
13	52.7	2337.1	544.8	12464.3	13.1	12.2	12.4 (600)	21.6 (334)
14	60.8	3556.4	914.2	14755.7	14.3	13.1	13.4 (621)	25.2 (277)

Note that as *n* increases linearly, the size of the search tree grows exponentially for all blind approaches, but the **A*Search** tree remains manageable. To be precise, the growth rates of these blind searches are estimated by the following functions:

$$BFS(n) \cong 0.24 * (n + 1)^{2.949}$$

$$DFS(n) \cong 1.43 * (n + 1)^{2.275}$$

$$DFS(2n) \cong 3.18 * (n + 1)^{3.164}$$

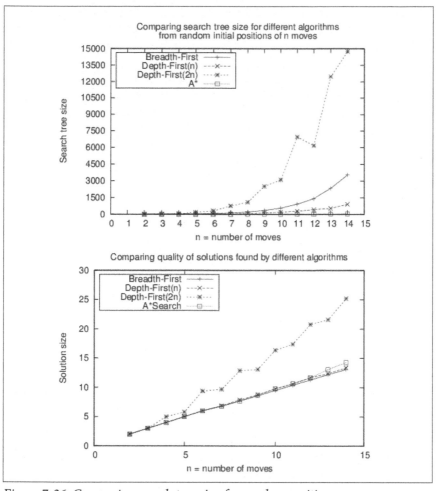

Figure 7-26. Comparing search tree size for random positions

Breadth-First Search always finds the shortest path to the solution, but note that **A*Search** is not far behind (because of the GoodEvaluator heuristic) even though it explores significantly fewer board states. In separate trials of **A*Search** with up to 30 random moves, the growth rate of the search tree was O($n^{1.5147}$); although not linear, this size is significantly smaller than for the blind searches. The actual exponent in each of these growth rate functions is dependent on the branching factor for the problem being solved. The results of Table 7-3 are shown graphically in Figure 7-26.

Finally, note how the horizon effect prevents **Depth-First Search** from solving numerous cases (recall that this happens when a board state node that is only a step away from the goal is added to the *closed* set). In fact, in this example run of 1,000 trials, **Depth-First Search** failed more than 60% of the time when using a maximum depth bound of 13.

Although all three searches have the potential to explore an exponential number of states, **A*Search** explores the smallest number given an admissible $h(n)$ estimation function.

There are other known ways to solve $n^2 - 1$ sliding tile puzzles besides relying on path finding. One ingenious approach proposed by Parberry (1995) is to use a Divide and Conquer strategy. That is, given an $n \times n$ puzzle, where $n > 3$, first complete the leftmost column and topmost row and then recursively solve the resulting $(n - 1)^2 - 1$ puzzle. When the inner problem to be solved is the 3×3 square, simply use brute force. This approach is guaranteed to find a solution that uses at most $5*n^3$ moves.

References

Barr, A. and E. Feigenbaum, *The Handbook of Artificial Intelligence*. William Kaufmann, Inc., 1981.

Berlekamp, E. and D. Wolfe, *Mathematical Go: Chilling Gets the Last Point*. A K Peters/CRC Press, 1994.

Botea, A., M. Müller, and J. Schaeffer, "Near optimal hierarchical path-finding," *Journal of Game Development*, 1(1): 2004, *http://www.cs.ualberta.ca/~mmueller/ps/hpastar.pdf*.

Hartmann, S., *Project Scheduling Under Limited Resources: Models, Methods, and Applications*. Springer, 1999.

Kaindl, H. and G. Kainz, "Bidirectional heuristic search reconsidered," *Journal of Artificial Intelligence Research*, 7: 283–317, 1997, *http://arxiv.org/pdf/cs/9712102.pdf*.

Korf, R. E., "Recent progress in the design and analysis of admissible heuristic functions," Proceedings, Abstraction, Reformulation, and Approximation: 4th International Symposium (SARA), Lecture notes in Computer Science #1864: 45–51, 2000, *http://www.aaai.org/Papers/AAAI/2000/AAAI00-212.pdf*.

Laramée, F. D., "Chess programming Part IV: Basic search," GameDev.net, August 26, 2000, *http://www.gamedev.net/reference/articles/article1171.asp*.

Michalewicz, Z. and D. Fogel, *How to Solve It: Modern Heuristics*. Second Edition. Springer, 2004.

Nilsson, N., *Problem-Solving Methods in Artificial Intelligence*. McGraw-Hill, 1971.

Parberry, I., "A real-time algorithm for the (n^2-1)-Puzzle," *Information Processing Letters*, 56(1):23–28, 1995, *http://dx.doi.org/10.1016/0020-0190(95)00134-X*.

Pearl, J., *Heuristics: Intelligent Search Strategies for Computer Problem Solving*. Addison-Wesley, 1984.

Pepicelli, G., "Bitwise optimization in Java: Bitfields, bitboards, and beyond," O'Reilly on Java.com, February 2, 2005, *http://www.onjava.com/pub/a/onjava/2005/02/02/bitsets.html*.

Reinefeld, A., "Complete solution of the 8-puzzle and the benefit of node ordering in IDA," Proceedings of the 13th International Joint Conference on Artificial Intelligence (IJCAI), Volume 1, 1993, *http://dl.acm.org/citation.cfm?id=1624060*.

Reinefeld, A. and T. Marsland, "Enhanced iterative-deepening search," *IEEE Transactions on Pattern Analysis and Machine Intelligence*, 16(7): 701–710, 1994, *http://dx.doi.org/10.1109/34.297950*.

Russell, S. J., "Efficient memory-bounded search methods," Proceedings, 10th European Conference on Artificial Intelligence (ECAI): 1–5, 1992.

Russell, S. J. and P. Norvig, *Artificial Intelligence: A Modern Approach*. Third Edition. Prentice Hall, 2009.

Samuel, A., "Some studies in machine learning using the game of checkers," *IBM Journal* 3(3): 210–229, 1967, *http://dx.doi.org/10.1147/rd.116.0601*.

Schaeffer, J., "Game over: Black to play and draw in checkers," *Journal of the International Computer Games Association* (ICGA), *https://ilk.uvt.nl/icga/journal/contents/Schaeffer07-01-08.pdf*.

Schaeffer, J., N. Burch, Y. Björnsson, A. Kishimoto, M. Müller, R. Lake, P. Lu, and S. Sutphen, "Checkers is solved," *Science Magazine*, September 14, 2007, 317(5844): 1518–1522, *http://www.sciencemag.org/cgi/content/abstract/317/5844/1518*.

Shannon, C., "Programming a computer for playing chess," *Philosophical Magazine*, 41(314): 1950, *http://tinyurl.com/ChessShannon-pdf*.

Wichmann, D. and B. Wuensche, "Automated route finding on digital terrains," Proceedings of IVCNZ, Akaroa, New Zealand, pp. 107–112, November 2004, *https://www.researchgate.net/publication/245571114_Automated_Route_Finding_on_Digital_Terrains*.

8

Network Flow Algorithms

Many problems can be presented as a network of vertices and edges, with a capacity associated with each edge over which commodities flow. The algorithms in this chapter spring from the need to solve these specific classes of problems. Ahuja (1993) contains an extensive discussion of numerous applications of network flow algorithms:

Assignment

> Given a set of tasks to be carried out and a set of employees, who may cost different amounts depending on their assigned task, assign the employees to tasks while minimizing the overall expense.

Bipartite matching

> Given a set of applicants who have been interviewed for a set of job openings, find a matching that maximizes the number of applicants selected for jobs for which they are qualified.

Maximum flow

> Given a network that shows the potential capacity over which goods can be shipped between two locations, compute the maximum flow supported by the network.

Transportation

> Determine the most cost-effective way to ship goods from a set of supplying factories to a set of retail stores.

Transshipment

> Determine the most cost-effective way to ship goods from a set of supplying factories to a set of retail stores, while potentially using a set of warehouses as intermediate holding stations.

Figure 8-1 shows how each of these problems can be represented as a network flow from one or more source nodes to one or more terminal nodes. The most general definition of a problem is at the bottom, and each of the other problems is a refinement of the problem beneath it. For example, the Transportation problem is a specialized instance of the Transshipment problem because transportation graphs do not contain intermediate transshipment nodes. Thus, a program that solves Transshipment problems can be applied to Transportation problems as well.

This chapter presents the **Ford–Fulkerson** algorithm, which solves the Maximum Flow problem. **Ford–Fulkerson** can also be applied to Bipartite Matching problems, as shown in Figure 8-1. Upon further reflection, the approach outlined in **Ford–Fulkerson** can be generalized to solve the more powerful Minimal Cost Flow problem, which enables us to solve the Transshipment, Transportation, and Assignment problems using that algorithm.

In principle, you could apply Linear Programming (LP) to all of the problems shown in Figure 8-1, but then you would have to convert these problems into the proper LP form, whose solution would then have to be recast into the original problem (we'll show how to do this at the end of the chapter). LP is a method to compute an optimal result (such as maximum profit or lowest cost) in a mathematical model consisting of linear relationships. In practice, however, the specialized algorithms described in this chapter outperform LP by several orders of magnitude for the problems shown in Figure 8-1.

Network Flow

We model a flow network as a directed graph $G = (V, E)$, where V is the set of vertices and E is the set of edges over these vertices. The graph itself is connected (though not every edge need be present). A special source vertex $s \in V$ produces units of a commodity that flow through the edges of the graph to be consumed by a sink vertex $t \in V$ (also known as the target or terminus). A flow network assumes the supply of units produced is infinite and that the sink vertex can consume all units it receives.

Each edge (u, v) has a flow $f(u, v)$ that defines the number of units of the commodity that flows from u to v. An edge also has a fixed capacity $c(u, v)$ that constrains the maximum number of units that can flow over that edge. In Figure 8-2, each vertex between the source s and the sink t is numbered, and each edge is labeled as f/c, showing the flow over that edge and the maximum allowed capacity. The edge between s and v_1, for example, is labeled 5/10, meaning that 5 units flow over that edge but it can sustain a capacity of up to 10. When no units are flowing over an edge (as is the case with the edge between v_5 and v_2), f is zero, and only the capacity is shown, outlined in a box.

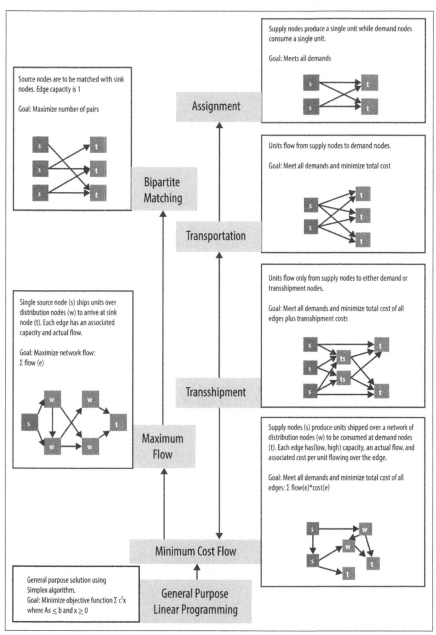

Figure 8-1. Relationship between network flow problems

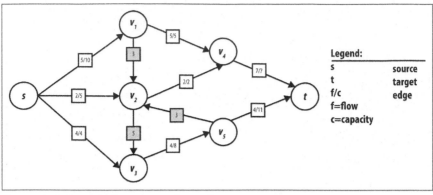

Figure 8-2. Sample flow network graph

The following criteria must be satisfied for any feasible flow *f* through a network:

Capacity constraint
> The flow $f(u, v)$ through an edge cannot be negative and cannot exceed the capacity of the edge $c(u, v)$. In other words, $0 \le f(u, v) \le c(u, v)$. If the network does not contain an edge from *u* to *v*, we define $c(u, v)$ to be 0.

Flow conservation
> Except for the source vertex *s* and sink vertex *t*, each vertex $u \in V$ must satisfy the property that the sum of $f(v, u)$ for all edges $(v, u) \in E$ (the flow into *u*) must equal the sum of $f(u, w)$ for all edges $(u, w) \in E$ (the flow out of *u*). This property ensures that flow is neither produced nor consumed in the network, except at *s* and *t*.

Skew symmetry
> The quantity $f(v, u)$ represents the opposite of the net flow from vertex *u* to *v*. This means that $f(u, v)$ must equal $-f(v, u)$.

In the ensuing algorithms, we refer to a network path that is a noncyclic path of unique vertices $< v_1, v_2, ..., v_n >$ involving *n-1* consecutive edges (v_i, v_j) in E. In the flow network shown in Figure 8-2, one possible network path is $< v_3, v_5, v_2, v_4 >$. In a network path, the direction of the edges can be ignored, which is necessary to properly construct *augmenting paths* as we will see shortly. In Figure 8-2, a possible network path is $< s, v_1, v_4, v_2, v_5, t >$.

Maximum Flow

Given a flow network, you can compute the maximum flow (*mf*) between vertices *s* and *t* given the capacity constraints $c(u, v) \ge 0$ for all directed edges $e = (u, v)$ in E. That is, compute the largest amount that can flow out of source *s*, through the network, and into sink *t* given specific capacity limits on individual edges. Starting with the lowest possible flow—a flow of 0 through every edge—**Ford–Fulkerson** successively locates an *augmenting path* through the network from *s* to *t* to which more flow can be added. The algorithm terminates when no augmenting paths can be found. The Max-flow Min-cut theorem (Ford and Fulkerson, 1962) guarantees that with non-negative integral flows and capacities, **Ford–Fulkerson** always terminates and identifies the maximum flow in a network.

The flow network is defined by a graph $G = (V, E)$ with designated start vertex s and sink vertex t. Each directed edge $e = (u, v)$ in E has a defined integer capacity $c(u, v)$ and actual flow $f(u, v)$. A *path* can be constructed from a sequence of n vertices from V, which we call $p_0, p_1, \ldots, p_{n-1}$, where p_0 is the designated *source* vertex of the flow network and p_{n-1} is its *sink* vertex. The path is constructed from *forward edges*, where the edge over consecutive vertices $(p_i, p_{i+1}) \in E$, and *backward edges*, where the edge $(p_{i+1}, p_i) \in E$ and the path traverses the edge opposite to its direction.

Input/Output

The flow network is defined by a graph $G = (V, E)$ with designated start vertex s and sink vertex t. Each directed edge $e = (u, v)$ in E has a defined integer capacity $c(u, v)$ and actual flow $f(u, v)$.

For each edge (u, v) in E, **Ford–Fulkerson** computes an integer flow $f(u, v)$ representing the units flowing through edge (u, v). As a side effect of its termination, **Ford–Fulkerson** computes the *min cut* of the network—in other words, the set of edges that form a bottleneck, preventing further units from flowing across the network from s to t.

Solution

The implementation of **Ford–Fulkerson** we'll describe here uses linked lists to store edges. Each vertex u maintains two separate lists: forward edges for the edges emanating from u and backward edges for the edges coming into u; thus each edge appears in two lists. The code repository provided with this book contains an implementation using a two-dimensional matrix to store edges, a more appropriate data structure to use for dense flow network graphs.

Ford–Fulkerson relies on the following structures:

FlowNetwork
> Represents the network flow problem. This abstract class has two subclasses, one based on adjacency lists and the other using an adjacency matrix. The getEdgeStructure() method returns the underlying storage used for the edges.

VertexStructure
> Maintains two linked lists (forward and backward) for the edges leaving and entering a vertex.

EdgeInfo
> Records information about edges in the network flow.

VertexInfo

> Records the augmenting path found by the search method. It records the previous vertex in the augmenting path and whether it was reached through a forward or backward edge.

Ford–Fulkerson Summary

Best, Average, Worst: O(E^*mf)

```
compute (G)
  while exists augmenting path in G do ❶
    processPath (path)
end

processPath (path)
  v = sink
  delta = ∞
  while v ≠ source do ❷
    u = vertex previous to v in path
    if edge(u,v) is forward then
      t = (u,v).capacity - (u,v).flow
    else
      t = (v,u).flow
    delta = min (t, delta)
    v = u

  v = sink
  while v ≠ source do ❸
    u = vertex previous to v in path
    if edge(u,v) is forward then ❹
      (u,v).flow += delta
    else
      (v,u).flow -= delta
    v = u
end
```

❶ Can loop up to *mf* times, making overall behavior O(E^*mf).

❷ Work backward from *sink* to find edge with lowest potential to increase.

❸ Adjust augmenting path accordingly.

❹ Forward edges increase flow; backward edges reduce.

Ford–Fulkerson is implemented in Example 8-1 and illustrated in Figure 8-4. A configurable Search object computes the augmented path in the network to which additional flow can be added without violating the flow network criteria. **Ford–Fulkerson** makes continual progress because suboptimal decisions made in earlier iterations of the algorithm can be fixed without having to undo all past history.

Example 8-1. Sample Java Ford–Fulkerson implementation

```java
public class FordFulkerson {
  FlowNetwork network;     /** Represents the FlowNetwork problem. */
  Search searchMethod;     /** Search method to use. */

  // Construct instance to compute maximum flow across given
  // network using given search method to find augmenting path.
  public FordFulkerson (FlowNetwork network, Search method) {
    this.network = network;
    this.searchMethod = method;
  }

  // Compute maximal flow for the flow network. Results of the
  // computation are stored within the flow network object.
  public boolean compute () {
    boolean augmented = false;
    while (searchMethod.findAugmentingPath (network.vertices)) {
      processPath (network.vertices);
      augmented = true;
    }
    return augmented;
  }

  // Find edge in augmenting path with lowest potential to be increased
  // and augment flows within path from source to sink by that amount.
  protected void processPath (VertexInfo []vertices) {
    int v = network.sinkIndex;
    int delta = Integer.MAX_VALUE;          // goal is to find smallest
    while (v != network.sourceIndex) {
      int u = vertices[v].previous;
      int flow;
      if (vertices[v].forward) {
        // Forward edges can be adjusted by remaining capacity on edge.
        flow = network.edge(u, v).capacity - network.edge(u, v).flow;
      } else {
        // Backward edges can be reduced only by their existing flow.
        flow = network.edge(v, u).flow;
      }
      if (flow < delta) { delta = flow; }   // smaller candidate flow.
      v = u;   // follow reverse path to source
    }

    // Adjust path (forward is added, backward is reduced) with delta.
    v = network.sinkIndex;
    while (v != network.sourceIndex) {
      int u = vertices[v].previous;
      if (vertices[v].forward) {
        network.edge(u, v).flow += delta;
      } else {
        network.edge(v, u).flow -= delta;
      }
```

```
        v = u;  // follow reverse path to source
    }
    Arrays.fill (network.vertices, null);   // reset for next iteration
  }
}
```

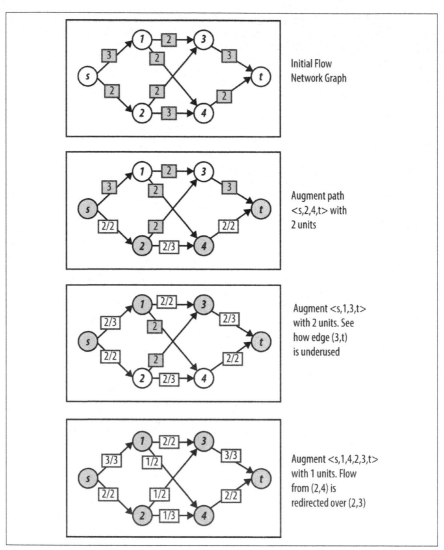

Figure 8-3. Ford–Fulkerson example

Any search method that extends the abstract Search class in Figure 8-5 can be used to locate an augmenting path. The original description of **Ford–Fulkerson** uses **Depth-First Search** while **Edmonds–Karp** uses **Breadth-First Search** (see Chapter 6).

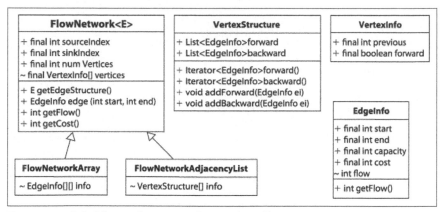

Figure 8-4. Modeling information for Ford–Fulkerson

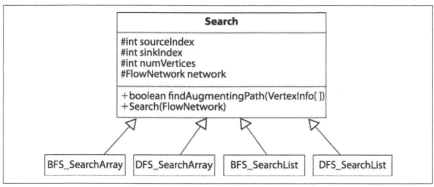

Figure 8-5. Search capability

The flow network example in Figure 8-3 shows the results of using **Depth-First Search** to locate an augmenting path; the implementation is listed in Example 8-2. The path structure contains a stack of vertices during its search. A potential augmenting path is extended by popping a vertex u from the stack and finding an adjacent unvisited vertex v that satisfies one of two constraints: (i) edge (u, v) is a forward edge with unfilled capacity; (ii) edge (v, u) is a backward edge with flow that can be reduced. If such a vertex is found, then v is appended to the end of path and the inner while loop continues. Eventually, the sink vertex t is visited or path becomes empty, in which case no augmenting path is possible.

Example 8-2. Using Depth-First Search to locate augmenting path

```
public boolean findAugmentingPath (VertexInfo[] vertices) {
  // Begin potential augmenting path at source.
  vertices[sourceIndex] = new VertexInfo (-1);
  Stack<Integer> path = new Stack<Integer>();
  path.push (sourceIndex);
```

Network
Flow
Algorithms

```
// Process forward edges from u; then try backward edges.
VertexStructure struct[] = network.getEdgeStructure();
while (!path.isEmpty()) {
  int u = path.pop();

  // try to make forward progress first...
  Iterator<EdgeInfo> it = struct[u].forward();
  while (it.hasNext()) {
    EdgeInfo ei = it.next();
    int v = ei.end;

    // not yet visited AND has unused capacity? Plan to increase.
    if (vertices[v] == null && ei.capacity > ei.flow) {
      vertices[v] = new VertexInfo (u, FORWARD);

      if (v == sinkIndex) { return true; }  // we have found one!
      path.push (v);
    }
  }

  // try backward edges
  it = struct[u].backward();
  while (it.hasNext()) {
    // try to find an incoming edge into u whose flow can be reduced.
    EdgeInfo rei = it.next();
    int v = rei.start;

    // now try backward edge not yet visited (can't be sink!)
    if (vertices[v] == null && rei.flow > 0) {
      vertices[v] = new VertexInfo (u, BACKWARD);
      path.push (v);
    }
  }
}

return false;     // nothing
}
```

As the path is expanded, the vertices array stores VertexInfo information about forward and backward edges enable the augmenting path to be traversed within the processPath method from Example 8-1.

The implementation of the **Breadth-First Search** alternative, known as **Edmonds–Karp**, is shown in Example 8-3. Here the path structure contains a queue of vertices during its search. The potential augmenting path is expanded by removing a vertex *u* from the head of the queue and expanding the queue by appending adjacent unvisited vertices through which the augmented path may exist. Again, either the sink vertex *t* will be visited or path becomes empty (in which case no augmenting path is possible). Given the same example flow network from Figure 8-3, the four augmenting paths located using **Breadth-First Search** are $< s, 1, 3, t >$, $< s, 1, 4, t >$, $< s, 2, 3, t >$, and $< s, 2, 4, t >$. The resulting maximum flow will be the same.

Example 8-3. Using Breadth-First Search to locate augmenting path

```java
public boolean findAugmentingPath (VertexInfo []vertices) {
  // Begin potential augmenting path at source with maximum flow.
  vertices[sourceIndex] = new VertexInfo (-1);
  DoubleLinkedList<Integer> path = new DoubleLinkedList<Integer>();
  path.insert (sourceIndex);

  // Process forward edges out of u; then try backward edges into u.
  VertexStructure struct[] = network.getEdgeStructure();
  while (!path.isEmpty()) {
    int u = path.removeFirst();

    Iterator<EdgeInfo> it = struct[u].forward();     // edges out from u
    while (it.hasNext()) {
      EdgeInfo ei = it.next();
      int v = ei.end;

      // if not yet visited AND has unused capacity? Plan to increase.
      if (vertices[v] == null && ei.capacity > ei.flow) {
        vertices[v] = new VertexInfo (u, FORWARD);
        if (v == sinkIndex) { return true; }  // path is complete.
        path.insert (v);                      // otherwise append to queue
      }
    }

    it = struct[u].backward();                 // edges into u
    while (it.hasNext()) {
      // try to find an incoming edge into u whose flow can be reduced.
      EdgeInfo rei = it.next();
      int v = rei.start;

      // Not yet visited (can't be sink!) AND has flow to be decreased?
      if (vertices[v] == null && rei.flow > 0) {
        vertices[v] = new VertexInfo (u, BACKWARD);
        path.insert (v);                       // append to queue
      }
    }
  }

  return false;     // no augmented path located.
}
```

When **Ford–Fulkerson** terminates, the vertices in V can be split into two disjoint sets, S and T (where $T = V - S$). Note that $s \in S$, whereas $t \in T$. S is computed to be the set of vertices from V that were visited in the final failed attempt to locate an augmenting path. The importance of these sets is that the forward edges between S

and T comprise a *min cut* or a bottleneck in the flow network. That is, the capacity that can flow from S to T is minimized, and the available flow between S and T is already at full capacity.

Analysis

Ford–Fulkerson terminates because the units of flow are non-negative integers (**Ford–Fulkerson**, 1962). The performance of **Ford–Fulkerson** using **Depth-First Search** is $O(E^*mf)$ and is based on the final value of the maximum flow, *mf*. Briefly, it is possible that each iteration adds only one unit of flow to the augmenting path, and thus networks with very large capacities might require a great number of iterations. It is striking that the running time is based not on the problem size (i.e., the number of vertices or edges) but on the capacities of the edges themselves.

When using **Breadth-First Search** (identified by name as the **Edmonds–Karp** variation), the performance is $O(V^*E^2)$. **Breadth-First Search** finds the shortest augmented path in $O(V + E)$, which is really $O(E)$ because the number of vertices is smaller than the number of edges in the connected flow network graph. Cormen et al. (2009) prove that the number of flow augmentations performed is on the order of $O(V^*E)$, leading to the final result that **Edmonds–Karp** has $O(V^*E^2)$ performance. **Edmonds–Karp** often outperforms **Ford–Fulkerson** by relying on **Breadth-First Search** to pursue all potential paths in order of length, rather than potentially wasting much effort in a depth-first "race" to the sink.

Optimization

Typical implementations of network-flow problems use arrays to store information. We choose instead to present each algorithm with lists because the code is more readable and readers can understand how the algorithm works. It is worth considering, however, how much performance speedup can be achieved by optimizing the resulting code; in Chapter 2 we showed a 50% performance improvement in optimizing the multiplication of *n*-digit numbers. It is clear that faster code can be written, but it may not be easy to understand or maintain if the problem changes. With this caution in mind, Example 8-4 contains an optimized Java implementation of **Ford–Fulkerson**.

Example 8-4. Optimized Ford–Fulkerson implementation

```java
public class Optimized extends FlowNetwork {
  int[][] capacity;      // Contains all capacities.
  int[][] flow;          // Contains all flows.
  int[] previous;        // Contains predecessor information of path.
  int[] visited;         // Visited during augmenting path search.

  final int QUEUE_SIZE; // Size of queue will never be greater than n.
  final int queue[];    // Use circular queue in implementation.

  // Load up the information
  public Optimized (int n, int s, int t, Iterator<EdgeInfo> edges) {
```

```java
    super (n, s, t);

    queue = new int[n];
    QUEUE_SIZE = n;
    capacity = new int[n][n];
    flow = new int[n][n];
    previous = new int[n];
    visited = new int [n];
    // Initially, flow is set to 0. Pull info from input.
    while (edges.hasNext()) {
      EdgeInfo ei = edges.next();
      capacity[ei.start][ei.end] = ei.capacity;
    }
  }

// Compute and return the maxFlow.
public int compute (int source, int sink) {
  int maxFlow = 0;
  while (search(source, sink)) { maxFlow += processPath (source, sink); }
  return maxFlow;
}

// Augment flow within network along path found from source to sink.
protected int processPath (int source, int sink) {
  // Determine amount by which to increment the flow. Equal to
  // minimum over the computed path from sink to source.
  int increment = Integer.MAX_VALUE;
  int v = sink;
  while (previous[v] != -1) {
    int unit = capacity[previous[v]][v] - flow[previous[v]][v];
    if (unit < increment) { increment = unit; }
    v = previous[v];
  }

  // push minimal increment over the path
  v = sink;
  while (previous[v] != -1) {
    flow[previous[v]][v] += increment;   // forward edges.
    flow[v][previous[v]] -= increment;   // don't forget back edges
    v = previous[v];
  }

  return increment;
}

// Locate augmenting path in the Flow Network from source to sink.
public boolean search (int source, int sink) {
  // clear visiting status. 0=clear, 1=actively in queue, 2=visited
  for (int i = 0 ; i < numVertices; i++) { visited[i] = 0; }

  // create circular queue to process search elements.
  queue[0] = source;
```

```
    int head = 0, tail = 1;
    previous[source] = -1;      // make sure we terminate here.
    visited[source] = 1;        // actively in queue.
    while (head != tail) {
      int u = queue[head]; head = (head + 1) % QUEUE_SIZE;
      visited[u] = 2;

      // add to queue unvisited neighbors of u with enough capacity.
      for (int v = 0; v < numVertices; v++) {
        if (visited[v] == 0 && capacity[u][v] > flow[u][v]) {
          queue[tail] = v;
          tail = (tail + 1) % QUEUE_SIZE;
          visited[v] = 1;        // actively in queue.
          previous[v] = u;
        }
      }
    }

    return visited[sink] != 0;  // did we make it to the sink?
  }
}
```

Related Algorithms

The Push/Relabel algorithm introduced by Goldberg and Tarjan (1986) improves the performance to $O(V{*}E{*}log(V^2/E))$ and also provides an algorithm that can be parallelized for greater gains. A variant of the problem, known as the Multi-Commodity Flow problem, generalizes the Maximum Flow problem stated here. Briefly, instead of having a single source and sink, consider a shared network used by multiple sources s_i and sinks t_i to transmit different commodities. The capacity of the edges is fixed, but the usage demanded for each source and sink may vary. Practical applications of algorithms that solve this problem include routing in wireless networks (Fragouli and Tabet, 2006). Leighton and Rao (1999) have written a widely cited reference for multicommodity problems.

There are several slight variations to the Maximum Flow problem:

Vertex capacities
What if a flow network places a maximum capacity $k(v)$ flowing through a vertex v in the graph? We can solve these problems by constructing a modified flow network G_m as follows. For each vertex v in G, create two vertices v^a and v^b. Create edge (v^a, v^b) with a flow capacity of $k(v)$. For each incoming edge (u, v) in G with capacity $c(u, v)$, create a new edge (u, v^a) with capacity $c(u, v)$. For each outgoing edge (v, w) in G, create edge (v^b, w) in G_m with capacity $k(v)$. A solution in G_m determines the solution to G.

Undirected edges
What if the flow network G has undirected edges? Construct a modified flow network G_m with the same set of vertices. For each edge (u, v) in G with

capacity $c(u, v)$, construct a pair of edges (u, v) and (v, u) each with the same capacity $c(u, v)$. A solution in G_m determines the solution to G.

Bipartite Matching

Matching problems exist in numerous forms. Consider the following scenario. Five applicants have been interviewed for five job openings. The applicants have listed the jobs for which they are qualified. The task is to match applicants to jobs such that each job opening is assigned to exactly one qualified applicant.

We can use **Ford–Fulkerson** to solve the Bipartite Matching problem. This technique is known in computer science as "problem reduction." We reduce the Bipartite Matching problem to a Maximum Flow problem in a flow network by showing (a) how to map the Bipartite Matching problem input into the input for a Maximum Flow problem, and (b) how to map the output of the Maximum Flow problem into the output of the Bipartite Matching problem.

Input/Output

A Bipartite Matching problem consists of a set of n elements, where $s_i \in S$; a set of m partners, where $t_j \in T$; and a set of p acceptable pairs, where $p_k \in P$. Each P pair associates an element $s_i \in S$ with a partner $t_j \in T$. The sets S and T are disjoint, which gives this problem its name.

The output is a set of (s_i, t_j) pairs selected from the original set of acceptable pairs, P. These pairs represent a maximum number of pairs allowed by the matching. The algorithm guarantees that no greater number of pairs can be matched (although there may be other arrangements that lead to the same number of pairs).

Solution

Instead of devising a new algorithm to solve this problem, we reduce a Bipartite Matching problem instance into a Maximum Flow instance. In Bipartite Matching, selecting the match (s_i, t_j) for element $s_i \in S$ with partner $t_j \in T$ prevents either s_i or t_j from being selected again in another pairing. Let n be the size of S and m be the size of T. To produce this same behavior in a flow network graph, construct $G = (V, E)$:

V contains n + m + 2 vertices
> Each element s_i maps to a vertex numbered i. Each partner t_j maps to a vertex numbered $n + j$. Create a new source vertex *src* (labeled 0) and a new target vertex *tgt* (labeled $n + m + 1$).

E contains n + m + k edges
> There are n edges connecting the new *src* vertex to the vertices mapped from S. There are m edges connecting the new *tgt* vertex to the vertices mapped from T. For each of the k pairs, $p_k = (s_i, t_j)$, add edge $(i, n + j)$. All of these edges must have a flow capacity of 1.

Computing the Maximum Flow in the flow network graph G produces a maximal matching set for the original Bipartite Matching problem, as proven in Cormen et al. (2009). For an example, consider Figure 8-6(a), where it is suggested that the two pairs (a, z) and (b, y) form the maximum number of pairs; the corresponding flow network using this construction is shown in Figure 8-6(b), where vertex 1 corresponds to a, vertex 4 corresponds to x, and so on. Upon reflection we can improve this solution to select three pairs, (a, z), (c, y), and (b, x). The corresponding adjustment to the flow network is made by finding the augmenting path <0,3,5,2,4,7>. Applying this augmenting path removes match (b, y) and adds match (b, x) and (c, y).

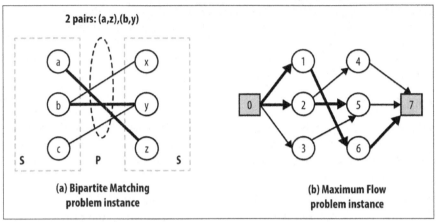

Figure 8-6. Bipartite Matching reduces to Maximum Flow

Once the Maximum Flow is determined, we convert the output of the Maximum Flow problem into the appropriate output for the Bipartite Matching problem. That is, for every edge (s_i, t_j) whose flow is 1, indicate that the pairing $(s_i, t_j) \in P$ is selected. In the code shown in Example 8-5, error checking has been removed to simplify the presentation.

Example 8-5. Bipartite Matching using Ford–Fulkerson

```
public class BipartiteMatching {
  ArrayList<EdgeInfo> edges;   /* Edges for S and T. */
  int ctr = 0;                 /* Unique id counter. */

  /* Maps that convert between problem instances. */
  Hashtable<Object,Integer> map = new Hashtable<Object,Integer>();
  Hashtable<Integer,Object> reverse = new Hashtable<Integer,Object>();

  int srcIndex;    /* Source index of flow network problem. */
  int tgtIndex;    /* Target index of flow network problem. */
  int numVertices; /* Number of vertices in flow network problem. */
  public BipartiteMatching (Object[] S, Object[] T, Object[][] pairs) {
```

```
    edges = new ArrayList<EdgeInfo>();

    // Convert pairs into input for FlowNetwork with capacity 1.
    for (int i = 0; i < pairs.length; i++) {
      Integer src = map.get (pairs[i][0]);
      Integer tgt = map.get (pairs[i][1]);
      if (src == null) {
        map.put (pairs[i][0], src = ++ctr);
        reverse.put (src, pairs[i][0]);
      }
      if (tgt == null) {
        map.put (pairs[i][1], tgt = ++ctr);
        reverse.put (tgt, pairs[i][1]);
      }

      edges.add (new EdgeInfo (src, tgt, 1));
    }

    // add extra "source" and extra "target" vertices
    srcIndex = 0;
    tgtIndex = S.length + T.length+1;
    numVertices = tgtIndex+1;
    for (Object o : S) {
      edges.add (new EdgeInfo (0, map.get (o), 1));
    }
    for (Object o : T) {
      edges.add (new EdgeInfo (map.get (o), tgtIndex, 1));
    }
  }

  public Iterator<Pair> compute() {
    FlowNetworkArray network = new FlowNetworkArray (numVertices,
            srcIndex, tgtIndex, edges.iterator());
    FordFulkerson solver = new FordFulkerson (network,
            new DFS_SearchArray(network));
    solver.compute();

    // retrieve from original edgeInfo set; ignore created edges to the
    // added "source" and "target". Only include in solution if flow == 1
    ArrayList<Pair> pairs = new ArrayList<Pair>();
    for (EdgeInfo ei : edges) {
      if (ei.start != srcIndex && ei.end != tgtIndex) {
        if (ei.getFlow() == 1) {
          pairs.add (new Pair (reverse.get (ei.start),
                               reverse.get (ei.end)));
        }
      }
    }

    return pairs.iterator();   // iterator generates solution
  }
}
```

Analysis

For a problem reduction to be efficient, it must be possible to efficiently map both the problem instance and the computed solutions. The Bipartite Matching problem $M = (S, T, P)$ is converted into a graph $G = (V, E)$ in $n + m + k$ steps. The resulting graph G has $n + m + 2$ vertices and $n + m + k$ edges, and thus the size of the graph is only a constant size larger than the original Bipartite Matching problem size. This important feature of the construction ensures we have an efficient solution to the Bipartite Matching problem. After **Ford–Fulkerson** computes the maximum flow, the edges in the network with a flow of 1 correspond to pairs in the Bipartite Matching problem that belong to the matching. Determining these edges requires k steps, or $O(k)$ extra processing, to "read" the solution to Bipartite Matching.

Reflections on Augmenting Paths

The Maximum Flow problem underlies solutions to all the remaining problems discussed earlier in this chapter in Figure 8-1. Each requires steps to represent it as a flow network, after which we can minimize the cost of that flow. If we associate with each edge (u, v) in the network a cost $d(u, v)$ that reflects the per-unit cost of shipping a unit over edge (u, v), the goal is to minimize

$$\Sigma f(u, v)^*d(u, v)$$

for all edges in the flow network. Now, for **Ford–Fulkerson**, we stressed the importance of finding an augmenting path that could increase the maximum flow through the network. But what if we modify the search routine to find the least costly augmentation, if one exists? We have already seen Greedy algorithms (such as **Prim's Algorithm** for building a Minimum Spanning Tree in Chapter 6) that iteratively select the least costly extension; perhaps such an approach will work here.

To find the least costly augmentation path, we cannot rely strictly on a breadth-first or a depth-first approach. As we saw with **Prim's Algorithm**, we must use a priority queue to store and compute the distance of each vertex in the flow network from the source vertex. We essentially compute the costs of shipping an additional unit from the source vertex to each vertex in the network, and we maintain a priority queue based on the ongoing computation:

1. As the search proceeds, the priority queue stores the ordered set of nodes that define the active searching focus.

2. To expand the search, retrieve from the priority queue the vertex u whose distance (in terms of cost) from the source is the smallest. Then locate a neighboring vertex v that has not yet been visited and that meets one of two conditions: either (a) the forward edge (u, v) still has remaining capacity to be increased, or (b) the backward edge (v, u) has flow that can be reduced.

3. If the sink index is encountered during the exploration, the search terminates successfully with an augmenting path; otherwise, no such augmenting path exists.

The Java implementation of ShortestPathArray is shown in Example 8-6. When this method returns true, the vertices parameter contains information about the augmenting path.

Example 8-6. Shortest path (in costs) search for Ford–Fulkerson

```java
public boolean findAugmentingPath (VertexInfo[] vertices) {
  Arrays.fill (vertices, null);   // reset for iteration

  // Construct queue using BinaryHeap. The inqueue[] array avoids
  // an O(n) search to determine if an element is in the queue.
  int n = vertices.length;
  BinaryHeap<Integer> pq = new BinaryHeap<Integer> (n);
  boolean inqueue[] = new boolean [n];

  // initialize dist[] array. Use INT_MAX when edge doesn't exist.
  for (int u = 0; u < n; u++) {
    if (u == sourceIndex) {
      dist[u] = 0;
      pq.insert (sourceIndex, 0);
      inqueue[u] = true;
    } else {
      dist[u] = Integer.MAX_VALUE;
    }
  }

  while (!pq.isEmpty()) {
    int u = pq.smallestID();
    inqueue[u] = false;

    // When reach sinkIndex we are done.
    if (u == sinkIndex) { break; }

    for (int v = 0; v < n; v++) {
      if (v == sourceIndex || v == u) continue;

      // forward edge with remaining capacity if cost is better.
      EdgeInfo cei = info[u][v];
      if (cei != null && cei.flow < cei.capacity) {
        int newDist = dist[u] + cei.cost;
        if (0 <= newDist && newDist < dist[v]) {
          vertices[v] = new VertexInfo (u, Search.FORWARD);
          dist[v] = newDist;
          if (inqueue[v]) {
            pq.decreaseKey (v, newDist);
          } else {
```

```
            pq.insert (v, newDist);
            inqueue[v] = true;
          }
        }
      }

      // backward edge with at least some flow if cost is better.
      cei = info[v][u];
      if (cei != null && cei.flow > 0) {
        int newDist = dist[u] - cei.cost;
        if (0 <= newDist && newDist < dist[v]) {
          vertices[v] = new VertexInfo (u, Search.BACKWARD);
          dist[v] = newDist;
          if (inqueue[v]) {
            pq.decreaseKey (v, newDist);
          } else {
            pq.insert (v, newDist);
            inqueue[v] = true;
          }
        }
      }
    }
  }
}

return dist[sinkIndex] != Integer.MAX_VALUE;
}
```

Armed with this strategy for locating the lowest-cost augmenting path, we can solve the remaining problems shown in Figure 8-1. To show the effect of this low-cost search strategy, Figure 8-7 illustrates the side-by-side computation on a small example comparing a straightforward Maximum Flow computation with a Minimum Cost Flow computation. Each iteration moving vertically down the figure is another pass through the while loop within the compute() method of **Ford–Fulkerson** (as seen in Figure 8-1). The result, at the bottom of the figure, is the maximum flow found by each approach.

In this example, you are the shipping manager in charge of two factories in Chicago (v_1) and Washington, D.C. (v_2) that can each produce 300 widgets daily. You must ensure that two customers in Houston (v_3) and Boston (v_4) each receive 300 widgets a day. You have several options for shipping, as shown in the figure. For example, between Washington, D.C. and Houston, you may ship up to 280 widgets daily at $4 per widget, but the cost increases to $6 per widget if you ship from Washington, D.C. to Boston (although you can then send up to 350 widgets per day along that route).

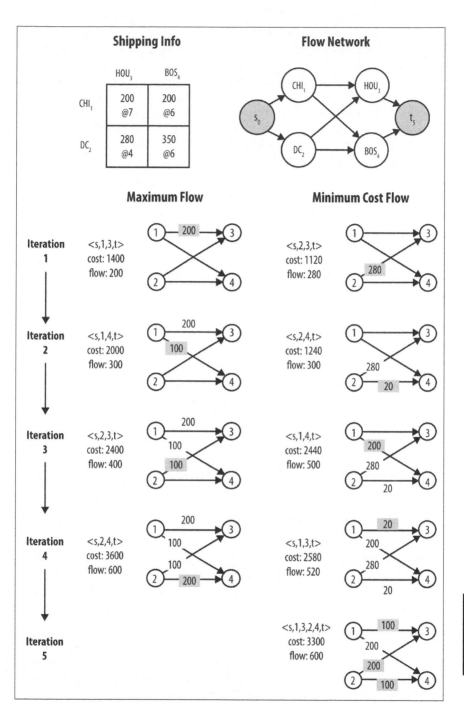

Figure 8-7. Side-by-side computation showing difference when considering the minimum cost flow

It may not even be clear that **Ford–Fulkerson** can be used to solve this problem, but note that we can create a graph G with a new source vertex s_0 that connects to the two factory nodes (v_1 and v_2), and the two customers (v_3 and v_4) connect to a new sink vertex t_5. To save space, the source and sink vertices s_0 and t_5 are omitted. On the lefthand side of Figure 8-7 we execute the **Edmonds–Karp** variation to demonstrate that we can meet all of our customer needs as requested, at the total daily shipping cost of \$3,600. During each of the four iterations by **Ford–Fulkerson**, the impact of the augmented path is shown (when an iteration updates the flow for an edge, the flow value is shaded gray).

Is this the lowest cost we can achieve? The righthand side of Figure 8-7 shows the execution of **Ford–Fulkerson** using `ShortestPathArray` as its search strategy, as described in Example 8-6. Note how the first augmented path found takes advantage of the lowest-cost shipping rate. Also `ShortestPathArray` only uses the costliest shipping route from Chicago (v_1) to Houston (v_3) when there is no other way to meet the customer needs; when this happens, the augmented path reduces the existing flows between Washington, D.C. (v_2) and Houston (v_3), as well as between Washington, D.C. (v_2) and Boston (v_4).

Minimum Cost Flow

To solve a Minimum Cost Flow problem we need only construct a flow network graph and ensure it satisfies the criteria discussed earlier—capacity constraint, flow conservation, and skew symmetry—as well as two additional criteria, *supply satisfaction* and *demand satisfaction*. These terms came into being when the problem was defined in an economic context, and they roughly correspond to the electical engineering concepts of a source and a sink:

Supply satisfaction
> For each source vertex $s_i \in S$, the sum of $f(s_i, v)$ for all edges $(s_i, v) \in E$ (the flow out of s_i) minus the sum of $f(u, s_i)$ for all edges $(u, s_i) \in E$ (the flow into s_i) must be less than or equal to $sup(s_i)$. That is, the supply $sup(s_i)$ at each source vertex is a firm upper bound on the net flow from that vertex.

Demand satisfaction
> For each sink vertex $t_j \in T$, the sum of $f(u, t_j)$ for all edges $(u, t_j) \in E$ (the flow into t_j) minus the sum of $f(t_j, v)$ for all edges $(t_j, v) \in E$ (the flow out of t_j) must be less than or equal to $dem(t_j)$. That is, the $dem(t_j)$ at each target vertex is a firm upper bound on the net flow into that vertex.

To simplify the algorithmic solution, we further constrain the flow network graph to have a single source vertex and sink vertex. This can be easily accomplished by taking an existing flow network graph with any number of source and sink vertices and adding two new vertices. First, add a new vertex (which we refer to as s_0) to be the source vertex for the flow network graph, and add edges (s_0, s_i) for all $s_i \in S$ whose capacity $c(s_0, s_i) = sup(s_i)$ and whose cost $d(s_0, s_i) = 0$. Second, add a new vertex (referred to as tgt, for target) to be the sink vertex for the flow network graph, and add edges (t_j, tgt) for all $t_j \in T$ whose capacity $c(t_j, tgt) = dem(t_j)$ and whose cost $d(t_0, t_j) = 0$. As you can see, adding these vertices and edges does not increase the cost of the network flow, nor do they reduce or increase the final computed flow over the network.

The supplies $sup(s_i)$, demands $dem(t_j)$, and capacities $c(u, v)$ are all greater than 0. The shipping cost $d(u, v)$ associated with each edge may be greater than or equal to zero. When the resulting flow is computed, all $f(u, v)$ values will be greater than or equal to zero.

We now present the constructions that allow us to solve each of the remaining flow network problems listed in Figure 8-1. For each problem, we describe how to reduce the problem to Minimum Cost Flow.

Transshipment

The inputs are:

- m supply stations s_i, each capable of producing $sup(s_i)$ units of a commodity
- n demand stations t_j, each demanding $dem(t_j)$ units of the commodity
- w warehouse stations w_k, each capable of receiving and reshipping (known as "transshipping") a maximum max_k units of the commodity at the fixed warehouse processing cost of wp_k per unit

There is a fixed shipping cost of $d(i, j)$ for each unit shipping from supply station s_i to demand stations t_j, a fixed transshipping cost of $ts(i, k)$ for each unit shipped from supply station s_i to warehouse station w_k, and a fixed transshipping cost of $ts(k, j)$ for each unit shipped from warehouse station w_k to demand station t_j. The goal is to determine the flow $f(i, j)$ of units from supply station s_i to demand station t_j that minimizes the overall total cost, which can be concisely defined as:

Total Cost (TC) = Total Shipping Cost (TSC) + Total Transshipping Cost (TTC)

$TSC = \Sigma_i \Sigma_j d(i, j)^* f(i, j)$

$TTC = \Sigma_i \Sigma_k ts(i, k)^* f(i, k) + \Sigma_j \Sigma_k ts(j, k)^* f(j, k)$

The goal is to find integer values for $f(i, j) \geq 0$ that ensure that TC is a minimum while meeting all of the supply and demand constraints. Finally, the net flow of units through a warehouse must be zero, to ensure no units are lost (or added). The supplies $sup(s_i)$ and demands $dem(t_i)$ are all greater than 0. The shipping costs $d(i, j)$, $ts(i, k)$, and $ts(k, j)$ may be greater than or equal to zero.

Network
Flow
Algorithms

Solution

We convert the Transshipment problem instance into a Minimum Cost Flow problem instance (as illustrated in Figure 8-8) by constructing a graph $G = (V, E)$ such that:

V *contains* $n + m + 2*w + 2$ *vertices*
> Each supply station s_i maps to a vertex numbered i. Each warehouse w_k maps to two different vertices, one numbered $m + 2*k - 1$ and one numbered $m + 2*k$. Each demand station t_j maps to $1 + m + 2*w + j$. Create a new source vertex src (labeled 0) and a new target vertex tgt (labeled $n + m + 2*w + 1$).

E *contains* $(w + 1)*(m + n) + m*n + w$ *edges*
> The Transshipment class in the code repository encodes the process for constructing edges for the Transshipment problem instance.

Briefly, the artificial *source* vertex is connected to the m supply vertices, with zero cost and capacity equal to the supplier capacity $sup(s_i)$. These m supply vertices are each connected to the n demand vertices with cost equal to $d(i, j)$ and infinite capacity. The n demand vertices are connected to the new artificial *target* vertex with zero cost and capacity equal to $dem(t_j)$. There are w warehouse nodes, each connected to the m supply vertices with cost equal to $ts(i, k)$ and capacity equal to the supplier capacity $sup(s_i)$; these warehouse nodes are also connected to the n demand vertices with cost equal to $ts(k, j)$ and capacity equal to the demand capacity $dem(t_j)$. Finally, edges between warehouses have capacities and costs based on the warehouse limits and costs.

Once the Minimum Cost Flow solution is available, the transshipment schedule can be constructed by locating those edges $(u, v) \in E$ whose $f(u, v) > 0$. The cost of the schedule is the sum total of $f(u, v)*d(u, v)$ for these edges.

Transportation

The Transportation problem is simpler than the Transshipment problem because there are no intermediate warehouse nodes. The inputs are:

- m supply stations s_i, each capable of producing $sup(s_i)$ units of a commodity
- n demand stations t_j, each demanding $dem(t_j)$ units of the commodity

There is a fixed per-unit cost $d(i, j) \geq 0$ associated with transporting a unit over the edge (i, j). The goal is to determine the flow $f(i, j)$ of units from supply stations s_i to demand stations t_j that minimizes the overall transportation cost, *TSC*, which can be concisely defined as:

$$\text{Total Shipping Cost } (TSC) = \Sigma_i \Sigma_j d(i, j)*f(i, j)$$

The solution must also satisfy both the total demand for each demand station t_j and the supply capabilities for supply stations s_i.

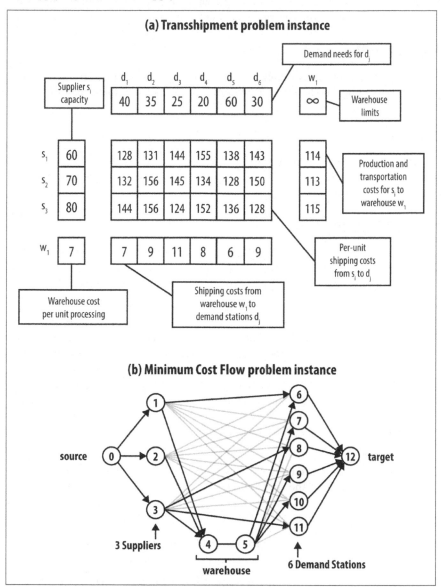

Figure 8-8. Sample Transshipment problem instance converted to Minimum Cost Flow problem instance

Solution

We convert the Transportation problem instance into a Transshipment problem instance with no intermediate warehouse nodes.

Assignment

The Assignment problem is simply a more restricted version of the Transportation problem: each supply node must supply only a single unit, and the demand for each demand node is also one.

Solution

We convert the Assignment problem instance into a Transportation problem instance, with the restriction that the supply nodes provide a single unit and the demand nodes require a single unit.

Linear Programming

The different problems described in this chapter can all be solved using Linear Programming (LP), a powerful technique that optimizes a linear objective function, subject to linear equality and inequality constraints (Bazaraa and Jarvis, 1977).

To show LP in action, we convert the Transportation problem depicted in Figure 8-8 into a series of linear equations to be solved by an LP solver. We use a general-purpose commercial mathematics software package known as Maple (*http://www.maplesoft.com*) to carry out the computations. As you recall, the goal is to maximize the flow over the network while minimizing the cost. We associate a variable with the flow over each edge in the network; thus the variable e13 represents $f(1,3)$. The function to be minimized is Cost, which is defined as the sum total of the shipping costs over each of the four edges in the network. This cost equation has the same constraints we described earlier for network flows:

Flow conservation
    The sum total of the edges emanating from a source vertex must equal its supply. The sum total of the edges entering a demand vertex must be equal to its demand.

Capacity constraint
    The flow over an edge $f(i, j)$ must be greater than or equal to zero. Also, $f(i, j) \leq c(i, j)$.

When executing the Maple solver, the computed result is {e13 = 100, e24 = 100, e23 = 200, e14 = 200}, which corresponds exactly to the minimum cost solution of 3,300 found earlier (see Example 8-7).

Example 8-7. Maple commands to apply minimization to Transportation problem

```
Constraints := [
# conservation of units at each node
e13+e14    = 300,  # CHI
e23+e24    = 300,  # DC

e13+e23    = 300,  # HOU
e14+e24    = 300,  # BOS

# maximum flow on individual edges
0 <= e13, e13 <= 200,
0 <= e14, e14 <= 200,
0 <= e23, e23 <= 280,
0 <= e24, e24 <= 350
];

Cost := 7*e13 + 6*e14 + 4*e23 + 6*e24;

# Invoke linear programming to solve problem
minimize (Cost, Constraints, NONNEGATIVE);
```

The **Simplex** algorithm designed by George Dantzig in 1947 makes it possible to solve problems such as those shown in Example 8-7, which involve hundreds or thousands of variables (McCall, 1982). **Simplex** has repeatedly been shown to be efficient in practice, although the approach can, under unfortunate circumstances, lead to an exponential number of computations. It is not recommended that you implement the **Simplex** algorithm yourself, both because of its complexity and because there are commercially available software libraries that do the job for you.

References

Ahuja, R. K., T. Magnanti, and J. Orlin, *Network Flows: Theory, Algorithms, and Applications*. Prentice Hall, 1993.

Bazaraa, M., J. Jarvis, and H. Sherali, *Linear Programming and Network Flows*. Fourth Edition. Wiley, 2009.

Cormen, T. H., C. Leiserson, R. Rivest, and C. Stein, *Introduction to Algorithms*. Third Edition. MIT Press, 2009.

Ford, L. R. Jr. and D. Fulkerson, *Flows in Networks*. Princeton University Press, 2010.

Fragouli, C. and T. Tabet, "On conditions for constant throughput in wireless networks," *ACM Transactions on Sensor Networks*, 2(3): 359–379, 2006, *http://dx.doi.org/10.1145/1167935.1167938*.

Goldberg, A. V. and R. Tarjan, "A new approach to the maximum flow problem," *Proceedings of the eighteenth annual ACM symposium on theory of computing*, pp. 136–146, 1986, *http://dx.doi.org/10.1145/12130.12144.*

Leighton, T. and S. Rao, "Multicommodity max-flow min-cut theorems and their use in designing approximation algorithms," *Journal of the ACM*, 46 (6):787–832, 1999. *http://dx.doi.org/10.1145/331524.331526.*

McCall, E. H., "Performance results of the simplex algorithm for a set of real-world linear programming models," *Communications of the ACM*, 25(3): 207–212, March 1982, *http://dx.doi.org/10.1145/358453.358461.*

Orden, A., "The Transhipment Problem," *Management Science*, 2(3): 276–285, 1956, *http://dx.doi.org/10.1287/mnsc.2.3.276.*

9

Computational Geometry

Computational geometry is the rigorous application of mathematics to compute geometric structures and their properties accurately and efficiently. We confine our discussion to solve problems involving two-dimensional structures represented in the Cartesian plane; there are natural extensions to n-dimensional structures. Mathematicians have investigated such problems for centuries, but the field has been recognized as a systematic study since the 1970s. This chapter presents the computational abstractions used to solve computational geometry problems. These techniques are by no means limited to geometry problems and have many real-world applications.

Algorithms in this category solve numerous real-world problems:

Convex hull
Compute the smallest convex shape that fully encloses a set of n two-dimensional points, P. This can be solved in $O(n \log n)$ instead of an $O(n^4)$ brute-force solution.

Intersecting line segments
Compute all intersections given a set of n two-dimensional line segments, S. This can be solved in $O((n + k) \log n)$ where k is the number of intersections, instead of an $O(n^2)$ brute-force solution.

Voronoi diagram
Partition a plane into regions based on distance to a set of n two-dimensional points, P. Each of the n regions consists of the Cartesian points closer to point $p_i \in P$ than any other $p_j \in P$. This can be solved in $O(n \log n)$.

Along the way we describe the powerful *Line Sweep* technique that can be used, ultimately, to solve all three of these problems.

Classifying Problems

A computational geometry problem inherently involves geometric objects, such as points, lines, and polygons. It is defined by the type of input data to be processed, the computation to be performed, and whether the task is static or dynamic.

Input Data

A computational geometry problem must define the input data. The following are the most common types of input data to be processed:

- Points in the two-dimensional plane
- Line segments in the plane
- Rectangles in the plane
- Polygons in the plane

Two-dimensional structures (lines, rectangles, and circles) have three-dimensional counterparts (planes, cubes, and spheres) and even *n*-dimensional counterparts (such as hyperplanes, hypercubes, and hyperspheres). Examples involving higher dimensions include:

Matching
> Using their Compatibility Matching System (U.S. Patent No. 6,735,568), the eHarmony matchmaking service predicts the long-term compatibility between two people. All users of the system (estimated to be 66 million in 2015) fill out a 258-question Relationship Questionnaire. eHarmony then determines closeness of match between two people based on 29-dimensional data.

Data imputation
> An input file contains 14 million records, where each record has multiple fields with text or numeric values. Some of these values are suspected to be wrong or missing. We can infer or impute "corrections" for the suspicious (or even missing) values by finding other records "close to" the suspect records.

This chapter describes a set of core interfaces for computational geometry and introduces classes that realize these interfaces. All algorithms are coded against these interfaces for maximum interoperability:

IPoint
> Represents a Cartesian point (x,y) using double floating-point accuracy. Implementations provide a default comparator that sorts by x, from left to right, and breaks ties by sorting y, from bottom to top.

IRectangle
> Represents a rectangle in Cartesian space. Implementations determine whether it contains an IPoint or an entire IRectangle.

ILineSegment

Represents a finite line segment in Cartesian space with a fixed start and end point. In "normal position," the start point will have a higher y coordinate than the end point, except for horizontal lines (in which case the leftmost end point is designated as the start point). Implementations can determine intersections with other ILineSegment or IPoint objects and whether an IPoint object is on its left or right when considering the orientation of the line from its end point to its start point.

These concepts naturally extend into multiple dimensions:

IMultiPoint

Represents an n-dimensional point with a fixed number of dimensions, with each coordinate value using double floating-point accuracy. The class can determine the distance to another IMultiPoint with the same dimensionality. It can return an array of coordinate values to optimize the performance of some algorithms.

IHypercube

Represents an n-dimensional solid shape with [*left, right*] bounding values for a fixed number of dimensions. The class can determine whether the hypercube intersects an IMultiPoint or contains an IHypercube with the same dimensionality.

Each of these interface types is realized by a set of concrete classes used to instantiate the actual objects (e.g., the class TwoDPoint realizes both the IPoint and IMulti Point interfaces).

Point values are traditionally real numbers that force an implementation to use floating-point primitive types to store data. In the 1970s, computations over floating-point values were relatively costly compared to integer arithmetic, but now this is no longer an obstacle to performance. Chapter 2 discusses important issues relating to floating-point computations, such as round-off error, that have an impact on the algorithms in this chapter.

Computation

There are three general tasks in computational geometry that are typically related to spatial questions, such as those shown in Table 9-1:

Query

Select existing elements within the input set based on a set of desired constraints (e.g., contained within, closest, or furthest); these tasks are most directly related to the search algorithms discussed in Chapter 5 and will be covered in Chapter 10.

Computation

Perform a series of calculations over the input set (e.g., line segments) to produce geometric structures that incorporate elements from the input set (e.g., intersections over these line segments).

Preprocessing

Embed the input set in a rich data structure to be used to answer a set of questions. In other words, the result of the preprocessing task is used as input for a set of other questions.

Table 9-1. Computational geometry problems and their applications

Computational geometry problem(s)	Real-world application(s)
Find the closest point to a given point.	Given a car's location, find the closest gasoline station.
Find the furthest point from a given point.	Given an ambulance station, find the furthest hospital from a given set of facilities to determine worst-case travel time.
Determine whether a polygon is simple (i.e., two nonconsecutive edges cannot share a point).	An animal from an endangered species has been tagged with a radio transmitter that emits the animal's location. Scientists would like to know when the animal crosses its own path to find commonly used trails.
Compute the smallest circle enclosing a set of points. Compute the largest interior circle of a set of points that *doesn't* contain a point.	Statisticians analyze data using various techniques. Enclosing circles can identify clusters, whereas large gaps in data suggest anomalous or missing data.
Determine the full set of intersections within a set of line segments, or within a set of circles, rectangles, or arbitrary polygons.	Very Large Scale Integration (VLSI) design rule checking.

Nature of the Task

A static task requires only that an answer be delivered on demand for a specific input data set. However, two dynamic considerations alter the way a problem might be approached:

- If multiple tasks are requested on a single input data set, preprocess the input set to improve the efficiency of each task

- If the input data set changes, investigate data structures that gracefully enable insertions and deletions

Dynamic tasks require data structures that can grow and shrink as demanded by changes to the input set. Arrays of fixed length might be suitable for static tasks, but dynamic tasks require the creation of linked lists or stacks of information to serve a common purpose.

Assumptions

For most computational geometry problems, an efficient solution starts by analyzing the assumptions and invariants about the input set (or the task to be performed). For example:

- Given an input set of line segments, can there be horizontal or vertical segments?

- Given a set of points, are any three of its points collinear? In other words, do they exist on the same mathematical line in the plane? If not, the points are said to be in *general position*, which means algorithms don't have to handle any special case involving collinear points.

- Does the input set contain a uniform distribution of points? Or is it skewed or clustered in a way that could force an algorithm into its worst-case behavior?

Most of the algorithms presented in this chapter have unusual boundary cases that are challenging to implement; we describe these situations in the code examples.

Convex Hull

Given a set of two-dimensional points P, the convex hull is the smallest convex shape that fully encloses all points in P (i.e., a line segment drawn between any two points within the hull lies totally within it). The hull is formed by computing a clockwise ordering of h points from P, which are labeled $L_0, L_1, \ldots, L_{h-1}$. Although any point can be the first (L_0), algorithms typically use the leftmost point in the set P; in other words, the one with the smallest x coordinate. If multiple such points exist in P, choose the one with the smallest y coordinate.

Given n points, there are $C(n, 3)$ or $n*(n - 1)*(n - 2)/6$ different possible triangles. Point $p_i \in P$ cannot be part of the convex hull if it is contained within a triangle formed by three other distinct points in P. For example, in Figure 9-1, point p_6 can be eliminated by the triangle formed by points p_4, p_7, and p_8. For each of these triangles T_i, a brute-force **Slow Hull** algorithm could eliminate any of the $n - 3$ remaining points from the convex hull if they exist within T_i.

Once the hull points are known, the algorithm labels the leftmost point L_0 and sorts all other points by the angle formed with a vertical line through L_0. Each sequence of three hull points L_i, L_{i+1}, L_{i+2} creates a right turn (note that this property holds for L_{h-2}, L_{h-1}, L_0 as well).

This inefficient approach requires $O(n^4)$ individual executions of the triangle detection step. We now present an efficient **Convex Hull Scan** algorithm that computes the convex hull in $O(n \log n)$.

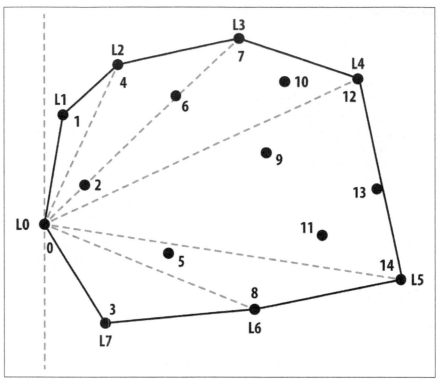

Figure 9-1. Sample set of points in plane with its convex hull drawn

Convex Hull Scan

Convex Hull Scan, invented by Andrew (1979), divides the problem by constructing a partial upper hull and a partial lower hull and then combining them. First, all points are sorted by their *x* coordinate (breaking ties by considering *y*). The partial upper hull starts with the leftmost two points in *P*. **Convex Hull Scan** extends the partial upper hull by finding the point $p \in P$ whose *x* coordinate comes next in sorted order after the partial upper hull's last point L_i. Computing the lower hull is similar; to produce the final results, join the partial results together by their end points.

If the three points L_{i-1}, L_i and the candidate point *p* form a right turn, **Convex Hull Scan** extends the partial hull to include *p*. This decision is equivalent to computing the determinant of the 3×3 matrix shown in Figure 9-2, which represents the cross product *cp*. If *cp* < 0, then the three points determine a right turn and **Convex Hull Scan** continues on. If *cp* = 0 (the three points are collinear) or if *cp* > 0 (the three points determine a left turn), then the middle point L_i must be removed from the partial hull to retain its convex property. **Convex Hull Scan** computes the convex upper hull by processing all points up to the rightmost point. The lower hull is similarly computed (this time by choosing points in decreasing *x* coordinate value), and the two partial hulls are joined together.

$$cp = \begin{vmatrix} L_{i-1}.x & L_{i-1}.y & 1 \\ L_i.x & L_i.y & 1 \\ p.x & p.y & 1 \end{vmatrix}$$

$$cp = (L_1.x - L_{i-1}.x)(p.y - L_{i-1}.y) - (L_1.y - L_{i-1}.y)(p.x - L_{i-1}.x)$$

Figure 9-2. Computing determinant decides whether points form right turn

Convex Hull Scan Summary

Best, Average, Worst: O(*n log n*)

```
convexHull (P)
  sort P ascending by x coordinate (break ties by sorting y) ❶
  if n < 3 then return P

  upper = {p0, p1} ❷
  for i = 2 to n-1 do
    append pi to upper
    while last three in upper make left turn do ❸
      remove middle of last three in upper ❹

  lower = {pn-1, pn-2} ❺
  for i = n-3 downto 0 do
    append pi to lower
    while last three in lower make left turn do
      remove middle of last three in lower

  join upper and lower (remove duplicate end points) ❻
  return computed hull
```

❶ Sorting points is the largest cost for this algorithm.

❷ Propose these two points as being on the upper hull.

❸ A left turn means the last three hull points form a nonconvex angle.

❹ Middle point was wrong choice so remove.

❺ Similar procedure computes lower hull.

❻ Stitch these together to form the convex hull.

Figure 9-3 shows **Convex Hull Scan** in action as it computes the partial upper hull. Note that the overall approach makes numerous mistakes as it visits every point in *P* from left to right, yet it adjusts by dropping—sometimes repeatedly—the middle of the last three points while it correctly computes the upper partial hull.

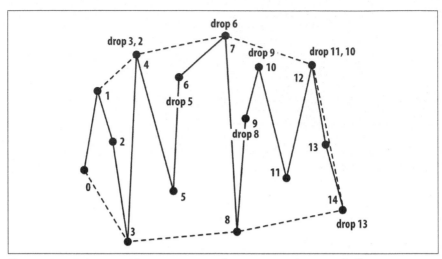

Figure 9-3. Incremental construction of upper partial convex hull

Input/Output

The input is a set of two-dimensional points P in a plane.

Convex Hull Scan computes an ordered list L containing the h vertices of the convex hull of P in clockwise order. The convex hull is a polygon defined by the points $L_0, L_1,..., L_{h-1}$, where h is the number of points in L. Note that the polygon is formed from the h line segments $<L_0, L_1>, <L_1, L_2>,..., <L_{h-1}, L_0>$.

To avoid trivial solutions, we assume $|P| \geq 3$. No two points are "too close" to each other (as determined by the implementation). If two points are too close to each other and one of those points is on the convex hull, **Convex Hull Scan** might incorrectly select an invalid convex hull point (or discard a valid convex hull point); however, the difference would be negligible.

Context

Convex Hull Scan requires only primitive operations (such as multiply and divide), making it easier to implement than **GrahamScan** (Graham, 1972), which uses trigonometric identities as demonstrated in Chapter 3. **Convex Hull Scan** can support a large number of points because it is not recursive.

The fastest implementation occurs if the input set is uniformly distributed and thus can be sorted in $O(n)$ using **Bucket Sort**, because the resulting performance would also be $O(n)$. Without such information, we choose **Heap Sort** to achieve $O(n \log n)$ behavior for sorting the initial points. The supporting code repository contains each of the described implementations that we benchmark for performance.

Solution

Example 9-1 shows how **Convex Hull Scan** first computes the partial upper hull before reversing direction and computing the partial lower hull. The final convex hull is the combination of the two partial hulls.

Example 9-1. Convex Hull Scan solution to convex hull

```
public class ConvexHullScan implements IConvexHull {
  public IPoint [] compute (IPoint[] points) {
    // sort by x coordinate (and if ==, by y coordinate).
    int n = points.length;
    new HeapSort<IPoint>().sort (points, 0, n-1, IPoint.xy_sorter);
    if (n < 3) { return points; }

    // Compute upper hull by starting with leftmost two points
    PartialHull upper = new PartialHull (points[0], points[1]);
    for (int i = 2; i < n; i++) {
      upper.add (points[i]);
      while (upper.hasThree() && upper.areLastThreeNonRight()) {
        upper.removeMiddleOfLastThree();
      }
    }

    // Compute lower hull by starting with rightmost two points
    PartialHull lower = new PartialHull (points[n-1], points[n-2]);
    for (int i = n-3; i >= 0; i--) {
      lower.add (points[i]);
      while (lower.hasThree() && lower.areLastThreeNonRight()) {
        lower.removeMiddleOfLastThree();
      }
    }

    // remove duplicate end points when combining.
    IPoint[] hull = new IPoint[upper.size()+lower.size()-2];
    System.arraycopy (upper.getPoints(), 0, hull, 0, upper.size());
    System.arraycopy (lower.getPoints(), 1, hull,
                      upper.size(), lower.size()-2);
    return hull;
  }
}
```

Because the first step of this algorithm must sort the points, we rely on **Heap Sort** to achieve the best average performance without suffering from the worst-case behavior of **Quicksort**. However, in the average case, **Quicksort** will outperform **Heap Sort**.

The Akl-Toussaint heuristic (1978) can noticeably improve the performance of the overall algorithm by discarding all points that exist within the extreme quadrilateral (the minimum and maximum points along both the x and y axes) computed from the initial set P. Figure 9-4 shows the extreme quadrilateral for the sample points from Figure 9-1. The discarded points are shown in gray; none of these points can belong to the convex hull.

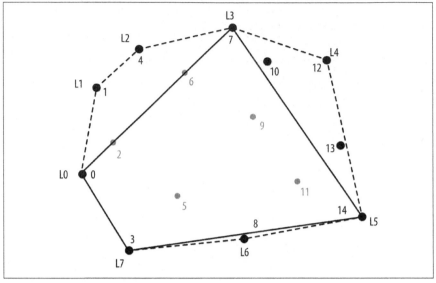

Figure 9-4. The Akl-Toussaint heuristic at work

To determine whether a point p is within the extreme quadrilateral, imagine a line segment s from p to an extreme point at $(p.x, -\infty)$, and count the number of times s intersects the four line segments of the quadrilateral; if the count is 1, p is inside and can be eliminated. The implementation handles special cases, such as when line segment s exactly intersects one of the end points of the extreme quadrilateral. This computation requires a fixed number of steps, so it is O(*1*), which means applying the Akl-Toussaint heuristic to all points is O(*n*). For large random samples, this heuristic can remove nearly half the initial points, and because these points are discarded before the sort operation, the costly sorting step in the algorithm is reduced.

Analysis

We ran a set of 100 trials on randomly generated two-dimensional points from the unit square, and the best and worst trials were discarded. Table 9-2 shows the average performance results of the remaining 98 trials. The table also shows the breakdown of average times to perform the heuristic plus some information about the solution that explains why **Convex Hull Scan** is so efficient.

As the size of the input set increases, nearly half of its points can be removed by the Akl-Toussaint heuristic. More surprising, perhaps, is the low number of points on the convex hull. The second column in Table 9-2 validates the claim by Preparata and Shamos (1985) that the number of points on the convex hull should be O(*log n*). Naturally, the distribution matters: if you choose points uniformly from a unit circle, for example, the convex hull contains on the order of the cube root of *n* points.

n	Average number of points on hull	Average time to compute	Average number of points removed by heuristic	Average time to compute heuristic	Average time to compute with heuristic
4,096	21.65	8.95	2,023	1.59	4.46
8,192	24.1	18.98	4,145	2.39	8.59
16,384	25.82	41.44	8,216	6.88	21.71
32,768	27.64	93.46	15,687	14.47	48.92
65,536	28.9	218.24	33,112	33.31	109.74
131,072	32.02	513.03	65,289	76.36	254.92
262,144	33.08	1168.77	129,724	162.94	558.47
524,288	35.09	2617.53	265,982	331.78	1159.72
1,048,576	36.25	5802.36	512,244	694	2524.30

The first step in **Convex Hull Scan** explains the cost of $O(n \log n)$ when the points are sorted using one of the standard comparison-based sorting techniques described in Chapter 4. The for loop that computes the upper partial hull processes $n - 2$ points, the inner while loop cannot execute more than $n - 2$ times, and the same logic applies to the loop that computes the lower partial hull. The total time for the remaining steps of **Convex Hull Scan** is thus $O(n)$.

Problems with floating-point arithmetic appear when **Convex Hull Scan** computes the cross-product calculation. Instead of strictly comparing whether the cross product $cp < 0$, PartialHull determines whether $cp < \delta$, where δ is 10^{-9}.

Variations

The sorting step of **Convex Hull Scan** can be eliminated if the points are already known to be in sorted order; in this case, **Convex Hull Scan** can perform in $O(n)$. Alternatively, if the input points are drawn from a uniform distribution, then one can use **Bucket Sort** (see "Bucket Sort" in Chapter 4) to also achieve $O(n)$ performance. Another convex hull variation known as **QuickHull** (Eddy, 1977) uses the Divide and Conquer strategy inspired by **Quicksort** to compute the convex hull in $O(n)$ performance on uniformly distributed points.

There is one final variation to consider. **Convex Hull Scan** doesn't actually need a sorted array when it constructs the partial upper hull; it just needs to iterate over all points in P in order, from smallest x coordinate to highest x coordinate. This behavior is exactly what occurs if one constructs a binary heap from the points in P and repeatedly removes the smallest element from the heap. If the removed points are stored in a linked list, the points can be simply "read off" the linked list to process

Computational Geometry

the points in reverse order from right to left. The code for this variation (identified as Heap in Figure 9-5) is available in the code repository accompanying this book.

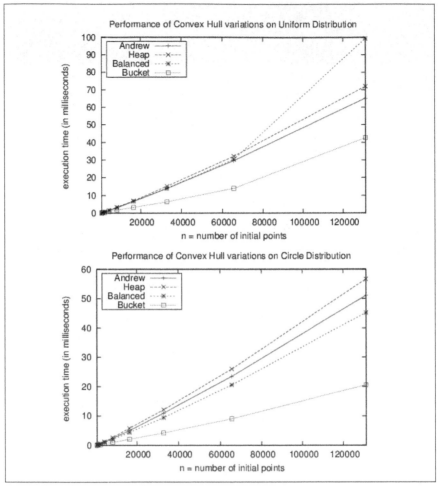

Figure 9-5. Performance of convex hull variations

The performance results shown in Figure 9-5 were generated from two data set distributions:

Circle data

n points distributed evenly over the edge of a unit circle. All points will belong to the convex hull, so this is an extreme case.

Uniform data

n points distributed evenly from the unit square. As n increases, the majority of these points will not be part of the convex hull, so this represents another extreme case.

We ran a series of trials using data sets with 512 to 131,072 points, the two data set distributions, the different implementations described in Example 9-1, and the code repository. We did not employ the Akl-Toussaint heuristic. For each data set size, we ran 100 trials and discarded the best- and worst-performing runs. The resulting average time (in milliseconds) of the remaining 98 trials is depicted in Figure 9-5. The implementation using balanced binary trees shows the best performance of the approaches that use comparison-based sorting techniques. Note that the implementation using **Bucket Sort** offers the most efficient implementation, but only because the input set is drawn from a uniform distribution. In the general case, computing a convex hull can be performed in $O(n \log n)$.

However, these implementations also suffer poor performance should the input data be skewed. Consider n points distributed unevenly with with points (0,0), (1,1) and $n - 2$ points clustered in thin slices just to the left of .502. This data set is constructed to defeat **Bucket Sort**. Table 9-3 shows how **Bucket Sort** degenerates into an $O(n^2)$ algorithm because it relies on **Insertion Sort** to sort its buckets.

The convex hull problem can be extended to three dimensions and higher where the goal is to compute the bounding polyhedron surrounding the three-dimensional point space. Unfortunately, in higher dimensions, more complex implementations are required.

Table 9-3. Timing comparison (in milliseconds) with highly skewed data

n	Andrew	Heap	Balanced	Bucket
512	0.28	0.35	0.33	1.01
1024	0.31	0.38	0.41	3.30
2048	0.73	0.81	0.69	13.54

Melkman (1987) developed an algorithm that produces the convex hull for a simple polyline or polygon in $O(n)$. Quite simply, it avoids the need to sort the initial points by taking advantage of the ordered arrangement of points in the polygon itself.

A convex hull can be maintained efficiently using an approach proposed by Overmars and van Leeuwen (1981). The convex hull points are stored in a tree structure that supports both deletion and insertion of points. The cost of either an insert or delete is known to be $O(\log^2 n)$, so the overall cost of constructing the hull becomes $O(n \log^2 n)$ while still requiring only $O(n)$ space. This result reinforces the principle that every performance benefit comes with its own trade-off.

GrahamScan was one of the earliest convex hull algorithms, developed in 1972 using simple trigonometric identities. We described this algorithm in Chapter 3. Using the determinant computation shown earlier, an appropriate implementation needs only simple data structures and basic mathematical operations. **GrahamScan** computes the convex hull in $O(n \log n)$, because it first sorts points by the angles they make with the point $s \in P$ with the smallest y coordinate and the x axis. One

Computational Geometry

challenge in completing this sort is that points with the same angle must be ordered by their distance from *s*.

Computing Line-Segment Intersections

Given a set of *n* line segments *S* in a two-dimensional plane, you might need to determine the full set of intersection points between all segments. In the example in Figure 9-6, there are two intersections (shown as small black circles) found in this set of four line segments. As shown in Example 9-2, a brute-force approach will compute all C(*n*,2) or $n*(n - 1)/2$ intersections of the line segments in *S* using O(n^2) time. For each pair, the implementation outputs the intersection, if it exists.

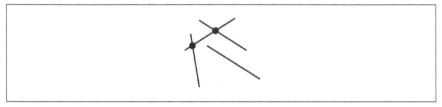

Figure 9-6. Three line segments with two intersections

Example 9-2. Brute Force Intersection implementation

```
public class BruteForceAlgorithm extends IntersectionDetection {
  public Hashtable<IPoint, List<ILineSegment>> intersections
          (ILineSegment[] segments) {
    initialize();
    for (int i = 0; i < segments.length-1; i++) {
      for (int j = i+1; j < segments.length; j++) {
        IPoint p = segments[i].intersection (segments[j]);
        if (p != null) {
          record (p, segments[i], segments[j]);
        }
      }
    }
    return report;
  }
}
```

This computation requires O(n^2) individual intersection computations and may require complex trigonometric functions.

It is not immediately clear that any improvement over O(n^2) is possible, yet this chapter presents the innovative **LineSweep** algorithm, which on average shows how to compute the results in O(($n + k$) *log n*) where *k* represents the number of reported intersection points.

LineSweep

There are numerous situations where we must detect intersections between geometric shapes. In VLSI chip design, precise circuits are laid out on a circuit board, and there must be no unplanned intersections. For travel planning, a set of roads could be stored in a database as line segments whose street intersections are determined by line-segment intersections.

Figure 9-7 shows an example with seven intersections between six line segments. Perhaps we don't have to compare all possible $C(n, 2)$ or $n*(n - 1)/2$ line-segment pairs. After all, line segments that are clearly apart from one another (in this example, S1 and S4) cannot intersect. **LineSweep** is a proven approach that improves efficiency by focusing on a subset of the input elements as it progresses. Imagine sweeping a horizontal line L across the input set of line segments from the top to the bottom and reporting the intersections when they are found by L. Figure 9-7 shows the state of line L as the sweep occurs from top to bottom (at nine distinct and specific locations).

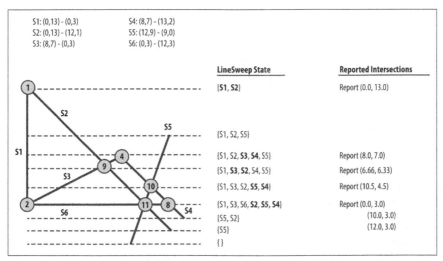

Figure 9-7. Detecting seven intersections for six line segments

The innovation of **LineSweep** is in recognizing that line segments can be ordered from left to right at a specific y coordinate. Horizontal segments are addressed by considering the left end point to be "higher" than the right end point. Line-segment intersections can then occur *only between neighboring segments in the state of the sweep line*. Specifically, for two line segments s_i and s_j to intersect, there must be some time during the line sweep when they are neighbors. **LineSweep** can efficiently locate intersections by maintaining this line state.

Looking closer at the nine selected locations of the horizontal sweep line in Figure 9-7, you will see that each occurs at (i) the start or end of a line segment, or (ii) an intersection. **LineSweep** doesn't actually "sweep" a line across the Cartesian plane; rather, it inserts the 2^*n segment end points into an event queue, which is a modified priority queue. All intersections involving start and end points of existing line segments can be detected when processing these points. **LineSweep** processes the queue to build up the state of the sweep line L to determine when neighboring line segments intersect.

Input/Output

LineSweep processes a set of n line segments S in the Cartesian plane. There can be no duplicate segments in S. No two line segments in S are collinear (i.e., overlap each other and have the same slope). The algorithm supports both horizontal and vertical line segments by carefully performing computations and ordering segments appropriately. No line segment should be a single point (i.e., a line segment whose start and end point are the same).

The output contains the k points representing the intersections (if any exist) between these line segments and, for each of these k points, p_i, the actual line segments from S that intersect at p_i.

Context

When the expected number of intersections is much smaller than the number of line segments, this algorithm handily outperforms a brute-force approach. When there are a significant number of intersections, the bookkeeping of the algorithm may outweigh its benefits.

A sweep-based approach is useful when you can (a) efficiently construct the line state, and (b) manage the event queue that defines when the sweep line is interpreted. There are numerous special cases to consider within the **LineSweep** implementation, and the resulting code is much more complex than the brute-force approach, whose worst-case performance is $O(n^2)$. Choose this algorithm because of the expected performance savings and improved worst-case behavior.

LineSweep produces partial results incrementally until the entire input set has been processed and all output results are produced. In the example here, the line state is a balanced binary tree of line segments, which is possible because we can impose an ordering on the segments at the sweep line. The event queue can also simply be a balanced binary tree of event points sorted lexicographically, meaning that points with a higher y value appear first (because the sweep line moves down the Cartesian plane from top to bottom); if there are two points with the same y value, the one with the lower x value appears first.

To simplify the coding of the algorithm, the binary tree used to store the line state is an augmented balanced binary tree in which only the leaf nodes contain actual information. The interior nodes store min and max information about the leftmost segment in the left subtree and rightmost segment in the right subtree. The ordering of segments within the tree is made based on the *sweep point*, the current EventPoint being processed from the priority queue.

LineSweep Summary

Best, Average, Worst: $O((n + k) \log n)$

```
intersection (S)
  EQ = new EventQueue
  foreach s in S do ❶
    ep = find s.start in EQ or create new one and insert into EQ
    add s to ep.upperLineSegments ❷

    ep = find s.end in EQ or create new one and insert into EQ
    add s to ep.lowerLineSegments

  state = new lineState
  while EQ is not empty do
    handleEvent (EQ, state, getMin(EQ))
end

handleEvent (EQ, state, ep)
  left = segment in state to left of ep
  right = segment in state to right of ep
  compute intersections in state between left to right ❸

  remove segments in state between left and right
  advance state sweep point down to ep

  if new segments start at ep then ❹
    insert new segments into state
    update = true
  if intersections associated with ep then ❺
    insert intersections into state
    update = true
  if update then
    updateQueue (EQ, left, left successor)
    updateQueue (EQ, right, right predecessor)
  else
    updateQueue (EQ, left, right)
end

updateQueue (EQ, A, B) ❻
  if neighboring A and B segments intersect below sweep point then
    insert their intersection point into EQ
end
```

❶   Initialize event queue with up to $2*n$ points.

❷   Event points refer to segments (upper or lower end points).

❸   Any intersection occurs between neighboring line segments.

❹   Maintain line state as new segments are discovered below sweep line.

⑤ At an intersection, neighboring line segments switch relative position.

⑥ Add intersection to event queue only if below sweep line.

Solution

The solution described in Example 9-3 depends on the EventPoint, EventQueue, and LineState classes found in the code repository.

Example 9-3. LineSweep Java implementation

```java
public class LineSweep extends IntersectionDetection {
  // Store line sweep state and event queue
  LineState lineState = new LineState();
  EventQueue eq = new EventQueue();

  /** Compute intersection of all segments from array of segments. */
  public Hashtable<IPoint,ILineSegment[]> intersections (
          ILineSegment[] segs) {
    // Construct Event Queue from segments. Ensure only unique
    // points appear by combining all information as it is discovered.
    for (ILineSegment ils : segs) {
      EventPoint ep = new EventPoint (ils.getStart());
      EventPoint existing = eq.event (ep);
      if (existing == null) { eq.insert (ep); } else { ep = existing; }

      // add upper line segments to ep (the object in the queue)
      ep.addUpperLineSegment (ils);

      ep = new EventPoint (ils.getEnd());
      existing = eq.event (ep);
      if (existing == null) { eq.insert (ep); } else { ep = existing; }

      // add lower line segments to ep (the object in the queue)
      ep.addLowerLineSegment (ils);
    }

    // Sweep top to bottom, processing each Event Point in the queue.
    while (!eq.isEmpty()) {
      EventPoint p = eq.min();
      handleEventPoint (p);
    }

    // return report of all computed intersections
    return report;
  }

  // Process events by updating line state and reporting intersections.
  private void handleEventPoint (EventPoint ep) {
```

```
// Find segments, if they exist, to left (and right) of ep in
// linestate. Intersections can happen only between neighboring
// segments. Start with nearest ones because as line sweeps down
// we will find any other intersections that (for now) we put off.
AugmentedNode<ILineSegment> left = lineState.leftNeighbor (ep);
AugmentedNode<ILineSegment> right = lineState.rightNeighbor (ep);

// determine intersections 'ints' from neighboring line segments and
// get upper segments 'ups' and lower segments 'lows' for this event
// point. An intersection exists if > 1 segment is associated with
// event point.
lineState.determineIntersecting (ep, left, right);
List<ILineSegment> ints = ep.intersectingSegments();
List<ILineSegment> ups = ep.upperEndpointSegments();
List<ILineSegment> lows = ep.lowerEndpointSegments();
if (lows.size() + ups.size() + ints.size() > 1) {
  record (ep.point, new List[] { lows, ups, ints } );
}

// Delete everything after left until left's successor is right.
// Then update the sweep point, so insertions will be ordered. Only
// ups and ints are inserted because they are still active.
lineState.deleteRange (left, right);
lineState.setSweepPoint (ep.point);
boolean update = false;
if (!ups.isEmpty()) {
  lineState.insertSegments (ups);
  update = true;
}
if (!ints.isEmpty()) {
  lineState.insertSegments (ints);
  update = true;
}

// If state shows no intersections at this event point, see if left
// and right segments intersect below sweep line, and update event
// queue properly. Otherwise, if there was an intersection, the order
// of segments between left & right have switched so we check two
// specific ranges, namely, left and its (new) successor, and right
// and its (new) predecessor.
if (!update) {
  if (left != null && right != null) { updateQueue (left, right); }
} else {
  if (left != null) { updateQueue (left, lineState.successor (left)); }
  if (right != null) { updateQueue (lineState.pred (right), right); }
}
}

// Any intersections below sweep line are inserted as event points.
private void updateQueue (AugmentedNode<ILineSegment> left,
                          AugmentedNode<ILineSegment> right) {
  // If two neighboring line segments intersect. make sure that new
```

```
    // intersection point is *below* the sweep line and not added twice.
    IPoint p = left.key().intersection (right.key());
    if (p == null) { return; }
    if (EventPoint.pointSorter.compare (p,lineState.sweepPt) > 0) {
      EventPoint new_ep = new EventPoint (p);
      if (!eq.contains (new_ep)) { eq.insert (new_ep); }
    }
  }
}
```

When the EventQueue is initialized with up to *2*n* EventPoint objects, each stores the ILineSegment objects that start (known as upper segments) and end (known as lower segments) at the stored IPoint object. When **LineSweep** discovers an intersection between line segments, an EventPoint representing that intersection is inserted into the EventQueue *as long as it occurs below the sweep line*. In this way, no intersections are missed and none are duplicated. For proper functioning, if this intersecting event point already exists within the EventQueue, the intersecting information is updated within the queue rather than being inserted twice. It is for this reason that **LineSweep** must be able to determine whether the event queue contains a specific EventPoint object.

In Figure 9-7, when the event point representing the lower point for segment S6 (technically the *rightmost* end point, because S6 is horizontal) is inserted into the priority queue, **LineSweep** only stores S6 as a lower segment; once it is processed, it will additionally store S4 as an intersecting segment. For a more complex case, when the event point representing the intersection of segments S2 and S5 is inserted into the priority queue, it stores no additional information. But after this event point is processed, it will store segments S6, S2, and S5 as intersecting segments.

The computational engine of **LineSweep** is the LineState class, which maintains the current sweep point as it sweeps from the top of the Cartesian plane downward. When the minimum entry is extracted from the EventQueue, the provided point Sorter comparator properly returns the EventPoint objects from top to bottom and left to right.

The true work of **LineSweep** occurs in the determineIntersecting method of LineState: the intersections are determined by iterating over those segments between *left* and *right*. Full details on these supporting classes are found in the code repository.

LineSweep achieves $O((n + k)\ log\ n)$ performance because it can reorder the active line segments when the sweep point is advanced. If this step requires more than $O(log\ s)$ for its operations, where s is the number of segments in the state, the performance of the overall algorithm will degenerate to $O(n^2)$. For example, if the line state was stored simply as a doubly linked list (a useful structure to rapidly find predecessor and successor segments), the insert operation would increase to require $O(s)$ time to properly locate the segment in the list, and as the set s of line segments increases, the performance degradation would soon become noticeable.

Similarly, the event queue must support an efficient operation to determine whether an event point is already present in the queue. Using a heap-based priority queue implementation—as provided by `java.util.PriorityQueue`, for example—also forces the algorithm to degenerate to $O(n^2)$. Beware of code that claims to implement an $O(n \log n)$ algorithm but instead produces an $O(n^2)$ implementation!

Analysis

LineSweep inserts up to $2*n$ segment end points into an event queue, a modified priority queue that supports the following operations in time $O(\log q)$, where q is the number of elements in the queue:

min
> Remove the minimum element from the queue.

insert (e)
> Insert e into its proper location within the ordered queue.

member (e)
> Determine whether e is a member of the queue. This operation is not strictly required of a generic priority queue.

Only unique points appear in the event queue—in other words, if the same event point is re-inserted, its information is combined with the event point already in the queue. Thus, when the points from Figure 9-7 are initially inserted, the event queue contains only eight event points.

LineSweep sweeps from top to bottom and updates the line state by adding and deleting segments in their proper order. In Figure 9-7, the ordered line state reflects the line segments that intersect the sweep line, from left to right, after processing the event point. To properly compute intersections, **LineSweep** determines the segment in the state to the left of (or right of) a given segment s_i. **LineSweep** uses an augmented balanced binary tree to process all of the following operations in time $O(\log t)$, where t is the number of elements in the tree:

insert (s)
> Insert line segment s into the tree.

delete (s)
> Delete segment s from the tree.

previous (s)
> Return segment immediately before s in the ordering, if one exists.

successor (s)
> Return segment immediately after s in the ordering, if one exists.

To properly maintain the ordering of segments, **LineSweep** swaps the order of segments when a sweep detects an intersection between segments s_i and s_j; fortunately, this too can be performed in $O(\log t)$ time simply by updating the sweep line point and then deleting and reinserting the line segments s_i and s_j. In Figure 9-7, for example, this swap occurs when the third intersection (6.66, 6.33) is found.

The initialization phase of the algorithm constructs a priority queue from the $2*n$ points (start and end) in the input set of n lines. The event queue must additionally be able to determine whether a new point p already exists within the queue; for this reason, we cannot simply use a heap to store the event queue, as is commonly done with priority queues. Since the queue is ordered, we must define an ordering of two-dimensional points. Point $p_1 < p_2$ if $p_1.y > p_2.y$; however, if $p_1.y = p_2.y$, then $p_1 < p_2$ if $p_1.x < p_2.x$. The size of the queue will never be larger than $2*n + k$, where k is the number of intersections and n is the number of input line segments.

All intersection points detected by **LineSweep** below the sweep line are added to the event queue, where they will be processed to swap the order of intersecting segments when the sweep line finally reaches the intersection point. Note that all intersections between neighboring segments will be found below the sweep line, and no intersection point will be missed.

As **LineSweep** processes each event point, line segments are added to the state when an upper end point is visited, and removed when a lower end point is visited. Thus, the line state will never store more than n line segments. The operations that probe the line state can be performed in O($log\ n$) time, and because there are never more than O($n + k$) operations over the state, our cost is O($(n + k)\ log\ (n + k)$). Because k is no larger than $C(n, 2)$ or $n*(n - 1)/2$, performance is O($(n + k)\ log\ n$), which becomes O($n^2\ log\ n$) in the worst case.

The performance of **LineSweep** is dependent on complex properties of the input (i.e., the total number of intersections and the average number of line segments maintained by the sweep line at any given moment). We can benchmark its performance given a specific problem and input data. We'll discuss two such problems now.

An interesting problem from mathematics is how to compute an approximate value of π using just a set of toothpicks and a piece of paper (known as Buffon's needle problem). If the toothpicks all are *len* units long, draw a set of vertical lines on the paper d units apart from one another where $d \geq len$. Randomly toss n toothpicks on the paper and let k be the number of intersections with the vertical lines. It turns out that the probability that a toothpick intersects a line (which can be computed as k/n) is equal to $(2*len)/(\pi*d)$.

When the number of intersections is much less than n^2, the brute-force approach wastes time checking lines that don't intersect (as shown in Table 9-4). When there are many intersections, the determining factor will be the average number of line segments maintained by LineState during the duration of **LineSweep**. When it is low (as might be expected with random line segments in the plane), **LineSweep** will be the winner.

Table 9-4. Timing comparison (in milliseconds) between algorithms on Buffon's needle problem

n	LineSweep	Brute force	Average number of intersections	Estimate for π	± Error
16	1.77	0.18	0.84	3.809524	9.072611
32	0.58	0.1	2.11	3.033175	4.536306
64	0.45	0.23	3.93	3.256997	2.268153
128	0.66	0.59	8.37	3.058542	1.134076
256	1.03	1.58	16.2	3.1644	0.567038
512	1.86	5.05	32.61	3.146896	0.283519
1,024	3.31	18.11	65.32	3.149316	0.14176
2,048	7	67.74	131.54	3.149316	0.07088
4,096	15.19	262.21	266.16	3.142912	0.03544
8,192	34.86	1028.83	544.81	3.12821	0.01772

For the second problem, consider a set S where there are $O(n^2)$ intersections among the line segments. **LineSweep** will seriously underperform because of the overhead in maintaining the line state in the face of so many intersections. Table 9-5 shows how brute force handily outperforms **LineSweep**, where n is the number of line segments whose intersection creates the $C(n, 2)$ or $n*(n-1)/2$ intersection points.

Table 9-5. Worst-case comparison of LineSweep versus brute force (in ms)

n	LineSweep (avg)	Brute force (avg)
2	0.17	0.03
4	0.66	0.05
8	1.11	0.08
16	0.76	0.15
32	1.49	0.08
64	7.57	0.38
128	45.21	1.43
256	310.86	6.08
512	2252.19	39.36

Computational Geometry

Variations

One interesting variation requires only that the algorithm report one of the intersection points, rather than all points; this would be useful to detect whether two polygons intersect. This algorithm requires only O($n \log n$) time, and may more rapidly locate the first intersection in the average case. Another variation considers an input set of red and blue lines where the only desired intersections are those between different colored line segments (Palazzi and Snoeyink, 1994).

Voronoi Diagram

In 1986, Fortune applied the line-sweep technique to solve another computational geometry problem, namely, constructing the Voronoi diagram for a set of points, P, in the Cartesian plane. This diagram is useful in a number of disciplines, ranging from the life sciences to economics (Aurenhammer, 1991).

A Voronoi diagram partitions a plane into regions based on each region's distance to a set of n two-dimensional points, P. Each of the n regions consists of the Cartesian points closer to point $p_i \in P$ than any other $p_j \in P$. Figure 9-8 shows the computed Voronoi diagram (black lines) for 13 sample points (shown as squares). The Voronoi diagram consists of 13 convex regions formed from edges (the lines in the figure) and vertices (where these lines intersect). Given the Voronoi diagram for a set of points, you can:

- Compute the convex hull
- Determine the largest empty circle within the points
- Find the nearest neighbor for each point
- Find the two closest points in the set

Fortune Sweep implements a line sweep similar to the one used to detect where line segments intersect. Recall that a line sweep inserts existing points into a priority queue and processes those points in order, thus defining a sweep line. The algorithm maintains a line state that can be updated efficiently to determine the Voronoi diagram. In **Fortune Sweep**, the key observation to make is that the sweeping line divides the plane into three distinct regions, as shown in Figure 9-9.

As the line sweeps down the plane, a partial Voronoi diagram is formed; in Figure 9-9, the region associated with point p_2 is fully computed as a semi-infinite polygon delimited by four line segments, shown in bold. The sweep line is currently ready to process point p_6 and points p_7 through p_{11} are waiting to be processed. The line-state structure currently maintains points { p_1, p_4, p_5, and p_3 }.

The challenge in understanding **Fortune Sweep** is that the line state is a complex structure called a *beach line*. In Figure 9-9, the beach line is the thin collection of curved fragments from left to right; the point where two parabolas meet is known as a *breakpoint*, and the dashed lines represent partial edges in the Voronoi diagram that have yet to be confirmed. Each of the points in the beach line state defines a

---

parabola with respect to the sweep line. The beach line is defined as the intersection of these parabolas closest to the sweep line.

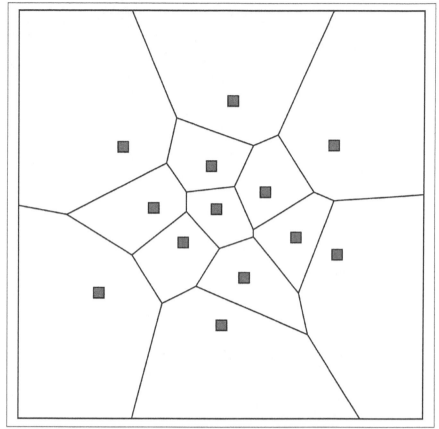

Figure 9-8. Sample Voronoi diagram

To explain the structure of the curved segments in the beach line, we need to define the *parabola* geometric shape. Given a focus point, *f*, and a line, *L*, a parabola is a symmetric shape composed of the Cartesian points that are *equidistant* from *f* and the line *L*. The vertex of the parabola, $v = (h, k)$, is the lowest point on the shape. *p* represents the distance between *L* and *v* as well as the distance between *v* and *f*. Given those variables, the equation $4p(y - k) = (x - h)^2$ defines the parabola's structure, which is easy to visualize when *L* is a horizontal line and the parabola opens upward as shown in Figure 9-10.

The sweep starts at the topmost point in *P* and sweeps downward, discovering points known as *sites* to process. The parabolas in the beach line change shape as the sweep line moves down, as shown in Figure 9-11, which means that breakpoints also change their location. Fortunately, the algorithm updates the sweep line only $O(n)$ times.

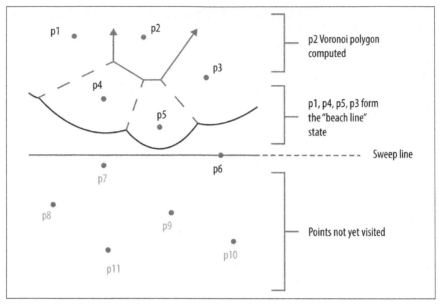

Figure 9-9. Elements of Fortune Sweep

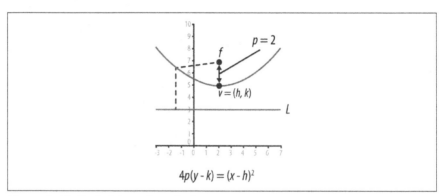

Figure 9-10. Definition of parabola

A vertex in the Voronoi diagram is computed by detecting three points in P that lie on a circle that doesn't contain any other points in P. The center of this circle defines the Voronoi vertex, because that is a point equidistant from the three points. The three rays that radiate from the center become edges in the Voronoi diagram because these lines define the points that are equidistant from two points in the collection. These edges *bisect* the chord line segments in the circle between the points. For example, line L_3 in Figure 9-12 is perpendicular to the line segment that would be drawn between (r_1, r_3).

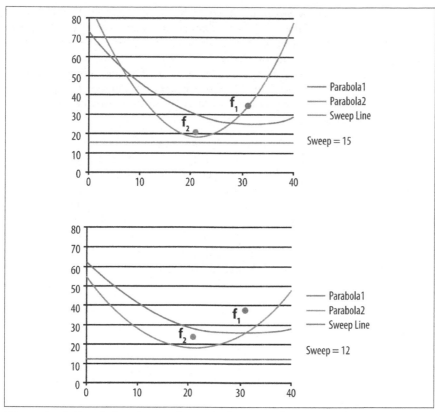

Figure 9-11. Parabolas change shape as the sweep line moves down

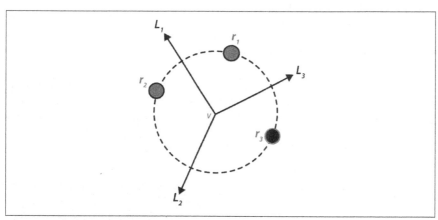

Figure 9-12. Circle formed by three points

We now show how **Fortune Sweep** maintains state information to detect these circles. The characteristics of the beach line minimize the number of circles **Fortune Sweep** checks; specifically, whenever the beach line is updated, **Fortune Sweep** needs to check only the neighboring arcs (to the left and to the right) where the update occurred. Figure 9-12 shows the mechanics of **Fortune Sweep** with just three points. These three points are processed in order from top to bottom, namely, r_1, r_2, and r_3. A circle is defined once the third point is processed and is known as the *circumcircle* of these three points.

Figure 9-13 shows the state of the beach line after processing points r_1 and r_2. The beach line is formed by the parabola segments that are closest to the sweep line; in this case, the state of the sweep line is represented as a binary tree where leaf nodes declare the associated parabola segment and internal nodes represent breakpoints. The beach line, from left to right, is formed by three parabolic segments, s_1, s_2 and then s_1 again, which are drawn from the parabolas associated with points r_1, r_2 and then r_1 again. The breakpoint $s_1{:}s_2$ represents the x coordinate where to its left, parabola s_1 is closer to the sweep line, and to its right, parabola s_2 is closer to the sweep line. The same characteristics holds for breakpoint $s_2{:}s_1$.

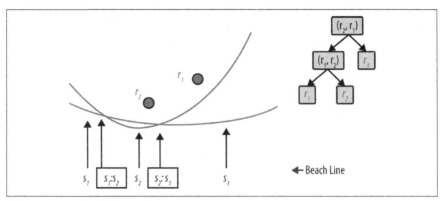

Figure 9-13. Beach line after two points

Figure 9-14 shows when the line-sweep processes the third point, r_3. By its location, a vertical line through r_3 intersects the beach line at the rightmost arc, s_1, and the updated beach line state is shown on the right side in Figure 9-14. There are four nonleaf nodes, representing the four intersections that occur on the beach line between the three parabolas. There are five leaf nodes, representing the five arc segments that form the beach line, from left to right.

Once this beach line is formed, observe that these three points form a circumcircle. The center of the circle *has the potential* to become a Voronoi point in the diagram, but this will happen only if no other point in P is contained within the circle. The algorithm handles this situation elegantly by creating a *circle event*, whose coordinates are the lowest point on this circle (shown in Figure 9-15), and inserting that event into the event priority queue. Should some other site event be processed before this circle event that "gets in the way," this circle event will be eliminated. Otherwise, it will be processed in turn and the center point of the circle becomes a vertex in the Voronoi diagram.

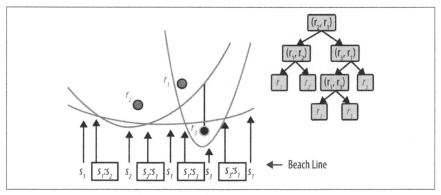

Figure 9-14. Beach line after three points

A key step in this algorithm is the removal of nodes from the beach line state that can have no other effect on the construction of the Voronoi diagram. Once the identified circle event is processed, the middle arc, associated with r_1 in this case, has no further effect on any other point in P, so it can be removed from the beach line. The resulting beach line state is shown in the binary tree on the right side of Figure 9-15.

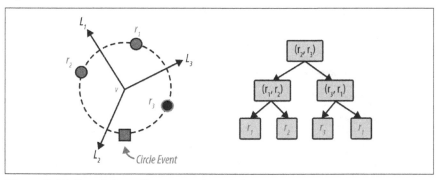

Figure 9-15. Beach line after processing circle event

Input/Output

The input is a set of two-dimensional points P in a plane.

Fortune Sweep computes a Voronoi diagram composed of n Voronoi polygons, each of which defines the region for one of the points in P. Mathematically, there may be partially infinite regions, but the algorithm eliminates these by computing the Voronoi diagram within a bounding box of suitable size to enclose all points in

P. The output will be a set of line segments and Voronoi polygons that are defined by edges in clockwise order around each point in *P*.

Some implementations assume *P* does not contain four cocircular points that form a circle.

Some implementations assume that no two points share the same *x* or *y* coordinate. Doing so eliminates many of the special cases. This is easy to implement when the input set (*x*, *y*) contains integer coordinates: simply add a random fractional number to each coordinate before invoking **Fortune Sweep**.

Solution

The implementation is complicated because of the computations needed to maintain the beach line's state; some of the special cases are omitted from the presentation here. The code repository contains functions that perform the geometric computations of intersecting parabolas. The classes that support this implementation are summarized in Figure 9-16. This implementation uses Python's heapq module, which provides heappop and heappush methods used to construct and process a priority queue.

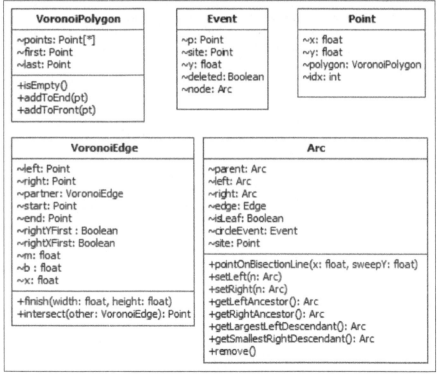

Figure 9-16. Classes supporting the code

As shown in Example 9-4, the process method creates site events for each of the input points and processes each event one at a time by descending y coordinate (ties are broken by smaller x coordinate).

Fortune Sweep Summary

Best, Average, Worst: O($n \log n$)

```
fortune (P)
  PQ = new Priority Queue
  LineState = new Binary Tree

  foreach p in P do ❶
    event = new SiteEvent(p)
    insert event into PQ

    while PQ is not empty do
      event = getMin(PQ)
      sweepPt = event.p ❷
      if event is site event then
        processSite(event)
      else
        processCircle(event)

    finishEdges() ❸

processSite(e) ❹
  leaf = find arc A in beach line bisected by e.p
  modify beach line and remove unneeded circle events ❺
  detect new potential circle events

processCircle(e) ❻
  determine (left,right) neighboring arcs in beach line
  remove unneeded circle events
  record Voronoi vertex and Voroni edges
  modify beach line to remove "middle" arc
  detect new potential circle events to left and right
```

❶ Priority queue orders events by descending y coordinate.

❷ Sweep line is updated by point associated with each event removed.

❸ Remaining breakpoints in beach line determine final edges.

❹ Update beach line with each new point...

❺ ...which might remove potential circle events.

❻ Compute Voronoi point and update beach line state.

Computational Geometry

Example 9-4. Voronoi Python implementation

```python
from heapq import heappop, heappush

class Voronoi:
  def process (self, points):
    self.pq = []
    self.edges = []
    self.tree = None
    self.firstPoint = None      # handle tie breakers with first point
    self.stillOnFirstRow = True
    self.points = []

    # Each point has unique identifier
    for idx in range(len(points)):
      pt = Point (points[idx], idx)
      self.points.append (pt)
      event = Event (pt, site=pt)
      heappush (self.pq, event)

    while self.pq:
      event = heappop (self.pq)
      if event.deleted:
        continue

      self.sweepPt = event.p
      if event.site:
        self.processSite (event)
      else:
        self.processCircle (event)

    # complete edges that remain and stretch to infinity
    if self.tree and not self.tree.isLeaf:
      self.finishEdges (self.tree)

      # Complete Voronoi Edges with partners
      for e in self.edges:
        if e.partner:
          if e.b is None:
            e.start.y = self.height
          else:
            e.start = e.partner.end
```

The implementation handles the special case when there are multiple points that share the same largest *y* coordinate value; it does so by storing the firstPoint detected within processSite.

The true details of **Fortune Sweep** are contained within the processSite implementation shown in Example 9-5 and processCircle shown in Example 9-6.

Example 9-5. Voronoi process site event

```
def processSite (self, event):
  if self.tree == None:
    self.tree = Arc(event.p)
    self.firstPoint = event.p
    return

  # Must handle special case when two points are at topmost y coordinate, in
  # which case the root is a leaf node. Note that when sorting events, ties
  # are broken by x coordinate, so the next point must be to the right.
  if self.tree.isLeaf and event.y == self.tree.site.y:
    left = self.tree
    right = Arc(event.p)

    start = Point(((self.firstPoint.x + event.p.x)/2, self.height))
    edge = VoronoiEdge (start, self.firstPoint, event.p)

    self.tree = Arc(edge = edge)
    self.tree.setLeft (left)
    self.tree.setRight (right)

    self.edges.append (edge)
    return

  # If leaf had a circle event, it is no longer valid
  # since it is being split
  leaf = self.findArc (event.p.x)
  if leaf.circleEvent:
    leaf.circleEvent.deleted = True

  # find point on parabola where event.pt.x bisects with vertical line,
  start = leaf.pointOnBisectionLine (event.p.x, self.sweepPt.y)

  # Potential Voronoi edges discovered between two sites
  negRay = VoronoiEdge (start, leaf.site, event.p)
  posRay = VoronoiEdge (start, event.p, leaf.site)
  negRay.partner = posRay
  self.edges.append (negRay)

  # modify beach line with new interior nodes
  leaf.edge = posRay
  leaf.isLeaf = False

  left = Arc()
  left.edge = negRay
  left.setLeft (Arc(leaf.site))
  left.setRight (Arc(event.p))

  leaf.setLeft (left)
```

```
leaf.setRight (Arc(leaf.site))

# Check whether there is potential circle event on left or right.
self.generateCircleEvent (left.left)
self.generateCircleEvent (leaf.right)
```

The processSite method modifies the beach line with each discovered *site* event to insert two additional interior nodes and two additional leaf nodes. The findArc method, in O(*log n*) time, locates the arc that must be modified by the newly discovered *site* event. In modifying the beach line, the algorithm computes two edges that will ultimately be in the final Voronoi diagram. These are attached with the breakpoint Arc nodes in the tree. Whenever the beach line state changes, the algorithm checks to the left and to the right to determine whether neighboring arcs form a potential circle event.

Example 9-6. Voronoi process circle event

```
def processCircle (self, event):
  node = event.node

  # Find neighbor on the left and right.
  leftA  = node.getLeftAncestor()
  left   = leftA.getLargestDescendant()
  rightA = node.getRightAncestor()
  right  = rightA.getSmallestDescendant()

  # Eliminate old circle events if they exist.
  if left.circleEvent:
    left.circleEvent.deleted = True
  if right.circleEvent:
    right.circleEvent.deleted = True

  # Circle defined by left - node - right. Terminate Voronoi rays.
  p = node.pointOnBisectionLine (event.p.x, self.sweepPt.y)
  leftA.edge.end = p
  rightA.edge.end = p

  # Update ancestor node in beach line to record new potential edges.
  t = node
  ancestor = None
  while t != self.tree:
    t = t.parent
    if t == leftA:
      ancestor = leftA
    elif t == rightA:
      ancestor = rightA

  ancestor.edge = VoronoiEdge(p, left.site, right.site)
  self.edges.append (ancestor.edge)
```

```
# Remove middle arc (leaf node) from beach line tree.
node.remove()

# May find new neighbors after deletion so must check for circles.
self.generateCircleEvent (left)
self.generateCircleEvent (right)
```

The processCircle method is responsible for identifying new vertices in the Voronoi diagram. Each circle event is associated with node, the topmost point in the circumcircle that generated the circle event in the first place. This method removes node from the beach line state since it can have no impact on future computations. In doing so, there may be new neighbors on the beach line, so it checks on the left and the right to see if any additional circle events should be generated.

These code examples depend on helper methods that perform geometrical computations, including the pointOnBisectionLine and the intersect line intersection methods. These details are found in the code repository. Much of the difficulty in implementing **Fortune Sweep** lies in the proper implementation of these necessary geometric computations. One way to minimize the number of special cases is to assume all coordinate values in the input (both x and y) are unique and that no four points are cocircular. Making these assumptions simplifies the computational processing, especially since you can ignore cases where the Voronoi diagram contains horizontal or vertical lines.

The final code example, generateCircleEvent, shown in Example 9-7, determines when three neighboring arcs on the beach line form a circle. If the lowest point of this circle is above the sweep line (i.e., it would already have been processed) then it is ignored; otherwise, an event is added to the event queue to be processed in order. It may yet be eliminated if another site to be processed falls within the circle.

Example 9-7. Voronoi generate new circle event

```
def generateCircleEvent (self, node):
    """
    There is possibility of a circle event with this new node
    being the middle of three consecutive nodes. If so, then add
    new circle event to the priority queue for further processing.
    """

    # Find neighbors on the left and right, should they exist.
    leftA = node.getLeftAncestor()
    if leftA is None:
        return
    left = leftA.getLargestLeftDescendant()

    rightA = node.getRightAncestor()
    if rightA is None:
        return
    right = rightA.getSmallestRightDescendant()
```

```
# sanity check. Must be different
if left.site == right.site:
  return

# If two edges have no valid intersection, leave now.
p = leftA.edge.intersect (rightA.edge)
if p is None:
  return

radius = ((p.x-left.site.x)**2 + (p.y-left.site.y)**2)**0.5

# make sure choose point at bottom of circumcircle.
circleEvent = Event(Point((p.x, p.y-radius)))
if circleEvent.p.y >= self.sweepPt.y:
  return

node.circleEvent = circleEvent
circleEvent.node = node
heappush (self.pq, circleEvent)
```

Analysis

The performance of **Fortune Sweep** is determined by the number of events inserted into the priority queue. At the start, the n points must be inserted. During processing, each new site can generate at most two additional arcs, thus the beach line is at most $2*n - 1$ arcs. By using a binary tree to store the beach line state, we can locate desired arc nodes in $O(log\ n)$ time.

Modifying the leaf node in processSite requires a fixed number of operations, so it can be considered to complete in constant time. Similarly, removing an arc node within the processCircle method is also a constant time operation. Updating the ancestor node in the beach line to record new potential edges remains an $O(log\ n)$ operation. The binary tree containing the line state is not guaranteed to be balanced, but adding this capability only increases the performance of insert and remove to $O(log\ n)$. In addition, after rebalancing a binary tree, its previously existing leaf nodes remain leaf nodes in the rebalanced tree.

Thus, whether the algorithm is processing a site event or a circle event, the performance will be bounded by $2*n*log(n)$, which results in $O(n\ log\ n)$ overall performance.

This complicated algorithm does not reveal its secrets easily. Indeed, even algorithmic researchers admit that this is one of the more complicated applications of the line-sweep technique. Truly, the best way to observe its behavior is to execute it step by step within a debugger.

References

Andrew, A. M., "Another efficient algorithm for convex hulls in two dimensions," *Information Processing Letters*, 9(5): 216–219, 1979, *http://dx.doi.org/ 10.1016/0020-0190(79)90072-3*.

Aurenhammer, F., "Voronoi diagrams: A survey of a fundamental geometric data structure," *ACM Computing Surveys*, 23(3): 345–405, 1991, *http://dx.doi.org/ 10.1145/116873.116880*.

Eddy, W., "A new convex hull algorithm for planar sets," *ACM Transactions on Mathematical Software*, 3(4): 398–403, 1977, *http://dx.doi.org/ 10.1145/355759.355766*.

Fortune, S., "A sweepline algorithm for Voronoi diagrams," Proceedings of the 2nd Annual Symposium on Computational Geometry. ACM, New York, 1986, pp. 313–322, *http://doi.acm.org/10.1145/10515.10549*.

Computational Geometry

10

Spatial Tree Structures

The algorithms in this chapter are concerned primarily with modeling two-dimensional structures over the Cartesian plane to conduct powerful search queries that go beyond simple membership, as covered in Chapter 5. These algorithms include:

Nearest neighbor
Given a set of two-dimensional points, P, determine which point is closest to a target query point, x. This can be solved in $O(log\ n)$ instead of an $O(n)$ brute-force solution.

Range queries
Given a set of two-dimensional points, P, determine which points are contained within a given rectangular region. This can be solved in $O(n^{0.5} + r)$ where r is the number of reported points, instead of an $O(n)$ brute-force solution.

Intersection queries
Given a set of two-dimensional rectangles, R, determine which rectangles intersect a target rectangular region. This can be solved in $O(log\ n)$ instead of an $O(n)$ brute-force solution.

Collision detection
Given a set of two-dimensional points, P, determine the intersections between squares of side s centered on these points. This can be solved in $O(n\ log\ n)$ instead of an $O(n^2)$ brute-force solution.

The structures and algorithms naturally extend to multiple dimensions, but this chapter will remain limited to two-dimensional structures for convenience. The chapter is named after the many ways researchers have been able to partition n-dimensional data using the intuition at the heart of binary search trees.

Nearest Neighbor Queries

Given a set of points, P, in a two-dimensional plane, you might need to determine the point in P that is *closest* to a query point x using Euclidean distance. Note that point x does not have to already exist in P, which differentiates this problem from the searching algorithms from Chapter 5. These queries also extend to input sets whose points are found in n-dimensional space.

The naïve implementation is to inspect all points in P, resulting in a linear $O(n)$ algorithm. Because P is known in advance, perhaps there is some way to structure its information to speed up queries by discarding large groups of its points during the search. Perhaps we could partition the plane into bins of some fixed size m by m, as shown in Figure 10-1(a). Here 10 input points in P (shown as circles) are placed into nine enclosing bins. The large shaded number in each bin reflects the number of points in it. When searching for the closest neighbor for a point x (shown as a small black square), find its enclosing bin. If that bin is not empty, we only need to search the bins that intersect the focus circle whose radius is $m^*sqrt(2)$.

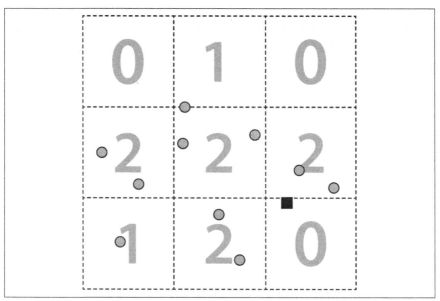

Figure 10-1. Bin approach for locating nearest neighbor

In this example, however, there are no points in the target bin, and the three neighboring bins will need to be examined. This ineffective approach is inappropriate because many bins may in fact be empty, and the algorithm would still have to search multiple neighboring bins. As we saw in Chapter 5, binary search trees reduce the effort by eliminating from consideration groups of points that could not be part of the solution. In this chapter, we introduce the idea of a *spatial tree* to partition the points in the two-dimensional plane to reduce the search time. The extra cost of preprocessing all points in P into an efficient structure is recouped later by savings of the query computations, which become O(*log n*). If the number of searches is small, then the brute-force O(*n*) comparison is best.

Range Queries

Instead of searching for a specific target point, a query could instead request all points in *P* that are contained within a given rectangular region of the two-dimensional plane. The brute-force solution checks whether each point is contained within the target rectangular region, resulting in O(*n*) performance.

The same data structure developed for nearest-neighbor queries also supports these queries, known as the "orthogonal range," because the rectangular query region is aligned with the *x* and *y* axes of the plane. The only way to produce better than O(*n*) performance is to find a way to both discard points from consideration, and include points in the query result. Using a *k*-d tree, the query is performed using a recursive traversal, and the performance can be O($n^{0.5} + r$), where *r* is the number of points reported by the query.

Intersection Queries

The input set being searched can typically be more complicated than a single *n*-dimensional point. Consider instead a set of rectangles *R* in a two-dimensional plane where each rectangle r_i is defined by a tuple (x_{low}, y_{low}, x_{high}, y_{high}). With this set *R* you might want to locate all rectangles that intersect a given point (*x*, *y*) or (more generally) intersect a target rectangle (x_1, y_1, x_2, y_2). Structuring the rectangles appears to be more complicated because the rectangles can overlap each other in the plane.

Instead of providing a target rectangle, we might be interested in identifying the intersections among a collection of two-dimensional elements. This is known as the *collision detection* problem, and we present a solution to detect intersections among a collection of points, *P*, using square-based regions centered around each point.

Spatial Tree Structures

Spatial tree structures show how to represent data to efficiently support the execution of these three common searches. In this chapter, we present a number of spatial tree structures that have been used to partition *n*-dimensional objects to improve the performance of search, insert, and delete operations. We now present three such structures.

k-d Tree

In Figure 10-2(a), the same 10 points from Figure 10-1 are shown in a *k*-d *tree*, so named because it can subdivide a *k*-dimensional plane along the perpendicular axes of the coordinate system. These points are numbered in the order in which they were inserted into the tree. The structure of the *k*-d tree from Figure 10-2(a) is depicted as a binary tree in Figure 10-2(b). For the remainder of this discussion we assume a two-dimensional tree, but the approach can also be used for arbitrary dimensions.

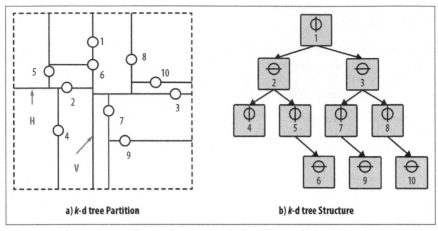

a) k-d tree Partition   b) k-d tree Structure

Figure 10-2. Division of two-dimensional plane using k-d tree

A k-d tree is a recursive binary tree structure where each node contains a point and a coordinate label (i.e., either x or y) that determines the partitioning orientation. The root node represents the rectangular region ($x_{low} = -\infty$, $y_{low} = -\infty$, $x_{high} = +\infty$, $y_{high} = +\infty$) in the plane partitioned along the vertical line V through point p_1. The left subtree further partitions the region to the left of V, whereas the right subtree further partitions the region to the right of the V. The left child of the root represents a partition along the horizontal line H through p_2 that subdivides the region to the left of V into a region above the line H and a region below the line H. The region ($-\infty$, $-\infty$, $p_1.x$, $+\infty$) is associated with the left child of the root, whereas the region ($p_1.x$, $\neq\infty$, $+\infty$, $+\infty$) is associated with the right child of the root. These regions are effectively nested, and we can see that the region of an ancestor node wholly contains the regions of any of its descendant nodes.

Quadtree

A *quadtree* partitions a set of two-dimensional points, P, recursively subdividing the overall space into four quadrants. It is a tree-like structure where each nonleaf node has four children, labeled **NE** (NorthEast), **NW** (NorthWest), **SW** (SouthWest), and **SE** (SouthEast). There are two distinct flavors of quadtrees:

Region-based

Given a 2^k by 2^k image of pixels where each pixel is 0 or 1, the root of a quadtree represents the entire image. Each of the four children of the root represents a 2^{k-1} by 2^{k-1} quadrant of the original image. If one of these four regions is not entirely 0s or 1s, then the region is subdivided into subregions, each of which is one-quarter the size of its parent. Leaf nodes represent a square region of pixels that are all 0s or 1s. Figure 10-3 describes the tree structure with a sample image bitmap.

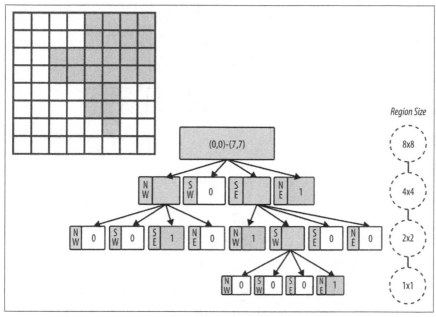

Figure 10-3. Quadtree using region-based partitioning

Point-based

Given a 2^k by 2^k space in the Cartesian plane, the quadtree directly maps to a binary tree structure, where each node can store up to four points. If a point is added to a full region, the region is subdivided into four regions each one-quarter the size of its parent. When no points are present in a quadrant for a node, then there is no child node for that quadrant, and so the shape of the tree depends on the order the points were added to the quadtree.

For this chapter, we focus on *point-based* quadtrees. Figure 10-4 shows an example containing 13 points in a 256 by 256 region. The quadtree structure is shown on the right side of the image. Note that there are no points in the root's SouthEast quadrant, so the root only has three children nodes. Also note the variable subdivisions of the regions based on which points have been added to the quadtree.

R-Tree

An *R-Tree* is a tree structure in which each node contains up to M links to children nodes. All actual information is stored by the leaf nodes, each of which can store up to M different rectangles. Figure 10-5 depicts an R-Tree where $M = 4$ and six rectangles have been inserted (labeled 1, 2, 3, 4, 5, and 6). The result is the tree shown on the right where the interior nodes reflect different rectangular regions inside of which the actual rectangles exist.

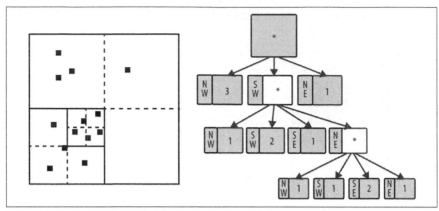

Figure 10-4. Quadtree using point-based partitioning

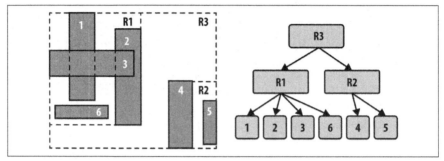

Figure 10-5. R-Tree example

The root node represents the smallest rectangular region (x_{low}, y_{low}, x_{high}, y_{high}) that includes all other rectangles in the tree. Each interior node has an associated rectangular region that similarly includes all rectangles in its descendant nodes. The actual rectangles in the R-Tree are stored only in leaf nodes. Aside from the root node, every rectangular region (whether associated with an interior node or a leaf node) is wholly contained by the region of its parent node.

We now use these various spatial structures to solve the problems outlined at the beginning of this chapter.

Nearest Neighbor Queries

Given a set of two-dimensional points, P, you are asked to determine which point in P is closest to a target query point, x. We show how to use k-d trees to efficiently perform these queries. Assuming the tree is effective in partitioning the points, each recursive traversal through the tree will discard roughly half of the points in the tree. In a k-d tree for points distributed in a normal manner, nodes on level i reflect rectangles that are roughly twice as large as the rectangles on level $i + 1$. This property will enable **Nearest Neighbor** to exhibit O($log\ n$) performance because it will be able to discard entire subtrees containing points that are demonstrably too far to be the closest point. However, the recursion is a bit more complex than for regular binary search trees, as we will show.

As shown in Figure 10-6, if the target point (shown as a small black square) were inserted, it would become a child of the node associated with point 9. Upon calling *nearest* with this selection, the algorithm can discard the entire left subtree because the perpendicular distance *dp* is not closer, so none of those points can be closer. Recursing into the right subtree, the algorithm detects that point 3 is closer. Further, it determines that the perpendicular distance to point 3 is closer than *min* so it must recursively investigate both subtrees rooted at points 7 and 8. Ultimately it determines that point 3 is the closest point.

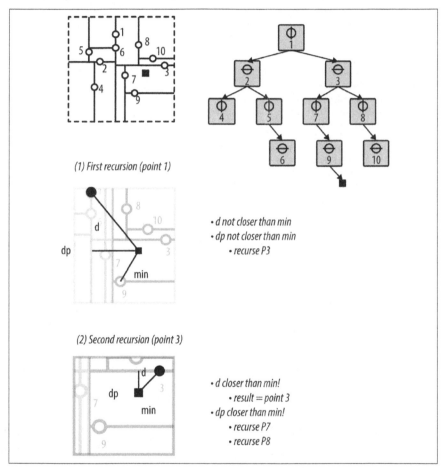

(1) First recursion (point 1)

• *d not closer than min*
• *dp not closer than min*
• *recurse P3*

(2) Second recursion (point 3)

• *d closer than min!*
• *result = point 3*
• *dp closer than min!*
• *recurse P7*
• *recurse P8*

Figure 10-6. Nearest Neighbor example

Nearest Neighbor Summary

Best, Average: O(*log n*) Worst: O(*n*)

```
nearest (T, x)
  n = find parent node in T where x would have been inserted
  min = distance from x to n.point ❶
  better = nearest (T.root, min, x) ❷
  if better found then return better
  return n.point
end

nearest (node, min, x)
  d = distance from x to node.point
  if d < min then
    result = node.point ❸
    min = d
  dp = perpendicular distance from x to node
  if dp < min then ❹
    pt = nearest (node.above, min, x)
    if distance from pt to x < min then
      result = pt
      min = distance from pt to x
    pt = nearest (node.below, min, x)
    if distance from pt to x < min then
      result = pt
      min = distance from pt to x
  else ❺
    if node is above x then
      pt = nearest (node.above, min, x)
    else
      pt = nearest (node.below, min, x)
    if pt exists then return pt
  return result
end
```

❶ Choose reasonable best guess for closest point.

❷ Traverse again from root to try to find better one.

❸ A closer point is found.

❹ If too close to call, check both *above* and *below* subtrees.

❺ Otherwise, can safely check only one subtree.

Input/Output

The input is a k-d tree formed from a set of two-dimensional points P in a plane. A set of nearest neighbor queries (not known in advance) is issued one at a time to find the nearest point in P to a point x.

For each query point x, the algorithm computes a point in P that is the closest neighbor to x.

If two points are "too close" to each other through floating-point error, the algorithm may incorrectly select the wrong point; however, the distance to the actual closest point would be so close that there should be no impact by this faulty response.

Context

When comparing this approach against a brute-force approach that compares the distances between query point x and each point $p \in P$, there are two important costs to consider: (1) the cost of constructing the k-d tree, and (2) the cost of locating the query point x within the tree structure. The trade-offs that impact these costs are:

Number of dimensions
> As the number of dimensions increases, the cost of constructing the k-d tree overwhelms its utility. Some authorities believe that for more than 20 dimensions, this approach is less efficient than a straight comparison against all points.

Number of points in the input set
> When the number of points is small, the cost of constructing the structure may outweigh the improved performance.

Binary trees can be efficient search structures because they can be balanced as nodes are inserted into and deleted from the tree. Unfortunately, k-d trees cannot be balanced easily, nor can points be deleted, because of the deep structural information about the dimensional plane they represent. The ideal solution is to construct the initial k-d tree so that either (a) the leaf nodes are at the same level in the tree, or (b) all leaf nodes are within one level of all other leaf nodes.

Solution

Given an existing k-d tree, **Nearest Neighbor** implementation is shown in Example 10-1.

Example 10-1. Nearest Neighbor implementation in KDTree

```
// KDTree method.
public IMultiPoint nearest (IMultiPoint target) {
  if (root == null||target == null) return null;

  // Find parent node to which target would have been inserted.
```

```
    // Best shot at finding closest point.
    DimensionalNode parent = parent (target);
    IMultiPoint result = parent.point;
    double smallest = target.distance (result);

    // Start back at the root to try to find closer one.
    double best[] = new double[] { smallest };

    double raw[] = target.raw();
    IMultiPoint betterOne = root.nearest (raw, best);
    if (betterOne != null) { return betterOne; }
    return result;
}

// DimensionalNode method. min[0] is best computed shortest distance.
IMultiPoint nearest (double[] rawTarget, double min[]) {
    // Update minimum if we are closer.
    IMultiPoint result = null;

    // If shorter, update minimum
    double d = shorter (rawTarget, min[0]);
    if (d >= 0 && d < min[0]) {
      min[0] = d;
      result = point;
    }

    // determine if we must dive into the subtrees by computing direct
    // perpendicular distance to the axis along which node separates
    // the plane. If d is smaller than the current smallest distance,
    // we could "bleed" over the plane so we must check both.
    double dp = Math.abs (coord — rawTarget[dimension-1]);
    IMultiPoint newResult = null;

    if (dp < min[0]) {
      // must dive into both. Return closest one.
      if (above != null) {
        newResult = above.nearest (rawTarget, min);
        if (newResult != null) { result = newResult; }
      }

      if (below != null) {
        newResult = below.nearest (rawTarget, min);
        if (newResult != null) { result = newResult; }
      }
    } else {
      // only need to go in one! Determine which one now.
      if (rawTarget[dimension-1] < coord) {
        if (below != null) {
          newResult = below.nearest (rawTarget, min);
        }
      } else {
        if (above != null) {
```

```
            newResult = above.nearest (rawTarget, min);
        }
    }

    // Use smaller result, if found.
    if (newResult != null) { return newResult; }
  }
  return result;
}
```

The key to understanding **Nearest Neighbor** is that we first locate the region where the target point would have been inserted, since this will likely contain the closest point. We then validate this assumption by recursively checking from the root back down to this region to see whether some other point is actually closer. This could easily happen because the rectangular regions of the k-d tree were created based on the set of input points. In unbalanced k-d trees, this checking process might incur an O(n) total cost, reinforcing the notion that the input set must be properly processed.

The example solution has two improvements to speed up its performance. First, the comparisons are made on the "raw" double array representing each point. Second, a shorter method in DimensionalNode is used to determine when the distance between two d-dimensional points is smaller than the minimum distance computed so far; this method exits immediately when a partial computation of the Euclidean distance exceeds the minimum found.

Assuming the initial k-d tree is balanced, the search can advantageously discard up to half of the points in the tree during the recursive invocations. Two recursive invocations are sometimes required, but only when the computed minimum distance is just large enough to cross over the dividing line for a node, in which case both sides need to be explored to find the closest point.

Analysis

The k-d tree is initially constructed as a balanced k-d tree, where the dividing line on each level is derived from the median of the points remaining at that level. Locating the parent node of the target query can be found in O(log n) by traversing the k-d tree as if the point were to be inserted. However, the algorithm may make two recursive invocations: one for the child above and one for the child below.

If the double recursion occurs frequently, the algorithm degrades to O(n), so it is worth understanding how often it can occur. The multiple invocations occur only when the perpendicular distance, dp, from the target point to the node's point is less than the best computed minimum. As the number of dimensions increases, there are more potential points that satisfy these criteria.

Table 10-1 provides some empirical evidence to show how often this occurs. A balanced k-d tree is created from $n = 4$ to 131,072 random two-dimensional points generated within the unit square. A set of 50 nearest point queries is issued for a random point within the unit square, and Table 10-1 records the average number of times two recursive invocations occurred (i.e., when $dp < min[0]$ and the node in question has children both above and below), as compared to single recursive invocations.

Table 10-1. Ratio of double-recursion invocations to single

n	d = 2 #Recursions	d = 2 #Double recursion	d = 10 #Recursion	d = 10 #Double recursion
4	1.96	0.52	1.02	0.98
8	3.16	1.16	1.08	2.96
16	4.38	1.78	1.2	6.98
32	5.84	2.34	1.62	14.96
64	7.58	2.38	5.74	29.02
128	9.86	2.98	9.32	57.84
256	10.14	2.66	23.04	114.8
512	12.28	2.36	53.82	221.22
1,024	14.76	3.42	123.18	403.86
2,048	16.9	4.02	293.04	771.84
4,096	15.72	2.28	527.8	1214.1
8,192	16.4	2.6	1010.86	2017.28
16,384	18.02	2.92	1743.34	3421.32
32,768	20.04	3.32	2858.84	4659.74
65,536	21.62	3.64	3378.14	5757.46
131,072	22.56	2.88	5875.54	8342.68

From this random data, the number of double recursions appears to be $.3*log(n)$ for two dimensions, but this jumps to $342*log(n)$ for 10 dimensions (a 1,000-fold increase). The important observation is that both of these estimation functions conform to $O(log\ n)$.

But what happens when d increases to be "sufficiently close" to n in some way? The data graphed in Figure 10-7 shows that as d increases, the number of double recursions actually approaches $n/2$. In fact, as d increases, the number of single recursions conforms to a normal distribution whose mean is very close to $log(n)$, which tells us that eventually all recursive invocations are of the double variety. The impact this discovery has on the performance of nearest-neighbor queries is that as d approaches $log(n)$, the investment in using k-d trees begins to diminish until the resulting performance is no better than $O(n)$, because the number of double recursions plateaus at $n/2$.

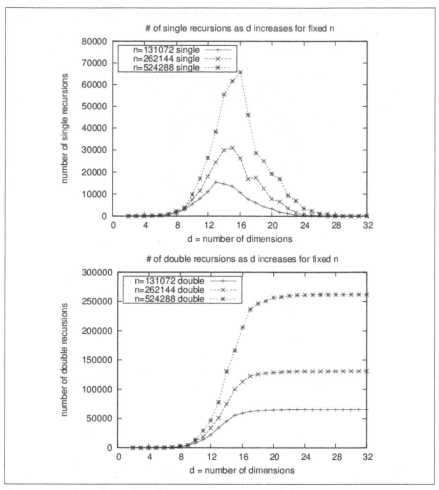

Figure 10-7. Number of double recursions as n and d increase

Certain input set data sets force **Nearest Neighbor** to work hard even in two dimensions. For example, let's change the input for Table 10-1 such that the *n* unique two-dimensional points are found on the edge of a circle of radius *r* > 1, but the nearest query points still lie within the unit square. When *n* = 131,072 points, the number of single recursions has jumped 10-fold to 235.8 while the number of double recursions has exploded to 932.78 (a 200-fold increase!). Thus, the nearest neighbor query will degenerate in the worst case to O(*n*) given specifically tailored queries for a given input set. Figure 10-8 demonstrates a degenerate *k*-d tree with 64 points arranged in a circle.

We can also evaluate the performance of *k*-d tree **Nearest Neighbor** against a straight brute-force O(*n*) comparison. Given a data set of size *n* = 131,072 points, where 128 searches random are to be executed, how large must the dimensionality *d*

of the input set be before the brute-force **Nearest Neighbor** implementation outperforms the k-d tree implementation?

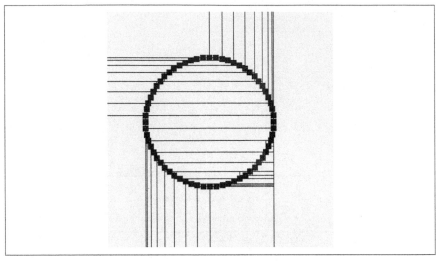

Figure 10-8. Circular data set leads to inefficient k-d tree

We ran 100 trials and discarded the best and worst trials, computing the average of
the remaining 98 trials. The results are graphed in Figure 10-9 and show that for
$d = 11$ dimensions and higher, the brute-force nearest neighbor implementation
outperforms the **Nearest Neighbor** k-d tree algorithm. The specific crossover point
depends on the machine hardware on which the code executes, the specific values of
n and d, and the distribution of points in the input set. We do not include in this
crossover analysis the cost of constructing the k-d tree, because that cost can be
amortized across all searches.

The results in Figure 10-9 confirm that as the number of dimensions increases, the
benefit of using **Nearest Neighbor** over brute force decreases. The cost of constructing the k-d trees is not a driving factor in the equation, because that is driven
primarily by the number of data points to be inserted into the k-d tree, not by the
number of dimensions. On larger data set sizes, the savings is more pronounced.
Another reason for the worsening performance as d increases is that computing
the Euclidean distance between two d-dimensional points is an $O(d)$ operation.
Although it can still be considered a constant time operation, it simply takes more
time.

To maximize the performance of k-d tree searches, the tree must be balanced.
Example 10-2 demonstrates the well-known technique for constructing a balanced
k-d tree using recursion to iterate over each of the coordinate dimensions. Simply
put, it selects the median element from a set of points to represent the node; the
elements below the median are inserted into the *below* subtree, whereas elements
above the median are inserted into the *above* subtree. The code works for arbitrary
dimensions.

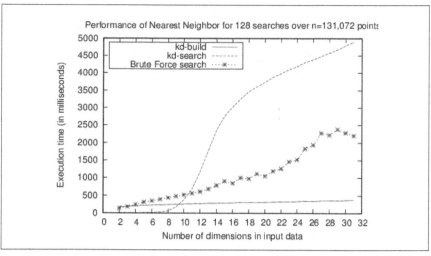

Figure 10-9. Comparing k-d tree versus brute-force implementation

Example 10-2. Recursively construct a balanced k-d tree

```
public class KDFactory {

  private static Comparator<IMultiPoint> comparators[];

  // Recursively construct KDTree using median method on points.
  public static KDTree generate (IMultiPoint []points) {
    if (points.length == 0) { return null; }

    // median will be the root.
    int maxD = points[0].dimensionality();
    KDTree tree = new KDTree(maxD);

    // Make dimensional comparators that compare points by ith dimension
    comparators = new Comparator[maxD+1];
    for (int i = 1; i <= maxD; i++) {
      comparators[i] = new DimensionalComparator(i);
    }
    tree.setRoot (generate (1, maxD, points, 0, points.length-1));
    return tree;
  }

  // generate node for d-th dimension (1 <= d <= maxD)
  // for points[left, right]
  private static DimensionalNode generate (int d, int maxD,
                                           IMultiPoint points[],
                                           int left, int right) {
    // Handle the easy cases first
    if (right < left) { return null; }
    if (right == left) { return new DimensionalNode (d, points[left]); }
```

```
    // Order the array[left,right] so mth element will be median and
    // elements prior to it will be <= median, though not sorted;
    // similarly, elements after will be >= median, though not sorted
    int m = 1+(right-left)/2;
    Selection.select (points, m, left, right, comparators[d]);

    // Median point on this dimension becomes the parent
    DimensionalNode dm = new DimensionalNode (d, points[left+m-1]);

    // update to the next dimension, or reset back to 1
    if (++d > maxD) { d = 1; }

    // recursively compute left and right subtrees, which translate
    // into 'below' and 'above' for n-dimensions.
    dm.setBelow (maxD, generate (d, maxD, points, left, left+m-2));
    dm.setAbove (maxD, generate (d, maxD, points, left+m, right));
    return dm;
  }
}
```

The select operation was described in Chapter 4. It can select the kth smallest number recursively in $O(n)$ time in the average case; however, it does degrade to $O(n^2)$ in the worst case.

Variations

In the implementation we have shown, the method nearest traverses from the root back down to the computed parent; alternate implementations start from the parent and traverse back to the root, in bottom-up fashion.

Range Query

Given a rectangular range R defined by $(x_{low}, y_{low}, x_{high}, y_{high})$ and a set of points P, which points in P are contained within a target rectangle T? A brute-force algorithm that inspects all points in P can determine the enclosed points in $O(n)$—can we do better?

For **Nearest Neighbor**, we organized the points into a k-d tree to process nearest-neighbor queries in $O(\log n)$ time. Using the same data structure, we now show how to compute **Range Query** in $O(n^{0.5} + r)$, where r is the number of points reported by the query. Indeed, when the input set contains d-dimensional data points, the solution scales to solve d-dimensional **Range Query** problems in $O(n^{1-1/d} + r)$.

Given target region, T, which covers the left half of the plane to just beyond point 7 in Figure 10-10, we can observe all three of these cases. Since T does not wholly contain the infinite region associated with the root node, **Range Query** checks whether T contains point 1, which it does, so that point is added to the result. Now T extends into both its *above* and *below* children, so both recursive calls are made. In the first recursion *below* point 1, T wholly contains the region associated with point 2. Thus, point 2 and all of its descendants are added to the result. In the second recursion, eventually point 7 is discovered and added to the result.

Range Query Summary

Best, Average: $O(n^{1-1/d} + r)$ **Worst:** $O(n)$

```
range (space)
  results = new Set
  range (space, root, results)
  return results
end

range (space, node, results)
  if space contains node.region then ❶
    add node.points and all of its descendants to results
    return

  if space contains node.point then ❷
    add node.point to results

  if space extends below node.coord then ❸
    range (space, node.below, results)
  if space extends above node.coord then
    range (space, node.above, results)
end
```

❶ Should a *k*-d tree node be wholly contained by search space, all descendants are added to results.

❷ Ensure point is added to results if contained.

❸ May have to search both *above* and *below*.

Input/Output

The input is a set of n points P in d-dimensional space and a d-dimensional hypercube that specifies the desired range query. The range queries are aligned properly with the axes in the d-dimensional data set because they are specified by d individual ranges, for each dimension of the input set. For $d = 2$, the range query has both a range over x coordinates and a range over y coordinates.

Range Query generates the full set of points enclosed by the range query. The points do not appear in any specific order.

Context

k-d trees become unwieldy for a large number of dimensions, so this algorithm and overall approach should be restricted to small dimensional data. For two-dimensional data, *k*-d trees offers excellent performance for **Nearest Neighbor** and **Range Query** problems.

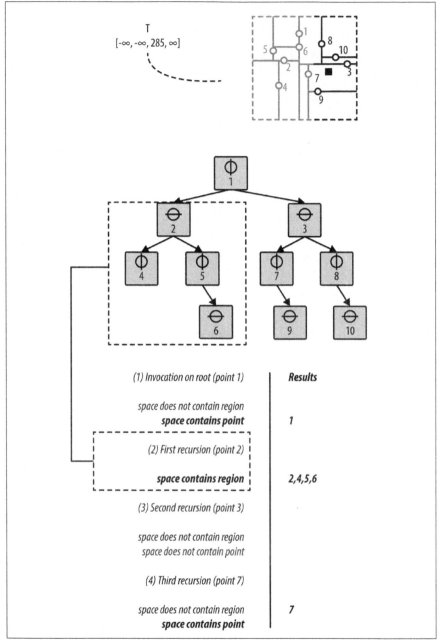

Figure 10-10. Range Query example

Solution

The Java solution shown in Example 10-3 is a method of the DimensionalNode class, which is simply delegated by the range(IHypercube) method found in KDTree. The key efficiency gain of this algorithm occurs when the region for a DimensionalNode is wholly contained within the desired range query. In this circumstance, all descendant nodes of the DimensionalNode can be added to the results collection because of the k-d tree property that the children for a node are wholly contained within the region of any of its ancestor nodes.

Example 10-3. Range Query implementation in DimensionalNode

```
public void range (IHypercube space, KDSearchResults results) {
  // Wholly contained? Take all descendant points
  if (space.contains (region)) {
    results.add (this);
    return;
  }

  // Is our point at least contained?
  if (space.intersects (cached)) {
    results.add (point);
  }

  // Recursively progress along both ancestral trees, if demanded.
  // The cost in manipulating space to be "cropped" to the proper
  // structure is excessive, so leave alone and is still correct.
  if (space.getLeft(dimension) < coord) {
    if (below != null) { below.range (space, results); }
  }
  if (coord < space.getRight(dimension)) {
    if (above != null) { above.range (space, results); }
  }
}
```

The code shown in Example 10-3 is a modified tree traversal that potentially visits every node in the tree. Because the k-d tree partitions the d-dimensional data set in hierarchical fashion, there are three decisions **Range Query** makes at each node n:

Is the region associated with node n fully contained within the query region?
When this happens, the range traversal can stop because all descendant points belong to the query result.

Does the query region contain the point associated with node n?
If so, add the point associated with n to the result set.

Along the dimension d represented by node n, does query region intersect n?
It can do so in two ways since the query region can intersect both the region associated with n's *below* subtree as well as the region associated with n's *above* subtree. The code may perform zero, one, or two recursive traversals of *range*.

Observe that the result returned is a `KDSearchResults` object that contains both individual points as well as entire subtrees. Thus, to retrieve all points you will have to traverse each subtree in the result.

Analysis

It is possible that the query region contains all points in the tree, in which case all points are returned, which leads to O(n) performance. However, when **Range Query** detects that the query region does not intersect an individual node within the k-d tree, it can prune the traversal. The cost savings depend on the number of dimensions and the specific nature of the input set. Preparata and Shamos (1985) showed that **Range Query** using k-d trees performs in $O(n^{1-1/d} + r)$, where r is the number of results found. As the number of dimensions increases, the benefit decreases.

Figure 10-11 graphs the expected performance of an $O(n^{1-1/d})$ algorithm; the distinctive feature of the graph is fast performance for small values of d that over time inexorably approaches O(n). Because of the addition of r (the number of points returned by the query), the actual performance will deviate from the ideal curve shown in Figure 10-11.

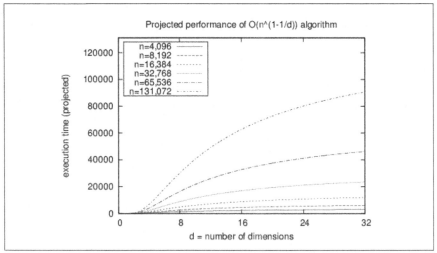

Figure 10-11. Expected performance for $O(n^{1-1/d})$ algorithm

It is difficult to produce sample data sets to show the performance of **Range Query**. We demonstrate the effectiveness of **Range Query** on a k-d tree by comparing its performance to a brute-force implementation that inspects each point against the desired query region. The d-dimensional input set for each of these situations contains n points whose coordinate values are drawn uniformly from the range [0, s], where s = 4,096. We evaluate three situations:

Query region contains all points in the tree

We construct a query region that contains all of the points in the k-d tree. This example provides the maximum speed-up supported by the algorithm; its performance is independent of the number of dimensions d in the k-d tree. The k-d tree approach takes about 5–7 times as long to complete; this represents the overhead inherent in the structure. In Table 10-2, the performance cost for the brute-force region query increases as d increases because computing whether a d-dimensional point is within a d-dimensional space is an $O(d)$ operation, not constant. The brute-force implementation handily outperforms the k-d tree implementation.

Table 10-2. Comparing Range Query execution times in milliseconds (k-d tree versus brute force) for all points in the tree

n	d = 2 RQ	d = 3 RQ	d = 4 RQ	d = 5 RQ	d = 2 BF	d = 3 BF	d = 4 BF	d = 5 BF
4,096	6.22	13.26	19.6	22.15	4.78	4.91	5.85	6
8,192	12.07	23.59	37.7	45.3	9.39	9.78	11.58	12
16,384	20.42	41.85	73.72	94.03	18.87	19.49	23.26	24.1
32,768	42.54	104.94	264.85	402.7	37.73	39.21	46.64	48.66
65,536	416.39	585.11	709.38	853.52	75.59	80.12	96.32	101.6
131,072	1146.82	1232.24	1431.38	1745.26	162.81	195.87	258.6	312.38

Fractional regions

Because the number of results found, r, plays a prominent role in determining the performance of the algorithm, we construct a set of scenarios to isolate this variable as the number of dimensions increases.

The uniformity of the input set discourages us from simply constructing a query region $[.5*s, s]$ for each dimension of input. If we did this, the total volume of the input set queried is $(1/2)^d$, which implies that as d increases the number of expected points, r, returned by the query region decreases. Instead, we construct query regions whose size increases as d increases. For example, in two dimensions the query region with $[.5204*s, s]$ on each dimension should return $.23*n$ points because $(1 - .5204)^2 = .23$. However, for three dimensions the query region must expand to $[.3873*s, s]$ on each dimension since $(1 - .3873)^3 = .23$.

Using this approach, we fix in advance the desired ratio k such that our constructed query will return $k*n$ points (where k is either 0.23, 0.115, 0.0575, 0.02875, or 0.014375). We compare the k-d tree implementation against a brute-force implementation as n varies from 4,096 to 131,072 and d varies from 2 to 15, as shown in Figure 10-12. The charts on the left side show the distinctive behavior of the $O(n^{1-1/d})$ k-d tree algorithm while the right side shows the linear performance of brute force. For a 0.23 ratio, the k-d tree implementation outperforms brute force only for $d = 2$ and $n \leq 8{,}192$; however, for a ratio of 0.014375, the k-d tree implementation wins for $d \leq 6$ and $n \leq 131{,}072$.

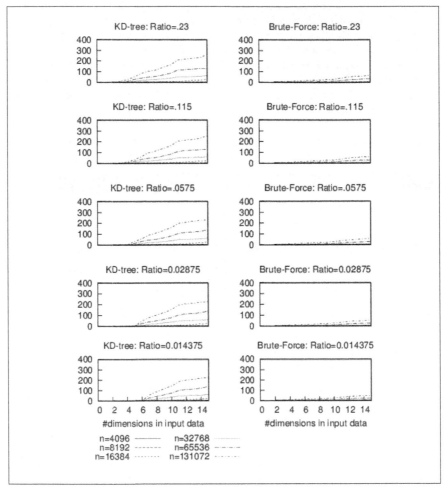

Figure 10-12. Comparing k-d tree versus brute force for fractional regions

Empty region

We construct a query region from a single random point drawn uniformly from the same values for the input set. Performance results are shown in Table 10-3. The k-d tree executes nearly instantaneously; all recorded execution times are less than a fraction of a millisecond.

Table 10-3. Brute-force Range Query execution times in milliseconds for empty region

n	d = 2 BF	d = 3 BF	d = 4 BF	d = 5 BF
4,096	3.36	3.36	3.66	3.83
8,192	6.71	6.97	7.3	7.5
16,384	13.41	14.02	14.59	15.16
32,768	27.12	28.34	29.27	30.53
65,536	54.73	57.43	60.59	65.31
131,072	124.48	160.58	219.26	272.65

Quadtrees

Quadtrees can be used to solve the following queries:

Range queries
> Given a collection of points in the Cartesian plane, determine the points that exist within a query rectangle. A sample application is shown in Figure 10-13 where a dashed rectangle is selected by the user, and points contained within the rectangle are highlighted. When a quadtree region is wholly contained by the target query, the application draws that region with a shaded background.

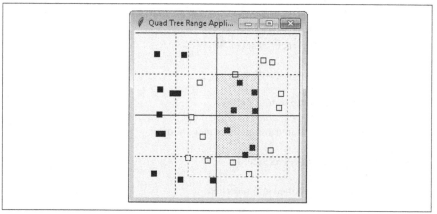

Figure 10-13. Range searching using a quadtree

Collision detection
> Given a collection of objects in the Cartesian plane, determine all intersections among the objects. A sample application is shown in Figure 10-14 that identifies the collisions among a number of moving squares that bounce back and forth within a window. Squares that intersect each other are highlighted.

Quadtree Summary

Best, Average, Worst: O(*log n*)

```
add (node, pt)
  if node.region does not contain pt then
    return false
  if node is leaf node then
    if node already contains pt then ❶
      return false
    if node has < 4 points then ❷
      add pt to node
      return true

  q = quadrant for pt in node
  if node is leaf node then
    node.subdivide() ❸
  return add(node.children[q], pt) ❹

range (node, rect, result)
  if rect contains node.region then ❺
    add (node, true) to result
  else if node is leaf node then
    foreach point p in node do
      if rect contains p then
        add (p, false) to result ❻
  else
    foreach child in node.children do
      if rect overlaps child.region
        range(child, rect, result) ❼
```

❶ Impose set semantics on quadtree.

❷ Each node can store up to four points.

❸ Leaf points are distributed among four new children.

❹ Insert new point into correct child.

❺ Entire subtree is contained and returned.

❻ Individual points returned.

❼ Recursively check each overlapping child.

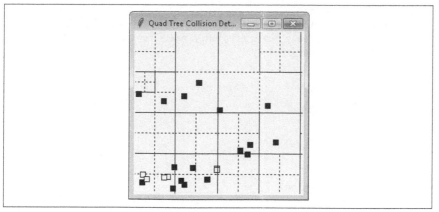

Figure 10-14. Collision detection using a quadtree

Input/Output

The input is a set of two-dimensional points *P* in a plane from which a quadtree is constructed.

For optimal performance, a range query returns the *nodes* in the quadtree, which allows it to return entire subtrees of points when the target rectangle wholly contains a subtree of points. The results of a collision detection are the existing points that intersect with a target point.

Solution

The basis of the Python implementation of quadtree is the QuadTree and QuadNode structures shown in Example 10-4. The smaller2k and larger2k helper methods ensure the initial region has sides that are powers of two. The Region class represents a rectangular region.

Example 10-4. Quadtree QuadNode implementation

```python
class Region:
  def __init__(self, xmin,ymin, xmax,ymax):
    """
    Creates region from two points (xmin,ymin) to (xmax,ymax). Adjusts if
    these are not the bottom-left and top-right coordinates for a region.
    """
    self.x_min = xmin if xmin < xmax else xmax
    self.y_min = ymin if ymin < ymax else ymax
    self.x_max = xmax if xmax > xmin else xmin
    self.y_max = ymax if ymax > ymin else ymin

class QuadNode:
  def __init__(self, region, pt = None, data = None):
    """Create empty QuadNode centered on origin of given region."""
```

```
      self.region = region
      self.origin = (region.x_min + (region.x_max - region.x_min)//2,
                     region.y_min + (region.y_max - region.y_min)//2)
      self.children = [None] * 4

      if pt:
        self.points = [pt]
        self.data = [data]
      else:
        self.points = []
        self.data = []
class QuadTree:
  def __init__(self, region):
    """Create QuadTree over square region whose sides are powers of 2."""
    self.root = None
    self.region = region.copy()

    xmin2k = smaller2k(self.region.x_min)
    ymin2k = smaller2k(self.region.y_min)
    xmax2k = larger2k(self.region.x_max)
    ymax2k = larger2k(self.region.y_max)

    self.region.x_min = self.region.y_min = min(xmin2k, ymin2k)
    self.region.x_max = self.region.y_max = max(xmax2k, ymax2k)
```

Points are added to the quadtree using the add method shown in Example 10-5. The add method returns False if the point is already contained within the quadtree, thus it enforces mathematical set semantics. Up to four points are added to a node if the point is contained within that node's rectangular region. When the fifth point is added, the node's region is subdivided into quadrants and the points are reassigned to the individual quadrants of that node's region; should all points be assigned to the same quadrant, the process repeats until all leaf quadrants have four or fewer points.

Example 10-5. Quadtree add implementation

```
class QuadNode:
  def add (self, pt, data):
    """Add (pt, data) to the QuadNode."""
    node = self
    while node:
      # Not able to fit in this region.
      if not containsPoint (node.region, pt):
        return False

      # if we have points, then we are leaf node. Check here.
      if node.points != None:
        if pt in node.points:
          return False
```

```
    # Add if room
    if len(node.points) < 4:
      node.points.append (pt)
      node.data.append (data)
      return True

  # Find quadrant into which to add.
  q = node.quadrant (pt)
  if node.children[q] is None:
    # subdivide and reassign points to each quadrant. Then add point.
    node.subdivide()
  node = node.children[q]

return False

class QuadTree:
  def add (self, pt, data = None):
    if self.root is None:
      self.root = QuadNode(self.region, pt, data)
      return True

    return self.root.add (pt, data)
```

With this structure, the range method in Example 10-6 demonstrates how to efficiently locate all points in the quadtree that are contained by a target region. This
Python implementation uses the yield operator to provide an iterator interface to
the results. The iterator contains tuples that are either individual points or entire
nodes. When a quadtree node is wholly contained by a region, that entire node is
returned as part of the result. The caller can retrieve all descendant values using a
preorder traversal of the node, provided by QuadNode.

Example 10-6. Quadtree Range Query implementation

```
class QuadNode:
  def range(self, region):
    """
    Yield (node,True) when node contained within region,
    otherwise (region,False) for individual points.
    """
    if region.containsRegion (self.region):
      yield (self, True)
    else:
      # if we have points, then we are leaf node. Check here.
      if self.points != None:
        for i in range(len(self.points)):
          if containsPoint (region, self.points[i]):
            yield ((self.points[i], self.data[i]), False)
      else:
        for child in self.children:
          if child.region.overlap (region):
```

```
        for pair in child.range (region):
            yield pair

class QuadTree:
    def range(self, region):
        """Yield (node,status) in Quad Tree contained within region."""
        if self.root is None:
            return None

        return self.root.range(region)
```

To support collision detection, Example 10-7 contains the `collide` method which searches through the quadtree to locate points in the tree that intersect a square with sides of length *r* centered at a given point, *pt*.

Example 10-7. Quadtree collision detection implementation

```
class QuadNode:
    def collide (self, pt, r):
        """Yield points in leaf that intersect with pt and square side r."""
        node = self
        while node:
            # Point must fit in this region
            if containsPoint (node.region, pt):
                # if we have points, then we are leaf node. Check here
                if node.points != None:
                    for p,d in zip(node.points, node.data):
                        if p[X]-r <= pt[X] <= p[X]+r and p[Y]-r <= pt[Y] <= p[Y]+r:
                            yield (p, d)

                # Find quadrant into which to check further
                q = node.quadrant (pt)
                node = node.children[q]

class QuadTree:
    def collide(self, pt, r):
        """Return collisions to point within Quad Tree."""
        if self.root is None:
            return None

        return self.root.collide (pt, r)
```

Analysis

Quadtrees partition the points in a plane using the same underlying structure of binary search trees. The region-based implementation presented here uses a fixed partitioning scheme that leads to efficient behavior when the collection of points is uniformly distributed. It may happen that the points are all clustered together in a small space, as shown in Figure 10-15. Thus, the search performance is logarithmic with respect to the tree size. The range query in Python is made efficient by return-

---

ing both individual points as well as entire nodes in the quadtree; however, you must still consider the time to extract all descendant values in the nodes returned by the range query.

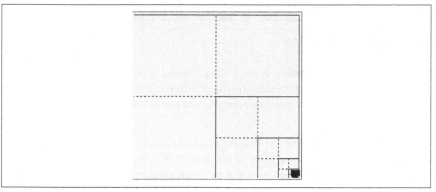

Figure 10-15. Degenerate quadtree

Variations

The quadtree structure presented here is a region quadtree. A point quadtree represents two-dimensional points. The *Octree* extends quadtree into three dimensions, with eight children (as with a cube) instead of four (Meagher, 1995).

R-Trees

Balanced binary trees are an incredibly versatile data structure that offer great performance for search, insert, and delete operations. However, they work best in primary memory using pointers and allocating (and releasing) nodes as needed. These trees can only grow as large as primary memory and they are not easily stored to secondary storage, such as a file system. Operating systems provide *virtual memory* so programs can operate using an assigned memory space, which might be larger than the actual memory. The operating system ensures a fixed-size block of memory (known as a *page*) is brought into primary memory as needed, and older unused pages are stored to disk (if modified) and discarded. Programs work most efficiently when consolidating read and write access using pages, which are typically 4,096 bytes in size. If you consider that a node in a binary tree might only require 24 bytes of storage, there would be dozens of such nodes packed to a page. It is not immediately clear how to store these binary nodes to disk especially when the tree is dynamically updated.

The B-Tree concept was developed by Bayer and McCreight in 1972, though it appears to have been independently discovered by vendors of database management systems and operating systems. A B-Tree extends the structure of a binary tree by allowing each node to store multiple values and multiple links to more than two nodes. A sample B-Tree is shown in Figure 10-16.

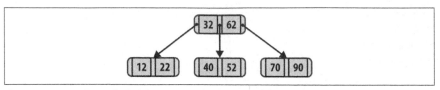

Figure 10-16. Sample B-Tree

Each node n contains a number of ascending values $\{\ k_1, k_2, ..., k_{m-1}\ \}$ and pointers $\{\ p_1, p_2, ..., p_m\ \}$ where m determines the maximum number of children nodes that n can point to. The value m is known as the *order* of the B-Tree. Each B-Tree node can contain $m-1$ values.

To maintain the *binary search tree property*, B-Tree nodes store key values such that all values in the subtree pointed to by p_1 are smaller than k_1. All values in the subtree pointed to by p_i are greater than or equal to k_i and smaller than k_{i+1}. Finally, all values in the subtree pointed to by p_m are greater than k_{m-1}.

Using Knuth's definition, a B-Tree of order m satisfies the following:

- Every node has at most m children.
- Every nonleaf node (except the root) has at least $\lceil m/2 \rceil$ children.
- The root has at least two children if it is not a leaf node.
- A nonleaf node with k children nodes contains $k - 1$ key values.
- All leaves appear in the same level.

Using this definition, a traditional binary tree is a degenerate B-Tree of order $m = 2$. Insertions and deletions in a B-Tree must maintain these properties. In doing so, the longest path in a B-Tree with n keys contains at most $log_m(n)$ nodes, leading to $O(log\ n)$ performance for its operations. B-Trees can be readily stored to secondary storage by increasing the number of keys in each node so that its total size properly aligns with the page size (e.g., storing two B-Tree nodes per page), which minimizes the number of disk reads to load nodes into primary memory.

With this brief sketch of B-Trees, we can now describe in more detail the R-Tree structure. An R-Tree is a height-balanced tree, similar to a B-Tree, that stores n-dimensional spatial objects in a dynamic structure that supports insert, delete, and query operations. It also supports *range queries* for locating objects that overlap with a target n-dimensional query. In this chapter, we describe the fundamental operations that maintain R-Trees to ensure efficient execution of the core operations.

An R-Tree is a tree structure in which each node contains links to up to M different children nodes. All information is stored by the leaf nodes, each of which can store up to M different n-dimensional spatial objects. An R-Tree leaf node provides an index into the actual repository that stores the objects themselves; the R-Tree only stores the unique identifier for each object and the n-dimensional bounding box, I, which is the smallest n-dimensional shape that contains the spatial object. In this presentation we assume two dimensions and these shapes are rectangles, but it can naturally be extended to n dimensions based on the structure of the data.

There is another relevant constant, $m \leq \lfloor M/2 \rfloor$, which defines the minimum number of values stored by a leaf node or links stored by interior nodes in the R-Tree. We summarize the R-Tree properties here:

- Every leaf node contains between m and M (inclusive) records [unless it is the root].

- Every nonleaf node contains between m and M (inclusive) links to children nodes [unless it is the root].

- For each entry $(I, child_i)$ in a nonleaf node, I is the smallest rectangle that spatially contains the rectangles in its children nodes.

- The root node has at least two children [unless it is a leaf].

- All leaves appear on the same level.

The R-Tree is a balanced structure that ensures the properties just listed. For convenience, the leaf level is considered level 0, and the level number of the root node is the height of the tree. The R-Tree structure supports insertion, deletion, and query in $O(\log_m n)$.

The repository contains sample applications for investigating the behavior of R-Trees. Figure 10-17 shows the dynamic behavior as a new rectangle 6 is added to the R-Tree that contains $M = 4$ shapes. As you can see, there is no room for the new rectangle, so the relevant leaf node R1 is *split* into two nodes, based on a metric that seeks to minimize the area of the respective new nonleaf node, R2. Adding this rectangle increases the overall height of the R-Tree by one since it creates a new root, R3.

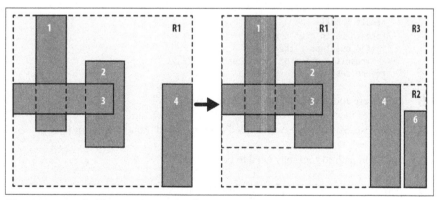

Figure 10-17. R-Tree insert example

R-Tree Summary

Best, Average: $O(log_m n)$ Worst: $O(n)$

```
add (R, rect)
  if R is empty then
    R = new RTree (rect)
  else
    leaf = chooseLeaf(rect)
    if leaf.count < M then  ❶
      add rect to leaf
    else
      newLeaf = leaf.split(rect)  ❷
      newNode = adjustTree (leaf, newLeaf)  ❸
      if newNode != null then
        R = new RTree with old Root and newNode as children  ❹
  end

search (n, t)
  if n is a leaf then  ❺
    return entry if n contains t otherwise False
  else
    foreach child c of n do  ❻
      if c contains t then
        return search(c, t)  ❼
  end

range (n, t)
  if target wholly contains n's bounding box then  ❽
    return all descendant rectangles
  else if n is a leaf
    return all entries that intersect t
  else
    result = null
    foreach child c of n do  ❾
      if c overlaps t then
        result = union of result and range(c, t)
    return result
```

❶   Entries are added to a leaf node if there is room.

❷   Otherwise, M + 1 entries are divided among the old leaf and a new node.

❸   Entries in path to root may need to be adjusted.

❹   R-Tree might grow in height after an add.

❺   Leaf nodes contain the actual entries.

❻   Recursively search *each child* since regions may overlap.

---

⑦   Once found the entry is returned.

⑧   Efficient operation for detecting membership.

⑨   May have to execute multiple recursive queries.

Input/Output

A two-dimensional R-Tree stores a collection of rectangular regions in the Cartesian plane, each with its own (optional) unique identifier.

R-Tree operations can modify the state of the R-Tree (i.e., insert or delete) as well as retrieve an individual rectangular region or a collection of regions.

Context

R-Trees were designed to index multidimensional information including geographical structures or more abstract n-dimensional data, such as rectangles or polygons. This is one of the few structures that offers excellent runtime performance even when the information is too large to store in main memory. Traditional indexing techniques are inherently one-dimensional and thus R-Tree structures are well-suited for these domains.

The operations on an R-Tree include insertion and deletion, and there are two kinds of queries. You can search for a specific rectangular region in the R-Tree or you can determine the collection of rectangular regions that intersect a query rectangle.

Solution

The Python implementation in Example 10-8 associates an optional identifier with each rectangle; this would be used to retrieve the actual spatial object from the database. We start with the RNode, which is the fundamental unit of an R-Tree. Each RNode maintains a bounding region and an optional identifier. An RNode is a leaf if node.level is zero. There are node.count children for an RNode and they are stored in the node.children list. When adding a child RNode, the parent node.region bounding box must be adjusted to include the newly added child.

Example 10-8. RNode implementation

```
class RNode:
  # Monotonically incrementing counter to generate identifiers
  counter = 0

  def __init__(self, M, rectangle = None, ident = None, level = 0):
    if rectangle:
      self.region = rectangle.copy()
    else:
      self.region = None
```

```
    if ident is None:
      RNode.counter += 1
      self.id       = 'R' + str(RNode.counter)
    else:
      self.id       = ident

    self.children   = [None] * M
    self.level      = level
    self.count      = 0

  def addRNode(self, rNode):
    """Add previously computed RNode and adjust bounding region."""
    self.children[self.count] = rNode
    self.count += 1

    if self.region is None:
      self.region = rNode.region.copy()
    else:
      rectangle = rNode.region
      if rectangle.x_min < self.region.x_min:
        self.region.x_min = rectangle.x_min
      if rectangle.x_max > self.region.x_max:
        self.region.x_max = rectangle.x_max
      if rectangle.y_min < self.region.y_min:
        self.region.y_min = rectangle.y_min
      if rectangle.y_max > self.region.y_max:
        self.region.y_max = rectangle.y_max
```

With this base in place, Example 10-9 describes the RTree class and the method for adding a rectangle to an R-Tree.

Example 10-9. RTree and corresponding add implementation

```
class RTree:
  def __init__(self, m=2, M=4):
    """Create empty R tree with (m=2, M=4) default values."""
    self.root = None
    self.m = m
    self.M = M

  def add(self, rectangle, ident = None):
    """Insert rectangle into proper location with (optional) identifier."""
    if self.root is None:
      self.root = RNode(self.M, rectangle, None)
      self.root.addEntry (self.M, rectangle, ident)
    else:
      # I1 [Find position for new record] Invoke ChooseLeaf to select
      # a leaf node L in which to place E. Path to leaf returned.
      path = self.root.chooseLeaf (rectangle, [self.root]);
      n = path[-1]
```

```
      del path[-1]

      # I2 [Add record to leaf node] If L has room for another entry,
      # install E. Otherwise invoke SplitNode to obtain L and LL containing
      # E and all the old entries of L.
      newLeaf = None
      if n.count < self.M:
        n.addEntry (self.M, rectangle, ident)
      else:
        newLeaf = n.split(RNode(self.M, rectangle, ident, 0),self.m,self.M)

      # I3 [Propagate changes upwards] Invoke AdjustTree on L, also
      # passing LL if a split was performed.
      newNode = self.adjustTree (n, newLeaf, path)

      # I4 [Grow tree taller] If node split propagation caused the root
      # to split, create a new root whose children are the two
      # resulting nodes.
      if newNode:
        newRoot = RNode(self.M, level = newNode.level + 1)
        newRoot.addRNode (newNode)
        newRoot.addRNode (self.root)
        self.root = newRoot
```

The comments in Example 10-9 reflect the steps in the algorithm published in Guttman's 1984 paper. Each RTree object records the configured m and M values and the root RNode object of the tree. Adding the first rectangle to an empty RTree simply creates the initial structure; thereafter, the add method finds an appropriate leaf node into which to add the new rectangle. The computed path list returns the ordered nodes from the root to the selected leaf node.

If there is enough room in the selected leaf node, the new rectangle is added to it and the bounding box changes are propagated up to the root using the adjustTree method. If, however, the selected leaf node is full, a newLeaf node is constructed and the $M + 1$ entries are split between n and newLeaf using a strategy to minimize the total area of the bounding boxes of these two nodes. In this case, the adjustTree method must also propagate the new structure upward to the root, which might further cause other nodes to be split in similar fashion. If the original root node self.root is split, then a new root RNode is created to be the parent of the original root and the newly created RNode object. Thus an RTree grows by only one level because existing nodes are split to make room for new entries.

Range queries can be performed as shown in Example 10-10. This implementation is brief because of Python's ability to write generator functions that behave like iterators. The recursive range method of RNode first checks whether the target rectangle wholly contains a given RNode; if so, the rectangles of all descendant leaf nodes will need to be included in the result. As a placeholder, a tuple (self, 0, True) is returned; the invoking function can retrieve all of these regions using a leafOrder generator defined by RNode. Otherwise, for nonleaf nodes, the function recursively yields those rectangles that are found in the descendants whose bounding rectangle intersects the target rectangle. Rectangles in leaf nodes are returned as (rectangle, id, False) if the target rectangle overlaps their bounding boxes.

Example 10-10. RTree/RNode implementation of Range Query

```
class RNode:
  def range (self, target):
    """Return generator (node,0,True) or (rect,id,False)
       of all qualifying identifiers overlapping target."""

    # Wholly contained for all interior nodes? Return entire node.
    if target.containsRegion (self.region):
      yield (self, 0, True)
    else:
      # check leaves and recurse
      if self.level == 0:
        for idx in range(self.count):
          if target.overlaps (self.children[idx].region):
            yield (self.children[idx].region, self.children[idx].id, False)
      else:
        for idx in range(self.count):
          if self.children[idx].region.overlaps (target):
            for triple in self.children[idx].range (target):
              yield triple

class RTree:
  def range (self, target):
    """Return generator of all qualifying (node,0,True) or
       (rect,id,False) overlapping target."""
    if self.root:
      return self.root.range (target)
    else:
      return None
```

Searching for an individual rectangle has the same structure as the code in Example 10-10; only the RNode search function is shown in Example 10-11. This function returns the rectangle and the optional identifier used when inserting the rectangle into the RTree.

Example 10-11. RNode implementation of search query

```
class RNode:
  def search (self, target):
    """Return (rectangle,id) if node contains target rectangle."""
    if self.level == 0:
      for idx in range(self.count):
        if target == self.children[idx].region:
          return (self.children[idx].region, self.children[idx].id)
    elif self.region.containsRegion (target):
```

```
      for idx in range(self.count):
        if self.children[idx].region.containsRegion (target):
          rc = self.children[idx].search(target)
          if rc:
            return rc
return None
```

To complete the implementation of R-Trees, we need the ability to delete a rectangle that exists in the tree. While the add method had to split nodes that were too full, the remove method must process nodes that have too few children, given the minimum number of children nodes, *m*. The key idea is that once a rectangle is removed from the R-Tree, any of the nodes from its parent node to the root might become "under-full." The implementation shown in Example 10-12 handles this using a helper method, condenseTree, which returns a list of "orphaned" nodes with fewer than *m* children; these values are reinserted into the R-Tree once the remove request completes.

Example 10-12. RNode implementation of remove operation

```
class RTree:
  def remove(self, rectangle):
    """Remove rectangle value from R Tree."""
    if self.root is None:
      return False

    # D1 [Find node containing record] Invoke FindLeaf to locate
    # the leaf node n containing R. Stop if record not found.
    path = self.root.findLeaf (rectangle, [self.root]);
    if path is None:
      return False

    leaf = path[-1]
    del path[-1]
    parent = path[-1]
    del path[-1]

    # D2 [Delete record.] Remove E from n
    parent.removeRNode (leaf)

    # D3 [Propagate changes] Invoke condenseTree on parent
    if parent == self.root:
      self.root.adjustRegion()
    else:
      parent,Q = parent.condenseTree (path, self.m, self.M)
      self.root.adjustRegion()

      # CT6 [Reinsert orphaned entries] Reinsert all entries
      # of nodes in set Q.
      for n in Q:
        for rect,ident in n.leafOrder():
```

```
self.add (rect, ident)

# D4 [Shorten tree.] If the root node has only one child after
# the tree has been adjusted, make the child the new root.
while self.root.count == 1 and self.root.level > 0:
  self.root = self.root.children[0]
if self.root.count == 0:
  self.root = None

return True
```

Analysis

The R-Tree structure derives its efficiency by its ability to balance itself when rectangles are inserted. Since all rectangles are stored in leaf nodes *at the same height in the R-Tree*, the interior nodes represent the bookkeeping structure. Parameters m and M determine the details of the structure, but the overall guarantee is that the height of the tree will be O($log\ n$) where n is the number of nodes in the R-Tree. The *split* method distributes rectangles among two nodes using a heuristic that minimizes the total area of the enclosing bounding boxes of these two nodes; there have also been other heuristics proposed in the literature.

The search performance of R-Tree methods depends on the number of rectangles in the R-Tree and the *density* of those rectangles, or the average number of rectangles that contain a given point. Given n rectangles formed from random coordinates in the unit square, about 10% of them intersect a random point, which means the *search* must investigate multiple subchildren in trying to locate an individual rectangle. Specifically, it must investigate every subchild whose region overlaps the target search query. With low-density data sets, searching an R-Tree becomes more efficient.

Inserting rectangles into an R-Tree may cause multiple nodes to be split, which is a costly operation. Similarly, when removing rectangles from an R-Tree, multiple orphaned nodes must have their rectangles reinserted into the tree. Deleting rectangles is more efficient than searching because while looking for the rectangles to delete the recursive calls are limited to subchildren that wholly contain the target rectangle being deleted.

Table 10-4 shows performance results on two rectangle data sets containing 8,100 rectangles. In Tables 10-4 through 10-6, we show different performance results for varying values of m and M (recall that $m \leq \lfloor M/2 \rfloor$). In the *sparse* set, the rectangles all have the same size but have no overlaps. In the *dense* set, the rectangles are formed from two random points drawn from the unit square. The entries record the total time to construct the R-Tree from the rectangles. The build time is slightly higher for the *dense* set because of the increased number of nodes that have to be split when inserting rectangles.

Table 10-5 shows the total time to search for all rectangles in the R-Tree. The dense data set is about 50 times slower than the sparse set. Additionally, it shows a marginal benefit of having the minimum number of children nodes to be $m = 2$.

Table 10-6 contains the corresponding performance for deleting all rectangles in the R-Tree. The performance spikes in the dense tree set are likely the result of the small size of the random data set.

Table 10-4. R-Tree-build performance on dense and sparse data sets

	Dense					Sparse				
M	m = 2	m = 3	m = 4	m = 5	m = 6	m = 2	m = 3	m = 4	m = 5	m = 6
4	1.32					1.36				
5	1.26					1.22				
6	1.23	1.23				1.2	1.24			
7	1.21	1.21				1.21	1.18			
8	1.24	1.21	1.19			1.21	1.2	1.19		
9	1.23	1.25	1.25			1.2	1.19	1.18		
10	1.35	1.25	1.25	1.25		1.18	1.18	1.18	1.22	
11	1.3	1.34	1.27	1.24		1.18	1.21	1.22	1.22	
12	1.3	1.31	1.24	1.28	1.22	1.17	1.21	1.2	1.2	1.25

Table 10-5. R-Tree search performance on dense and sparse data sets

	Dense					Sparse				
M	m = 2	m = 3	m = 4	m = 5	m = 6	m = 2	m = 3	m = 4	m = 5	m = 6
4	25.16					0.45				
5	21.73					0.48				
6	20.98	21.66				0.41	0.39			
7	20.45	20.93				0.38	0.46			
8	20.68	20.19	21.18			0.42	0.43	0.39		
9	20.27	21.06	20.32			0.44	0.4	0.39		
10	20.54	20.12	20.49	20.57		0.38	0.41	0.39	0.47	
11	20.62	20.64	19.85	19.75		0.38	0.35	0.42	0.42	
12	19.7	20.55	19.47	20.49	21.21	0.39	0.4	0.42	0.43	0.39

Table 10-6. R-Tree delete performance on dense and sparse data sets

M	Dense					Sparse				
	m = 2	m = 3	m = 4	m = 5	m = 6	m = 2	m = 3	m = 4	m = 5	m = 6
4	19.56					4.08				
5	13.16					2.51				
6	11.25	18.23				1.76	4.81			
7	12.58	11.19				1.56	3.7			
8	8.31	9.87	15.09			1.39	2.81	4.96		
9	8.78	11.31	14.01			1.23	2.05	3.39		
10	12.45	8.45	9.59	18.34		1.08	1.8	3.07	5.43	
11	8.09	7.56	8.68	12.28		1.13	1.66	2.51	4.17	
12	8.91	8.25	11.26	14.8	15.82	1.04	1.52	2.18	3.14	5.91

We now fix $M = 4$ and $m = 2$ and compute the performance of search and deletion as n increases in size. In general, higher values of M are beneficial when there are lots of deletions, since it reduces the number of values to be reinserted into the R-Tree because of under-full nodes, but the true behavior is based on the data and the balancing approach used when splitting nodes. The results are shown in Table 10-7.

Table 10-7. R-Tree search and delete performance (in milliseconds) on sparse data set as n doubles

n	Search	Delete
128	0.033	0.135
256	0.060	0.162
512	0.108	0.262
1,024	0.178	0.320
2,048	0.333	0.424
4,096	0.725	0.779
8,192	1.487	1.306
16,384	3.638	2.518
32,768	7.965	3.980
65,536	16.996	10.051
131,072	33.985	15.115

References

Bayer, R. and E. McCreight, "Organization and maintenance of large ordered indexes," Acta Inf. 1, 3, 173-189, 1972, *http://dx.doi.org/10.1007/bf00288683*.

Comer, D., "Ubiquitous B-Tree," *Computing Surveys*, 11(2): 123–137, 1979. *http://dx.doi.org/10.1145/356770.356776*.

Guttman, A., "R-trees: a dynamic index structure for spatial searching," in Proceedings of the SIGMOD international conference on management of data, 1984, pp. 47–57, *http://dx.doi.org/10.1145/971697.602266*.

Meagher, D. J. (1995). US Patent No. EP0152741A2. Washington, DC: U.S. Patent and Trademark Office, *http://www.google.com/patents/EP0152741A2?cl=en*.

11

Emerging Algorithm Categories

Earlier chapters described algorithms that solve common problems. Obviously, you will encounter challenges in your programming career that do not fit into any common category, so this chapter presents four algorithmic *approaches* to solving problems.

Another change in this chapter is its focus on randomness and probability. These were used in previous chapters when analyzing the average-case behavior of algorithms. Here the randomness can become an essential part of an algorithm. Indeed, the probabilistic algorithms we describe are interesting alternatives to deterministic algorithms. Running the same algorithm on the same input at two different times may provide very different answers. Sometimes we will tolerate wrong answers or even claims that no solution was found.

Variations on a Theme

The earlier algorithms in this book solve instances of a problem by giving an exact answer on a sequential, deterministic computer. It is interesting to consider relaxing these three assumptions:

Approximation algorithms
   Instead of seeking an exact answer for a problem, accept solutions that are close to, but not necessarily as good as, the true answer.

Parallel algorithms
   Instead of being restricted to sequential computation, create multiple computational processes to work simultaneously on subproblem instances.

Probabilistic algorithms
> Instead of computing the same result for a problem instance, use randomized computations to compute an answer. When run multiple times, the answers often converge on the true answer.

Approximation Algorithms

Approximation algorithms trade off accuracy for more efficient performance. As an example where a "good enough" answer is sufficient, consider the *Knapsack Problem*, which arises in a variety of computational domains. The goal is to determine the items to add to a backpack that maximize the value of the entire backpack while not exceeding some maximum weight, W. This problem, known as **Knapsack 0/1**, can be solved using Dynamic Programming. For the **Knapsack 0/1** problem, you can only pack one instance of each item. A variation named **Knapsack Unbounded** allows you to pack as many instances of a particular item that you desire. In both cases, the algorithm must return the maximum value of the items given space constraints.

Consider having the set of four items {4, 8, 9, 10} where each item's cost in dollars is the same value as its weight in pounds. Thus, the first item weighs 4 pounds and costs $4. Assume the maximum weight you can pack is $W = 33$ pounds.

As you will recall, Dynamic Programming records the results of smaller subproblems to avoid recomputing them and combines solutions to these smaller problems to solve the original problem. Table 11-1 records the partial results for **Knapsack 0/1** and each entry $m[i][w]$ records the maximum value to be achieved by allowing the first i items (the rows below) to be considered with a maximum combined weight of w (the columns below). The maximum value for given weight W using up to four items as shown in the lower-right corner is $31. In this case, one instance of each item is added to the backpack.

Table 11-1. Performance of Knapsack 0/1 on small set

...	13	14	15	16	17	18	19	20	21	22	23	24	25	26	27	28	29	30	31	32	33
1	4	4	4	4	4	4	4	4	4	4	4	4	4	4	4	4	4	4	4	4	4
2	12	12	12	12	12	12	12	12	12	12	12	12	12	12	12	12	12	12	12	12	12
3	13	13	13	13	17	17	17	17	21	21	21	21	21	21	21	21	21	21	21	21	21
4	13	14	14	14	17	18	19	19	21	22	23	23	23	23	27	27	27	27	31	31	31

For the **Knapsack Unbounded** variation, Table 11-2 records the entry $m[w]$, which represents the maximum value attained for weight w if you are allowed to pack any number of instances of each item. The maximum value for given weight W as shown in the rightmost entry below is $33. In this case, there are six instances of the four-pound item and one nine-pound item.

Table 11-2. Performance of Knapsack Unbounded on small set

...	13	14	15	16	17	18	19	20	21	22	23	24	25	26	27	28	29	30	31	32	33
...	13	14	14	16	17	18	19	20	21	22	23	24	25	26	27	28	29	30	31	32	33

Knapsack 0/1 Summary

Best, Average, Worst: O($n*W$)

```
Knapsack 0/1 (weights, values, W)
  n = number of items
  m = empty (n+1) x (W+1) matrix ❶
  for i=1 to n do
    for j=0 to W do
      if weights[i-1] <= j then ❷
        remaining = j - weights[i-1]
        m[i][j] = max(m[i-1][j], m[i-1][remaining] + values[i-1])
      else
        m[i][j] = m[i-1][j] ❸
  return m[n][W] ❹
end

Knapsack unbounded(weights, values, W)
  n = number of items
  m = empty (W+1) vector ❺
  for j=1 to W+1 do
    best = m[j-1]
    for i=0 to n-1 do
      remaining = j - weights[i]
      if remaining >= 0 and m[remaining] + values[i] > best then
        best = m[remaining] + values[i]
      m[j] = best
  return m[W]
```

❶ $m[i][j]$ records maximum value using first i items without exceeding weight j.

❷ Can we increase value by adding item $i - 1$ to previous solution with weight (j – that item's weight)?

❸ Item $i - 1$ exceeds weight limit and thus can't improve solution.

❹ Return computed best value.

❺ For unbounded, $m[j]$ records maximum value without exceeding weight j.

Input/Output

You are given a set of items (each with an integer weight and value) and a maximum weight, W. The problem is to determine which items to pack into the knapsack so the total weight is less than or equal to W and the total value of the packed items is as large as possible.

Context

This is a type of resource allocation problem with constraints that is common in computer science, mathematics, and economics. It has been studied extensively for over a century and has numerous variations. Often you need to know the actual selection of items, not just the maximum value, so the solution must also return the items selected to put into the knapsack.

Solution

We use Dynamic Programming, which works by storing the results of simpler subproblems. For **Knapsack 0/1**, the two-dimensional matrix $m[i][j]$ records the result of the maximum value using the first i items without exceeding weight j. The structure of the solution in Example 11-1 matches the expected double loops of Dynamic Programming.

Example 11-1. Python implementation of Knapsack 0/1

```python
class Item:
  def __init__(self, value, weight):
    """Create item with given value and weight."""
    self.value = value
    self.weight = weight

def knapsack_01 (items, W):
  """
  Compute 0/1 knapsack solution (just one of each item is available)
  for set of items with corresponding weights and values. Return total
  weight and selection of items.
  """
  n = len(items)
  m = [None] * (n+1)
  for i in range(n+1):
    m[i] = [0] * (W+1)

  for i in range(1,n+1):
    for j in range(W+1):
      if items[i-1].weight <= j:
        valueWithItem = m[i-1][j-items[i-1].weight] + items[i-1].value
        m[i][j] = max(m[i-1][j], valueWithItem)
      else:
        m[i][j] = m[i-1][j]

  selections = [0] * n
  i = n
  w = W
  while i > 0 and w >= 0:
```

```
    if m[i][w] != m[i-1][w]:
        selections[i-1] = 1
        w -= items[i-1].weight
    i -= 1

return (m[n][W], selections)
```

This code follows the Dynamic Programming structure by computing each subproblem in order. Once the nested `for` loops compute the maximum value, `m[n][W]`, the subsequent `while` loop shows how to recover the actual items selected by "walking" over the `m` matrix. It starts at the lower righthand corner, `m[n][W]`, and determines whether the ith item was selected, based on whether `m[i][w]` is different from `m[i-1][w]`. If this is the case, it records the selection and then moves left in `m` by removing the weight of i and continuing until it hits the first row (no more items) or the left column (no more weight); otherwise it tries the previous item.

The **Knapsack Unbounded** problem uses a one-dimensional vector `m[j]` to record the result of the maximum value not exceeding weight j. Its Python implementation is shown in Example 11-2.

Example 11-2. Python implementation of Knapsack unbounded

```
def knapsack_unbounded (items, W):
    """
    Compute unbounded knapsack solution (any number of each item is
    available) for set of items with corresponding weights and values.
    Return total weight and selection of items.
    """
    n = len(items)
    progress = [0] * (W+1)
    progress[0] = -1
    m = [0] * (W + 1)
    for j in range(1, W+1):
        progress[j] = progress[j-1]
        best = m[j-1]
        for i in range(n):
            remaining = j - items[i].weight
            if remaining >= 0 and m[remaining] + items[i].value > best:
                best = m[remaining] + items[i].value
                progress[j] = i
        m[j] = best

    selections = [0] * n
    i = n
    w = W
    while w >= 0:
        choice = progress[w]
        if choice == -1:
            break
        selections[choice] += 1
```

```
    w -= items[progress[w]].weight

  return (m[W], selections)
```

Analysis

These solutions are not O(*n*) as one might expect, because that would require the overall execution to be bounded by $c*n$, where c is a constant for sufficiently large *n*. The execution time depends on *W* as well. That is, in both cases, the solution is O(*n*W*), as clearly shown by the nested for loops. Recovering the selections is O(*n*), so this doesn't change the overall performance.

Why does this observation matter? In **Knapsack 0/1**, when *W* is much larger than the weights of the individual items, the algorithm must repeatedly perform wasted iterations, because each item is only chosen once. There are similar inefficiencies for **Knapsack Unbounded**.

In 1957, George Dantzig proposed an approximate solution to **Knapsack Unbounded**, shown in Example 11-3. The intuition behind this approximation is that you should first insert items into the knapsack that maximize the value-to-weight ratio. In fact, this approach is guaranteed to find an approximation that is no worse than half of the maximum value that would have been found by Dynamic Programming. In practice, the results are actually quite close to the real value, and the code is noticeably faster.

Example 11-3. Python implementation of Knapsack unbounded approximation

```
class ApproximateItem(Item):
  """
  Extends Item by storing the normalized value and the original position
  of the item before sorting.
  """
  def __init__(self, item, idx):
    Item.__init__(self, item.value, item.weight)
    self.normalizedValue = item.value/item.weight
    self.index = idx

def knapsack_approximate (items, W):
  """Compute approximation to knapsack problem using Dantzig approach."""
  approxItems = []
  n = len(items)
  for idx in range(n):
    approxItems.append (ApproximateItem(items[idx], idx))
  approxItems.sort (key=lambda x:x.normalizedValue, reverse=True)

  selections = [0] * n
  w = W
  total = 0
  for idx in range(n):
```

```
item = approxItems[idx]

if w == 0:
  break

# find out how many fit
numAdd = w // item.weight
if numAdd > 0:
  selections[item.index] += numAdd
  w -= numAdd * item.weight
  total += numAdd * item.value

return (total, selections)
```

The implementation iterates over the items in reverse order by their normalized value (i.e., the ratio of value to weight). The cost of this algorithm is $O(n \log n)$ because it must sort the items first.

Returning to the original set of four items {4, 8, 9, 10} in our earlier example, observe that the ratio of value to weight is 1.0 for each item, which means they are all "equivalent" in importance according to the algorithm. For the given weight $W = 33$, the approximation chooses to pack eight instances of the item weighing four pounds, which results in a total value of $32. It is interesting that all three algorithms came up with a different value given the same items and overall weight constraint.

The following table compares the performance of the **Knapsack Unbounded Approximation** with **Knapsack Unbounded** as W grows in size. Each of the items in the set of $n = 53$ items has a different weight and each item's value is set to its weight. The weights range from 103 to 407. As you can see, as the size of W doubles, the time to execute **Knapsack Unbounded** also doubles, because of its $O(n*W)$ performance. However, the performance of **Knapsack Approximate** doesn't change as W gets larger because its performance is determined only by $O(n \log n)$.

Reviewing the final two columns, you can see that for $W = 175$, the approximate solution is 60% of the actual answer. As W increases, the approximate solution converges to be closer to the actual answer. Also, the approximation algorithm is almost 1,000 times faster.

Table 11-3. Performance of Knapsack variations

W	Knapsack Unbounded Time	Knapsack Approximate Time	Actual Answer	Approximate Answer
175	0.00256	0.00011	175	103
351	0.00628	0.00011	351	309
703	0.01610	0.00012	703	618
1407	0.03491	0.00012	1407	1339

W	Knapsack Unbounded Time	Knapsack Approximate Time	Actual Answer	Approximate Answer
2815	0.07320	0.00011	2815	2781
5631	0.14937	0.00012	5631	5562
11263	0.30195	0.00012	11263	11227
22527	0.60880	0.00013	22527	22454
45055	1.21654	0.00012	45055	45011

Parallel Algorithms

Parallel algorithms take advantage of existing computational resources by creating and managing different threads of execution.

Quicksort, presented in Chapter 4, can be implemented in Java as shown in Example 11-4, assuming the existence of a partition function to divide the original array into two subarrays based on a pivot value. As you recall from Chapter 4, values to the left of pivotIndex are ≤ the pivot value while values to the right of pivotIndex are ≥ the pivot value.

Example 11-4. Quicksort implementation in Java

```
public class MultiThreadQuickSort<E extends Comparable<E>> {

  final E[]     ar;  /** Elements to be sorted. */
  IPivotIndex   pi;  /** Partition function. */

  /** Construct an instance to solve quicksort. */
  public MultiThreadQuickSort (E ar[]) {
    this.ar = ar;
  }

  /** Set the partition method. */
  public void setPivotMethod (IPivotIndex ipi) { this.pi = ipi; }

  /** Single-thread sort of ar[left,right]. */
  public void qsortSingle (int left, int right) {
    if (right <= left) { return; }

    int pivotIndex = pi.selectPivotIndex (ar, left, right);
    pivotIndex = partition (left, right, pivotIndex);

    qsortSingle (left, pivotIndex-1);
    qsortSingle (pivotIndex+1, right);
  }
}
```

The two subproblems qsortSingle (left, pivotIndex-1) and qsortSingle (pivotIndex+1, right) are independent problems and, theoretically, can be solved at the same time. The immediate question is how to use multiple threads to solve this problem. You cannot simply spawn a helper thread with each recursive call since that would overwhelm the resources of the operating system. Consider the rewrite, qsort2, shown in Example 11-5:

Example 11-5. Multithreaded Java Quicksort implementation

```
/** Multi-thread sort of ar[left,right]. */
void qsort2 (int left, int right) {
  if (right <= left) { return; }

  int pivotIndex = pi.selectPivotIndex (ar, left, right);
  pivotIndex = partition (left, right, pivotIndex);

  qsortThread (left, pivotIndex-1);
  qsortThread (pivotIndex+1, right);
}

/**
 * Spawn thread to sort ar[left,right] or use existing thread
 * if problem size is too big or all helpers are being used.
 */
private void qsortThread (final int left, final int right) {
  // are all helper threads working OR is problem too big?
  // Continue with recursion if so.
  int n = right + 1 - left;
  if (helpersWorking == numThreads || n >= threshold) {
    qsort2 (left, right);
  } else {
    // otherwise, complete in separate thread
    synchronized (helpRequestedMutex) {
      helpersWorking++;
    }

    new Thread () {
      public void run () {
        // invoke single-thread qsort
        qsortSingle (left, right);

        synchronized (helpRequestedMutex) {
          helpersWorking--;
        }
      }
    }.start();
  }
}
```

For each of the two qsortThread subproblems, there is a simple check to see whether the primary thread should continue the recursive qsortThread function call. The separate helper thread is dispatched to compute a subproblem only if a thread is available and the size of the subproblem is smaller than the specified threshold value. This logic is applied when sorting the left subarray as well as the right subarray. The threshold value is computed by calling setThresholdRatio(r), which sets the threshold problem size to be n/r where n is the number of elements to be sorted. The default ratio is 5, which means a helper thread is only invoked on subproblems that are smaller than 20% of the original problem size.

The helpersWorking class attribute stores the number of active helper threads. Whenever a thread is spawned, the helpersWorking variable is incremented, and the thread itself will decrement this same value on completion. Using the mutex variable, helpRequestedMutex, and the ability in Java to synchronize a block of code for exclusive access, this implementation safely updates the helpersWorking variable. qsort2 invokes the single-threaded qsortSingle method within its helper threads. This ensures only the primary thread is responsible for spawning new threads of computation.

For this design, helper threads cannot spawn additional helper threads. If this were allowed to happen, the "first" helper thread would have to synchronize with these "second" threads, so the "second" threads would only begin to execute after the "first" helper thread had properly partitioned the array.

Figures 11-1 and 11-2 compare the Java single-helper solution against a single-threaded solution sorting random integers from the range [0, 16777216]. We consider several parameters:

Size n of the array being sorted
This falls in the range {65,536 to 1,048,576}.

Threshold n/r
This determines the maximum size of the problem for which a helper thread is spawned. We experimented with values of r in the range {1 to 20} and MAX-INT, which effectively denies using helper threads.

Number of helper threads available
We experimented with 0 to 9 helper threads.

Partition method to use
We tried both "select a random element" and "select the rightmost element."

The parameter space thus amounts to 2,000 unique combinations of these parameters. In general, we found there is a noticeable performance slowdown of about 5% in using the random number generator across all experiments, so we now focus only on the "rightmost" partition method. In addition, for **Quicksort**, having more than one helper thread available did not improve the performance, so we focus only on having a single helper thread.

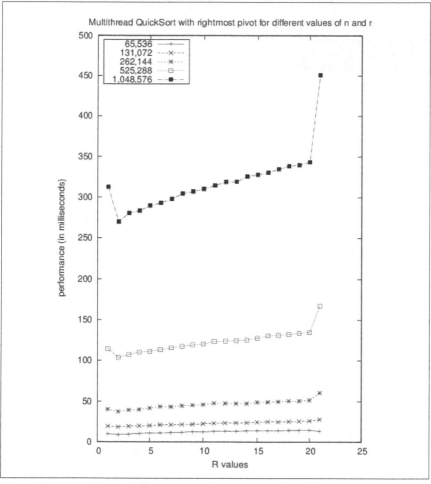

Figure 11-1. Multithreaded Quicksort for varying n and r

Reading the graph from left to right, you can see that the first data point ($r = 1$) reports the performance that tries to immediately begin using the helper thread, while the last data point ($r = 21$) reports the result when no helper thread is ever used. When we compute the *speedup factor* from time T1 to a smaller time T2, we use the equation T1/T2. Simply using an extra thread shows a speedup factor of about 1.3. This is a very nice return on investment for a small programming change, as shown in Table 11-4.

Table 11-4. Speedup of having one helper thread for (r = 1) versus
(r = MAXINT)

n	Speedup of Multi-thread to no thread
65,536	1.24
131,072	1.37
262,144	1.35
524,288	1.37
1,048,576	1.31

Returning to Figure 11-1, you can see that the best improvement occurs near where $r = 2$. There is a built-in overhead to using threads, and we shouldn't automatically dispatch a new thread of execution without some assurance that the primary thread will not have to wait and *block* until the helper thread completes its execution. These results will differ based on the computing platform used.

In many cases, the speedup is affected by the number of CPUs on the computing platform. Figure 11-2 contains the speedup tables on two different computing platforms—a dual-core CPU and a quad-core CPU. Each row represents the potential number of available threads while each column represents a threshold value r. The total number of elements sorted is fixed at $n = 1,048,576$. The quad-core results demonstrate the effectiveness of allowing multiple threads, achieving a speedup of 1.5; the same cannot be said of the dual-core execution, whose performance increases by no more than 5% when allowing multiple threads.

Research in speedup factors for parallel algorithms shows there are inherent limitations to how much extra threading or extra processing will actually help a specific algorithmic implementation. Here the multithreaded **Quicksort** implementation achieves a nice speedup factor because the individual subproblems of recursive **Quicksort** are entirely independent; there will be no contention for shared resources by the multiple threads. If other problems share this same characteristic, they should also be able to benefit from multithreading.

Probabilistic Algorithms

A probabilistic algorithm uses a stream of random bits (i.e., random numbers) as part of the process for computing an answer, so you will get different results when running the algorithm on the same problem instance. Often, assuming access to a stream of random bits leads to algorithms that are faster than any current alternatives.

For practical purposes, we should be aware that streams of random bits are very difficult to generate on deterministic computers. Though we may generate streams of quasi-random bits that are virtually indistinguishable from streams of truly random bits, the cost of generating these streams should not be ignored.

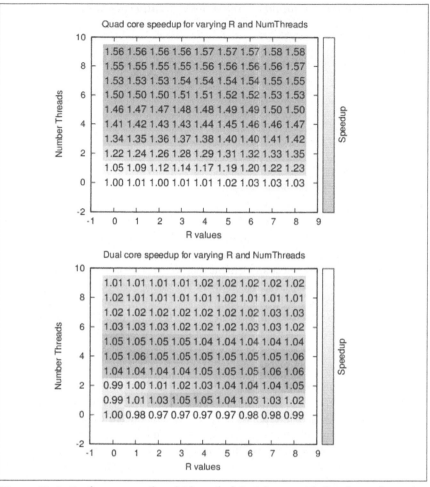

Figure 11-2. Performance of multithreaded Quicksort with fixed n and varying r and number of threads

Estimating the Size of a Set

As an example of the speedup that can be obtained in allowing probabilistic algorithms, assume we want to estimate the size of a set of *n* distinct objects (i.e., we want to estimate the value *n* by observing individual elements). It would be straightforward to count all the objects, at a cost of O(*n*). Clearly this process is guaranteed to yield an exact answer. But if an incorrect estimate of the value of *n* is tolerable, assuming it could be computed more quickly, the algorithm described in Example 11-6 is a faster alternative. This algorithm is similar to the mark-and-recapture experiments biologists use to estimate the size of a spatially limited population of organisms. The approach here is to use a generator function that returns a random individual in the population.

Example 11-6. Implementation of probabilistic counting algorithm

```
def computeK(generator):
    """
    Compute estimate of using probabilistic counting algorithm.
    Doesn't know value of n, the size of the population.
    """
    seen = set()

    while True:
        item = generator()
        if item in seen:
            k = len(seen)
            return 2.0*k*k/math.pi
        else:
            seen.add(item)
```

Let's start with some intuition. We must have the ability to pick random elements from the set and mark them as being seen. Since we assume the set is finite, at some point we must eventually select an element that we have seen before. The longer it takes to choose a previously selected element, the larger the size of the original set must be. In statistics, this behavior is known as "sampling with replacement" and the expected number of selections, k, we can make until seeing a previously selected element is

$$k = \sqrt{\pi * n/2}$$

As long as the *generator* function returns an element that has already been seen (which it must do because the population is finite) the while loop will terminate after some number of selections, k. Once k is computed, rearrange the preceding formula to compute an approximation of n. Clearly, the algorithm can never give the exact value of n, because $2*k^2/\pi$ can never be an integer, but this computation is an unbiased estimate of n.

In Table 11-5 we show a sample run of the algorithm that records the results of performing the computation repeatedly for a number of trials, $t = \{32, 64, 128, 256, 512\}$. From these trials, the lowest and highest estimates were discarded, and the average of the remaining t-2 trials is shown in each column.

Table 11-5. Results of probabilistic counting algorithm as number of trials increase

n	Average of 30	Average of 62	Average of 126	Average of 254	Average of 510
1,024	1144	1065	1205	1084	1290
2,048	2247	1794	2708	2843	2543
4,096	3789	4297	5657	5384	5475

n	Average of 30	Average of 62	Average of 126	Average of 254	Average of 510
8,192	9507	10369	10632	10517	9687
16,384	20776	18154	15617	20527	21812
32,768	39363	29553	40538	36094	39542
65,536	79889	81576	76091	85034	83102
131,072	145664	187087	146191	173928	174630
262,144	393848	297303	336110	368821	336936
524,288	766044	509939	598978	667082	718883
1,048,576	1366027	1242640	1455569	1364828	1256300

Because of the random nature of the trials, it is not at all guaranteed that the final accurate result can be achieved simply by averaging over an increasing number of independent random trials. Even increasing the number of trials does little to improve the accuracy, but that misses the point; this probabilistic algorithm efficiently returns an estimate based on a small sample size.

Estimating the Size of a Search Tree

Mathematicians have long studied the 8-Queens Problem, which asks whether it is possible to place eight queens on a chessboard so that no two queens threaten each other. This was expanded to the more general problem of counting the number of unique solutions to placing n nonthreatening queens on an n-by-n chessboard. No one has yet been able to devise a way to mathematically compute this answer; instead you can write a brute-force program that checks all possible board configurations to determine the answer. Table 11-6 contains some of the computed values taken from the On-Line Encyclopedia of Integer Sequences (*https://oeis.org/ A000170*). As you can see, the number of solutions grows extremely rapidly.

Table 11-6. Known count of solutions for n-Queens Problem with our computed estimates

n	Actual number of solutions	Estimation with T = 1,024 trials	Estimation with T = 8,192 trials	Estimation with T = 65,536 trials
1	1	1	1	1
2	0	0	0	0
3	0	0	0	0
4	2	2	2	2
5	10	10	10	10
6	4	5	4	4

n	Actual number of solutions	Estimation with T = 1,024 trials	Estimation with T = 8,192 trials	Estimation with T = 65,536 trials
7	40	41	39	40
8	92	88	87	93
9	352	357	338	351
10	724	729	694	718
11	2,680	2,473	2,499	2,600
12	14,200	12,606	14,656	13,905
13	73,712	68,580	62,140	71,678
14	365,596	266,618	391,392	372,699
15	2,279,184	1,786,570	2,168,273	2,289,607
16	14,772,512	12,600,153	13,210,175	15,020,881
17	95,815,104	79,531,007	75,677,252	101,664,299
18	666,090,624	713,470,160	582,980,339	623,574,560
19	4,968,057,848	4,931,587,745	4,642,673,268	4,931,598,683
20	39,029,188,884	17,864,106,169	38,470,127,712	37,861,260,851

To count the number of exact solutions to the 4-Queens Problem, we expand a search tree (shown in Figure 11-3) based on the fact that each solution will have one queen on each row. Such an exhaustive elaboration of the search tree permits us to see that there are two solutions to the 4-Queens Problem. Trying to compute the number of solutions to the 19-Queens Problem is much harder because there are 4,968,057,848 nodes at level 19 of the search tree. It is simply prohibitively expensive to generate each and every solution.

However, what if you were interested only in approximating the number of solutions, or in other words, the number of potential board states on level n? Knuth (1975) developed a novel alternative approach to estimate the size and shape of a search tree. His method corresponds to taking a random walk down the search tree. For the sake of brevity, we illustrate his technique for the 4-Queens Problem, but clearly it could just as easily be applied to approximate the number of solutions to the 19-Queens Problem. Instead of counting all possible solutions, create a single board state containing n queens and estimate the overall count by totaling the potential board states *not followed*, assuming each of these directions would be equally productive.

Figure 11-4 demonstrates Knuth's approach on a 4x4 chessboard. Each of the board states has an associated estimate in a small circle for the number of board states in the entire tree *at that level*. Starting with the root of the search tree (no queens placed), each board state expands to a new level based on its number of children. We will conduct a large number of random walks over this search tree, which will never be fully constructed during the process. In each walk we will select moves at random until a solution is reached or no moves are available. By averaging the number of solutions returned by each random walk, we can approximate the actual count of states in the tree. Let's perform two possible walks starting from the root node at level 0:

- Choose the leftmost board state in the first level. Because there are four children, our best estimate for the total number of states at level 1 is 4. Now again, choose the leftmost child from its two children, resulting in a board state on level 2. From its perspective, assuming each of the other three children of the root node are similarly productive, it estimates the total number of board states on level 2 to be 4*2 = 8. However, at this point, there are no more possible moves, so from its perspective, it assumes no other branch is productive, so it estimates there are 0 board states at level 3 and the search terminates with no solution found.

- Choose the second-to-left board state in the first level. Its best estimate for the number of states at level 1 is 4. Now, in each of the subsequent levels there is only one valid board state, which leads to the estimate of 4*1 = 4 for the number of board states at each subsequent level, assuming all of the other original paths were similarly productive. Upon reaching the lowest level, it estimates there are four solutions in the entire tree.

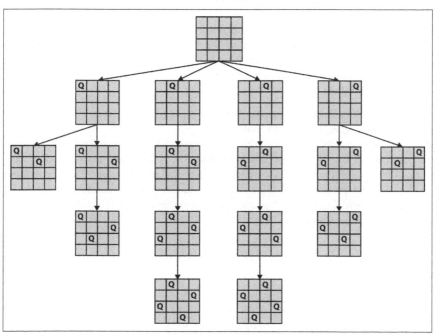

Figure 11-3. Final solution for 4-Queens Problem with four rows extended

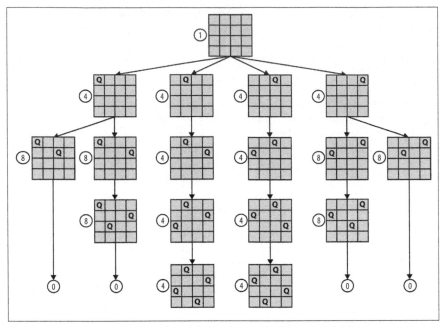

Figure 11-4. Estimating number of solutions of 4-Queens Problem

Neither of these estimates is correct, and it is typical of this approach that different walks lead to under- and overestimates of the actual count. However, if we perform a large number of random walks, the average of the estimates will converge on the value. Each estimate can be computed quickly, thus this refined (averaged) estimate can also be computed quickly.

If you refer back to Table 11-6, we show the computed results from our implementation for 1,024, 8,192, and 65,536 trials. No timing information is included, because all results were computed in less than a minute. The final estimate for the 19-Queens problem with T = 65,536 trials is within 3% of the actual answer. Indeed, all of the estimates for T = 65,536 are within 5.8% of the actual answer. This algorithm has the desirable property that the computed value is more accurate as more random trials are run. Example 11-7 shows the implementation in Java for a single estimate of the *n*-Queens problem.

Example 11-7. Implementation of Knuth's randomized estimation of n-Queens problem

```
/**
 * For an n-by-n board, store up to n nonthreatening queens and
 * search along the lines of Knuth's random walk. It is assumed the
 * queens are being added row by row starting from 0.
 */
public class Board {
```

```java
boolean [][] board;    /** The board. */
final int n;           /** board size. */

/** Temporary store for last valid positions. */
ArrayList<Integer> nextValidRowPositions = new ArrayList<Integer>();

public Board (int n) {
  board = new boolean[n][n];
  this.n = n;
}

/** Start with row and work upwards to see if still valid. */
private boolean valid (int row, int col) {
  // another queen in same column, left diagonal, or right diagonal?
  int d = 0;
  while (++d <= row) {
    if (board[row-d][col]) { return false; }
    if (col >= d && board[row-d][col-d]) { return false; }
    if (col+d < n && board[row-d][col+d]) { return false; }
  }
  return true; // OK
}

/**
 * Find out how many valid children states are found by trying to add
 * a queen to the given row. Returns a number from 0 to n.
 */
public int numChildren (int row) {
  int count = 0;
  nextValidRowPositions.clear();
  for (int i = 0; i < n; i++) {
    board[row][i] = true;
    if (valid (row, i)) {
      count++;
      nextValidRowPositions.add (i);
    }
    board[row][i] = false;
  }

  return count;
}

/** If no board is available at this row then return false. */
public boolean randomNextBoard (int r) {
  int sz = nextValidRowPositions.size();
  if (sz == 0) { return false; }

  // select one randomly
  int c = (int) (Math.random()*sz);
  board[r][nextValidRowPositions.get (c)] = true;
  return true;
}
```

```
}

public class SingleQuery {
  /** Generate table. */
  public static void main (String []args) {
    for (int i = 0; i < 100; i++) {
      System.out.println(i + ": " + estimate(19));
    }
  }

  public static long estimate (int n) {
    Board b = new Board(n);

    int r = 0;
    long lastEstimate = 1;
    while (r < n) {
      int numChildren = b.numChildren (r);

      // no more to go, so no solution found.
      if (!b.randomNextBoard (r)) {
        lastEstimate = 0;
        break;
      }

      // compute estimate based on ongoing tally and advance
      lastEstimate = lastEstimate*numChildren;
      r++;
    }

    return lastEstimate;
  }
}
```

References

Armstrong, J., *Programming Erlang: Software for a Concurrent World*. Second Edition. Pragmatic Bookshelf, 2013.

Berman, K. and J. Paul, *Algorithms: Sequential, Parallel, and Distributed*. Course Technology, 2004.

Christofides, N., "Worst-case analysis of a new heuristic for the traveling salesman problem," Report 388, Graduate School of Industrial Administration, CMU, 1976.

Knuth, D. E., "Estimating the efficiency of backtrack programs," *Mathematics of Computation*, 29(129): 121–136, 1975.

12

Epilogue: Principles of Algorithms

While we have reached the end of this book, there is no limit to the amount of information you can find on algorithms about which you're interested. Indeed, there is no end to the kind of problems to which you can apply the techniques presented in this book.

We finally have the opportunity to step back and review the nearly three dozen algorithms we described in detail and by example. We hope you agree that we have accomplished what we set out to do. To show the breadth of material that we've covered, we now summarize the principles behind the algorithms presented in this book. In doing so, we can demonstrate the similarities of different algorithms that were designed to solve different problems. Instead of simply summarizing each of the previous chapters, we'll end this book by focusing on key principles that were instrumental in designing these algorithms in the first place. We also take this opportunity to summarize the concepts used by each algorithm. Thus, we provide a quick summary and make it possible to cross-index this book in terms of shared concepts across different algorithms.

Know Your Data

This book discussed a variety of common actions you might need to perform on some data. You might need to sort data to produce a specific ordering. You might need to search through data to locate a specific piece of information. Your data may be accessible in random access (where you can fetch any piece of information at any time) or sequentially using an Iterator (where each element is generated one at a time). Without specific knowledge about your data, it is only possible to recommend algorithms in the most general way.

Often properties about the input data have a significant impact. In Chapter 9, many special cases can simply be eliminated if you know you are computing the intersections among line segments containing no vertical lines; similarly, computing the Voronoi diagram is simplified if no two points share the same x or y coordinate. **Dijkstra's Algorithm**, found in Chapter 6, will run forever if a cycle exists whose sum of all edge weights is negative. Make sure you understand the special cases and assumptions of the algorithms you choose.

As we have argued, there is no single algorithm that consistently delivers the best performance for all circumstances. Choose the most appropriate algorithm based on your data as you become more familiar with the available options. Table 12-1 summarizes the results of the sorting algorithms presented in Chapter 4. Naturally you will focus on the worst-case performance of each algorithm, but also pay attention to the *concepts* that arise when implementing or using these algorithms.

Table 12-1. Sorting algorithms

Algorithm	Best	Average	Worst	Concepts	Page
Bucket Sort	n	n	n	Hash	"Bucket Sort" on page 74
Heap Sort	$n \log n$	$n \log n$	$n \log n$	Recursion, Binary Heap	"Heap Sort" on page 62
Insertion Sort	n	n^2	n^2	Greedy	"Transposition Sorting" on page 57
Merge Sort	$n \log n$	$n \log n$	$n \log n$	Recursion, Stable, Divide and Conquer	"Merge Sort" on page 81
Quicksort	$n \log n$	$n \log n$	n^2	Recursion, Divide and Conquer	"Partition-Based Sorting" on page 67
Selection Sort	n^2	n^2	n^2	Greedy	"Selection Sort" on page 61

Decompose a Problem into Smaller Problems

When designing an efficient algorithm to solve a problem, it is helpful if the problem can be decomposed into two (or more) smaller subproblems. It is no mistake that **Quicksort** remains one of the most popular sorting algorithms. Even with the well-documented special cases that cause problems, **Quicksort** offers the best average-case for sorting large collections of information. Indeed, the very concept of an O($n \log n$) algorithm is based on the ability to (a) decompose a problem of size n into two subproblems of about $n/2$ in size, and (b) recombine the solution of the two subproblems into a solution for the original problem. To design an O($n \log n$) algorithm, it must be possible for both of these steps to execute in O(n) time.

Quicksort was the first in-place sorting algorithm to demonstrate O($n \log n$) performance. It succeeds by the novel (almost counterintuitive) approach for dividing the problem into two halves, each of which can be solved recursively by applying **Quicksort** to the smaller subproblems.

Problems often can be simply cut in half, leading to impressive performance savings. Consider how **Binary Search** converts a problem of size n into a problem of size $n/2$. **Binary Search** takes advantage of the repetitive nature of the search task to develop a recursive solution to the problem.

Sometimes a problem can be solved by dividing it into two subproblems without resorting to recursion. **Convex Hull Scan** produces the final convex hull by constructing and merging together two partial hulls (the upper and lower).

Sometimes a problem can be decomposed into the repeated iteration of a different (seemingly unconnected) smaller problem over the same input data. **Ford–Fulkerson** computes the maximum flow in a flow network by repeatedly locating an augmenting path to which flow can be added. Eventually, no augmenting paths are possible and the original solution is solved. **Selection Sort** repeatedly locates the maximum value in an array and swaps it with the rightmost element in the array; upon completing n iterations, the array is sorted. Similarly, **Heap Sort** repeatedly swaps the largest element in the heap with its proper location in the array.

Observe that Dynamic Programming decomposes problems into smaller problems, but its overall behavior is typically $O(n^2)$ or $O(n^3)$ because the smaller problems are typically just one size smaller than the original problem, rather than half its size.

Table 12-2 contains a comparison of the searching algorithms discussed in Chapter 5. These algorithms offer different approaches to answer the fundamental question of membership in a collection. In analyzing their performance, we used a technique to *amortize* the costs of a series of operations, which allows us to accurately characterize the *average* performance given a random search query.

Table 12-2. Searching algorithms

Algorithm	Best	Average	Worst	Concepts	Page
AVL Binary Search Tree	1	$log\ n$	$log\ n$	Binary Tree, Balanced	"Binary Search Tree" on page 119
Sequential Search	1	n	n	Brute Force	"Sequential Search" on page 92
Binary Search	1	$log\ n$	$log\ n$	Divide and Conquer	"Binary Search" on page 95
Bloom Filter	k	k	k	False Positive	"Bloom Filter" on page 114
Hash-Based Search	1	1	n	Hash	"Hash-Based Search" on page 99
Binary Search Tree	1	$log\ n$	n	Binary Tree	"Binary Search Tree" on page 119

Choose the Right Data Structure

The famed algorithm designer Robert Tarjan was once quoted as saying that any problem can be solved in $O(n\ log\ n)$ time with the right data structure. Many algorithms need to use a priority queue to store partial progress and direct future computations. One of the most common means of implementing a priority queue is through a binary heap, which allows for $O(log\ n)$ behavior for removing the element with lowest priority from the priority queue. However, a binary heap offers no ability to determine whether it contains a specific element. We expanded on this very point in the discussion of **LineSweep** (Chapter 9). This algorithm can provide

O($n \log n$) performance because it uses an augmented binary tree to implement the priority queue and still provides O($\log n$) performance for removing the minimum element. Another way to state this principle is to avoid selecting an inappropriate data structure that will prevent an algorithm from achieving its best performance.

In Chapter 6, we showed when to use an adjacency list or an adjacency matrix to represent a graph, based on whether the graph was *sparse* or *dense*. This single decision has the greatest impact on the performance of these algorithms. Table 12-3 shows the graph algorithms discussed in Chapter 6.

Table 12-3. Graph algorithms

Algorithm	Best	Average	Worst	Concepts	Page
Bellman-Ford Algorithm	V^*E	V^*E	V^*E	Weighted Directed Graph, Overflow	"All-Pairs Shortest Path" on page 159
Breadth-First Search	$V + E$	$V + E$	$V + E$	Graph, Queue	"Breadth-First Search" on page 143
Depth-First Search	$V + E$	$V + E$	$V + E$	Graph, Recursion, Backtracking	"Depth-First Search" on page 137
Dijkstra's Algorithm PQ	$(V + E) \log V$	$(V + E) \log V$	$(V + E) \log V$	Weighted Directed Graph, Priority Queue, Overflow	"Single-Source Shortest Path" on page 147
Dijkstra's Algorithm DG	$V^2 + E$	$V^2 + E$	$V^2 + E$	Weighted Directed Graph, Overflow	"Single-Source Shortest Path" on page 147
Floyd–Warshall Algorithm	V^3	V^3	V^3	Dynamic Programming, Weighted Directed Graph, Overflow	"All-Pairs Shortest Path" on page 159
Prim's Algorithm	$(V + E) \log V$	$(V + E) \log V$	$(V + E) \log V$	Weighted Graph, Binary Heap, Priority Queue, Greedy	"Minimum Spanning Tree Algorithms" on page 163

When working with complex n-dimensional data, you need more complicated recursive structures to store the data. Chapter 10 describes sophisticated *spatial tree* structures to efficiently support standard search queries as well as more complicated range queries. These structures were carefully designed by extending *binary trees*, the fundamental recursive data structure in computer science.

Make the Space versus Time Trade-Off

Many of the computations carried out by the algorithms are optimized by storing information that reflects the results of past computations. **Prim's Algorithm** for computing the minimum spanning tree for a graph uses a priority queue to store the unvisited vertices in order of their shortest distance to an initial vertex s. During a key step in the algorithm, we must determine whether a given vertex has already been visited. Because the binary heap implementation of the priority queue fails to provide this operation, a separate Boolean array records the status of each vertex. In the same algorithm, another array stores the computed distances to avoid having to search again through the priority queue. This extra storage on the order of $O(n)$ is required to ensure the efficient implementation of the algorithm. In most situations, as long as the overhead is $O(n)$, you are going to be safe.

Sometimes an entire computation can be cached so it never needs to be recomputed. In Chapter 6, we discussed how the hash function for the java.lang.String class stores the computed hash value to speed up its performance.

Sometimes the nature of the input set demands a large amount of storage, such as the dense graphs described in Chapter 6. By using a two-dimensional matrix to store the edge information—rather than using simple adjacency lists—certain algorithms exhibit reasonable performance. You may also note that for undirected graphs, the algorithms can be simplified by having twice as much storage and use a two-dimensional matrix to store information for edgeInfo[i][j] as well as edge Info[j][i]. It would be possible to eliminate this extra information if we always queried for edgeInfo[i][j] using $i \leq j$, but this would further complicate every algorithm that simply desired to know whether edge (i, j) exists.

Sometimes an algorithm is unable to operate without some higher-than-expected storage. **Bucket Sort** can sort in linear time simply by storing up to $O(n)$ extra storage, if the input set is uniformly distributed. Given that today's modern computers often have very large random access memory present, you should consider **Bucket Sort** for uniform data even though its memory requirements are so high.

Table 12-4 shows the spatial tree algorithms discussed in Chapter 10.

Table 12-4. Spatial Tree algorithms

Algorithm	Best	Average	Worst	Concepts	Page
Nearest Neighbor Query	$log\ n$	$log\ n$	n	k-d tree, Recursion	"Nearest Neighbor Summary" on page 290
Quadtree	$log\ n$	$log\ n$	$log\ n$	Quadtree	"Quadtree" on page 286
Range Queries	$n^{1-1/d} + r$	$n^{1-1/d} + r$	n	k-d tree, Recursion	"Range Query" on page 298
R-Tree	$log\ n$	$log\ n$	$log\ n$	R-Tree	"R-Tree" on page 287

Construct a Search

Early pioneers in the field of artificial intelligence (AI) were often characterized as trying to solve problems for which no known solution existed. One of the most common approaches to solving problems was to convert the problem into a search over a very large graph. We dedicated an entire chapter to this approach because it is an important and general technique for solving numerous problems. But be careful to apply it only when no other computational alternative is available! You could use the path-finding approach to discover a sequence of element transpositions that starts from an unsorted array (the initial node) and produces a sorted array (the goal node), but you shouldn't use an algorithm with exponential behavior because numerous $O(n \log n)$ algorithms exist to sort data.

Table 12-5 shows the path–finding algorithms discussed in Chapter 7. These all exhibit exponential performance, but these are still the preferred approach for implementing intelligent game-playing programs. While these algorithms identify the structure for finding a solution, they succeed because of sophisticated heuristics that truly make the search process intelligent.

Table 12-5. Path finding in AI

Algorithm	Best	Average	Worst	Concepts	Page
Depth-First Search	$b*d$	b^d	b^d	Stack, Set, Backtracking	"Depth-First Search" on page 192
Breadth-First Search	b^d	b^d	b^d	Queue, Set	"Breadth-First Search" on page 198
A*Search	$b*d$	b^d	b^d	Priority Queue, Set, Heuristics	"A*Search" on page 201
Minimax	b^{ply}	b^{ply}	b^{ply}	Recursion, Backtracking, Brute Force	"Minimax" on page 174
NegMax	b^{ply}	b^{ply}	b^{ply}	Recursion, Backtracking, Brute Force	"NegMax" on page 180
AlphaBeta	$b^{ply/2}$	$b^{ply/2}$	b^{ply}	Recursion, Backtracking, Heuristics	"AlphaBeta" on page 183

Reduce Your Problem to Another Problem

Problem reduction is a fundamental approach used by computer scientists and mathematicians to solve problems. As a simple example, suppose you wanted to locate the fourth largest element in a list. Instead of writing this special-purpose code, you could use any sorting algorithm to sort the list and then return the fourth element in the sorted list. Using this approach, you have defined an algorithm whose performance time is $O(n \log n)$, although this is not the most efficient way to solve the problem.

When using **Fortune Sweep** to compute the Voronoi diagram, the convex hull can be readily computed by finding those points that share an infinite Voronoi edge within their polygons. In this regard, the algorithm computes more information than necessary, but the output can be used for a number of interesting problems, such as computing a planar triangulation of the points in the collection.

Chapter 8 presented a set of problems that all seemed related, but there didn't seem to be any easy way to tie them all together. It is possible to reduce all of these problems to linear programming (LP) and use commercially available software packages, such as Maple, to compute solutions. However, the reductions are complicated, and the general-purpose algorithms used to solve LP problems can be outperformed, often significantly, by the **Ford–Fulkerson** family of algorithms. We show in Chapter 8 how to solve a single problem type, namely computing the minimum-cost maximum flow in a flow network. With this algorithm in hand, the five other problems are immediately solved. Table 12-6 shows the network flow algorithms described in Chapter 8.

Table 12-6. Network flow algorithms

Algorithm	Best	Average	Worst	Concepts	Page
Ford–Fulkerson	E^*mf	E^*mf	E^*mf	Weighted Directed Graph, Greedy	"Maximum Flow" on page 220
Edmonds–Karp	V^*E^2	V^*E^2	V^*E^2	Weighted Directed Graph, Greedy	"Maximum Flow" on page 220

Writing Algorithms Is Hard—Testing Algorithms Is Harder

Because the algorithms we describe are predominantly deterministic (except for those from Chapter 11), it was rather straightforward to develop test cases to ensure they behaved properly. In Chapter 7, we began to encounter difficulties because we were using path-finding algorithms to locate potential solutions that we did not know in advance. For example, although it was straightforward to write test cases to determine whether the GoodEvaluator heuristic was working properly for the 8-puzzle, the only way to test an **A*Search** using that heuristic is to invoke the search and manually inspect the explored tree to validate that the proper move was selected. Thus, testing **A*Search** is complicated by having to test the algorithm in the context of a specific problem and heuristic. We have extensive test cases for the path-finding algorithms, but in many cases they exist only to ensure a reasonable move was selected (for either game or search trees), rather than to ensure a specific move was selected.

Testing the algorithms in Chapter 9 was further complicated because of floating-point computations. Consider our approach to test **Convex Hull Scan**. The original idea was to execute the brute-force **Slow Hull** algorithm, whose performance was $O(n^4)$, and compare its output with the output from Andrew's **Convex Hull Scan**.

During our extensive testing, we randomly generated two-dimensional data sets uniformly drawn from the [0, 1] unit square. However, when the data sets grew sufficiently large, we invariably encountered situations where the results of the two algorithms were different. Was there a subtle defect exposed by the data, or was something else at work? We eventually discovered that the floating-point arithmetic used by **Slow Hull** produced slightly (ever so slightly) different results when compared with **Convex Hull Scan**. Was this just a fluke? Unfortunately, no. We also noticed that the **LineSweep** algorithm produced slightly different results when compared with the **Brute-Force Intersection** algorithm.

Which algorithm produced the "right" result? It's not that simple, as using floating-point values led us to develop a consistent notion of comparing floating-point values. Specifically, we (somewhat) arbitrarily defined `FloatingPoint.epsilon` to be the threshold value below which it becomes impossible to discern differences between two numbers. When the resulting computations lead to values near this threshold (which we set to 10^{-9}), unexpected behavior would often occur. Eliminating the threshold entirely won't solve the problem, either. We ultimately resorted to statistically checking the results of these algorithms, rather than seeking absolute and definitive answers for all cases.

Table 12-7 summarizes the algorithms presented in Chapter 9. Each algorithm shares the challenges in working with two-dimensional geometric structures and accurately performing geometric computations.

Table 12-7. Computational geometry

Algorithm	Best	Average	Worst	Concepts	Page
Convex Hull Scan	n	$n \log n$	$n \log n$	Greedy	"Convex Hull Scan" on page 250
LineSweep	$(n + k) \log n$	$(n + k) \log n$	n^2	Priority Queue, Binary Tree	"LineSweep" on page 259
Voronoi Diagram	$n \log n$	$n \log n$	$n \log n$	LineSweep, Priority Queue, Binary Tree	"Voronoi Diagram" on page 268

Accept Approximate Solutions When Possible

In many circumstances, an approximate result is acceptable if it can be computed much faster than an accurate result and it has a known error from the correct result. The **Knapsack unbounded** problem provides such a scenario, since the approximation is no worse than 50% of the actual result. These approximations can use randomness to compute an estimate of an actual answer, as we saw with the example for counting the number of solutions to the N-Queens Problem. Use this approach when you know that repeated trials increase the precision of the estimate.

A **Bloom Filter** is carefully designed so it can return false positives, but never false negatives, when searching for an element in a collection. At first glance, it may seem useless to have an algorithm that returns an incorrect answer. But a **Bloom Filter** can dramatically reduce the execution time of searching algorithms involving secondary storage or database systems. When it returns negative, it truly means the element does not exist in the collection, so there is no need to pursue a more costly search. Of course, it might mean that sometimes the **Bloom Filter** allows a search to continue that will fail, but this won't affect the correctness of the overall application.

Add Parallelism to Increase Performance

The algorithms presented in this book compute their results assuming a single, sequential computer. If you can identify subproblems that can be independently computed, you might be able to design a multithreaded solution using the available resources provided by modern computers. For instance, Chapter 11 showed how to parallelize **Quicksort** to achieve a nice speedup. What other algorithms in this book can benefit from parallelism? Recall that **Convex Hull Scan** has a sorting substep followed by two independent problems: constructing the lower partial hull and and the upper partial hull. Each of these tasks can be parallelized to achieve improved performance. Table 12-8 shows the impressive speedup (review the `algs.model.problems.convexhull.parallel` code in the repository). Despite the impressive performance, the algorithm still performs in O($n \log n$) time, although with better constants.

Table 12-8. Performance improvements of multithreaded Convex Hull Scan

n	single-threaded	1 helper thread	2 helpers	3 helpers	4 helpers
2,048	0.8571	0.5000	0.6633	0.5204	0.6020
4,096	1.5204	0.7041	0.7041	0.7755	0.7857
8,192	3.3163	0.9592	1.0306	1.0306	1.0816
16,384	7.3776	1.6327	1.6327	1.5612	1.6939
32,768	16.3673	3.0612	2.8980	2.9694	3.1122
65,536	37.1633	5.8980	6.0102	6.0306	6.0408
131,072	94.2653	13.8061	14.3776	14.1020	14.5612
262,144	293.2245	37.0102	37.5204	37.5408	38.2143
524,288	801.7347	90.7449	92.1939	91.1633	91.9592
1,048,576	1890.5612	197.4592	198.6939	198.0306	200.5612

Most serial algorithms cannot achieve theoretic maximal speedup because only part of the algorithm can be parallelized among multiple threads; this is known as *Amdahl's law*. Don't try to use as many threads as possible in a solution. Adding multiple helper threads requires more complicated programs than adding a single helper thread. So with only a small increase in complexity, using a single helper thread can provide noticeable improvement.

However, not every algorithm can be improved with parallelism. In the k-d tree **Nearest Neighbor**, for example, there may be double recursions as the algorithm seeks to find the closest point in the collection to a target point. Parallelizing these separate method invocations will slow down the overall performance because of the need to synchronize these helper threads so they both complete together.

A

Benchmarking

Each algorithm in this book is accompanied by data about its performance. Because it's important to use the right benchmarks to get accurate performance, we present our infrastructure to evaluate algorithm performance in this appendix. This should also help to address any questions or doubts you might have concerning the validity of our approach. We try to explain the precise means by which empirical data is computed, in order to enable you both to verify that the results are accurate and to understand where the assumptions are appropriate given the context in which the algorithm is intended to be used.

There are numerous ways by which algorithms can be analyzed. Chapter 2 presented a theoretical, formal treatment, introducing the concepts of worst-case and average-case analysis. These theoretic results can be empirically evaluated in some cases, but not all. For example, consider evaluating the performance of an algorithm to sort 20 numbers. There are $2.43*10^{18}$ permutations of these 20 numbers, and we cannot simply exhaustively evaluate each of these permutations to compute the average case. Additionally, we cannot compute the average by measuring the time to sort all of these permutations. We must rely on statistical measures to assure ourselves we have properly computed the expected performance time of the algorithm.

Statistical Foundation

This chapter focuses on essential points for evaluating the performance of algorithms. Interested readers should consult any of the large number of available textbooks on statistics for more information on the relevant statistical information used to produce the empirical measurements in this book.

To compute the performance of an algorithm, we construct a *suite* of T independent *trials* for which the algorithm is executed. Each trial is intended to execute an algorithm on an input problem of size n. Some effort is made to ensure these trials are all reasonably *equivalent* for the algorithm. When the trials are actually identical, the intent of the trial is to quantify the *variance* of the underlying implementation of the algorithm. This may be suitable, for example, if it is too costly to compute a large number of independent equivalent trials.

The suite is executed and millisecond-level timings are taken before and after the observable behavior. When the code is written in Java, the system garbage collector is invoked immediately prior to launching the trial; although this effort can't guarantee that the garbage collector does not execute during the trial, it may reduce this risk of spending extra time unrelated to the algorithm. From the full set of T recorded times, the best and worst performing times are discarded as being "outliers." The remaining $T - 2$ time records are averaged, and a standard deviation is computed using the following formula:

$$\sigma = \sqrt{\frac{\sum_i (x_i - x)^2}{n - 1}}$$

where x_i is the time for an individual trial and x is the average of the $T - 2$ trials. Note here that n is equal to $T - 2$, so the denominator within the square root is $T - 3$. Calculating averages and standard deviations will help predict future performance, based on Table A-1, which shows the probability (between 0 and 1) that the actual value will be within the range $[x - k^*\sigma, x + k^*\sigma]$, where σ represents the standard deviation computed in the equation just shown. The probability values become *confidence intervals* that declare the confidence we have in a prediction.

Table A-1. Standard deviation table

k	Probability
1	0.6827
2	0.9545
3	0.9973
4	0.9999
5	1

For example, in a randomized trial, it is expected that 68.27% of the time the result will fall within the range $[x-\sigma, x+\sigma]$.

When reporting results, we never present numbers with greater than four decimal digits of accuracy, so we don't give the mistaken impression that we believe the accuracy of our numbers extends any farther. This process will convert a computation such as 16.897986 into the reported number 16.8980.

Example

Assume we wanted to benchmark the addition of the numbers from 1 to n. An experiment is designed to measure the times for $n = 8,000,000$ to $n = 16,000,000$ in increments of two million. Because the problem is identical for n and doesn't vary, we execute for 30 trials to eliminate as much variability as possible.

The hypothesis is that the time to complete the sum will vary directly in relation to n. We show three programs that solve this problem—in Java, C, and Python—and present the benchmark infrastructure by showing how it is used.

Java Benchmarking Solutions

On Java test cases, the current system time (in milliseconds) is determined immediately prior to, and after, the execution of interest. The code in Example A-1 measures the time it takes to complete the task. In a perfect computer, the 30 trials should all require exactly the same amount of time. Of course, this is unlikely to happen, because modern operating systems have numerous background processing tasks that share the same CPU on which the performance code executes.

Example A-1. Java example to time execution of task

```java
public class Main {
  public static void main (String[] args) {
    TrialSuite ts = new TrialSuite();
    for (long len = 8000000; len <= 16000000; len += 2000000) {
      for (int i = 0; i < 30; i++) {
        System.gc();
        long now = System.currentTimeMillis();

        /** Task to be timed. */
        long sum = 0;
        for (int x = 1; x <= len; x++) {
          sum += x;
        }

        long end = System.currentTimeMillis();
        ts.addTrial(len, now, end);
      }
    }
    System.out.println (ts.computeTable());
  }
}
```

The `TrialSuite` class stores trials by their size. After all the trials have been added to the suite, the resulting table is computed. To do this, the running times are added together to find the total sum, minimum value, and maximum value. As described earlier, the minimum and maximum values are removed from the set when computing the average and standard deviation.

Example | 357

Linux Benchmarking Solutions

For C test cases, we developed a benchmarking library to be linked with the code to test. In this section, we briefly describe the essential aspects of the timing code and refer the interested reader to the code repository for the full source.

Primarily created for testing sort routines, the C-based infrastructure can be linked to existing source code. The timing API takes over responsibility for parsing the command-line arguments:

```
usage: timing [-n NumElements] [-s seed] [-v] [OriginalArguments]
       -n declares the problem size        [default: 100,000]
       -v verbose output                   [default: false]
       -s # set the seed for random values [default: no seed]
       -h print usage information
```

The timing library assumes a problem will be attempted whose input size is defined by the [-n] flag. To produce repeatable trials, the random seed can be set with [-s seed]. To link with the timing library, a test case provides the following functions:

void problemUsage()
: Report to the console the set of [OriginalArguments] supported by the specific code. Note that the timing library parses the declared timing parameters, and remaining arguments are passed along to the prepareInput function.

void prepareInput (int size, int argc, char **argv)
: For some problems, this function is responsible for building the input set to be processed within the execute method. Note that this information is not passed directly to execute via a formal argument, but instead is stored as a static variable within the test case.

void postInputProcessing()
: If any validation is needed after the input problem is solved, that code can execute here.

void execute()
: This method contains the body of code to be timed. Because the code is run once as part of the evaluation time, it can have a small impact on the reported time. When the execute method is empty, the overhead is considered to have no impact on the overall reporting.

The test case in Example A-2 shows the code task for the addition example.

Example A-2. Task describing addition of n numbers

```
extern int numElements;    /* size of n */
void problemUsage() { /* none */ }
void prepareInput() { /* none */ }
void postInputProcessing() { /* None */ }
```

```
void execute() {
  int x;
  long sum = 0;
  for (x = 1; x <= numElements; x++) { sum += x; }
}
```

Each execution of the C function corresponds to a single trial, so we have a set of shell scripts to repeatedly execute the code being tested to generate statistics. For each suite, a configuration file name *config.rc* is created to represent the trial suite run. Example A-3 shows the file for the value-based sorting used in Chapter 4.

Example A-3. Sample configuration file to compare sort executions

```
# configure to use these BINS
BINS=./Insertion ./Qsort_2_6_11 ./Qsort_2_6_6 ./Qsort_straight

# configure suite
TRIALS=10
LOW=1
HIGH=16384
INCREMENT=*2
```

This specification file declares that the set of executables will be three variations of **QuickSort** with one **Insertion Sort**. The suite consists of problem sizes ranging from *n = 1* to *n = 16,384*, where *n* doubles after each run. For each problem size, 10 trials are executed. The best and worst performers are discarded, and the resulting generated table will have the averages (and standard deviations) of the remaining eight trials.

Example A-4 contains the *compare.sh* script that generates an aggregate set of information for a particular problem size *n*.

Example A-4. compare.sh benchmarking script

```
#!/bin/bash
#
#  This script expects TWO arguments:
#     $1  -- size of problem n
#     $2  -- number of trials to execute
#  This script reads its parameters from the $CONFIG configuration file
#     BINS    set of executables to execute
#     EXTRAS  extra command line arguments to use when executing them
#
#  CODE is set to directory where these scripts are to be found
CODE=`dirname $0`

SIZE=20
NUM_TRIALS=10
if [ $# -ge 1 ]
```

Example | 359

```
then
  SIZE=$1
  NUM_TRIALS=$2
fi

if [ "x$CONFIG" = "x" ]
then
  echo "No Configuration file (\$CONFIG) defined"
  exit 1
fi

if [ "x$BINS" = "x" ]
then
  if [ -f $CONFIG ]
  then
     BINS=`grep "BINS=" $CONFIG | cut -f2- -d'='`
    EXTRAS=`grep "EXTRAS=" $CONFIG | cut -f2- -d'='`
  fi

  if [ "x$BINS" = "x" ]
  then
     echo "no \$BINS variable and no $CONFIG configuration "
     echo "Set \$BINS to a space-separated set of executables"
  fi
fi

echo "Report: $BINS on size $SIZE"
echo "Date: `date`"
echo "Host: `hostname`"
RESULTS=/tmp/compare.$$
for b in $BINS
do
  TRIALS=$NUM_TRIALS

  # start with number of trials followed by totals (one per line)
  echo $NUM_TRIALS > $RESULTS
  while [ $TRIALS -ge 1 ] do
    $b -n $SIZE -s $TRIALS $EXTRAS | grep secs | sed 's/secs//' >> $RESULTS
    TRIALS=$((TRIALS-1))
  done

  # compute average/stdev
  RES=`cat $RESULTS | $CODE/eval`
  echo "$b $RES"
  rm -f $RESULTS
done
```

compare.sh makes use of a small C program, eval, that computes the average and standard deviation using the method described at the start of this chapter. This *compare.sh* script is repeatedly executed by a manager script, *suiteRun.sh*, which iterates

---

over the desired input problem sizes specified within the *config.rc* file, as shown in
Example A-5.

Example A-5. suiteRun.sh benchmarking script

```bash
#!/bin/bash
CODE=`dirname $0`

# if no args then use default config file, otherwise expect it
if [ $# -eq 0 ]
then
  CONFIG="config.rc"
else
  CONFIG=$1
  echo "Using configuration file $CONFIG..."
fi

# export so it will be picked up by compare.sh
export CONFIG

# pull out information
if [ -f $CONFIG ]
then
   BINS=`grep "BINS=" $CONFIG | cut -f2- -d'='`
   TRIALS=`grep "TRIALS=" $CONFIG | cut -f2- -d'='`
   LOW=`grep "LOW=" $CONFIG | cut -f2- -d'='`
   HIGH=`grep "HIGH=" $CONFIG | cut -f2- -d'='`
   INCREMENT=`grep "INCREMENT=" $CONFIG | cut -f2- -d'='`
else
  echo "Configuration file ($CONFIG) unable to be found."
  exit -1
fi

# headers
HB=`echo $BINS | tr ' ' ','`
echo "n,$HB"

# compare trials on sizes from LOW through HIGH
SIZE=$LOW
REPORT=/tmp/Report.$$
while [ $SIZE -le $HIGH ]
do
  # one per $BINS entry
  $CODE/compare.sh $SIZE $TRIALS | awk 'BEGIN{p=0} \
      {if(p) { print $0; }} \
      /Host:/{p=1}' | cut -d' ' -f2 > $REPORT

  # concatenate with, all entries ONLY the average. The stdev is
  # going to be ignored
  # ----------------------------
  VALS=`awk 'BEGIN{s=""}\
```

Example | 361

```
    {s = s "," $0 }\
    END{print s;}' $REPORT`
rm -f $REPORT

echo $SIZE $VALS

# $INCREMENT can be "+ NUM" or "* NUM", it works in both cases.
SIZE=$(($SIZE$INCREMENT))
done
```

Python Benchmarking Solutions

The Python code in Example A-6 measures the performance of computing the addition problem. It uses the timeit module, a standard for measuring the execution time of Python code fragments and entire programs.

Example A-6. Python example to time execution of task

```python
import timeit

def performance():
    """Demonstrate execution performance."""
    n = 8000000
    numTrials = 10
    print ("n", "Add time")
    while n <= 16000000:
        setup = 'total=0'
        code  = 'for i in range(' + str(n) + '): total += i'
        add_total = min(timeit.Timer(code, setup=setup).repeat(5,numTrials))

        print ("%d %5.4f " % (n, add_total ))
        n += 2000000

if __name__ == '__main__':
    performance()
```

The timeit module returns a list of values reflecting the execution time in seconds of the code fragment. By applying min to this list, we extract the best performance of any of these trials. The timeit module documentation explains the benefits of using this approach to benchmark Python programs.

Reporting

It is instructive to review the actual results of the performance of three different implementations (in different programming languages) of the same program when computed on the same platform. We present three tables (Table A-2, Table A-4, and Table A-5), one each for Java, C, and Python. In each table, we present the millisecond results and a brief histogram table for the Java results.

Table A-2. Timing results of computations in Java

n	average	min	max	stdev
8,000,000	7.0357	7	12	0.189
10,000,000	8.8571	8	42	0.5245
12,000,000	10.5357	10	11	0.5079
14,000,000	12.4643	12	14	0.6372
16,000,000	14.2857	13	17	0.5998

The aggregate behavior of Table A-2 is shown in detail as a histogram in Table A-3. We omit from the table rows that have only zero values; all nonzero values are shaded in the table.

Table A-3. Individual breakdowns of timing results

time (ms)	8,000,000	10,000,000	12,000,000	14,000,000	16,000,000
7	28	0	0	0	0
8	1	7	0	0	0
9	0	20	0	0	0
10	0	2	14	0	0
11	0	0	16	0	0
12	1	0	0	18	0
13	0	0	0	9	1
14	0	0	0	3	22
15	0	0	0	0	4
16	0	0	0	0	2
17	0	0	0	0	1
42	0	1	0	0	0

To interpret these results for Java, we turn to statistics, referring to the *confidence intervals* described earlier. We assume the timing of each trial is independent. If we are asked to predict the performance of a proposed run for $n = 12,000,000$, observe that its average performance, x, is 12.619 and the standard deviation, σ, is 0.282. Consider the range of values $[x - 2^*\sigma, x + 2^*\sigma]$, which covers values that are plus or minus two standard deviations from the average. As you can see from Table A-1, the probability of being in this range of [9.5199, 11.5515] is 95.45%.

Table A-4. Timing results (in milliseconds) of computations in C

n	average	min	max	stdev
8,000,000	8.376	7.932	8.697	.213
10,000,000	10.539	9.850	10.990	.202
12,000,000	12.619	11.732	13.305	.282
14,000,000	14.681	13.860	15.451	.381
16,000,000	16.746	15.746	17.560	.373

A few years ago, there would have been noticeable differences in the execution times of these three programs. Improvements in language implementations (especially just-in-time compilation) and computing hardware allows them to converge on pretty much the same performance for this specific computation. The histogram results are not as informative, because the timing results include fractional milliseconds, whereas the Java timing strategy reports only integer values. Comparing more realistic programs would show greater differences between the programming languages.

Table A-5. Timing results of computations in Python

n	Execution time (ms)
8,000,000	7.9386
10,000,000	9.9619
12,000,000	12.0528
14,000,000	14.0182
16,000,000	15.8646

Precision

Instead of using millisecond-level timers, we could use nanosecond timers. On the Java platform, the only change in the earlier timing code would be to invoke `System.nanoTime()` instead of accessing the milliseconds. To understand whether there is any correlation between the millisecond and nanosecond timers, we changed the code to that shown in Example A-7.

Example A-7. Using nanosecond timers in Java

```
TrialSuite tsM = new TrialSuite();
TrialSuite tsN = new TrialSuite();
for (long len = 8000000; len <= 16000000; len += 2000000) {
    for (int i = 0; i < 30; i++) {
        long nowM = System.currentTimeMillis();
        long nowN = System.nanoTime();
```

```
        long sum = 0;
        for (int x = 1; x <= len; x++) { sum += x; }
        long endM = System.currentTimeMillis();
        long endN = System.nanoTime();
        tsM.addTrial(len, nowM, endM);
        tsN.addTrial(len, nowN, endN);
    }
}
System.out.println (tsM.computeTable());
System.out.println (tsN.computeTable());
```

Table A-2, shown earlier, contains the millisecond results of the timings, whereas Table A-6 contains the results when using the nanosecond timer in C, and Table A-7 shows the Java performance. For these computations, the results are quite accurate. Because we don't find that using nanosecond-level timers adds much extra precision or accuracy, we continue to use millisecond-level timing results within the benchmark results reported in the algorithm chapters. We also continue to use milliseconds to avoid giving the impression that our timers are more accurate than they really are. Finally, nanosecond timers on Unix systems are not yet standardized, and there are times when we wanted to compare execution times across platforms, which is another reason we chose to use millisecond-level timers throughout this book.

Table A-6. Results using nanosecond timers in C

n	average	min	max	stdev
8,000,000	6970676	6937103	14799912	20067.5194
10,000,000	8698703	8631108	8760575	22965.5895
12,000,000	10430000	10340060	10517088	33381.1922
14,000,000	12180000	12096029	12226502	27509.5704
16,000,000	13940000	13899521	14208708	27205.4481

Table A-7. Results using nanosecond timers in Java

n	average	min	max	stdev
8,000,000	6961055	6925193	14672632	15256.9936
10,000,000	8697874	8639608	8752672	26105.1020
12,000,000	10438429	10375079	10560557	31481.9204
14,000,000	12219324	12141195	12532792	91837.0132
16,000,000	13998684	13862725	14285963	124900.6866

Index

Symbols

* (multiplication operator), 32
** (exponentiation operator), 31
15-puzzle, 173
8-puzzle, 189
8-Queens Problem, 339
== operator, 94
"Big O" notation, 18
≅ (approximately equal), 40

A

A*Search algorithm, 201
adjacency lists, 135-137, 167
adjacency matrix, 135, 152, 167
Akl-Toussaint heuristic, 253-255
algorithms
    Addition, 22-25
    approximation algorithms, 325-331
    Bentley–Faust–Preparata, 5
    Bisection, 21
    blind-search, 192
    building blocks of, 35-42
    Counting Search, 17
    dealing with computational abstrac-
        tions (see computational geometry
        algorithms)
    dealing with networks of vertices and
        edges (see network flow algo-
        rithms)
    defined, 2
    emerging categories of, 325-342
    expected computation time, 9
    (see also mathematics)
    Exponentiation by Squaring, 32
    for search queries (see spatial tree
        structures)
    GCD, 28-31
    Graham's Scan, 42-46, 252
    graph (see graph algorithms)
    Guessing, 20
    Hash Sort, 79-81
    Insertion Sort, 12, 57-60, 74
    logarithmic, 19
    Merge Sort, 54
    parallel algorithms, 325, 332-336, 353
    principles governing, 345-354
    probabilistic algorithms, 326, 336-342
    Quicksort, 12, 69-74, 332-336
    searching (see searching algorithms)
    Sequential Search, 11, 17
    sorting (see sorting algorithms)
    steps in selecting, 1-8
    template example, 42-46
    testing, 351
all-pairs shortest path problem, 159-163
AlphaBeta algorithm
    versus Minimax, 188
    versus NegMax, 188
Amdahl's law, 353
analysis in best, average, and worst cases
    average case, 16
    best case, 17
    lower and upper bounds, 18
    overview of, 14
    sorting algorithms, 87
    worst case, 16

AND/OR trees (see game trees)
approximation algorithms, 325-331
artificial intelligence (AI), 170, 350
    (see also path-finding approach)
Assignment problem, 217, 242
associative lookup query, 91
asymptotic growth, 31
asymptotically equivalent, 10
augmenting path, 220, 234-238
AVL trees, 122-126, 130

B

B-trees, 311
backward edges, 221
Bellman–Ford algorithm, 154-159
benchmark operations
    ** operator, 31
    example, 357
    graph algorithms, 157
    Java, 357
    Linux, 358
    overview of, 355
    precision, 364
    Python, 362
    reporting, 362
    sorting algorithms, 85-86
    statistical foundation, 355
Bentley–Faust–Preparata algorithm, 5
binary decision trees, 88, 286, 311
binary heaps, 150
Binary Search algorithm, 95-99, 346
    versus Sequential Search, 98
Binary Search Tree algorithm, 119-131
Bipartite Matching problem, 217, 231-234
Bisection algorithm, 21
bitboards, 173
blind-search algorithms, 192
Bloom Filter, 114-118
Bloom Filter algorithm, 352
Blum-Floyd-Pratt-Rivest-Tarjan (BFPRT), 73, 86
branching factor, 174
Breadth-First Search algorithm, 143-146
    to locate augmenting path, 226
Bucket Sort algorithm, 74-81, 252, 349
Buffon's needle problem, 266

C

collision detection, 283, 285, 305
computational geometry
    assumptions for problems, 249
    defined, 245
    input data, 246
    static versus dynamic tasks, 248
    tasks related to spatial questions, 247
computational geometry algorithms
    Akl-Toussaint heuristic, 253-255
    applications of, 245, 247
    computing line-segment intersections, 258
    Convex Hull Scan, 250-258, 347
    Fortune Sweep, 268-280, 351
    LineSweep, 245, 259-268, 347
    problem classification, 246-249
    QuickHull, 255
    Voronoi diagram, 268-280
computing platforms, 10
Connect Four game, 174
constant behavior, 19
convex hull problem, 245, 249
Convex Hull Scan algorithm, 250-258, 347
counting algorithms, 337
Counting Search algorithm, 17

D

demand satisfaction, 238
dense graphs, 158, 348
    (see also Dijkstra's Algorithm)
Depth-First Search algorithm, 137-143
    evaluation of, 196
    to locate augmenting path, 228
Dijkstra's Algorithm
    for dense graphs, 152-158
    input data, 345
    with priority queue, 147-151
directed graphs, 135
"disjoint-set" data structure, 167
double hashing, 110
Dynamic Programming, 48-51, 159-163, 326

E

edges, 133

Edmonds–Karp algorithm, 226
8-puzzle, 189
8-Queens Problem, 339
empirical evaluation format, 37
evaluating board state, 191
existence query, 91
expansion depth, 174
exponential performance, 31
Exponentiation by Squaring algorithm, 32
exponentiation operator (**), 31

F

15-puzzle, 173
floating-point computation
    arithmetic errors, 40
    comparing values, 40
    modern computer processing of, 38
    performance, 38
    rounding error, 39
    special quantities, 41
Floyd–Warshall algorithm, 159-163
Ford–Fulkerson algorithm, 218, 220-231,
    347, 351
    (see also network flow algorithms)
Fortune Sweep algorithm, 268-280, 351
forward edges, 221
functions, rate of growth of, 10

G

game-tree algorithms, 169-173
GCD algorithm, 28-31
generating valid moves, 191
generator functions, 338
Graham's Scan algorithm, 42, 252
graph algorithms
    adjacency list versus adjacency matrix,
        167
    all-pairs shortest path, 159-163
    Bellman–Ford, 154-159
    benchmark data, 157
    Breadth-First Search, 143-146
    cost estimate comparison, 157-159
    data structure design, 137
    Depth-First Search, 137-143
    Dijkstra's Algorithm for dense graphs,
        152-158
    Floyd–Warshall, 159-163

Kruskal's, 167
    minimum spanning tree, 163-167
    operations on graphs, 137
    overview of, 348
    Prim's, 163-167, 349
    single-source shortest path, 147-151
    storage issues, 167
    terminology used, 133
    types of graphs, 134-137
Guessing algorithm, 20

H

Hash Sort algorithm, 79-81
    versus Quicksort, 80
    string benchmark results, 86
hash tables (see Hash-based Search)
Hash-based Search algorithm, 99-114
heap property, 64
Heap Sort algorithm, 62-67, 252, 347
heuristic functions, 192, 206
HPA* (Hierarchical Path-Finding A*),
    211

I

IDA* (IterativeDeepeningA*) algorithm,
    210
IEEE Standard for Binary Floating-Point
    Arithmetic (IEEE 754), 38
IGameMove interface, 172
IGameState interface, 171
IHypercube interface, 247
ILineSegment interface, 247
IMove interface, 191
IMultiPoint interface, 247
INode interface, 191
INodeSet interface, 191
Insertion Sort algorithm, 12, 57-60
    versus Quicksort, 74
instance size, 9
intersection queries, 283, 285
    (see also line-segment intersections)
IntroSort algorithm, 74
IPlayer interface, 172
IPoint interface, 246
IRectangle interface, 246
IterativeDeepeningA* algorithm (IDA*),
    210

K

k-d trees, 285
Knapsack Problem, 326-331
Knapsack Unbounded algorithm, 326, 352
Knapsack Unbounded Approximation, 330
Knuth's randomized estimation, 340
Kruskal's algorithm, 167

L

line-segment intersections, 245, 258
linear probing, 110
Linear Programming (LP), 218, 242, 351
linear search (see Sequential Search)
linearithmic performance, 25
LineSweep algorithm, 245, 259-268, 347
log n behavior, 19-21
logarithmic algorithms, 19
lower bound notations, 18

M

managing state, 191
matching problems (see Bipartite Matching problem)
mathematics
    analysis in best, average, and worst cases, 14-18
    benchmark operations, 31
    performance families, 18-31
    problem instance size, 9
    rate of growth of functions, 10-14
Max-flow Min-cut theorem, 220
maximum expansion depth, 174
Maximum Flow problem, 217, 220-231
Merge Sort algorithm, 54, 81-85
    string benchmark results, 86
Minimax algorithm, 174-180
    versus AlphaBeta, 188
Minimum Cost Flow problem, 236, 238
minimum edit distance, 48-51
moves
    calculating available, 174
    generating valid, 191
MST (minimum spanning tree) algorithms, 163-167
Multi-Commodity Flow problem, 230

multithreading (see parallel algorithms)

N

n-way trees, 131
Nearest Neighbor algorithm, 283-285, 288-298
NegMax algorithm, 180-182
    versus AlphaBeta, 188
network flow algorithms
    applications of, 217
    Assignment, 242
    augmenting path discovery, 234-238
    Bipartite Matching, 231-234
    Edmonds–Karp, 226
    Ford–Fulkerson, 220-231, 347, 351
    Linear Programming approach, 242, 351
    Maximum Flow, 220-231
    Minimum Cost Flow, 238
    modeling flow networks, 218
    Push/Relabel, 230
    Simplex, 243
    Transportation, 240
    Transshipment, 239

O

Octrees, 311
On-Line Encyclopedia of Integer Sequences, 339
open addressing delete method, 112
open addressing hash tables, 111

P

parallel algorithms, 325, 332-336, 353
partition-based sorting, 67-74
path-finding approach
    A*Search, 201-211
    AlphaBeta, 183-189
    Breadth-First Search, 198-201
    comparison of algorithms, 211-214
    Depth-First Search, 192-197
    game trees, 169-173
    Minimax, 174-180
    NegMax, 180-182
    overview of, 169, 350
    path-finding concepts, 173

search trees, 189-192
path-length heuristic functions, 192, 206
paths, 133
  augmenting, 220
  constructing in flow networks, 221
perfect hash function, 103, 114
performance
  asymptotically equivalent costs, 10
  floating-point computation, 38
  increasing with parallelism, 353
performance families
  asymptotic growth, 31
  classifications, 18
  constant behavior, 19
  exponential, 31
  linear, 22-25
  linearithmic, 25
  quadratic, 26-29
  sublinear, 22
point-based quad trees, 287
Prim's Algorithm, 163-167, 349
principles
  governing algorithm design, 345-354
priority keys, 164
priority queue (PQ), 147-151, 234
probabilistic algorithms, 326, 336-342
problem reduction, 350
programming problems
  all-pairs shortest path, 159-163
  Assignment, 217, 242
  Bipartite Matching, 217
  Buffon's needle, 266
  collision detection, 285
  convex hull, 245, 249
  8-Queens, 339
  instance size, 9
  intelligent solutions to, 3
  Knapsack, 326-331
  line-segment intersections, 245, 258
  Maximum Flow, 217, 220-231
  Minimum Cost Flow, 236, 238
  Multi-Commodity Flow, 230
  queries, 283-285
    (see also spatial tree structures)
  representing as network flow between
    nodes, 218
  shared concepts in solving, 345-354
  single-source shortest path, 147-151,
    157-159

solving by approximation, 5
solving by Divide and Conquer
    approach, 4, 47
solving by Dynamic Programming
    approach, 48-51, 159-163, 326
solving by generalization, 7
solving by Greedy approach, 4, 46
solving by parallel approach, 5, 332,
    353
Transportation, 217, 240
Transshipment, 217, 239
Traveling Salesman Problem, 158
Voronoi diagram, 245, 268-280, 345
without clear computation solutions
    (see path-finding approach)
pseudocode
  template format, 36
Push/Relabel algorithm, 230
Python
  Exponentiation by Squaring algo-
    rithm, 32
  exponentiation operator (**), 31

Q

quadratic performance, 26-28
quadratic probing, 110
quadtrees, 286, 305-311
queries, 283-285
  (see also spatial tree structures)
QuickHull algorithm, 255
Quicksort algorithm, 12, 332-336, 346
  versus Hash Sort, 80
  versus Insertion Sort, 74
  optimizing, 14
  partition-based sorting with, 69-74
  string benchmark results, 86

R

R-trees, 287, 311-322
range queries, 283-285, 305, 312
Range Query algorithm, 298-304
rate of growth of functions, 10
Red-Black trees, 131
region-based quad trees, 286
rehashing, 108
representing state, 173
rounding error, 39

Rubik's Cube, 174

S

search trees, estimating size of, 339
"search-or-insert" operation, 99
search-tree algorithms, 119, 189-192
    (see also Binary Search Tree algorithm)
    compared, 211
searching algorithms
    beyond simple membership (see spatial tree structures)
    Binary Search, 95-99, 346
    Binary Search Tree, 119-131
    Bloom Filter, 114-118, 352
    criteria for choosing, 91
    fundamental queries supported, 91
    Hash-based Search, 99-114
    Sequential Search, 92-95
Selection Sort algorithm, 61, 347
Sequential Search algorithm, 11, 92-95
    average case analysis, 17
    best case analysis, 17
    versus Binary Search, 98
sets, estimating size of, 337
shape property, 64
significand, 39
Simplex algorithm, 243
Simplex Method, 31
Simplified Memory Bounded A* (SMA*), 211
single-source shortest path problem, 147-151, 157-159
SMA* (Simplified Memory Bounded A*), 211
sorting algorithms
    analysis techniques, 87
    Bucket Sort, 74-81, 252, 349
    concepts arising from use, 346
    criteria for choosing, 56
    evaluating, 12
    Hash Sort, 86
    Heap Sort, 62-67, 252, 347
    Merge Sort, 81-85, 86
    overview, 53-56
    partition-based sorting, 67-74
    Quicksort, 86, 332-336, 346
    Selection Sort, 61, 347
    sorting with extra storage, 81-85
    sorting without comparisons, 74
    string benchmark results, 85-86
    transposition sorting, 57-60
sparse graphs, 158, 348
    (see also Dijkstra's Algorithm)
spatial tree structures
    applications of, 283
    B-trees, 311
    collision detection, 283, 285, 305
    intersection queries, 283, 285
    k-d trees, 285
    Nearest Neighbor algorithm, 283-285, 288-298
    Octree, 311
    overview of, 348
    quadtrees, 286, 305-311
    R-trees, 287, 311-322
    range queries, 283, 305, 312
    Range Query algorithm, 298-304
speedup factor, 335
state
    evaluating, 191
    hierarchical versus flat, 211
    managing, 191
    representing, 173
static evaluation functions, 172
string benchmark results, 85

T

templates
    algorithm format, 35
    example, 42-46
    pseudocode format, 36
Tic-tac-toe, 169-189
Transportation problem, 217, 240
transposition sorting, 57-60
transposition tables, 211
Transshipment problem, 217, 239
travel planning, 259
    (see also LineSweep algorith)
Traveling Salesman Problem, 158

U

undirected, unweighted graphs, 134
upper bound notation, 18

V

vertices, 133
virtual memory, 311
Voronoi diagram, 7, 245, 268-280, 345

W

weight, 133
weighted graphs, 135

About the Authors

George T. Heineman is an associate professor of computer science at Worcester Polytechnic Institute. His research interests are in software engineering and the modular synthesis of software systems. He co-edited the 2001 book *Component-Based Software Engineering: Putting the Pieces Together* (Addison-Wesley). Aside from his professional pursuits, George is an avid puzzler. He invented Sujiken, a Sudoku variation played on a right-triangle arrangement of cells in which numbers cannot repeat in a horizontal row, vertical column, or diagonal in any direction. Books published include *Sudoku on the Half Shell: 150 Addictive Sujiken® Puzzles* (Puzzlewright Press, 2011).

Gary Pollice is a self-labeled curmudgeon (that's a crusty, ill-tempered, usually old man) who spent more than 35 years in industry trying to figure out what he wanted to be when he grew up. Even though he hasn't grown up yet, he did make the move in 2003 to the hallowed halls of academia, where he has been corrupting the minds of the next generation of software developers with radical ideas like "develop software for your customer," "learn how to work as part of a team," "design and code quality and elegance and correctness counts," and "it's OK to be a nerd as long as you are a great one."

Gary retired from full-time teaching in 2015 and now teaches one online course per year from his retirement home in Cuenca, Ecuador.

Stanley Selkow, a professor emeritus of computer science at Worcester Polytechnic Institute, received a B.S. in electrical engineering from Carnegie Institute of Technology in 1965, and a Ph.D. in the same area from the University of Pennsylvania in 1970. From 1968 to 1970, he was in the public health service at the National Institutes of Health at Bethesda, Maryland. Since 1970, he has been on the faculty at universities in Knoxville, Tennessee, and Worcester, Massachusetts, as well as Montreal, Chonqing, Lausanne, and Paris. His major research has been in graph theory and algorithm design.

Colophon

The animal on the cover of *Algorithms in a Nutshell* is a hermit crab (*Pagurus bernhardus*). More than 500 species of hermit crabs exist. Mostly aquatic, they live in saltwater in shallow coral reefs and tide pools. Some hermit crabs, however, especially in the tropics, are terrestrial. The robber crab, which can grow as large as a coconut, is one such example. Even terrestrial hermit crabs carry a small amount of water in their shells to help them breathe and keep their abdomens moist.

Unlike true crabs, hermit crabs do not have a hard shell of their own and must seek refuge from predators in the abandoned shells of gastropods (snails). They are particularly fond of the discarded shells of periwinkles and whelks. As they grow bigger, they have to find a new shell to inhabit. Leaving any part of themselves exposed would make them more susceptible to predators; in addition, not having a well-fitted shell stunts their growth. Because intact gastropod shells are limited, shell competition is an issue.

Hermit crabs are decapod (which literally means "ten footed") crustaceans. Of their five pairs of legs, the first two are pincers, or grasping claws, the larger one of which they use to defend themselves and shred food. The smaller claw is used for eating. The second and third pairs of legs help them walk, and the final two pairs help keep them in their shells.

Characteristic of crustaceans, hermit crabs do not have an internal skeleton but rather a hard exoskeleton of calcium. They also have two compound eyes, two pairs of antennae (which they use to sense smells and vibration), and three pairs of mouthparts. Near the base of their antennae is a pair of green glands that excretes waste.

Sea anemones (water-dwelling, predatory animals) are often found attached to hermit crabs' shells. In exchange for transportation and a helping of the hermit crab's leftovers, sea anemones help to ward off the hermit crab's marine predators, such as fish and octopus. Other predators include birds, other crabs, and some mammals (man included).

Known as the "garbage collectors of the sea," hermit crabs will eat mostly anything, including dead and rotting material on the seashore, and thus they play an important role in seashore cleanup. As omnivores, their diet is varied and includes everything from worms to organic debris, such as grass and leaves.

The cover image is from Johnson's *Library of Natural History*, Volume 2. The cover font is Adobe ITC Garamond. The text font is Linotype Birka; the heading font is Adobe Myriad Condensed; and the code font is LucasFont's TheSansMonoCondensed.

Have it your way.

O'Reilly eBooks

- Lifetime access to the book when you buy through oreilly.com
- Provided in up to four, DRM-free file formats, for use on the devices of your choice: PDF, .epub, Kindle-compatible .mobi, and Android .apk
- Fully searchable, with copy-and-paste, and print functionality
- We also alert you when we've updated the files with corrections and additions.

oreilly.com/ebooks/

Safari Books Online

- Access the contents and quickly search over 7000 books on technology, business, and certification guides
- Learn from expert video tutorials, and explore thousands of hours of video on technology and design topics
- Download whole books or chapters in PDF format, at no extra cost, to print or read on the go
- Early access to books as they're being written
- Interact directly with authors of upcoming books
- Save up to 35% on O'Reilly print books

See the complete Safari Library at safaribooksonline.com

©2014 O'Reilly Media, Inc. O'Reilly logo is a registered trademark of O'Reilly Media, Inc. 14373

Get even more for your money.

Join the O'Reilly Community, and register the O'Reilly books you own. It's free, and you'll get:

- $4.99 ebook upgrade offer
- 40% upgrade offer on O'Reilly print books
- Membership discounts on books and events
- Free lifetime updates to ebooks and videos
- Multiple ebook formats, DRM FREE
- Participation in the O'Reilly community
- Newsletters
- Account management
- 100% Satisfaction Guarantee

Signing up is easy:

1. Go to: oreilly.com/go/register
2. Create an O'Reilly login.
3. Provide your address.
4. Register your books.

Note: English-language books only

To order books online:
oreilly.com/store

For questions about products or an order:
orders@oreilly.com

To sign up to get topic-specific email announcements and/or news about upcoming books, conferences, special offers, and new technologies:
elists@oreilly.com

For technical questions about book content:
booktech@oreilly.com

To submit new book proposals to our editors:
proposals@oreilly.com

O'Reilly books are available in multiple DRM-free ebook formats. For more information:
oreilly.com/ebooks

O'REILLY®

©2014 O'Reilly Media, Inc. O'Reilly logo is a registered trademark of O'Reilly Media, Inc. 14373

CPSIA information can be obtained at www.ICGtesting.com
Printed in the USA
BVOW06s1505200316

440645BV00005B/5/P

9 781491 948927